an introduction to

Social
Psychology

an introduction to

Social Psychology

second edition

James A. Schellenberg

Western Michigan University

Random House • New York

Library of Congress Cataloging in Publication Data

Schellenberg, James A   1932–
    An introduction to social psychology.

    Bibliography: p.
    1. Social psychology. I. Title. [DNLM: 1. Psychology, Social.   HM251 S322i 1974]
HM251.S299 1974   301.1   73-19749
ISBN 0-394-31829-3

Manufactured in the United States of America

Second Edition 987654

TABLE CREDITS

Table 1 adapted from August B. Hollingshead, *Elmtown's Youth: The Impact of Social Classes on Adolescents.* New York: Wiley, 1949. Reprinted by permission of the publisher. Table 23 adapted from and Table 24 from Marvin E. Shaw, "Communication Networks," in L. Berkowitz (ed.), *Advances in Experimental Social Psychology,* I, 111–147. New York: Academic Press, 1964. Reprinted by permission of the author and the publisher. Table 27 from Stanley Lieberson and Arnold R. Silverman, "The Precipitants and Underlying Conditions of Race Riots," *American Sociological Review,* 30(1965), 889. Reprinted by permission of the authors and the American Sociological Association.

Preface

Since this book is an introduction to social psychology, not an encyclopedic review of the field, I have been quite selective in what has been chosen for discussion. The purpose is not so much to "cover the field" as it is to encourage students to develop social psychological insights. To help develop social psychological insights, I have emphasized certain features in the organization and presentation of materials. These might be summarized as (1) a focus upon the sense of the problematic, (2) an exploration, and not just a citation, of relevant empirical data, and (3) a standing invitation to the reader to participate in some rather elementary theory building as we go along.

I have organized the materials of this book primarily with the above considerations in mind. In other words, considerations of effectiveness for learning have taken precedence over considerations of strictly logical order.

In this revised edition, materials are grouped around seven general topics (affiliation, aggression, social influence, attitudes, groups, social norms, and personality in society), with four chapters on each of these topics. Within a typical chapter a few selected studies are explored, and we build gradually on the foundation of these studies. Every fourth chapter is a review and discussion chapter, which seeks to bring the main points of previous materials together into a systematic framework.

Because this is an introductory book, no previous study in the field of social psychology can be assumed. Background in psychological and sociological theories and in research methods is introduced as needed. This is done in theoretical and methodological "pointers" presented as asides to the main line of discussion. By the end of the book the student should have enough of a background to be able, with effort, to comprehend most journal articles presenting current theory and research in social psychology.

Behind the selection of topics in this book is the conception of social psychology as the study of interpersonal behavior. This suggests that social psychology is both sociology and psychology, but that it also has its own distinctive focus in person-to-person behavior. Therefore, while the subject of personality is introduced in several places, the assumption is that the study of individual personality is primarily the domain of other fields, especially of certain fields in psychology. Likewise, while group behavior is explored in several chapters, the assumption is that the organization of groups in society is a matter primarily for other fields, especially for sociology. However, this is not to suggest any rigid lines around social psychology. The division of labor is only approximate, for social psychologists borrow widely from, and contribute to, all the behavioral and social sciences. I wish only to indicate my view that social psychology has a central home base in interpersonal behavior, which is precisely where the conventional domains of psychology (the study of the behavior of individuals) and sociology (the study of the behavior of groups) intersect.

Since this book is written for the beginning student, many points discussed are considerably simplified. Also, the studies and topics have been arranged to suggest particular interpretations. Students should be warned that this is the case, and they should expect an instructor to point to some of these simplications and to introduce somewhat different interpretations. I have tried to introduce the perspectives and intellectual tools that would provide the most useful introduction to social psychology as this discipline is most frequently conceived in American higher education. But I have tried to do this in such a way as to open the issues for further evidence and interpretation—not to close them out.

J. A. S.

Kalamazoo, Mich.
November 1973

Contents

part one: AFFILIATION

In all everywhere
See thyself.
Abandon this thy ignorant conceit
Which holds that thou are separate from other men.

Ancient Sanskrit poem

If any subject is basic to social psychology, it is surely the one focusing on the way persons establish relationships with each other. This is the central concern of the materials of this first part.

We start with studies of people helping other people. Under what conditions do we find persons more willing to help others? What factors are most important in determining whether or not a person in need gets help? Such questions as these are explored in Chapter 1 ("Helping People").

Interpersonal attraction is the subject of Chapter 2 ("Liking People"). Here we seek to identify some general patterns behind the often unexpected quirks of human affections.

The early development of social attachment is the subject of Chapter 3 ("Origins of Affiliation"). Here we examine some of the foundations of human sociability in the early experience of infants.

In Chapter 4 ("Affiliation: Review and Discussion") we bring together some of the main findings of the first three chapters and try to derive a few key generalizations regarding the nature of human affiliation.

Studies discussed in Part One are selected to give a cross section of the varieties of research in social psychology. Although the actual procedures of research are not discussed in detail, the broad familiarity gained here with the different kinds of studies will provide background for more intensive examination of different forms of research in Part Two.

1
Helping People

THE CASE OF THE SILENT WITNESSES

It was about 3 A.M. one night in March 1964. Kitty Genovese was coming home from work when she was attacked by a crazed young man who repeatedly raped and stabbed her. This was not done clandestinely in some hidden alley, but in the street near her apartment in Queens, a borough of New York City. As Kitty screamed, her neighbors came to their windows to see what was going on. They saw her being murdered. What did they do about it? They watched. Did they come to her aid as she lay dying? No. Did anyone even call the police? No, not until the girl had already been dead for half an hour.

A *New York Times* reporter (Rosenthal, 1964)* later identified thirty-eight persons who had heard Kitty Genovese scream and had watched some part of the attack. But not one of them did a thing to help her. How horrible! Not just the murder, but also the reaction of those who watched and did nothing. This incident, widely reported, inspired numerous Sunday sermons on the moral callousness of our age. Scholars, too, were horrified by this and similar incidents, and they seized the opportunity to expound on the alienation and apathy of modern man.

But, as the saying goes, what good does it do to curse the darkness? Let us rather suggest what light systematic research may shed upon this phenomenon of *bystander apathy*. In so doing we may illustrate the characteristic way in which a social psychologist proceeds in his work, namely:

1. He identifies a key intellectual problem about social behavior. (For example, why do bystanders so often fail to come to the aid of a person in distress?)
2. He conceptualizes the main factor to be explained as a variable. (For example, bystander apathy becomes conceptualized as "probability of coming to the aid of a person in distress" or "amount of help given a person in need.")
3. He systematically studies different conditions that may affect this variable and then carefully measures whatever effects may

* References throughout this text will be cited in full in the bibliographical list at the back of the book.

be observed. (For example, in what kinds of situations are
witnesses less apt to come to the aid of a person in distress?
And what kinds of people are most apt to help?)

4. He attempts to formulate a theory that will summarize his
findings and predict other observations. (For example, he might
sum up observations concerning when a person in distress is
helped in terms of a theory of costs and rewards of helping.)

WHO HELPS THE LADY IN DISTRESS?

Among those whose attention was drawn to the case of Kitty Genovese
were two social psychologists, John Darley and Bibb Latané. To begin
with, they were suspicious of some of the generalizations easily made
about the so-called apathy and indifference of our age. As they put it:

> The 38 witnesses to Kitty Genovese's murder did not merely look
> at the scene once and then ignore it. Instead they continued to
> stare out of their windows at what was going on. Caught,
> fascinated, distressed, unwilling to act but unable to turn away,
> their behavior was neither helpful nor heroic; but it was not
> indifferent or apathetic either (Latané and Darley, 1969, p. 244).

What then were some of the features of this situation that can help
to explain the lack of helpfulness? Latané and Darley found a number
of clues in examining the general characteristics of emergency situations. Emergencies typically involve dangers; seldom are there opportunities for improved good fortune for anybody. Emergencies are rare,
and the actions that would be helpful in one situation differ greatly
from those that would be helpful in another. Furthermore, because
emergencies are not foreseen they usually require instant action; therefore, there is no chance to plan appropriate behavior. Given these
features of emergencies, is it not understandable that most bystanders
might remain standing by?

But enough speculating. Let us find situations where we can actually
observe what bystanders do in response to an emergency. For example,
imagine yourself in the following situation.

You have been contacted by phone to take part in a bit of market
research for the Consumer Testing Bureau at Columbia University. You
understand that you must come in to help them discover game and
puzzle preferences, and that for your efforts you will be paid two
dollars.

You arrive at the Consumer Testing Bureau, where you are met by
an attractive young woman. She takes you through the cluttered main
office to an adjacent testing room. There she gives you a questionnaire
to fill out, which you are now answering.

You glance around the room. A variety of games are lying about.
There is not much else in the room except the table you are seated at
and a few chairs. The questionnaire is not very interesting, but the
woman said it would only take about ten minutes to complete. Then
she went next door to work in her office. She must be busy there now,
for you hear a drawer open and papers being shuffled. Now it sounds

like she's climbing up on a chair to get at something high on the bookcase. Suddenly you heard a loud crash and a scream next door. The chair apparently collapses and the woman falls to the floor. She can be heard moaning now. Some words can be made out among her moans: "Oh, my God, my foot . . . I . . . can't move . . . Oh . . . my ankle . . . can't get this . . . off me."

What do you do?

Do you rush next door to help the young lady? Do you shout for someone else to help? Do you call to the woman to ask if she needs help? Or do you just sit there and continue to fill out that questionnaire?

You have only a little more than a minute to do something. If you do nothing, the woman will by then have struggled to crawl to the door in the next room and have left. Or so it will seem from the sounds that reach you. What will actually happen is that she will turn off the tape recorder from which all those sounds of distress have been issuing. For, you see, this was a test to see what you would do. The bit about market research on games and puzzles was just a cover story. The real question was: Would you come to the aid of the lady in distress? And if so, how quickly would you make your move to help?

This experiment, carried out by Latané and Rodin (1969), was one of a series done by Latané, Darley, and their associates to investigate the bystander apathy problem. Among other experimental situations they have used are the following (described more fully in Latané and Darley, 1970): (1) while filling out a questionnaire, a subject sees smoke begin to issue from a wall vent; (2) customers in a discount beer store are made witnesses to a staged theft of a case of beer; (3) a subject is speaking over an intercom with a person in the next room who suddenly seems to have a violent seizure. In each case careful attention was given to whether, when, and how the unknowing subjects attempted to give aid.

Typical of the findings were those of the lady-in-distress case in which we have asked you to imagine yourself. A number of different conditions were tried with different sets of subjects. Under what conditions would you as a bystander be most apt to help the lady?

1. If you were alone in the room, you probably helped (70 percent did).
2. If you were with another subject, a stooge who only shrugged his shoulders and went on with the questionnaire, you probably did not help (only 7 percent did).
3. If you were with another subject, a stranger to you but a real subject, not a stooge, neither of you probably helped (in only 40 percent of the cases did either help).
4. But if you were with a friend who was participating in the study with you, the chances are that one of you would respond to the lady's distress (in 70 percent of these cases at least one person moved to help).

From such results we may begin to form some generalizations. One generalization is that if an individual is in the company of a friend, he is more apt to offer help than if he is in the company of a stranger. Another is that an individual is more apt to help if he is alone than if he is with others. However, the chances that *one* of the two friends would give aid are no better than if any individual is alone. This tendency was also found in the other experiments by Latané and Darley. Persons are less apt to give aid when other persons are present than when they are alone. Why? Latané and Darley reason that two different processes may be working in this direction. One might be called the social influence hypothesis. When in an unexpected situation, we look to others who may be present to help us interpret what is happening. When this monitoring of cues from each other is going on, persons may be less apt to act than if they were alone. And observing others fail to act may give the individual the idea that the situation is less serious than he first thought.

Another way of explaining the greater inaction of groups may be called the diffusion-of-responsibility hypothesis. If a group is present in an emergency, they share and thus diffuse responsibility for acting to such a degree that no one individual may take on the job of helping. When an individual is alone, he feels a greater responsibility for taking action.

Do such studies as these make more understandable the silence of the thirty-eight witnesses to the Kitty Genovese murder? Latané and Darley believe that they do, but not by any process of dehumanization in large cities. Rather, they conclude that their studies show that situational factors, that is, factors about the immediate social environment, are more important in determining an individual's behavior in an emergency than such general concepts as apathy or alienation due to urbanization. They suggest that bystanders' relationships with each other, or the lack thereof, provide the key for understanding their unresponsiveness.

Why do we find that such incidents of apparent indifference occur most frequently in large urban centers? Latané and Darley (1970) have a ready answer:

> When an emergency occurs in a large city, many people are likely to be present. The people are likely to be strangers. It is likely that no one will be acquainted with the victim. The bystanders may be unfamiliar with the locale of the emergency. These are exactly the conditions that made helping least likely in our experiments (p. 127).

GOING UNDERGROUND

Imagine yourself now in another situation. You are on the subway; to be exact, the 8th Avenue IND train between 59th Street and 125th Street in New York City. Among the people getting on at the last stop was a man you hadn't particularly noticed until this moment, as he unsteadily leans against a post near the end of the car. Suddenly, before your eyes, he collapses to the floor, rolls over on his back, and lies still. Is he unconscious? That's hard to say. He appears to be staring at the ceiling. Maybe he needs help of some kind—but what should anyone do? Maybe in a minute he'll get up, and everything will be O.K. You hope so, for he's really a mess lying there like that. Someone should do something about it. Isn't that man near him going to help? Maybe if you went on to the next car you could find a more pleasant place to sit . . .

In just such a situation as this approximately 4,450 men and women in 1968 unwittingly served as subjects for an experiment by Irving Piliavin and associates (Piliavin, Rodin, and Piliavin, 1969). These subjects were bystanders in a car where the man-who-collapses-on-the-floor act was staged. Also in the same car were two college students, discreetly placed to observe what happened, and one other person who would eventually help the victim if nobody else did so. This experimental team of four repeated their act, with certain planned variations, more than a hundred times during a period of ten weeks.

There were several main variations in the experiment. One of these had to do with the props carried by the victim and his appearance. Sometimes he carried a white cane, suggesting blindness as an explanation of his unsteadiness. At other times he smelled of alcohol and carried a liquor bottle in a paper bag, suggesting quite another explanation for his lack of physical grace.

Another key variation was that of the victim's race. In some cases the victim was black and in other cases white. With the racial composition of these trains fairly evenly divided between blacks and whites, this would allow study of race as a possible variable in helping behavior.

Still another variation occurred quite naturally in the subway simply by virtue of the time of day that the experiment was conducted. Sometimes the car was crowded and sometimes it was nearly empty. Did this make any difference for coming to the aid of the victim?

For results, let us note first that most of the time someone did come to aid the victim within the first minute after he fell. This was especially true when the victim carried a white cane, for a full 100 percent of the seemingly blind victims were given help by subway travelers. Only about two-thirds of the drunk victims were so aided.

Did race make a difference? Apparently it did not contribute significantly to the outcome. Whites and blacks in the car were about equally likely to come to the aid of the victim. Furthermore, in the blind condition there was apparently no relationship between race of victim and race of helper; in the drunk condition, however, there was a tendency for help to come first from someone of the same race as the victim.

More important than race differences were those of sex. Approximately 90 percent of those who offered help first were males, although only about 60 percent of the people in the car were males. This suggests that in this particular kind of situation (including a male victim), help was much more likely to come from males than females.

And what about the degree of crowding? Here we come to a result that seems to contradict the earlier experiments of Latané and Darley. When there were more persons in the part of the car where the victim fell, he was apt to be helped more quickly than when fewer persons were present. Rather than a diffusion-of-responsibility effect, greater numbers of bystanders appeared to create a stimulation-of-helping effect. How can this be reconciled with the earlier studies by Latané and Darley? In part, Piliavin suggests, by noting some possibly key differences in the design of the conditions obtaining in the studies. Perhaps diffusion of responsibility is less apt to occur when the victim is immediately present and his misfortune may be seen directly. This was the case in the 8th Avenue subway studies, in contrast to the studies by Latané and Darley. Perhaps the diffusion of responsibility applies mainly as we go from one person to two or three (the main comparisons of earlier studies) rather than in the somewhat larger groups found in the subway cars. Here, at any rate, is an issue left inconclusive by this research: When will a larger number of bystanders inhibit the giving of help, and when might they stimulate it? Under what conditions might we appropriately apply that new adage of "the more the warier"?

But we should be able to do better than just pull out a few generalizations from the results of each study. If we are to develop the ability to generalize from study to study and from research studies to everyday life, we need a framework for fitting the findings together. We need, in other words, a theoretical model. Such a theoretical model of responding to emergency situations is outlined by Piliavin, Rodin, and Piliavin (1969). It may be summarized by the following propositions.

1. Observing an emergency tends to be accompanied by emotional arousal. This arousal is greater (a) the closer one is to a victim physically, (b) the greater the psychological identification with the victim, and/or (c) the longer the emergency continues.
2. Bystanders in such situations seek ways of reducing their emotional arousal. This can be done by (a) helping directly, (b) going to get help, (c) leaving the situation, and/or (d) psychologically rejecting the victim as unworthy of help.
3. Persons will reduce their arousal in whatever manner they find most rewarding or least costly. Included in the rewards and costs must be: (a) rewards for helping, such as a good self-evaluation, (b) rewards for not helping, such as being able to continue whatever else one is doing, (c) costs for helping, such as embarrassment or possible physical harm, and (d) costs for not helping, such as being criticized by self or others.

Such a theoretical model does not tell us directly what will happen in a particular situation, but it does give us a guide for making some general predictions. However, one thing should give us pause about making predictions about responses to emergencies; this is that an emergency in real life is by its very nature not predictable.

Interestingly enough, this lack of anticipation of emergencies came to plague the Piliavin subway study in a very special way. In fact, it caused the study to end before all the planned trials had been carried out. Just as these teams of Columbia University students were becoming seasoned professionals at staging their man-who-collapses-on-the-floor act, another kind of emergency developed up above ground level. This was the 1968 student strike at Columbia University, and Irving Piliavin's fall guys were among those involved in the strike. Without the help of these student teams, the study was forced to end abruptly in June, leaving New York subway travelers with only real drunks and blind men to help.

FURTHER FACTORS IN HELPING

We have suggested that the relationships among bystanders is an important factor in determining whether or when help will be given in an emergency. Further research has underlined another important factor; that is, the example offered by the behavior of the other people who are present. For example, Jacqueline Macaulay (in Macaulay and Berkowitz, 1970, pp. 43–59) has shown that the intake of public contributions to a charity is boosted not only by a generous donor but also by a person who unpleasantly refuses to give anything at all. Apparently the response of another person not only may give an example of appropriate action, but also may serve to focus attention and sentiment. In Macaulay's studies the mere presence of a Santa Claus at a collection box for needy children in December served to increase giving by about tenfold, and even a gruff refusal to give to a Biafra-Nigeria Relief Committee stimulated others to give. When a focus of attention is given to an opportunity for helping, it is apparently harder to pass it by.

Also important is whether or not an individual identifies with others in the situation. Smith and associates (Smith, Smythe, and Lien, 1972) have shown that a planted nonresponsive bystander had a different effect on subjects depending on whether they saw him as similar or dissimilar to themselves. When the nonresponsive bystander was seen as dissimilar, the other people in the situation were more apt to help a feigning fainting victim.

The relationship to the victim is also important. Liebhart (1972) has shown that the tendency to help a victim of an apparent explosion is stronger when subjects believe themselves acquainted with him. And Langer and Abelson (1972) have suggested that when the victim is not known, the way in which he asks for help may be very important in determining whether or not he gets it. They indicate that this may also be affected by whether or not a request for help is considered legitimate. When a victim asks a legitimate favor, the chances of getting help are improved if he begins the appeal with victim-oriented phrases (for example, "My knee is killing me, I think I sprained it. Would you do something for me? . . ."). When a victim asks for help that might be considered illegitimate, phrases oriented to the person approached are more likely to elicit help (for example, "Would you do something for me? Please do me a favor and . . ."). Langer and Abelson subtitle their report "How to Succeed in Getting Help without Really Dying"; it may be a good bit of research to remember if you ever want to approach a passerby for help in a future personal emergency.

Another important factor in determining whether or not help will be given is the severity of the emergency. Having their students go down into the subway again, this time in Philadelphia, Piliavin and Piliavin (1972) had the prospective fall-down victim take along some red food coloring in addition to his white cane. In half of the trials the victim would pop a dropper full of red food coloring into his mouth just before staging his act. Then when he fell, out of his mouth would trickle what could only be perceived as blood. The other half of the trials constituted the no blood condition. What effect did the sight of blood have upon gaining help? It made immediate help less likely, but increased the likelihood that observers would try to go and get help from someone else. This leads to the conclusion that as the severity of the emergency increases, the likelihood that direct help will be given decreases while the probability of indirect help increases. But, alas, another underground Piliavin study had to be cut short before all the planned trials were completed, so our data are not quite as complete as we would like. The reasons mentioned by the authors for termination of the study must remind us of the dangers in making an experiment too realistic:

> Problems encountered included discovery and harassment by transit authority police; irrational actions on the part of real bystanders, such as attempting to pull the emergency cord to stop the train; and impending panic during some blood trials (p. 356).

There is some evidence that mood or temporary disposition is an important factor in coming to the aid of another person. Isen (1970) has demonstrated that persons are more generous and helpful after a temporary success than after an experimentally induced failure. Temporary elation, rather than depression, has been shown by Aderman (1972) to be associated with helping behavior. And Ragan and associates (1972) have presented evidence to suggest that temporary arousal of guilt feelings leads to an increased tendency to help.

Given the evidence for the importance of temporary mood, we might expect that the more enduring patterns of personality would be related to the amount and kind of helping. However, what evidence we have on personality factors does not in fact suggest that they are very important. After reviewing their evidence, Latané and Darley (1970) concluded:

> None of the personality tests we have investigated have related to helping, and autobiographical information seems to do little better. These findings suggest that anybody can be led either to help or not to help in a specific situation. Characteristics of the immediate situation may have a more important influence on what the bystander does than his personality or life history (pp. 119–120).

If variations in providing help to others in emergency situations are not determined to any meaningful or predictable extent by individual character or personal background, how can we make general sense out of such helping behavior? How can we sum up the "characteristics of the immediate situation" that are apparently so important? There is no good single theory that will summarize nicely all the results we have mentioned. But for a useful framework, let us remind ourselves of the theoretical model suggested by Piliavin, Rodin, and Piliavin (1969). This leads us to focus upon the factors in a situation that might affect the costs or rewards of helping. Anything that generally serves to emphasize the importance of the opportunity to help, as is seen in the studies by Macaulay, is apt to increase helping. However, if signs of danger are involved, such as blood trickling from the victim's mouth (Piliavin and Piliavin, 1972), the costs of immediate helping (and also of doing nothing at all) will appear increased. The result will be a more emotionally charged dilemma in deciding to help or not to help—sometimes resolved nicely by getting help from someone else. Identification with other unresponsive bystanders will reduce the costs of not helping, as suggested by the results of Smith and associates (1972), but identification (or even only slight acquaintance) with the victim will increase the costs of not helping. The manner of asking for help may be especially important in drawing attention to certain rewards and costs, as the research by Langer and Abelson (1972) suggests. Finally, mood may be interpreted as predisposing a person to be relatively more sensitive to rewards (in a good mood) or to costs (in a bad mood). The special case of guilt arousal may be seen as making the potential benefits of self-esteem temporarily much higher, given the generally low state of self-regard that accompanies guilt feelings; thus people who feel guilty are more apt to help—providing the helping behavior can be seen as genuinely doing good.

In an after-the-fact kind of reasoning we can thus make sense of most of the findings of the various studies we have cited about helping behavior. But there is one question still left hanging: Is help more or less likely to come when there are more bystanders present? Apparently this depends on additional features of the situation, which have yet to be identified. Immediate presence of the victim, as Piliavin (1969) suggests, may be one important factor. But what else?

SUGGESTED EXERCISE

Team up with another individual, with one of you playing the role of victim and the other one acting as observer.

The victim should be walking along with an armful of books. At an appropriate place he will stumble in a predetermined manner and drop most of his books. This stumbling-and-book-dropping act must be carefully standardized so that it can be performed in exactly the same way on different occasions.

The observer should follow at a discreet distance and record information regarding whether the victim is helped and, if so, how, how quickly, and by whom.

This act should be repeated in different kinds of settings. Note particularly variations in numbers of persons immediately present in the same kind of setting to see if this variable is related to the tendency to help.

With imagination you can devise new variations to test for additional factors in helping behavior. Ask your instructor to help you plan a systematic experiment.

A word of caution: If you do the book-dropping act repeatedly, try to use expendable books. Librarians would rightfully frown upon library books being thrown around in the fashion necessary for such an experiment.

2
Liking People

THE WELCOME WEEK EXPERIMENT

Incoming freshmen at the University of Minnesota have traditionally had a week of specially planned events known as "Welcome Week." Scheduled for the final day of this week one recent year was to be a dance with partners selected by a computer. "Here's your chance to meet someone who has the same expressed interests as yourself," said the advertising piece. Tickets were sold at the rate of one dollar per person to the first 376 male and 376 female students who appeared. In taking part in this social event, students were also, without their knowledge, taking part in an experiment conducted by Elaine Walster and her associates (Walster, Aronson, Abrahams, and Rottmann, 1966).[1]

In the process of getting properly registered for this dance, students met four persons. One sold tickets; a second person down the same table checked identification cards and told the students to proceed to another room; here a third person met the students and gave them questionnaires; a fourth person showed them to seats where they could fill out their questionnaires. These four persons (two males and two females, all sophomores) were the same individuals throughout registration for the dance, and they had another less obvious task in addition to helping students register. This was to make an independent evaluation of the physical attractiveness of each of the 752 freshmen buying tickets.

In filling out advance questionnaires, students supplied general information about themselves and their preferences. Also included "only for research purposes and not for matching purposes" were questions designed to measure four variables: self-report of popularity, nervousness, general self-esteem, and expectations of date's attractiveness. Actually, the only information used at all in matching partners was height: no males were matched with taller females. Aside from this requirement, the matching was done on a purely random basis.

Of the 376 couples arranged, all but 44 showed up for the dance.

[1] Elaine Walster, Vera Aronson, Darcy Abrahams, and Leon Rottman, "Importance of Physical Attractiveness in Dating Behavior," *Journal of Personality and Social Psychology*, 4 (1966), 508–516. Copyright 1966 by the American Psychological Association. Quotations from this source are reprinted with permission of the publisher.

During the intermission, ticket stubs were collected for a fifty-dollar drawing while participants individually filled out questionnaires rating their partners. In a follow-up, the investigators contacted participants several months later to see whether or not there had been any attempts by the computer partners to date each other. Fifteen couples either could not be contacted later or failed to fill out all materials at intermission, leaving 317 couples for final analysis.

As the reader may guess, the intermission ratings of dance partners supplied the basic "moment of truth" for this experiment. This was when the measures of the main dependent variable, interpersonal attraction, were obtained. Supplementing these ratings were the follow-up data concerning whether further dating followed.

And what led to attractiveness toward a partner? What kinds of persons found their partners most attractive, and what kinds of partners were considered to be the most attractive dates?

A variety of personality measures were available to the investigators. These included a scale of self-acceptance derived from preliminary questionnaire material, and several variables (for example, social introversion and masculinity-femininity) were obtained from testing-service files. Also obtained were measures of intelligence and high school scholastic achievement. However, none of these variables appeared to have much to do with attraction at the computer dance. While some of the patterns may be interesting (persons with higher indications of social maturity and masculinity and lower indications of introversion and high school scholastic achievement tend to be the better liked as dating partners), the correlations between personality measures and attraction were generally so low that little significance should be attached to them.

But the investigators were not just interested in these gross relationships. They had another approach, with a more specific set of hypotheses. Their general theory was that satisfaction with a partner would be relative to level of aspiration, and level of aspiration would in turn be related to one's own attractiveness. They cited work of Kurt Lewin to suggest that goals a person can expect to attain are usually lower than what would be most desirable. They reasoned further that

> In romantic choices, attractiveness and availability would also seem to be negatively correlated. The more abstractly desirable a potential romantic object is, the more competition there probably is for him (or her), and the less likely it is that a given individual will be able to attain his friendship. Thus, one's *realistic* social choices should be less "socially desirable" than one's fantasy skills. In addition . . . we would expect that the individual's own social attractiveness would affect his level of aspiration (pp. 508–509).

Not only would unusually attractive persons be unrealistic dates for less attractive persons, but interaction between such persons should be less satisfying than between those more equal in personal attractiveness. Or at least so speculated the investigators.

From such considerations Walster and associates derived the following three hypotheses:

1. Individuals who are themselves very socially desirable will require that an appropriate partner possess more social desirability than will a less socially desirable individual.
2. If couples varying in social desirability meet in a social situation, those couples who are similar in social desirability will most often attempt to date one another.
3. An individual will not only *choose* a date of approximately his own social desirability, but also after actual experience with potential dates of various desirabilities an individual will express the most *liking* for a partner of approximately his own desirability (p. 509).

In this study only one aspect of attractiveness was evaluated—physical attractiveness. It was not assumed to be the same as attractiveness in general; rather, it was used to indicate the form of attractiveness that could be most easily assessed (by the four sophomores in the registration procedure).

Let us now see what degree of support the investigators found for their hypotheses. The first hypothesis was strongly supported. The more physically attractive persons had less liking for their randomly selected partners than the less attractive persons felt toward their partners. This was clearly the trend for both males and females.

The second and third hypotheses, however, were not supported by the findings. Rather, what was found was that persons generally liked most those partners who had the highest physical attractiveness.

These results seem somewhat inconsistent. More attractive persons are less apt to reciprocate their partner's liking; nevertheless, such liking does not decrease. Isn't it reasonable to expect liking to decline when it isn't reciprocated? Or doesn't the emotional response of liking or even loving someone work in this fashion? The investigators speculated:

> It may be that our findings are limited to large group situations, where young people are in very brief contact with one another. Perhaps if individuals had been exposed to one another for long periods of time, similarity of interests, beliefs, and reciprocal liking would come to be more important than physical appearances in determing liking (p. 516).

Perhaps. But later research by Walster and associates (Berscheid, Dion, Walster, and Walster, 1971) provides clearer evidence that persons in dating situations do tend to pair off in terms of social desirability.

That similarity of physical attractiveness does continue to characterize couples after initial dating is suggested by further research by Murstein (1972). In two different studies of actual couples who were going steady or were engaged, he found a significant degree of similarity between partners in terms of ratings of physical attractiveness. Murstein concludes that persons "with equal market value for physical attractiveness are more likely to associate in an intimate relationship such as premarital engagement than individuals with disparate values" (p. 11).

DATING AT ELMTOWN

The theory we have been dealing with in this chapter is a theory about general social desirability. However, the main kind of social desirability examined so far is that of physical attractiveness. Would the same pattern of attraction to those with similar levels of desirability hold if we used a broader conception of social desirability? In answer to this question, let us examine some data that is available to us as part of a study of an Illinois town, nicknamed "Elmtown," by August B. Hollingshead (1949).

During April 1942 Hollingshead attempted to obtain as complete a record as possible of who dated whom during that month among all the adolescents of Elmtown. This appears as no small task when it is pointed out that Elmtown had, by Hollingshead's own count, 735 adolescents. Nevertheless, he was able to record 967 dates for this month. Of these, 553 dates were between high school students; and of these 553 dates, slightly over half (51 percent) were with persons of the same school class. Of those outside the school class, most of the girls dated boys of a higher level in school, and most of the boys dated girls of a lower school class—reflecting the cultural preference that males be at least as old as the females they date or marry.

However, Hollingshead's main interest was in another kind of class, social class; and the role of social class appears even stronger than that of school class in determining dating patterns. He divided members of the community into five social classes. Because the highest class had so few members, he usually combined it with the next social class for purposes of analysis. For simplicity, we shall represent these social class levels as classes A, B, C, and D, from highest to lowest.

The Nature of Social Class

THEORETICAL POINTER

Social class has a variety of meanings in contemporary social science, but all have reference to a hierarchical placement of persons in the structure of society.

Often social class is identified by economic criteria such as income, occupation, or the degree of affluence represented by one's residence. Another frequent means of identification is amount of education, which correlates closely with economic variables. Such criteria of socioeconomic status can be used to compare persons with one another, and the divisions that such comparisons are broken into are called social classes. With such a procedure, social classes are often considered as simply arbitrary divisions of a continuum of socioeconomic status.

Other writers use the concept of social class to refer to actual groupings of a community. The key delineator of social class in this view is the reputation a family has in the community. Furthermore, it is held that such reputations of families come to be clustered around different levels of the prestige continuum. The term *social class* is then used to represent the strata into which major clusterings of families are to be found on the prestige scale of a given community.

This latter approach to social class is the one used by Hollingshead. To obtain his social class designations he had certain members of the community give comparative evaluations of other families in terms of (1) the way the family lived, (2) income and possessions, (3) participation in community affairs, and (4) prestige or standing in the community. From such ratings he developed a class ranking for all families in the community who had adolescent children.

Still somewhat different is the traditional conception of social class, which has its roots in Europe's feudal period. This was a division of social positions ranging from titled nobility to the serfs. It had its reference in the society at large and not just in a local community, and the divisions were formally recognized in the legal structure. As this system evolved, a middle class of tradesmen and other city dwellers came into prominence between the traditionally dominant upper class of the titled nobility and the numerically dominant but relatively powerless lower class of peasants. On the modern American scene this approach sees a much more informal class structure consisting of a small elite, a large middle class of business and white collar persons, and

an equally large lower- or working-class group.

Somewhat similar is the Marxian conception of social classes as based on ownership or nonownership of productive property. This approach, though more specifically based upon the economic system, also presents a society-wide basis of dividing social class.

All three of these main conceptions of social class—(1) as an arbitrary division of a continuum of socioeconomic status, (2) as a grouping of families based on their reputations in a particular community, and (3) as the modern counterpart of a historical division of society into formally recognized segments—provide means of describing differences in status among different people. The set of categories developed by one of these approaches has produced results that correlate quite closely with those of another approach. But the theoretical roots of these three approaches are actually quite different.

Considering these social class designations as matters of family background and place in the community, we can see that such matters of family and community entered into dating patterns in an important way. Altogether, 61 percent of dates were within the same social class level. A detailed breakdown of dating by social class levels is given in Table 1. In this table we see not only the preponderance of dating with the same social class but also that most of the other dates were between persons of adjacent social classes.

Table 1 also points to another phenomenon. While the class-level dating patterns of boys and girls were about the same, the girls showed a consistently higher frequency of dating. This is true even though there were fewer boys than girls in high school. This means that the girls, far more than the boys, dated with nonschool persons. In fact, most of the girls' dates were with boys out of school, whereas less than one-fourth of the boys' dates were outside the school. In dating nonstudents, girls from the upper social classes dated primarily Elmtown high school graduates; whereas lower-class girls dated primarily boys who had dropped out of school.

Parental influence had an important part to play in supporting such a concentration of dating within one's social class. But the adolescents themselves were also upholders of this class structure. Their informal

TABLE 1   DATING PATTERNS OF ELMTOWN HIGH SCHOOL STUDENTS
IN APRIL 1942, BY SOCIAL CLASS

	Social Class Level	Mean No. of Dates (month)	Percent of Dates with Persons of Social Class			
			A	B	C	D
BOYS:	A	3.4	50	35	15	0
	B	2.8	15	58	27	0
	C	2.9	4	16	74	6
	D	1.9	0	9	33	58
GIRLS:	A	5.2	54	38	8	0
	B	3.3	18	53	27	2
	C	3.4	3	11	79	7
	D	4.6	0	2	28	70

SOURCE: Adapted from Hollingshead (1949), pp. 229 and 231.

cliques were major influences on who dated whom. An illustration of this may be seen in the case of Joan Meyers and Melvin Swigart. Joan was a member of the G.W.G.'s, a relatively high-class club of Elmtown's teenagers, but she accepted a date to a high school dance with Melvin Swigart of class D. Two days later she was seen going for a ride in Melvin's jalopy during the noon hour. For these indiscretions she was given the "silent treatment" by her former friends. She did not continue dating Melvin, and, after a short period of inactivity, became involved once again with the G.W.G.'s. She explained her situation as follows:

> You see, I'm in the G.W.G.'s, but I don't run around with the
> G.W.G.'s all the time. I'm kind of in-between the G.W.G.'s and
> the other kids. I was out of the G.W.G.'s for a while because they
> made me mad. They drew the social line too fine. I dated a boy
> they didn't like. We went to a dance, and they just ignored me.
> I just couldn't stand that. It hurt me, so I pulled out of there;
> but now I've more or less started to go back with them (p. 235).

A class D girl made the following summary of this incident: "Joan should not have dated Melvin if she wanted to run with those upper kids. A girl like her cannot do that kind of a thing" (p. 235).

The dating observed by Hollingshead took place in a more natural way than that in the experiments designed by Walster and associates. Also, social class suggests a broader conception of social desirability than does physical attractiveness. Elmtown may therefore provide an even better test of Walster's hypothesis that persons come to choose persons roughly equal in social desirability to themselves. If we accept social class status as an index of such desirability, we find in Hollingshead's study rather direct evidence that this does indeed occur. Elmtown adolescents did select persons of similar social class backgrounds for dates.

Of course, we have no good evidence in Hollingshead's study that these adolescents actually came to *like* better those of similar social desirability—especially as compared to those of greater desirability. They might still have preferred those who were beyond their reach.

However, if marriage is any evidence of liking, Hollingshead has produced in a later study of another town (1950) rather compelling evidence that persons do marry others of similar social background, including social class.

THEORETICAL
POINTER

The Compromise Process

Carl Backman and Paul Secord (1964) report further evidence that persons do come to choose *and like* persons similar to themselves in general social desirability. In studying a college sorority, they found that mutual preferences for each other tended to come from girls of the same general level of popularity in the group.

Deriving some basic ideas from Thibaut and Kelley (1959) and Homans (1961), Backman and Secord suggest that it would be useful to view liking "as a function of the degree to which persons achieve in their interaction with others a reward-cost ratio in excess of some minimum level" (p. 21). Rewards here refer to anything that brings satisfaction, and costs may refer to any trouble or disadvantages suf-

fered, including rewards forgone. The mutuality of social choice may thus be seen as a situation produced by each person "obtaining his best available cost-reward outcomes."

But why not prefer someone higher on the ladder of social desirability? Such a person might not be so available to become a friend, for there are others seeking such friendship. Also, the costs of being rejected, and even those of simply anticipating rejection, are high. Much greater, then, may be the rewards of seeking friendship with someone at one's own level. Apparently this is the compromise solution often accepted—accepted at least often enough to help stabilize the patterns of relationships within groups.

"BIRDS OF A FEATHER"?

So far in this chapter we have established that persons of a similar level of social desirability are apt to be more attracted to each other than persons of different levels of desirability. The interpretation suggested has been formulated primarily on a social system level rather than on an individual level. In the market system of human beings wanting other human beings, there is a tendency for transactions to occur when both parties, given their own limited resources, can best afford the interaction—which is usually at similar levels of social desirability.

At this point many readers will be restless. They did not come to this book for a lesson on economics, and a chapter on "Liking People" should allow more for the uniqueness of individual preferences than has been indicated so far. But patience! There is more to come.

One way to interpret the results regarding attraction at similar levels of social desirability is as just one aspect of the more general theme of similarity. "Like attracts like"—so goes the popular saying; or "birds of a feather flock together." Are there not basic psychological needs that are satisfied by attraction to someone similar to oneself?

Many research studies have documented the role of similarity in attraction. A review such as that given by Berscheid and Walster in their book, *Interpersonal Attraction* (1969, pp. 69–91), gives ample evidence that, as a general rule, persons are attracted to others who are similar to themselves in important respects. Let us take just one of these studies and examine it in some detail.

ACQUAINTANCE AT ANN ARBOR

Most studies of friendship record data either when the process is just starting (as in the Welcome Week study) or after friendship is already formed (as in Hollingshead's Elmtown study). Very rare are systematic studies of friendship formation that follow the process from the very beginnings of acquaintance through a period of actual friendship. The problems of doing such a study are obvious. How can you know which friendships are going to be formed? And if this problem could be overcome, how can one presume to follow closely enough or long enough to capture the dynamics of the process?

One notable attempt to study friendship formation in process—rare in its attention to systematic data-gathering on friendship formation—was conducted by Theodore Newcomb (1956; 1961) in 1954–1956 at Ann Arbor, home of the University of Michigan.

During each of two different school years a house was rented near the university campus. This was to be a rooming house for seventeen male students and, at the same time, a laboratory for the study of interpersonal processes.

Each year a separate set of students was offered this opportunity for free rent in exchange for their willingness to be subjects for frequent questionnaires and interviews. All persons involved were transfer students, strangers to the university who had no previous acquaintance with one another. In fact, care was taken to see that no two persons who would be in the house had ever lived in the same city. They were allowed to develop their own arrangements, within university regulations, to conduct their house, including provisions for cooking and eating meals. However, they were not given any choice over room assignments; these were made in advance by the investigators.

All seventeen men arrived at approximately the same time, and the first questionnaire was presented almost immediately—before they had a chance to become acquainted with one another. Further questionnaires and interviews followed, at semiweekly intervals, throughout the period of a semester.

Newcomb's principal research objective was to study "changing interrelationships, over time, between attraction and similarity of attitudes" (1956, p. 570). For this it was important to get a variety of measures of attitudes, both at the very beginning and throughout the period of acquaintance. It was important to bring together persons without previous acquaintance, so that friendship could be observed in the process of formation.

While generally curious about "what would happen," Newcomb also had a rather definite theoretical orientation that he brought to the study. He had in mind some theoretical generalizations about interpersonal relations, which he hoped to be able to test by data gathered on the acquaintance process. These generalizations were largely derived from Heider's theory of balance (Heider, 1944; 1958), and they dealt primarily with the relationships of attitudes to interpersonal perception and attraction. Newcomb had a general expectation that interpersonal attraction would follow a similarity of attitudes, at least when the object of attitudes had common relevance for the persons involved. This in turn was based on the general expectation of balance theory that we will have similar sentiments about things that we regard as belonging together. In other words, where we perceive similar attitudes we will perceive ourselves to be more closely associated with another person; and when we feel closely associated, some of our own positive self-feeling should also be associated with the other person.

More formally, we may follow some of the terms used by Newcomb to indicate his theoretical expectations. Let us consider two persons, A and B, with a common object of orientation, X. If A is attracted to B, he will tend to have the same attitude toward X that he perceives B has. Likewise, if A has a favorable attitude toward X and he perceives that B does too, he will tend to be attracted to B. Also, if A is attracted to B and is favorable toward X, he will tend to perceive B as also favorable to X. To summarize, let us represent these three elements as angles of a triangle.

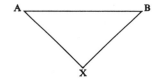

Here the line AB represents A's liking (or disliking) of B, the line AX represents A's favorable (or unfavorable) attitude toward object X, and the line BX represents A's perception of B's attitude toward X. (Note that all of this is to be located in the mind of A.)

From this model, three main kinds of effects would be predicted: (1) we should tend to be attracted to those persons whose attitudes we perceive as being most like our own; (2) we should tend to develop attitudes that are similar to those of persons toward whom we are attracted; and (3) we should tend to see persons to whom we are attracted as more similar to ourselves in attitudes than is the case in reality.

If any two lines of this triangle represent positive association in the mind of A, the third line, according to the theory of balance, should also tend toward positive association. For example, if Abner likes Betty, who in turn likes symphonic music, there would be at least some tendency for Abner to like symphonic music too. If any two lines represent negative association, the third line, to balance these, should tend toward positive association. For example, if Abner dislikes opera and he perceives that Betty dislikes opera too, he will be slightly more attracted to Betty as a result. Finally, if one line represents positive association and another represents negative association, the third line should also represent negative association. For example, if Abner likes

Betty but dislikes hillbilly music, there will be a tendency for him to perceive her as disliking such music too. Although Newcomb gives some evidence relative to all of these predictions in his Ann Arbor study, we shall limit our attention primarily to the prediction that attitude similarity leads to interpersonal attraction.

However, before we examine the specific data on attitudes as related to attraction, let us take note of the influence of some other factors. Among possible background factors that might relate to interpersonal attraction, Newcomb examined five in particular: age, college at the university in which the student was enrolled, religious preference, rural-urban background, and room assignment. In neither of the two years that the study was conducted was similarity in regard to any of these five variables significantly related to interpersonal attraction during the initial week of the study. But in the first year a tendency had developed by the end of the term for mutual friends to be similar in age and residential background (rural or urban). And in the study of the second-year group, college enrollment, room assignment, and residential background all showed significant relationships to interpersonal attraction by the end of the term. Newcomb suggests that such background factors may have worked largely to facilitate attraction through common attitudes.

But what of the evidence specifically related to attitudes? Are persons with similar attitudes attracted to one another, as Newcomb hypothesized?

Newcomb obtained attitude responses to a wide variety of objects. These included such things as attitudes toward house policies, particular university policies, sexual behavior, other personal standards, religion, race relationships, and public affairs. He then developed an index of agreement of a potential pair of subjects on this miscellaneous collection of attitudes. Our next question is whether such an index of attitude similarity is related to interpersonal attraction.

Table 2 presents a breakdown of attraction separately for those persons showing especially high similarity in attitudes and those not showing such similarity. By comparing the two rows we see that attraction during the first week of the term had little relationship to initial agreement on attitudes (30 percent is not significantly different from 26 percent). But by the end of the term a strong difference could be observed—persons with high initial agreement on attitudes (and these attitudes showed little change during the period of study) were at least twice as likely (58 percent vs. 25 percent) to show high attrac-

TABLE 2 ATTRACTION AS RELATED TO SIMILARITY OF MISCELLA-NEOUS ATTITUDES

Initial Agreement on Attitudes	*Number of Pairs (both years)*	**Percent of Pairs Showing High Attraction**	
		First Week	*Last Week*
High	43	30	58
Moderate or low	229	26	25

SOURCE: Adapted from Newcomb (1961), pp. 80 and 81.

tion to each other as those with less agreement on attitudes.

These attitude items, however, represented quite a mixture. It may be recalled that Newcomb's prediction was that attraction would develop when persons had similar attitudes *toward objects of common relevance.* Many of the elements in the attitude questionnaires would not have much common relevance for any particular pair of persons; but there are some attitude objects that would necessarily be of common relevance. For instance, what could be of more common relevance than the rest of the persons living in the house? Would persons with similar attitudes toward other house members also tend to show high attraction toward each other? Indeed, yes; this is what Newcomb found. Here the relationships were even stronger than those indicated for miscellaneous attitudes. Persons with high agreement about the attractiveness of other house members were at least four times as likely to be mutual friends as those with low agreement. Of course here it is quite likely that we are dealing with both cause and effect at the same time: persons who shared the same view of other house members were more likely to become friends, and persons who became friends were more likely to develop similar views about other house members.

But perhaps not all objects of common relevance are equally important. Agreement on some things may be primary and on others less crucial. Let us therefore broaden the generalization to say that persons will become attracted to each other when they share similar attitudes toward *mutually important* objects of common relevance. And what would be an especially important object of common relevance? Probably most important of all would be two persons' views of each other. From the standpoint of a particular person this becomes the question: Does he have the same view of me as I have of myself? Assuming that most persons are attracted to themselves, a most crucial question is whether the other is attracted. And very early this does show its importance in Newcomb's data—within the very first few days. He has reported:

> Whatever the causal direction, our data show that an individual's distribution of General Liking among his associates is related to their liking for him. The relationship is almost as close on the fourth day as at the end of the fourth month, and as a general tendency is highly significant, though there are individual exceptions. One can predict an individual's liking for another individual with much better than chance accuracy if one knows the latter's liking for the former, at any time after the fourth day.
>
> The prediction will be a good deal more accurate, however, if it is made from an individual's *estimate* of how well he is liked by the other. At any time from the second week on (when such estimates were first made), about three of every four estimates of another person's liking for oneself were in the same half of the distribution as own liking for that other person (1956, p. 581).

Many years ago W. I. Thomas made the observation that situations defined as real are real in their consequences. Newcomb's data suggests the importance of such a definition-of-the-situation idea: those who *thought* another was attracted were usually attracted in turn—whether or not the other really was attracted.

If a sharing of common attitudes (about things in general, about other people in particular, and especially about each other) is an important basis of attraction, we would expect that attraction to be most stable after there is an opportunity for acquaintance. It takes time for an exploration of mutual concern to discover what has common relevance. We therefore would expect that friendship patterns early in the term would show less stability than those near the end of the period. And this is exactly what Newcomb found. Only 27 percent of the pair relationships showed stability over the initial two weeks of the study, but 55 percent showed stability over the final two weeks.

Generally, the evidence given by Newcomb supports the idea that we are selectively attracted toward those persons who share common attitudes with us—especially when these attitudes deal with things that we consider important.

THE LIMITS OF SIMILARITY

Using more artificial and more precisely controlled laboratory conditions than Newcomb, Donn Byrne (1969; 1971) has reported even more conclusive evidence concerning the role of similar attitudes in attraction. From the evidence of his series of experiments, it appears that attraction toward a previously unknown individual is directly related to (expressed more precisely mathematically as "a linear function of") the proportion of attitudes of the other that are perceived to be similar to one's own. Byrne's theoretical interpretation of his results differs from that of Newcomb. Byrne prefers a reinforcement theory formulation (with agreement in attitudes seen as positive reinforcement) rather than a balance theory model. But the primary findings of Newcomb and Byrne are the same: similarity in attitudes is a key basis of predicting interpersonal attraction.

However, to say that a similarity of attitudes promotes attraction is not to say that this will prove to be equally true for all persons or for all attitudes. This is well exemplified in a study by Touhey (1972). Although Touhey found that, in general, similarity in attitudes was associated with heterosexual attraction, more interesting were certain differences between males and females. Males, much more than females, were attracted to prospective dates on the basis of similarity of attitudes regarding sex. Females, on the other hand, were more attracted on the basis of similarity of attitudes regarding religion.

Also, evidence of similarity of personality as a basis of attraction is far less clear than that of similarity of attitudes. Although most studies of friends and mates have indicated a positive correlation on personality traits, there remain several possible interpretations. Similarity of personality may be a cause, an effect, or only indirectly associated with attraction. Persons who are similar may be more apt to provide rewards for each other. Or, on the other hand, persons who interact a great deal may become more similar through their association. In the first of these cases similarity would be a cause of attraction; in the second it would be more of a result. Or perhaps the association is only accidental: persons who are similar in personality may be more apt to move in the same circles and thereby meet each other. Most research gives us no basis for sorting out the relative importance of these three possibilities.

There is also evidence to suggest that personalities match on other bases besides similarity. There is of course the factor of sex; males and females are attracted to each other on the basis of very central characteristics that differ. Winch (1958) has extended the idea of attraction through personality differences to formulate a theory of *complementary needs*, and he presents evidence that certain patterns of personality needs (for example, dominance or nurturance) may lead to attraction toward a different rather than a similar person for marriage or close friendship. In another study Hendrick and Brown (1971) have shown that on some measures of attraction, introverts are more attracted to extroverts than to other introverts.

How can such evidence for personality differences be harmonized with the more predominant evidence for similarity? One way has been suggested by Carl Backman and Paul Secord (1962). In studying a sorority group they report evidence for what they call a theory of *interpersonal congruency*. This theory (see also Secord and Backman, 1961) holds that an individual engages in interaction with others in such a way as to maximize the consistency between the following three elements: (1) his own self-concept, (2) his behavior toward others, and (3) the way others seem to relate to him. Essentially, this suggests that he will try to behave toward others in such a way that their response will support his own self-image. Also, suggest Backman and Secord, he will be especially attracted toward those persons who do in fact respond in such a way as to confirm his self-image.

While their research results do give strong support for a congruency theory of attraction, the evidence also suggests a role for similarity in attraction over and above that required for interpersonal congruency. Some of this may be due to the influence of similar social backgrounds, making persons who are in a position to be attracted to each other more likely to be similar; but Schellenberg (1960) has found evidence for similarity even after controlling for similar social backgrounds. Why this added impetus for similarity as such? Perhaps, other things being equal, we just find it easier to associate with persons who are like us. If so, this would turn out to be another manifestation of balance theory: we adopt similar attitudes toward those things we see as "belonging" together, and similarity of self and other may be one of the ingredients for this sense of belonging. Therefore the same high regard we (usually) have for ourselves is more apt than not to be extended to those we see as being like ourselves.

ATTRACTION AS A PROCESS

We have examined two main themes in this chapter. The first theme was that of the importance of similar levels of social desirability in interpersonal attraction. The second was the importance of similarity in personal characteristics, such as attitudes and personality. Both of these themes have been qualified, but both still remain strongly supported by evidence. Let us now attempt to put them together.

Interpersonal attraction may be seen as a process that has several phases. Levinger and Snoek (1972) identify key transition phases in a developing relationship as: (1) approach (becoming aware of another person); (2) affiliation (developing a basis for limited interaction); and (3) attachment (developing a basis of significant and enduring mutuality).

Using the terms of Levinger and Snoek for present convenience, let us suggest that physical attractiveness and similar levels of social desirability will be especially important for the approach phase. We are more apt to initiate some contact if another person is seen as being of a similar status level (in whatever manner status may be evaluated for that particular setting).

Similarity in attitudes, and perhaps in other personal characteristics, is apt to be particularly important for the affiliation phase. Interaction will be more likely to continue if similar attitudes suggest that the individuals have significant things in common. Also probably important here is the possibility of a gain in self-esteem associated with the other person; this factor has been given special emphasis in studies by Aronson (1969).

For the attachment phase our analysis does not so clearly point to key factors. Continuing mutuality in attitudes is no doubt important. Interpersonal congruency may be even more important. But probably most important of all is a reciprocity of commitments. Each individual commits some important part of his life to another. Such commitments may be facilitated by the rather impersonal press of circumstances, as in the case with many work partners. Frequently, however, significant emotional involvements with one another are also a part of the process.

WHAT ABOVE LOVE?

We have almost finished this chapter on "Liking People" with hardly a word about love. It is not that romantic love is not an important part of interpersonal attraction. Rather, the problem is that love is difficult to subject to systematic and objective study. Much easier is it for a social psychologist to content himself with "liking ratings of a stimulus person."

Part of the problem is the ambiguity of what is meant by love. There is in our society such a strongly positive sentiment toward the idea of love that a great variety of experiences are hopefully presented as examples. The result may well lead the observer today to the same conclusion as that early student of the subject (Finck, 1891) who said: "Love is such a tissue of paradoxes, and exists in such an endless variety of forms and shades, that you may say almost anything about it that you please, and it is likely to be correct" (p. 224).

But we cannot quite end on this note, for it would be unfair to what social psychologists have done in this area. Perhaps what a social psychologist can demonstrate about love is insignificant as compared to what a good novelist can imply, but social psychologists have at least begun to investigate the subject.

Consider, for example, the work of Zick Rubin on "Measurement of Romantic Love" (1970). Based on a survey of previous work, Rubin collected a large number of questionnaire items to indicate some form of attraction. He then had individuals judge these items in terms of their ability to distinguish between liking and loving. The outcome was two scales of thirteen items each, one a liking scale and the other a love scale. After validating these scales in a study of 158 dating couples, Rubin set up an experiment. The experiment divided couples on the basis of whether they were high or low on the love scale and allowed observation of their patterns of interaction. The results indicated that couples whose scale scores indicated high love for one another did express it in their interaction, in such forms as gazing into one another's eyes.

Rubin's work may help us measure romantic love, but it does not do much to help us understand why love occurs. Perhaps a study by Stephan and associates (Stephan, Berscheid, and Walster, 1971) may offer some clues on this question. Under the pretext of rating reading materials for another study, half of the subjects (all unattached male undergraduates) were given sexually arousing material to read. The other half read about the sex life of herring gulls; presumably, most of this group were not erotically stimulated by this. Shortly after completing their reading all subjects were presented with information about a female and asked to rate her on several dimensions. Generally, the sexually aroused rated her as more attractive than did those who were not aroused. And when subjects believed that they would have a date with the female rated, aroused subjects were more likely to see her as sexually receptive. All in all, this study appears to give hard evidence for what we have always suspected: sexual arousal may increase the tendency to idealize a prospective partner. Or, to put the matter into even broader terms, it appears that "high drive initiates an 'autistic' process operating in the direction of gratification" (Stephan, Berscheid, and Walster, 1971, p. 99). Certainly this might be one basis of romantic love.

But is sexual arousal a necessary precursor to love? In a speculative essay, Walster and Berscheid (1971) suggest that any kind of arousal might lead to romantic love—provided that a person subjectively associates the arousal experience with his object of love. Physiological arousal may be facilitated by frustration, fear, pain, sex, or joy. Whatever the basis of arousal, if the situational cues are such that the individual identifies his arousal as love, then he will feel himself to be "in love."

Can you formulate a better theory?

3
Origins of Affiliation

To consider the beginnings of human affection we will take note of some of the work of Harry F. Harlow and his associates at the University of Wisconsin. In a series of bold experiments, Harlow manipulated the early social environments of infants to see the effects of varied patterns of early experience. He very carefully observed the behavior of infants with different degrees of opportunity for contact with peers and of those who were subject to different kinds of mothering. To explore the effects of artificial mothering, some of the infants were taken from their mothers shortly after birth.

On the basis of years of such work, Harlow has identified a number of stages in the development of early social relationships, what he refers to as stages in the development of *affectional systems* (Harlow and Harlow, 1965; 1966). We will review the stages the Harlows identify as typical stages of development of the infant's affection for his mother (the *infant-mother affectional system*) and of affection for peers (the *peer affectional system*). Our discussion will be based particularly on their review article titled "Learning to Love" (1966).[1]

STAGES OF EARLY AFFECTION

The infant-mother affectional system has stages that are identified by Harlow and Harlow (1966, pp. 248–253) as (1) the reflex stage, (2) the stage of comfort and attachment, (3) the security stage, and (4) the separation stage. Let us take a brief look at each.

Many of the behaviors Harlow and associates observed in newborns are of a reflex nature. These include such things as sucking and grasping. Although relatively brief, the period of the reflex stage aids survival through physical adjustment to the mother. And although this is primarily a stage of physical adjustment rather than socialization, socialization too begins at this time.

During the latter half of the first month the beginnings of a second stage of development, the stage of comfort and attachment, can typically be seen. In this stage true affectional bonds and basic social

[1] Harry F. Harlow and Margaret K. Harlow, "Learning to Love," *American Scientist*, 54 (1966), 244–272. Quotations from this source are reprinted with permission of the authors and the publisher of *American Scientist*, journal of The Society of the Sigma Xi.

patterns are established. Especially prominent are responses of nursing and clinging, which Harlow sees as natural correlates to each other in the way the infant attaches to the mother. Also of interest is *primary object following*, which typically includes both a visual fixation on the mother and actual physical following of the mother when possible. Thus "when the mother explores a physical object, so does the infant; when the mother mouths and ingests a food substance, so does the infant; when the mother is startled or frightened, the infant clings to the mother's body and observes" (1966, p. 250). In such manner is laid the foundations of an imitation that facilitates the learning of the younger generation from the older.

From this comfort and attachment, and from the mother's corresponding attachment and protection, the infant seems to develop a strong sense of safety and security when in the mother's presence. "All the mother-infant interactions related to nursing, bodily contact, and following-imitation contribute to security, although there is evidence that sheer bodily contact-comfort is the dominant variable," according to Harlow and Harlow (1966, p. 250). Harlow's work indicates that this sense of security may also be centered in a mother surrogate—even a specially constructed "cloth mother" in the case of certain infants reared experimentally without real mothers. "During this period the infant, in the presence of the mother, surrogate or real, shows a growing tendency to go out and explore the inanimate and animate world about it, returning from time to time to the mother's body for comfort and reassurance" (1966, p. 251). This is especially important, in Harlow's view, "in the self-assurance it provides the infant in its exploration of the animate world, particularly the animate world of the infant's own age-mates or peers." Gradually the frequency of contact with the mother declines, and the sight of the mother more and more substitutes for direct bodily contact as a source of security.

Finally comes a gradual separation from the mother. This separation stage may be characterized as a period during which associations with peers are gaining in importance relative to infant-mother relationships. This is in part made possible by the maternal security of the previous stage. Equally important is the curiosity of the young, attracting them to what is novel and interesting—especially toward what may be learned in the company of peers.

The peer affectional system, which in normal cases comes to replace the infant-mother system as the most dominant form of association, also may be identified in terms of four stages. Harlow and Harlow (1965, pp. 253–263) identify these as follows: (1) the reflex stage, (2) the manipulation stage, (3) the stage of interactive play, and (4) the mature interaction stage.

Early in the first year of life infants may begin to fix their vision on each other and to make rough efforts toward approaching each other. This, the Harlows suggest, is originally on a reflex basis. When contact is allowed between infants at this stage, the main manifestations are clinging to and following (visually and physically) each other. Taking note of their experiments that have provided opportunity for extensive peer contact very early (and with minimal mothering), they report that "the pattern appears to be that of utilizing the partner or partners for bodily contact, and this behavior tends to become fixated and to persist long after the clinging reflex disappears if the infants are kept together continuously from early infancy" (1965, p. 255). However, with normal mothering this clinging cannot long continue, for mothers both discourage continuous clinging to themselves and prevent infants from being with each other enough to engage in much early body contact.

Very early in the first year of life, signs of a second stage of peer development, a manipulation stage, are evident. This is also basically a presocial period, but it establishes the foundation for more developed peer relationships as infants "explore each other with eyes, hands, mouth and body, and they alternate manipulation of age-mates with manipulation of the physical environment." The Harlows also report that infants in their experimental conditions "spend steadily increasing time in proximity to each other and make progressively increasing numbers of physical contacts. Gradually they come to respond to each other as social objects instead of physical objects, and social play emerges from the matrix of manipulatory play" (1965, p. 255).

The third stage of development of peer affectional relations, that of interactive play, thus emerges from the manipulation stage. Within the interactive play stage there is a progressive introduction of new styles of interaction. First is a kind of rough-and-tumble play involving wrestling and close body contact. Then is evident a kind of "approach-withdrawal" play with age-mates chasing each other, often alternating roles of chasing and chased. A third development of interactive play is the gradual integration of these patterns of peer interaction into more continuous sequences. And finally there emerges more and more evidence of aggression. From late infancy to the early juvenile period, Harlow and Harlow report, contests between age-mates take on an increasingly aggressive quality as an ordering of dominance within peer groups gradually shows itself. Also noted in the interactive play stage is a tendency toward sexual separation. Most everyday play of males comes to be with other males, and most play of females is with other females.

A final stage in peer affectional development is labeled by the Harlows as that of mature interaction. Even as play decreases, they point out, "there are ample indicators of the continuance of affectional ties among members, both like-sexed and opposite-sexed. Thus, while original peer ties develop in play, these ties may continue to function after play no longer is an important social behavior" (1965, p. 261). This is evident in patterns of association observed in periods of rest and at meal times as well as in other everyday activities.

Earlier we mentioned that some of Harlow's work involved experiments in which infants were systematically deprived of normal mothering. In some cases infants had, for extended periods of time, been denied both normal mothering and contact with peers. In some cases visual contact was allowed, but not physical contact; in other cases not even visual contact was allowed.

The reader probably considers that such experimental procedures are no fit way to treat human beings. The Harlows would agree. It is therefore time that it be made clear that these studies were not of humans at all, but rather of rhesus monkeys. In fact, all the preceding discussion in this chapter has been based on these studies of monkeys. We have avoided saying so until now in order to encourage the reader to see parallels to human development. In their own discussion, the Harlows make clear that they see the stages of development outlined as applying generally (though of course with somewhat different emphases and different time periods) to apes and to men as well as to monkeys. These they see as typical features of primate development, and humans share this primate heritage.

Let us leave aside for the moment the argument concerning whether these studies may or may not have much to suggest about human development and return to what the Harlows report as the effects upon monkeys in their studies of social deprivation:

> As would be expected, total social deprivation produces more dramatic and pervasive effects than partial social deprivation although we now know, somewhat to our surprise, that the differences between these two forms of social deprivation are not nearly as great as we would have predicted, primarily because partial social deprivation is more damaging than we had anticipated (1966, p. 264).

In a series of experiments newborn monkeys were subjected to total social deprivation for different periods of time. Some were isolated for three months, some for six months, and some for a full year. Harlow and Harlow summarize the results of these studies as follows:

> Two studies show that release of the animals after three months of essentially total social deprivation leaves them in a state of emotional shock. Their initial responses are characterized by self-clutching and crouching, which resembles a postural expression of human autistic children. If, however, the monkeys can survive the immediate emotional trauma of release from total social deprivation and are then allowed to interact with control age-mates 30 minutes a day in our playroom situation, they very rapidly establish effective social relationships with their peers. Such long-term studies as we have to date point to essentially complete social recovery, normal learning, and normal sexual adjustment in adolescence. . . .
>
> We have much more definitive data on the effects of 6 and 12 months of total social isolation. The results clearly indicate that even 6 months of total social isolation leaves the monkeys unable to interact socially with age-mates when pairs of them are placed with pairs of controls raised in partial social deprivation and tested in our playroom situation. . . .
>
> Twelve months of total social deprivation, compared with 6 months, produces even more socially devastating results. The 12-month isolates display essentially no social interaction with each other or with controls, as illustrated for the simplest form of play—activity play. Indeed, in this experiment we had to conclude the social tests after 10 weeks because the control animals were increasingly abusing the social isolates, and we were convinced that the isolates would have been killed if testing had continued.
>
> Despite the social ineptitude of both the 6- and 12-month social

isolates, their intellectual abilities appear to have been spared. Like the 3-month isolates, the 6- and 12-month isolates were tested on discrimination learning set problems in the second year of life. They performed at a level not statistically different from that of control subjects of the same age. . . .

We now have a long-term follow-up of animals subjected to 6 and 12 months of total social isolation. As preadolescents and adolescents, they were individually paired in separate tests with a single normal adult, a normal age-mate, and a normal young juvenile. The total social isolates showed fear of adults, age-mates, and even juveniles, but while showing fear, the 6-month isolates—not the 12-month isolates—also demonstrated, completely to our surprise, violent and abnormal aggressive behaviors. These included aggresson against juveniles, a pattern of response seldom or never seen in normal adolescent monkeys, particularly normal adolescent female monkeys, and brief outbursts of suicidal aggression against adults—aggressions which they never displayed more than once, since the bursts of aggression were always unsuccessful; these isolates learned the social facts of life the hard and bloody way. The 12-month isolates, on the other hand, showed no aggression, apparently because fear inhibited its external expression in these animals (1966, pp. 264–268).

The investigators also raised baby monkeys without mothers or with substitute mothers. In some cases the substitute or surrogate mother consisted of a cloth-covered apparatus. They report that monkeys raised with cloth surrogate mothers, compared to those with real mothers, "were somewhat slow in forming adequate play patterns with their peers, but by the end of a year they were interacting effectively, and they have made normal heterosexual adjustments with age-mates as juveniles and preadolescents" (1966, p. 269). In some cases, however, as Harlow earlier described (1962), there was considerable retardation in the development of adult sexuality.

Babies reared without any mothers whatsoever (not even cloth substitutes) showed even greater disturbances in their development, such as a lack of play when young and exaggerated tendencies to cling to other young monkeys. Nevertheless, adult sexual behavior appears to develop in fairly normal sequence for these monkeys, especially if they are reared with age-mates.

Finally, mention may be made of an experiment in which infants were raised with mothers but without peer contacts for varying degrees of time. When finally put together with peers, such monkeys tended to show both extreme cautiousness concerning their age-mates and heightened aggressiveness.

From this whole line of studies Harlow and Harlow draw the following general conclusions:

Both normal mothering and normal infant-infant affectional development are extremely important variables in the socialization of rhesus monkeys and presumably of the higher primates. These variables are interactive, and they interact in a totally orderly sequential manner. Interference with either variable may not of necessity socially destroy an infant monkey if it is subsequently allowed to lead a normal or more or less normal life, but there can be no doubt that the easier and safer way to become a normal monkey is to learn to love and live with both mothers and age-mates (1966, p. 272).

THEORETICAL
POINTER

Animals and Men

Do studies of animals other than humans belong in social psychology? The answer to this question depends on the view that is taken of the field of social psychology and on the evaluation that is made of the distinctiveness of human behavior.

Most social psychologists see their field as limited to the social behavior of humans. This is not the case, however, for most fields of psychology. Psychology is typically seen as the study of the behavior of organisms, with human beings viewed as being only one variety of organisms that may be studied—albeit an especially interesting variety. Chapters on learning in a general psychology text are as apt to cite a study of white rats as a study of college sophomores. But if animal studies are introduced in social psychology (or in sociology), it is usually by means of only a few scattered references or, perhaps even more typically, in a separate chapter devoted to animal behavior as an evolutionary background for the study of humans. Human beings are apparently the real objects of study in social psychology.

Logically, studies of the social behavior of animals other than man should have just as much legitimacy to the title of social psychology as studies of humans. That these are usually placed in a field called *ethology* (when done by persons trained as zoologists) or *compara-* *tive psychology* (when done by persons trained as psychologists) is perhaps simply an accident of nomenclature. But accidental or not, conventions have developed that associate social psychology with the behavior of humans, thus leaving the study of the social behavior of other animals largely to other fields. There is a general justification sometimes given for this—that is, the symbolic adjustment of humans to each other makes their social relationships sufficiently different from other animals to warrant separate attention. But couldn't the same rationale be provided for other fields, such as learning?

In the present book we too have followed the basic assumption that our subject matter is human social behavior. But at the same time it is recognized that insight into human behavior may sometimes be furthered by animal studies. If, as Harry Harlow believes, the early stages of normal social development are roughly similar for various species of primates (including man), then considerable human insight may come from the study of the social development of rhesus monkeys. A special motive for such studies of primates is that experimental procedures (such as total social deprivation) may be used in their study that would not be tolerated for studying human beings.

HOSPITALISM

Some years ago René Spitz (1945; 1946) reported observations on two child-care establishments. One was a foundling home that had infants whose parents could not or would not provide care. The other was the nusery of a penal institution for delinquent girls. These will be referred to as Foundling Home and Nursery, respectively.

When Spitz first visited Foundling Home it had ninety-one children. Two years later thirty-four of these had died, twenty-three had been taken back by their parents, nine were placed elsewhere, four could not be accounted for, and twenty-one remained at the institution. Of those remaining at the institution, Spitz (1946, pp. 114–115)[2] reported the following data on their development:

Bodily Development
    Incapable of any locomotion 5
    Can sit up but not walk 3
    Can walk assisted 8
    Can walk unassisted 5
                                                                    ——
                                                                    21

Speech Development
    Cannot talk at all 6
    Vocabulary of 2 to 5 words 14
    Uses sentences 1
                                                                    ——
                                                                    21

It should be noted that all of these twenty-one children were over two years of age, with the oldest just over four years. Nevertheless, only three of them had attained the normal weight range, and only two had attained the normal height, for *two-year-old* children. "In other words," comments Spitz, "the physical picture of these children impresses the casual observer as that of children half their age" (1946, p. 115).

In contrast is the case of the Nursery, where the outcome was much closer to normal. Spitz studied the Nursery for a period of three and one-half years. Of 122 infants involved, not a single one died, and few suffered any more than very mild illnesses. Those who were in the Nursery for over a year showed physical and intellectual development at least as advanced as that of most children of comparable age.

How can we account for these marked differences in outcome of Foundling Home and Nursery? If the moral character of parents could be considered a factor, it would hardly favor the Nursery, for all mothers here were imprisoned as delinquent girls. The conditions of general care that are described by Spitz (1945)[3] appear to show few significant differences between the two institutions:

> Housing Conditions. Both institutions are situated outside the city, in large spacious gardens. In both hygienic conditions are carefully maintained. In both infants at birth and during the first 6 weeks are segregated from the older babies in a special new-

[2] René A. Spitz, "Hospitalism: A Follow-up Report," in A. Freud, H. Hartmann, and E. Kriss (eds.), *The Psychoanalytic Study of the Child*, II. New York: International Universities Press, 1946. Quotations from this source are reprinted with permission of the author and publisher.

[3] René A. Spitz, "Hospitalism," in A. Freud, H. Hartmann, and E. Kris (eds.), *The Psychoanalytic Study of the Child*, I. New York: International Universities Press, 1945. Quotations from this source are reprinted with permission of the author and publisher.

borns' ward, to which admittance is only permitted in a freshly sterilized smock after hands are washed. In both institutions infants are transferred from the newborns' ward after 2 to 3 months to the older babies' wards, where they are placed in individual cubicles which in Nursery are completely glass enclosed, in Foundling Home glass enclosed on three sides and open at the end. In Foundling Home the children remain in their cubicles up to 15 to 18 months; in Nursery they are transferred after the 6th month to rooms containing four to five cots each. . . .

Food. In both institutions adequate food is excellently prepared and varied according to the needs of the individual child at each age; bottles from which children are fed are sterilized. In both institutions a large percentage of the younger children are breast-fed. In Nursery this percentage is smaller, so that in most cases a formula is soon added, and in many cases weaning takes place early. In Foundling Home all children are breast-fed as a matter of principle as long as they are under 3 months unless disease makes a deviation from this rule necessary.

Clothing. Clothing is practically the same in both institutions. The children have adequate pastel-colored dresses and blankets. The temperature in the rooms is appropriate. We have not seen any shivering child in either set-up.

Medical care. Foundling Home is visited by the head physician and the medical staff at least once a day, often twice, and during these rounds the chart of each child is inspected as well as the child itself. For special ailments a laryngologist and other specialists are available; they also make daily rounds. In Nursery no daily rounds are made, as they are not necessary. The physician sees the children when called (1945, pp. 61–62).

Such differences as have just been indicated would appear, if anything, to favor the Foundling Home. But the Foundling Home was the institution with 38 percent deaths, whereas the Nursery had no deaths—to mention only one of the dramatic differences in outcome. Were there not other differences that clearly favored the Nursery? Spitz does note several such differences. More of the Nursery children had toys. Children in the Nursery could look out the window, whereas vision in the Foundling Home was limited to the children's cubicles and the corridor in which they were placed. But the most significant difference was in the human environment. Spitz reports further:

In Foundling Home there is a head nurse and five assistant nurses for a total of forty-five babies. These nurses have the *entire* care of the children on their hands, except for the babies so young that they are breast-fed. The latter are cared for to a certain extent by their own mothers or by wetnurses; but after a few months they are removed to the single cubicles of the general ward, where they share with at least seven other children the ministrations of *one* nurse. It is obvious that the amount of care one nurse can give to an individual child when she has eight children to manage is small indeed. These nurses are unusually motherly, baby-loving women; but of course the babies of Foundling Home nevertheless lack all human contact for most of the day.

Nursery is run by a head nurse and her three assistants, whose duties do not include the care of the children, but consist mainly in teaching the children's mothers in child care, and in supervising them. The children are fed, nursed and cared for by their own mothers or, in those cases where the mother is separated from her child for any reason, by the mother of another child, or by a pregnant girl who in this way acquires the necessary experience for the care of her own future baby. Thus in Nursery each child has the full-time care of his own mother, or at least that of the substitute which the very able head nurse tries to change about until she finds someone who really likes the child (1946, p. 64).

As Dr. Spitz further comments:

It would take an exacting experimenter to invent an experiment with conditions as diametrically opposed in regard to the mother-child relationship as they are in these two institutions. Nursery provides each child with a mother to the nth degree, a mother who gives the child everything a good mother does and, beyond that, everything else she has. Foundling Home does not give the child a mother, nor even a substitute-mother, but only an eighth of a nurse (1946, p. 65).

The particular term Spitz uses to characterize the symptoms of the Foundling Home children is that of *hospitalism*. Apparently, an institution such as a hospital does not make a very good substitute mother.

ANNA AND ISABELLE

If a child is isolated from contacts with other people during his early years—even more completely deprived of social contact than the Foundling Home children described by Spitz—what chance does he have to develop into a normal human being? The cases of Anna and Isabelle reported by Kingsley Davis (1940; 1947) offer some further evidence on this question—as well as some interesting contrasts between the two cases.

Anna was confined to an upstairs room for almost all of her first six years. The second illegitimate child of a mentally subnormal woman, she was kept there by her mother in deference to the grandfather's stern disapproval of the child's existence. Apparently the mother gave almost no care to Anna, feeding her only milk.

When found and removed from the grandfather's house at the age of six, Anna was extremely undernourished and very apathetic; she could not walk or talk and appeared to be mentally blank. Taken first to a county home, then to a foster home, and finally to a school for retarded children, she improved very slowly. She recovered physically until she was large for her age. In two years she learned to walk, understand simple commands, feed herself, achieve some neatness, and remember people; however, she still could not talk and generally acted much like an infant of about one and one-half years. During the next two years toilet habits were established, she learned to dress herself, and began to develop speech at about the two-year level. At the age of ten and one-half she died of hemorrhagic jaundice.

Isabelle was also an illegitimate child and hidden for that reason. For her first six and one-half years she was confined in a dark room with her mother, a deaf-mute. When found, she was rachitic and her legs were badly bowed. She reacted with fear and hostility to strangers, especially men. She acted in many ways like an infant and at first appeared to be deaf. Her intelligence was measured as equivalent to a normal intelligence of nineteen months.

Very soon Isabelle was given systematic and skillful training. Her first gradual responses accelerated into rapid progress through the learning stages usually attained between ages one and six. By the age of eight and one-half her I.Q. reached a normal level. At fourteen she had passed the sixth grade in public school and appeared bright, cheerful, and energetic.

How do we explain the different outcomes of these two cases that appeared so similar at discovery? One might speculate that Anna was congenitally deficient while Isabelle was not; that Isabelle's closer contacts with her mother posed an important difference in the two cases; or that the specialized training given Isabelle was the key to her greater progress.

In any event, both cases dramatically underline the necessity of human communication and other social contacts for the development of what we ordinarily conceive of as being human nature.

METHODOLOGICAL POINTER

Natural Experiments

Discussions of experimental methodology frequently distinguish between laboratory experiments and field experiments. Both are generally considered to be planned by the investigator, who manipulates key variables in either kind of setting. The difference is that in the laboratory the entire setting is the investigator's creation, whereas in the field the investigator controls only a few variables in an otherwise normal real-life setting.

The studies by Spitz and by Davis that have just been discussed represent still another category, which may be called natural experiments. In one sense these are not experiments at all, for the investigator did not manipulate any variables in these settings. But in another sense, nature has manipulated the variables—albeit by accident rather than through planned design. The investigator, by selecting comparison cases of what has actually already happened, re-creates from these natural occurrences what amounts to an ex post facto experiment.

Laboratory studies of extensive social deprivation of human infants are not possible. Scientific freedom does not extend this far. So for this kind of experimentation, perhaps the best we can do is to turn to systematic studies of other primates, as Harlow has provided. But Spitz and Davis show us another way—to take advantage of some data that nature has provided through instances of early deprivation. From this we learn further that for normal development it is vital to establish early contact with others of the species.

NEEDS AND IMITATION

The tendency of the infant to tie himself to his mother is strengthened by his helplessness. The newborn human is an especially helpless creature, and his indepedence is long delayed.

What are the important needs that the mother—with the help of the other humans around—supplies? Food, of course, is the most obvious. But the studies mentioned in this chapter suggest that it is by no means the end of the story. Foundling Home babies were given perfectly good food, but they still did not develop normally. Although Harlow's studies were not with humans, it is interesting to note that in one experimental variation young monkeys became comforted more by artificial cloth mothers than by other artificial mothers that provided food. Is it then physical contact that is more important than nutrition for early social development? Harlow's work does emphasize the importance of early body contact and social stimulation for normal development. Would it be less so for the even more sensitive social animal, man?

Then there are needs for activity and for stimulation from a varied environment. Infants are not just passive beings. When awake, they normally are eager for experience—for things to look at, for things to handle. And other humans typically provide them with such opportunities.

Finally, we might talk about broad mental needs. Perhaps the term *cognitive needs* sounds too broad, yet something of this order is required for normal development, even in infancy. The brain, we are more and more learning, is not just a passive organ, but—given any significant degree of stimulation—will show spontaneous patterns of activity (Pribram, 1964). Certainly this spontaneous mental activity is no less a pattern of infants than adults.

To satisfy all of the infant's needs—food, body contact, physical movement, visual stimulation, cognitive exercise—the mother and father are instrumental. And as parents engage in behaviors to satisfy these needs, an interesting thing begins to happen. The infant begins to show some behaviors like those of his parents. He begins to imitate some of their sounds and gestures. He seems to follow them with special attention and exhibits more and more of their behavior in his own actions.

Imprinting and Critical Periods

THEORETICAL
POINTER

Konrad Lorenz, whose studies of animal behavior make delightful reading (especially 1952), has introduced into the scientific world the concept of *imprinting*. His studies of the greyleg goose showed that a newly hatched gosling will develop a strong tendency to follow any kind of large moving object seen at this early period. If this happens to be a human rather than a mother goose, then throughout life these geese will follow the human as they otherwise would a mother goose. These patterns of fol- lowing seemed so quickly developed and so irreversible that Lorenz sought to formulate a concept (imprinting) that would set such social learning off from ordinary learning.

Other biologists suggest that this learning may not involve basically different principles from those of other learning, but rather that its significance comes from the special openness for learning that comes at particular points early in the life cycle. Thus Scott (1958) prefers to emphasize the nature of the *critical periods* at which time what he calls *primary socialization* takes place. Scott's work with dogs has suggested that a key feature of primary socialization is a return to familiar places and individuals after experiencing an unfamiliar setting (Scott, 1967).

All highly social species seem to have a period of primary socialization early in life (apparently lasting for varied amounts of time in different species—from a few hours to a few months). The objects experienced during this period determine the kind of animal to which the individual will be attached throughout his life. In most normal cases the mother represents this main source of primary socialization.

Is the theory concerning the existence of such critical periods of primary socialization also applicable to man? Harlow's discussion of his work with monkeys suggests such a possibility. And Spitz, in his recent work (1965), is even more explicit in the view that something like such primary socialization also takes place in man.

A word of caution is in order, however. In man the learning process is much less specifically determined by built-in mechanisms than is the case in other species. It is likely that primary socialization will be more varied in humans than in other species. Perhaps it is so much so that a notion of a critical period for human identification may not be very useful. Whether or not humans have a critical period for primary socialization is therefore still an open question.

AN EXPERIMENTAL STUDY OF IDENTIFICATION

Somehow early in life the infant forms a strong interpersonal bond with the person or persons primarily responsible for his care. As a part of this relationship, he finds that many of his basic needs are met. In this relationship he also shows behavior that is apparently copied from the most important other persons around him. This much seems clear from what has been discussed in this chapter. But this leads us to a further question: What, more specifically, contributes to this copying and imitation? Generally we can say that this imitation, so important for later social development, grows out of a process of identification, and identification in turn grows out of the condition of heightened dependency. But what of the dynamics of this process of identification? For instance, what specifically about a parent and his relationship to the infant leads the infant to choose the parent as an object of identification and imitation?

An experimental study that may throw some light on this question has been done by Bandura, Ross, and Ross (1963). This experiment deals specifically with the selection of a model for imitative behavior. In this study the investigators also attempt to provide a comparative test for several current theories about identification.

The three theories of identification that the experiment by Bandura and associates is designed to test are the *status envy* theory, the *social power* theory, and the *secondary reinforcement* theory. Each of these theories gives a distinctive explanation of the process of identification with whoever becomes the focus of imitative behavior. Let us examine briefly each of these three theories.

The status envy theory of identification points to the selection of a successful rival as a model. Freud (1924) saw this as the outcome of the oedipal situation in which the child and his parent of the same sex compete for the affection of the other parent. As the competing parent is too formidable a competitor, the best solution for the child is to become like his successful parent. The more like the successful parent he may become, the more may he associate such success with himself. More recently John W. M. Whiting (1960) has further developed this theory of identification. Whiting's theory is somewhat broader than Freud's in that he sees many different kinds of rewards, and not just those of sex and affection, as possibilities for the emergence of rivalry. Whenever another is successful in attaining desired rewards and oneself is not, Whiting suggests, the basis of using the other as a model will be present.

The social power theory of identification suggests that anyone who has power over important rewards will be selected as a model for imitation. In this theory the important thing is not so much that another enjoys such rewards, but rather that he can affect whether the child will receive them. It is not clear whether the motive here is to please the person with power or to share vicariously in this power, or perhaps both. In any event, according to this view, it is the person with power, especially the power over important rewards, who becomes a model for the child.

The secondary reinforcement theory of identification holds that the association with being rewarded is the key to identification. We associate with reward whatever customarily accompanies such rewards. Thus by a process of conditioning, the repeated association of parental figures with early biological and social rewards leads the child to attach reward value to the actions of parents. And as the child himself can perform some of these actions, he also comes to feel rewarded. The more his acts approach those of the model, the greater the association with the model, who in turn has become associated with primary reward. Mowrer (1960) considers such processes as the basis of identification in general and the learning of language in particular.

All three of these theories of identification have some basic assumptions in common. All appear to presuppose an early experience in which basic rewards have been closely associated with other people. All assume an early dependency on the part of the infant accompanied by an active capacity for learning. Where they differ is primarily in the precise means of arousing the early learning that is most clearly imitative in nature.

All three of these theories also predict a similar outcome for the normal family setting. All three would predict that parents will become primary models for their children. However, the question of why a parent becomes a model would receive a different answer according to each theory. The status envy theory would hold that the important thing is the child's recognition of rewards a parent enjoys; the social power theory would hold that the important thing is the child's recognition of the parent's power; and the secondary reinforcement theory would hold that the important thing is that the child associates his parent with his own satisfactions. However, all would predict the same basic outcome: if a child develops an early involvement with parents, which under normal circumstances is hard to avoid, he will come to copy the behavior of parental figures.

Would it be possible to test these theories to decide which is the best explanation of identification? This would require a special manipulation of variables, for the usual family setting leaves the key variables of these theories confounded. Such a special manipulation, and in a rather ingenious fashion, is precisely what Bandura, Ross, and Ross attempted. Let us examine carefully how they did this.[4]

The investigators used as subjects seventy-two children enrolled in the Stanford University Nursery School. Half were boys and half were girls, and all were about four years old. Each subject was assigned to one of three experimental treatments. In each of these treatments three adults were involved, whom we will designate respectively as the "experimenter," the "controller," and the "other adult." In all cases the controller was introduced as the "owner" of a special "surprise room" of the nursery school. On the way to this surprise room the experimenter and the child met the other adult, who was also interested in the surprise room. ·

In one treatment (with other adult as consumer) the other adult was given permission by the controller to play with the toys in the room while the child was occupied with two small toys at one table. This the other adult did with great enthusiasm for twenty minutes while the controller provided him with a wealth of amusements, including a dart game, a pinball machine, and all the cookies he wished.

In another treatment (with child as consumer) the child had the opportunity to enjoy the rich variety of toys in the room while the other adult was ignored. He was left to read a book while the controller provided materials for the child to play with.

A third treatment was that of a control group. Here subjects did not have previous interaction with either of the two adults (controller or other adult), but were led directly to an imitation task situation. Therefore, the distinction between controller and other adult was irrelevant for this treatment.

An imitation task situation was the culminating event for all three treatments. This was described as a game in which the experimenter would hide a picture sticker in one of two boxes, and the players would have to guess which box it was in. The two adults took turns first, after which the child was to take his turn. In the course of his behavior in this game, each adult performed a great variety of distinctive motor and verbal responses. These were irrelevant so far as the discrimination problem was concerned but were deliberately planned to provide incidental features that the child might later imitate. The actions of the two adult models were distinctively different but equated in terms of type, number, and interest value.

[4] Albert Bandura, Dorothea Ross, and Sheila A. Ross, "A Comparative Test of the Status Envy, Social Power, and Secondary Reinforcement Theories of Identificatory Learning," *Journal of Abnormal and Social Psychology,* 67 (1963), 527–534. Copyright 1963 by the American Psychological Association. Quotations from this source are reprinted with permission of the publisher.

In addition to the guess-the-box game, a picture preference test was also given to the two adults while the child watched. Then the child had his chance at both the guess-the-box game and the picture preference exercise.

Here was the crucial part of the experiment. Which adult model would the child tend to imitate? In an adjoining room three observers watched through a one-way window and carefully noted the child's behavior. From their observations was derived an imitation score to represent the extent to which the child's choices and mannerisms matched those provided previously by either of the two adult models.

Incidentally, it may be pointed out that the particular adult playing a given role was varied from session to session. Half the subjects in the one treatment had a male controller and half a female controller. Also, half the subjects in each treatment were male and half were female, thus including equally every possible sex combination of a potential model and child.

Before we examine the results of this experiment, let us pause to consider what would be predicted by different theories of identification. Consider first the status envy theory. This would lead us to expect that the child would imitate most the behavior of the adult consumer (rather than the controller) in the other-adult-as-consumer treatment. It would also predict that imitation would be higher in this treatment (where there was the basis of status envy) than in the treatment where the child himself played with the materials.

In contrast, the secondary reinforcement theory would predict more imitation in the child-as-consumer treatment than in the other-adult-as-consumer treatment; for in the former treatment the child himself enjoyed the play materials, whereas in the latter he could only observe their enjoyment. Furthermore, the adult most imitated would be the one most associated with the child's own enjoyment, the controller rather than the other adult.

Still somewhat different would be the predictions from the social power theory. This theory would not predict any significant difference between the two experimental treatments. Rather, in each treatment the controller would be the adult imitated, for it is he who had the power over rewards.

Table 3 summarizes the expectations of each of these theories. The status envy theory predicts that the highest imitation will be of the other adult when he is the consumer. The social power theory predicts that highest imitation will be of the controller, regardless of who the consumer may be. And the secondary reinforcement theory predicts

TABLE 3 PREDICTIONS OF HIGH IMITATION ACCORDING TO EACH OF THREE THEORIES

Treatment	Object of Imitation	
	Controller	*Other Adult*
Other adult as consumer	Social power	Status envy
Child as consumer	Secondary reinforcement, social power	

SOURCE: Adapted from Bandura, Ross, and Ross (1963).

that the controller will be the highest object of imitation only when the child is himself the consumer.

In Table 4 we see how well the results correspond to the various predictions. The pattern of results departs most markedly from the predictions of a status envy theory. When the other adult is the consumer and the child must watch, we see the least, not the most, imitation of this adult.

Although the results are in the direction predicted by the secondary reinforcement theory, this theory also fails to predict the most dramatic differences. As we would expect from a theory of secondary reinforcement, children do show somewhat more imitation when they consume the rewards than when they watch someone else enjoy them. And when they do consume the rewards, there is some tendency to imitate more the adult most associated with the rewards (the controller rather than the other adult). But there is not in this secondary reinforcement theory the basis for predicting the great difference between imitating the two adults in the other-adult-as-consumer treatment. This failure to obtain evidence for a secondary reinforcement theory is somewhat ironic, because such evidence had been obtained in a previous experiment by Bandura (Bandura and Huston, 1961).

The theory that best anticipates the results shown in Table 4 is the social power theory of identification. The strongest pattern in the data is that of the imitation of the controller in preference to the other adult. This is precisely what the social power theory would predict. Also, imitation of the adult controller seems to be about the same whether the other adult or the child had been the consumer of the rewards. Again, this is what would be predicted if social power is the key to the process of identification.

TABLE 4 MEAN NUMBER OF IMITATIVE RESPONSES PERFORMED BY CHILDREN

Treatment	Object of Imitation	
	Controller	Other Adult
Other adult as consumer	26.9	13.6
Child as consumer	27.5	22.4
Control group	18.9 (per adult)	

SOURCE: Bandura, Ross, and Ross (1963), p. 531.

METHODOLOGICAL POINTER

What Does a Single Experiment Prove?

Just as there is reason to doubt that a single case study is suitable evidence for a generalization about behavior, so we may doubt if very much can be proved by a single experiment.

The experiment by Bandura, Ross, and Ross is rather unusual from the point of view of the care that was taken to present a test case for different theories. Here we have three different theories tested in the same experiment. Does this then prove that social power is the key to the process of identification, as this is the theory that best fits the results?

The evidence in this experiment supporting a social power theory of identification is clear. It would be hard to imagine such a pattern of results as that obtained if the social power theory was completely without validity. But perhaps this just leads us to press the question: What was there in the behavior of the controller that was most instrumental in making him a model for the child? Was it his specific ownership of the play materials, or was it his general prominence in the play situation, or what? Social power is not necessarily a simple phenomenon, and it may be that not all manifestations of social power are equally likely to produce imitation. For example, if power is exerted primarily through punishment rather than reward, we might expect avoidance rather than imitation.

But what about the other theories of identification? Does this experiment disprove them? With even less certainty than we can say that the social power theory is proved can we say that alternative theories are clearly disproved. In the first place, there are theories of identification that are not specifically examined in this study—for example, Sears's suggestion that withholding of love might be the key to identification or Stotland's similarity theory (Secord and Backman, 1964b, pp. 532–540). Furthermore there are always difficulties of representing a theory in a particular experiment. Perhaps, in some way not now apparent, the procedures failed to create some of the conditions necessary to give proper emphasis to a status envy or secondary reinforcement condi-

tion. Finally, there is no reason to hold that there is just *one* theoretical basis of identification. It is possible that fundamentally different conditions can alike lead to identification and imitation, and more than one or two experiments are necessary to examine these various possibilities.

The contrast between the findings of this experiment and the earlier support for a secondary reinforcement interpretation of imitation (Bandura and Huston, 1961) underscores the importance of continued experimentation on a problem. It is common in social psychological research to find that earlier findings are not replicated by later studies. There may be many possible causes: small but significant differences of experimental procedures, different experimental samples, different nuances in an experimenter's behavior, or even differences in the way chance probabilities happen to sort themselves out. All of these variables emphasize the importance of preferring the evidence of a series of experiments over that of a single experiment.

The experiment by Bandura, Ross, and Ross is unusual in the way it combines theories for a comparative test. But no single experiment can give the final answer for a scientific problem. Indeed, there can be no final answer for a scientific problem—just further analysis of observed relationships directed to ever more precise and comprehensive explanations.

In their discussion of this experiment, Bandura, Ross, and Ross have some instructive comments about the idea that children choose a single primary model at a given age level and that this model becomes the source of uncritical imitation. Their comments should leave us with a healthy skepticism concerning an all-or-nothing view of identification:

Theories of identificatory learning have generally assumed that
within the family setting the child's initial identification is confined to his mother, and that during early childhood boys must
turn from the mother as the primary model to the father as the
main source of imitative behavior. However, throughout the
course of development children are provided with ample opportunities to observe the behavior of both parents. The results of
the present experiment reveal that when children are exposed
to multiple models they may select one or more of them as the
primary source of behavior, but rarely reproduce all the elements
of a single model's repertoire or confine their imitation to that
model. Although the children adopted many of the characteristics
of the model who possessed rewarding power, they also repro-
duced some of the elements of behavior exhibited by the model
who occupied the subordinate role. Consequently, the children
were not simply junior-size replicas of one or the other model;
rather, they exhibited a relatively novel pattern of behavior representing an amalgam of elements from both models. Moreover, the
specific admixture of behavior elements varied from child to
child. These findings provide considerable evidence for the seemingly paradoxical conclusion that imitation can in fact produce
innovation of social behavior, and that within the same family
even same-sex siblings may exhibit quite different response patterns, owing to their having selected for imitation different elements of their parents' response repertoires (pp. 533–534).

4
Affiliation: Review and Discussion

"Man is by nature a social animal." This assertion is as old as Aristotle, and it has a nice profound ring to it. It underlines for us the truism that man's way of relating to other men has deep roots in his biology and history. But such an appeal to nature can actually explain very little. It does not say what aspect of man's nature is responsible for what forms of social behavior, nor does it specify the conditions under which different forms of social behavior will occur.

Social psychologists early gave up trying to explain forms of social behavior in terms of any inherent nature of man. Behavior is too varied and changing to be simply expressive of some stable internal principle. Much more popular with social scientists has been the attempt to identify specific social conditions that are associated with the development of particular forms of behavior. This has usually been done under the heading of *socialization*. Socialization may be generally conceived as the process of an individual's adjustment to living with other people. This adjustment is in part an adjustment to particular individuals, in part an adjustment to groups, and in part an adjustment to broader cultural values and norms. In reality these three aspects of adjustment (individuals, groups, and culture) are not separate but rather are all tied together. However, for convenience in these opening chapters dealing with affiliation we have selected for discussion those aspects that focus upon adjustment to other individuals. Later in this book we will deal with aspects of socialization relating more directly to groups and to culture.

Considering affiliation as a part of the more general process of socialization, we may view it as developing on three levels. These can be described as (1) primary socialization, (2) self-selective interaction, and (3) situational orientations.

LEVELS OF SOCIALIZATION

The most primitive sense of being a human being and of belonging to other people develops very early. This primary socialization is a result of the biological dependence of the human infant on his mother. The bond is forged before the infant is able to reflect about what is going on. Thus, quite literally, before he knows it, he is firmly bound to relationships with other persons.

Chapter 3 dealt with this primary level of socialization. The question was there raised, and not fully answered, of the extent to which the pattern of primary socialization in humans is similar to that of other animals. Harlow's studies of affectional development in monkeys and the work of ethologists on imprinting and critical periods in other species all offer suggestive speculations about general patterns of primary socialization. Although the pattern of early human socialization may be more flexible than that of other species, early social deprivation clearly retards development in humans no less than in monkeys. This much is indicated by reports by Spitz and Davis on early social deprivation.

Chapter 3 also dealt with the more distinctively human aspects of imitation and identification. An experiment by Bandura and associates that attempted to isolate the primary causes of human identification was discussed in some detail. Although we cannot simply conclude that the social power of parents is *the* cause of a child's identification with them, the evidence of this study does suggest that parental power is clearly a key part of the process.

After the human being forms a sense of identity and develops a capacity for imaginative action, his social relationships take on a more self-selective character. His associations are not just given by nature or the accidents of social arrangements. These of course still provide the setting, but within this setting some relationships are consciously chosen and cultivated in preference to others.

Chapter 2 dealt with this level of socialization, which may be identified as self-selective interaction. Its most obvious manifestation is the selection of friends and mates. In this chapter three studies of interpersonal attraction were given special attention: the Welcome Week study by Walster and associates, Hollingshead's analysis of dating in Elmtown, and Newcomb's study of the acquaintance process among residents of a rooming house in Ann Arbor. To expand upon and qualify the themes found in these three studies, a number of other studies focusing on interpersonal attraction were cited in less detail.

Together, these studies of Chapter 2 point to some significant features of interpersonal attraction. For one thing, the value that an individual sees in others depends on the value he sees in himself. Persons who are in a position to place a high value on themselves are apt to be more particular in their choice of other persons, as the studies by Walster and Hollingshead suggest. In relatively unstructured situations, such as that studied by Walster, this is apt to emphasize temporary features of attractiveness; in situations that are more firmly rooted in social structure, as in Hollingshead's Elmtown, attraction may be ordered much more by social conventions about appropriate relationships. Also, we are generally attracted to persons who share our own attitudes and values. This does not mean that simple similarity is basically descriptive of attraction patterns; heterosexuality is a strong argument to the contrary. Rather, our attraction is toward those whose impressions and actions are congruent with our own. Newcomb's evidence concerning the process of peer attraction indicates that a similarity of attitudes toward matters of common relevance is one of the strongest links binding persons together.

Finally, we may point to situational orientations as a third level of socialization. This suggests that socialization is always going on when-ever we are with other people. Chapter 1 dealt with one way in which situational orientations may be studied: in terms of the tendency to offer help to another person. Studies such as those of Latané and Darley have identified conditions under which helping behavior is least apt to occur—when bystanders are unfamiliar with the locale, the victim, and, above all, each other. As the reverse side of the same coin, more familiar settings and persons are more likely to be associated with helping behavior. Other studies, such as those by Piliavin and associates, indicate that conditions of reward and cost immediately present in the situation are especially important for understanding such behavior.

Although our studies of helping behavior have dealt with only one aspect of situational orientations, they do show the crucial role that the immediate situation may play in determining the form of social behavior expressed.

TOWARD MORE GENERAL PRINCIPLES

In the remainder of this chapter we shall attempt to develop a more general framework for describing the dynamics of affiliation, whatever the particular form it may take. For this purpose three basic com-ponents will be identified: (1) satisfaction, (2) dependence, and (3) commitment.

SATISFACTION

One of the most thoroughly documented principles of the behavioral sciences is that reinforcement or reward strengthens a response ten-dency. Not only does reinforcement make a response more likely to occur again, but it also attracts the organism to the kind of situation in which the reinforcement occurred.

Applying these basic principles of conditioning to interpersonal relationships, we see that the greater the satisfactions associated with another person, the greater will be the tendency to seek out this per-son for future interaction. Satisfaction brings, in a word, attraction.

But perhaps this is belaboring the obvious. It is probably also obvious that most human satisfactions are associated with other human beings; therefore, it is clear that social relationships must be especially significant for the human pursuit of happiness. What may be less obvious is precisely how we are satisfied in interpersonal rela-tionships—or to put the question in learning-theory terms, how are we reinforced in affiliative responses?

That some basic biological needs lie at the root of our reinforcement by other people is suggested by studies such as those of Harlow, Spitz, and Davis. Others of our species seem to be necessary to instigate and support those responses we look upon as human nature. Clearly more than the need for food provides the biological base for this association. Needs for physical comfort, movement, and visual variety may be as important as the need for food in underwriting the budding sociability of infants. But whatever the biological base, other humans early come to dominate the attentions of the normal human infant.

Later, human individuals come to identify more clearly the things around them that they need to satisfy their wants, and it turns out that nearly all of these require the cooperation of other humans if they are to be met. Persons, such as parents, who have special abilities to promote such satisfactions may become objects of identification and imitation. And still later, the budding sexual appetites encourage reorganization of social interests.

All this may be summarized in the statement that we become dependent upon others for need satisfaction.

DEPENDENCE

We may summarize the basic ways we can be satisfied by other people as consisting of three kinds of dependence: (1) instrumental dependence, (2) orientational dependence, and (3) ego dependence. In instrumental dependence other persons serve as means to help us obtain specific things we want (for example, money or prestige). In orientational dependence other people help us understand the world around us (for example, by suggesting how we might evaluate something experienced unexpectedly). In ego dependence other people help us understand ourselves (for example, by suggesting through their reactions what a particular act means).

There is another central feature of the concept of dependence that has not yet been mentioned. This is the role of alternatives. We are dependent on a thing, on a person, or on a relationship to a group not only insofar as this is a source of satisfaction but also insofar as there are not alternatives available that might also yield such satisfaction.

The basic distinction we are making has also been expressed in different terms by Thibaut and Kelley (1959). Satisfaction in a social relationship is a result of the goodness of outcomes relative to one's *comparison level*, whereas the continuance of a relationship depends on the outcomes relative to the *comparison level of alternatives*. In other words, the base upon which satisfaction rests (whether things are better or worse than one is prepared for) is somewhat different from the base upon which rests the stability of social relationships (whether this relationship is better or worse than some alternative state of affairs).

The meaning of this may be further explored in terms of examples from dating and mate selection. There are many values that one might look for in a dating partner that would enhance the desirability of such a person. But a date would not take place simply because this person is desirable; he or she must also be available. A similar point could be made by distinguishing between social *preferences* and social *choices*. Preferences represent images of what we want; choices represent what we are able to get. One may prefer that the girl he marries be "as soft and as sweet as a nursery" or perhaps "just like the girl that married dear old Dad," but in either case the girl actually married may turn out to be slightly different. This need not cast doubt on the assertions of preferences; it only suggests that, in choosing, a compromise was made necessary by the realities at hand—perhaps the softest and sweetest girl turned out to have a few rough edges after all, or the girl most like the one who married dear old Dad turned out to be already married.

Preferences are often highly individualized matters. Especially is this true for preferences in close personal relationships. This is fortunate, for otherwise many persons might be left without close friends. But there are also factors of group evaluation present in most individual preferences. Even some of our most private evaluations reflect the suggestions of other persons. Thus in evaluations of a desirable date or mate, there are also social definitions of the true, the good, and the beautiful that enter into our preferences. In the study by Walster and associates, physical attractiveness turned out to be more predictive of preferences than anything else—and these evaluations of physical attractiveness reflected general judgments of other persons, not just one's own personal judgment. And in Hollingshead's study of Elmtown, general social status turned out to be highly predictive of dating patterns—again a matter of general consensus rather than simply a reflection of idiosyncratic values.

Choice, reflecting what is available as well as what is desirable, is also conditioned by both individual and group factors. A person's opportunities for choice depend on who he is and what individual attributes he possesses. The tall, handsome athlete may have different dating opportunities than the stubby grind who gets consistent A's in his social psychology class. But there are also opportunity structures rooted in group factors—in such things as the population make-up of a given college, which fraternity schedules social events with which sorority, or even which families may happen to live in the same neighborhood. Such group factors set the stage for choices of dates and mates as surely as social values enter into individual preferences.

COMMITMENT

We have summarized affiliative tendencies as due to our satisfaction with and dependence on certain persons. Other things being equal, we become attached most to those relationships that are most rewarding. Also, our attachment to a relationship is inversely related to the availability of desirable alternatives. But there are also psychological features of interpersonal attachment that cannot be easily reduced to either satisfaction or dependence. Some of these features may be pointed to as products of commitment.

Every time we make a choice, we are to some degree committing ourselves. Some of our actions tie us to other persons, and these too become commitments. Some of these commitments are of small and only temporary significance, such as stepping aside to allow another person to pass first through a doorway. Other commitments, such as choice of a marriage partner, have far greater consequences. But whether choices be major or minor, adjustment requires that we make them, and make them in such a way as to make them clear to ourselves and to others. Even a little thing like deciding to stand aside at a doorway can be a source of considerable discomfort if one is unable to make the choice decisively and follow through with it.

So, by and large, we develop the ability to live with whatever choices we make. A part of this living with our choices is to adopt, at least temporarily, the attitudes that will see the choice through. And sometimes these attitudes have a way of hanging on or even growing once we sense that a commitment has been made.

Particularly is this true with commitments to other persons. Sometimes, in fact, a commitment may be made—and made in very strong fashion—without ever consciously choosing a particular associate. Examples may be seen among parents and children. Parents do not exactly choose which children they will have, nor do children choose their parents. In such cases the impact of the relationship is so great that the binding power is very strong—even though not a matter of specific choice.

We tend to develop the attitudes toward other persons that will support us in our social commitments. We therefore become more and more closely linked with those to whom we are drawn in social commitments. In a real sense, such persons become parts of the self system. This may not be noticed until something occurs to disturb a relationship to which we are adjusted—illness or death, for example. Then it becomes apparent that a part of the self was very much involved.

AFFILIATION AND AGGRESSION

At first glance, affiliation and aggression may seem like antithetical topics. Hurting others is the opposite of helping them. Therefore, for balance it may seem fitting to follow the major topic of affiliation with that of aggression.

But it is misleading to think of affiliative and aggressive responses as necessarily opposed. A great deal of aggression is expressed toward persons with whom we are closely affiliated. The most frequent victim of a murderer's gun, police statistics tell us, is a friend or relative. And acts of brutal aggression frequently have strongly affiliative motives—such as loyalty to friends or nation.

Human association always has its mixed blessings of bitterness as well as kindness, of tearing apart as well as putting together, of conflict as well as cooperation. Although the affiliative processes are at the core of the fabric of society, aggression is woven into the same fabric. And it is only analytically that we may take one process out of the living web of social life to examine it more fully.

part two: AGGRESSION

Aggressive or hostile "impulses" do not suffice to account for social conflict. Hatred, just as love, needs some object.

Lewis A. Coser

Most students come to the study of social psychology with a central interest in personality. When we want to know what makes people behave the way they do, there are frequently certain persons we have especially in mind (above all, ourselves). It is therefore convenient to continue our introduction to social psychology through the study of a particular person. The case study of Julia Wilson in Chapter 5 ("Fighter") provides an opportunity for this. At the same time that we try to analyze how Julia came to acquire her aggressive tendencies, we will also deal with issues of interpreting early influences upon personality formation.

A single case study is not enough to conclude very much about the development of aggressive behavior. Therefore, in Chapter 6 ("Seeds of Aggression") we focus upon a study of several hundred persons in trying to unravel determinants of aggression. In the process we will also explore a number of important methodological questions as they become relevant to the study under discussion.

While Chapters 5 and 6 focus upon aggression as a property of persons, Chapter 7 ("Aggression in the Laboratory") shifts attention to a situational perspective. In so doing, Chapter 7 also encourages further understanding of the procedures of laboratory experimentation.

In Chapter 8 ("Aggression: Review and Discussion") we bring together the insights gained in the previous three chapters. A major theme of this chapter, and indeed of this entire book, is that behavior is always a product of both the person and his social situation.

5
Fighter

We continue our study of social psychology with a case study. The subject of this case is Julia Wilson, described by Allison Davis and John
Dollard in their book, *Children of Bondage* (1940).[1] Note what kind of
a person Julia seems to be, and consider how she may have become
what she is. Davis and Dollard describe her as a

> . . . dark-skinned girl of sixteen with a slender figure which she
> regards as a handicap in her campaign against men. She attends
> the first year of high school but shows little or no interest in her
> work. Her family is upper-lower class, having fallen from lower-
> middle-class position. She lives with her mother, father, and two
> younger brothers in a four-room house near the railroad tracks
> in New Orleans. Her parents own the house, one room of which
> they rent to male lodgers. She also has two older sisters who are
> married and live in New Orleans. Julia is the third child; there is
> a difference of about two years in age between each child and the
> next younger. . . .
>
> At school, Julia's acquaintances (she has only one intimate
> friend and does not believe in forming a circle of close asso-
> ciates) call her not Julia, but "Raddie" Wilson. Her nickname
> means "rowdy" or "troublemaker," and she is regarded by both
> pupils and teachers as a "show-off." Julia herself boasts that the
> people at school, as well as the boy friends whom she curses and
> fights, think she is "crazy"; that is, that she will do "anything"—
> fight a man, curse a teacher, or kiss a boy in the schoolyard—
> without regard for the usual restrictions upon a girl and upon
> a pupil.
>
> Her own mother says that Julia thinks of herself as the "Big
> I am," and that she has never been able to play cooperatively
> with other girls or to get along congenially with anyone except
> her next older sister. But Julia is a fighter and she does not bar
> even her mother. She replies that her mother does not like her
> and has never liked her. Nor does she pretend to like her mother.
> Her mother, Julia insists, likes only her son, Earl, who is two
> years younger than Julia.
>
> In spite of her rather pleasant smile and her somewhat mid-

---

[1] Allison Davis and John Dollard, *Children of Bondage: The Personality Development of Negro Youth in the Urban South.* Washington, D.C.: American Council
on Education, 1940. Quotations from this source are reprinted with permission of
the publisher.

dle-class "front," there is no doubt that Julia deserves her reputation as a fighter. A slender but tigerish Amazon, who fights with her fists rather than with a knife, she harasses her boy friends with insatiable aggression until a curse and a slap lead to a knockdown drag-out fight. She fights not only the bantams at school, but even the white girls who "meddle" with her; she curses and slaps the older boy friends who drive her to school in their cars; and she engages grown men in public fights and cursing duels in her own neighborhood. . . .

Julia is not only a chronic fighter, she is a clever and unrelenting exploiter of men. What she wants from men is their money. To attain this goal, which to her is all important, she holds out her sexual lures to a great variety of men but she has sex relations with few or none. Over a period of four months she furnished the interviewer with detailed accounts of fourteen boys and men whom she remembers having successfully gouged of money and presents. In this list is her father, whom she values more highly than her mother "because he has always given me things," but whom she nevertheless has blackmailed for years with the threat of revealing his love affairs to her mother. There is also an easily gullible married man of about thirty, from whom Julia has been extracting rather large sums of money since she was fourteen. She boasts that she has kept him under control by her "craziness" (her constant fight-picking) and her refusal to have sex relations with him. "That's the way to do," Julia triumphantly points out. "When you get a sucker, bump his head."

To Julia, men are a class of people who have more money than women and who are therefore capable of giving one the more vital needs of life: candy and clothes and money and automobile rides. They are beings who also have a strange and apparently headlong desire for sexual responses from women, a weakness in their nature which Julia regards as universal to their sex, and as originally designed for her specific aggrandizement. It is this curious and simple-minded passion of men, she feels, which makes them susceptible to her various baits and lures; it enables her to use them and at the same time to keep them writhing at a safe distance. As she sums up the case of Fred, her married suitor, "I know he likes me 'cause I can get anything I want out of him. I can get things when his wife can't. Yes, I know he loves me, but I don't care for him, and he knows it, too. He told me that once. He said, 'I know you don't love me, but I'm crazy about you.' " Men are apparently not sex objects to Julia; they are necessary instrumental steps to the attainment of money and gifts.

This thirst of hers to be given things, or to take them, is not directed only toward men, however. She wishes to use women in the same way—to extract presents from them, for example, and to cajole or browbeat her mother into giving her more attention or gifts than the other children in her family. Since women have little money to give and since they are competitors with Julia for the rich haul which men do have, she spends relatively little time with girls. Instead, she takes their boy friends from them and taunts them with the fact that it is their hard luck if they are unable to keep them.

In the face of the convincing evidence that Julia is really a "tough" girl who fights anything two-footed, and that she is a persistent exploiter of both men and women, there are nevertheless strange inconsistencies both in her report of her life and in her overt behavior. She is extremely afraid of the unpredictable pain of illness or accident. She has no hesitation in admitting that she cannot bear much pain and that she still cries "for the least little thing that hurts me." Except for the memories of her father's gifts to her, moreover, all of her earliest childhood recollections are of terrifying experiences: of a flood in which she and her family were swept out of their house, of her childhood diseases, of the illness of her mother, of the fights between her parents, and of accidents and sudden deaths which came to relatively unknown people. She has exceedingly vivid and lacerating memories of the killing of an uncle and three white children by snakes and she claims to have seen their dead bodies with the snakes around their necks.

Even more unexpected, in view of her continual pursuit of men, is the strong aversion which she expresses to exposing her body to any man, or to having full sexual relationships. She gives as the worst experience of her life the times when she was compelled to submit to medical examinations; she says that she turned her head in shame on each occasion and was always afraid thereafter that she would meet the physicians on the street. Unlike most lower-class girls of her age, she insists that she has never had sex relations, except with her husband; there have been only three such occasions, she claims, in their year of courtship and marriage. At these times, she always felt ashamed of her action and could not face her husband afterward. Dreams and strange accounts of attempts by unknown men to attack her or to abduct her are as numerous in her record as her stories of sex fights.

There are even more puzzling aspects of Julia's behavior than her fear of accidents, sickness, and sexual attack. This Amazon from the battlefield of "across-the-tracks," who has had boys stabbed for her and has fought men and women on the streets, displays behavior which is often childlike, almost infantile. At times, even now at the age of sixteen, she plays "dolls" and "keeping house" with the little children in her neighborhood. Until she was twelve or thirteen, she regularly played with dolls, and even at that age played "mamma and children" with much younger girls, always forcing them to grant her the position of "mamma." Julia says, furthermore, "I am always trying to get my mamma to do things for me. She does them for me too. I rub up against her and feel her breasts until she does." She adds that she likes to play with her mother's breasts, and that she attempts the same behavior toward her next older sister, who slaps her hands. Mrs. Wilson herself says that Julia insisted upon keeping her pacifier until she was eight or nine years old, although the mother had tried to break her of this infantile habit when she was two years old (pp. 23–28).

From the above record of Julia, we get the picture of a tough-minded young female out to get whatever she can for herself. Davis and Dollard summarize her personality as "self-centered, exploitative, and chronically aggressive" (p. 28).

How can we explain the development of such a personality? And how can we explain those other features—her fear of pain and sex and her curious instances of infantile behavior—so apparently inconsistent with the dominant picture of tough-mindedness?

THEORETICAL
POINTER

Personality and Social Psychology

Personality is not the central focus of social psychology. Most social psychologists are more interested in the regularities of particular kinds of behavior of people in general than they are in detailed studies of particular personalities. And it is the interaction *between* persons, rather than events within them, that is the central focus of social psychology. It is in the fields of clinical psychology, psychology of personality, and psychiatry that personality is the main area of concern.

Nevertheless, even though personality is not the central focus of study for most social psychologists, it remains a part of everything they study. Sometimes personality may not be explicitly studied, but more often some recognition in research must be made of the fact that different persons are different—and that these differences affect the behavior being studied.

Furthermore, the very nature of personality makes it impossible to exclude it from the main interest in interpersonal interaction of most social psychologists. Personality largely evolves out of an interpersonal matrix, as we shall soon see as we proceed further with the case of Julia. And much of personality is directly interpersonal in its expression—as, for example, the characteristic of aggressiveness.

There is no fully satisfactory theory of personality. Or, more accurately, there are many good theories of personality, but they are often in disagreement with one another; and all theories leave uncharted at least as much of the mystery of personality as they uncover.

A beginning student in social psychology might be well served to adopt both a broad view of personality and a tolerant attitude toward the various theories of personality. Personality may be simply considered as the organization of behavior characteristic of a particular person. Furthermore, this behavior goes on at different levels at the same time, and we may expect different theories to give primary attention to different levels. Something of the nature of these different levels of the organization of the behavior of an individual may be suggested by the following classification:

1. The organism—the organization of physiological, including neurological, activity
2. The private identity—the self-concept, the set of definitions a person has of himself and of the meaning of his behavior
3. The public identity—the combination of roles a person plays in his various groups, organizations, and interpersonal relationships

Only occasionally do social psychologists focus on the level of the organism. Nerves and muscles, like molecules and atoms, may be active in all social behavior, but social psychologists usually see the organism in the background rather than the foreground.

Most of the interest of social psychologists in personality is in the relationship between private and public identities. By and large, most sociologically trained social psychologists give the larger emphasis to the public identity, and those with a strong background in clinical psychology are apt to emphasize the private identity.

EARLY CHILD TRAINING

One approach to explaining personality development is to focus upon very early learning experiences. Many psychiatrists, following the lead of Sigmund Freud, give special attention to such things as early feeding, weaning, and toilet-training experiences in their analyses of individual cases. Davis and Dollard, also assuming that "the earliest learning of human beings is the most basic learning" (p. 28), supply information regarding some of the early experiences of Julia.

Freud's Views on Early Development

THEORETICAL
POINTER

According to the influential views of Sigmund Freud (1859–1939), the earliest years are the crucial ones for personality development. It is during the first five years that the ego and superego become differentiated from the more primitive thrust of pleasure seeking, the id. The mature personality becomes a constellation of these three subsystems—the id (developing around pleasure-seeking impulses) the ego (developing around modifications imposed by the adjustment to reality), and the superego (a specialized aspect of adjustment representing an uncritical acceptance of social values and prohibitions)—and how these subsystems become differentiated determines the basic structure of the adult personality.

As the interplay between impulse and reality constitutes the building material of personality, so also the nature of infantile pleasure seeking becomes a central consideration in Freudian theory. According to Freud, the basic pleasure-seeking impulses proceed through a sequence of development that can be represented by reference to parts of the body.

1. During the first year the mouth is the central focus for pleasure seeking, and this is called the *oral* stage. Basic patterns of dependence on other people become developed during this time.

2. During the second year elimi-native functions come more to the center of attention. During this *anal* stage, basic patterns of relating oneself to things become formed. During this time the ego shows its first instances of self-conscious mastery over id impulses.

3. During the third and fourth years the child develops an interest in his genitals. This represents the *phallic* stage. During this time he also forms something of a sexual attraction toward the parent of the opposite sex—a key element of what Freud called the "Oedipus complex." But the sexual wishes of this stage are doomed to failure, and the superego the child develops to control these early sexual desires and also to check his aggressive impulses (drawing heavily on an identification with his parent of the same sex) forms the basis of his sense of right and wrong.

Following these stages of development are a *latency* stage of repressed sexuality and the *genital* stage that comes with adolescence. But by the end of the phallic stage the main pattern of personality is already set.

A key to the process of development is the kind of reality parents present for the child's adjustment. Procedures of weaning, toilet training, and discouraging sexual play thus take on an obvious significance.

In Davis and Dollard's description of Julia's early training, one of the things first noted is the abruptness of her weaning. At only a little over one month of age her mother's breast "was suddenly no longer there. Instead she was handed a bottle" (p. 28). Without being gradually taught to substitute the bottle for the breast, she went for two days without nourishment. In speculating what this must have meant to the young infant, Davis and Dollard suggest that "Julia learned from this experience that even the most gratifying and well-fixed habits could be inexplicably interrupted by deprivation and suffering. She learned in a scarcely conscious manner that the 'world,' which to her was the mother, could not be depended upon *to bring necessary things to you*" (p. 29).

Furthermore, we learn that "as the result of an incorrect formula for bottle feeding, Julia had persistent colic during her first year of life." What did Julia learn from this? Davis and Dollard suggest that she "learned to expect pain after sucking and developed an ambivalent feeling toward eating and toward people." With such an experience "the pleasure of eating is constantly followed by physical suffering," and a child with colic "can therefore only expect that all fixed habits, no matter how basic to life, will be interrupted by loss and suffering" (p. 29).

Mrs. Wilson used a direct approach in Julia's toilet training as well as in her weaning. She began by spanking her, when she was about three months old, for rolling off the bed pad and wetting the bed. "I did that for a couple of months till she wouldn't roll off that pad'" (p. 29).

We are also told that Julia was punished for her early discovery and manipulation of her genitals, though the details of the punishments are not clear. This occurred around the age of two, at the same time that a new baby arrived.

> Her little brother, Earl, was born just at the time when her mother and sister were actively scorning and rejecting her for an infantile habit whose adult social meaning she did not know. . . . At the same instant when, as a result of the baby's sudden appearance, Julia was being denied her former privileges of sitting in the mother's lap and having the mother's attention and care, she was also being frightened, punished, and severely rejected because she continued her gratifying but (for some reason unknown to her) disapproved behavior. Mrs. Wilson tells us that Julia's behavior changed very markedly at this time, and that these changes later became strongly fixed in her habits. . . .
>
> What Julia actually did, according to her mother, was (1) to begin to cling to and cry for the mother, as an infant does; (2) to insist upon keeping her pacifier, and to try to take the mother's breast again; (3) to push the baby out of the mother's lap, to beat it when the mother's back was turned, and to criticize and attack the mother. Mrs. Wilson reports, "Julia never did like Earl—ever since he was born. She was a good girl till my boy came, an' then she started acting more like a baby than she did when she was younger. She hated him. An' ever since then, my biggest trouble was tryin' to keep Julia from beating Earl every time my back wuz turned. She would always take things from him and beat

him." She also states that Julia called her names and attacked her when she tried to protect Earl from Julia's blows (pp. 30–31).

Summarizing the probable impact of her early training upon Julia, Davis and Dollard say:

> Upon the basis of her long and hard experience that even the people closest to her would not give her what she needed or let her keep it, Julia began to depend upon herself alone. She took what she wanted and fought to get it. Since she expected only hostility and deprivation from her family, she acted not as they wanted her to, but as they—especially her mother and Earl—did *not* want her to act. She was henceforth in business for herself (p. 33).

The Impact of Early Training

CAUTION

While individual cases like Julia's may suggest the value of attention to early child training for understanding personality development, the evidence is by no means all on the side of Freudian hypotheses. There is considerable doubt that personality is so completely formed so early, that instinctively based pleasure seeking has such an important role to play, and that particular child-rearing practices have the kind of effects that are assumed in much of the psychoanalytic literature.

Among those who have questioned the psychoanalytic theories about early child training is William Sewell, a sociologist. Sewell (1952)[2] has pointed out that

for the most part the evidence brought to bear on these assumptions by the psychoanalytic school has been based on clinical observations of adults, with subsequent reconstruction of training experiences as an infant, rather than on empirical studies of the relation between observed experiences of infancy and personality traits. The danger in this procedure is that the reconstruction of infant experiences may be erroneous, and even if not there is no way of knowing that those who are clinically treated differ from the general population in the infant training they have undergone (p. 150).

Apparently, what is needed is a more direct attempt to investigate both early personality and child-training practices in a more typical set of young persons. This Sewell has done in a study of 162 Wisconsin farm children of age five or six.

Personal interviews with mothers yielded information on child-training practices such as nursing, weaning, bowel and bladder training, and early sleeping arrangements. Personality data included an objective pencil-and-paper personality test taken by the child, a projective test administered to each child, a behavior-rating scale filled out by the child's teacher, and information obtained from interviewing the mother. These various measures yielded almost five hundred specific tests of possible relationships between child-training practices and early personality. Of these, the number of relationships that showed statistical significance was only about what

---

[2] William Sewell, "Infant Training and the Personality of the Child," *American Journal of Sociology*, 58 (1952), 150–159. Copyright 1952 by The University of Chicago. Quotations from this source are reprinted with permission of The University of Chicago Press.

would be expected from random variation. Sewell reports that "such practices as breast feeding, gradual weaning, demand schedule, and easy and late induction to bowel and bladder training, which have been so much emphasized in the psychoanalytic literature, were almost barren in terms of relation to personality adjustment as measured in this study" (p. 158). He concludes:

Certainly the results of this study cast serious doubts on the validity of the psychoanalytic claims regarding the importance of the infant disciplines and on the efficacy of prescriptions based on them. However, it should not be concluded that these results unequivocally refute the claim that infancy is an important period in the development of the individual's personality, or even that the particular training practices studied have a bearing on personality formation and adjustments. To establish the first point would demand both controlled experiments and the study of other aspects of infancy. To establish the second point would demand the corroboration of the results of this study by many and better-designed studies of different culture and age groups (pp. 158–159).

And quite significantly Sewell points out:

It is entirely possible that the significant and crucial matter is not the practices themselves but the whole personal-social situation in which they find their expression, including the attitudes and behavior of the mother. This aspect of the mother-child relationship was purposely excluded from this paper (p. 159).

This would suggest that it is not the weaning or toilet-training practices that are themselves important, but rather the meanings they convey within their specific interpersonal context.

INTERPERSONAL RELATIONSHIPS

In addition to the child-training practices, we must consider the effect of the quality of interpersonal relationships surrounding the child. Who are the most significant other people for the young child? What is the nature of these interpersonal relationships? And how do these interpersonal relationships change as the child grows?

In the case of Julia, we have already begun to gather some impressions concerning her relationship to her mother. Her mother apparently had a very direct approach to disciplining her, which to Julia must have been terrifying. But in other ways Mrs. Wilson was grudgingly indulgent, or at least till she suddenly decided that enough was enough. Davis and Dollard report the matter of Julia's pacifier:

> For six years after the birth of her brother, she had insisted upon keeping a pacifier; indeed she had fought her mother, her oldest sister, and her teasing, contemptuous schoolmates in order to keep it. Moreover, her mother had consented to her using it and was continually buying her new pacifiers because she lost them regularly. At the age of seven, she had also been allowed by her mother to stop the first grade because she was afraid of school and would leave the building whenever the teacher's back was turned. The mother taught her at home for two years. Then at the age of nine, Julia was suddenly confronted with a mother who was no longer indulgent and protecting, but unaccountably enraged and violent.

"I tell you how I stopped her, an' I wish I would've did that before. One day I had jus' finished whippin' some of my children an' wuz tired an' mad, too. Julia came up and jumped up on my lap an' started cryin'. I jus' jerked that string from aroun' her neck an' threw that nipple so far! An' then I tol' her, 'You'd bettuh not ask for no nipple no more!' An' she never did. She ain't asked for that nipple from that day on. When I jerked that nipple from aroun' her neck, she jus' looked at me an' trembled —she was so scared!" (pp. 32–33).

For her part, Julia apparently tried early to relate to her mother with a combination of infantile behavior and aggression—infantile behavior to obtain the protection and privileges of a baby so far as her mother's indulgence would allow, and aggression to fight her mother for what she wanted. In the end, hostility and disobedience became the dominant feature of her response to her mother. "My mamma don't like me, and I don't like her, 'cause she's too mean to me—I don't do what she says noway" (p. 32).

Although Mrs. Wilson was the dominant member of Julia's family, we must also consider Julia's relationship to other family members. Her father was a roustabout and laborer on the river and thus was often many miles from home. But when he was home, he presented both an ally in Julia's struggle against her mother and an otherwise interesting example.

Julia's father is not only a fighter and a bootlegger who allowed his customers to give Julia drinks at the age of ten, he not only curses freely in his home and threatens to "stomp" his children to death, but he is preeminently a "woman chaser." Julia remembers many free-for-all fights in her home over this point, with the mother and all the children joining in against the father. One Christmas, when her mother and father were shopping downtown, her father met one of his "girl friends" and had a fight with her in the mother's presence. When he came home, Julia's next older sister hit him on the head with an axe, and all the family except Julia tried to "beat him good." He is like a stranger in the house now, and is barely spoken to by his wife or children.

Although Julia shares her mother's feeling that the father has disgraced them and now exhibits some hostility to him on this account, she used to get along with him excellently and to prize his free spending and violent living. She constantly emphasized to the interviewer the "free-heartedness" of her father, as contrasted with the stinginess of her mother. Equally constant is her insistence that the father was lenient with her; he allowed her to go out at night, did not try to discipline her, and aligned with her against the mother's discipline. Even now Julia goes to night clubs with her father and his "girl friends."

In the father's way of life, and under his protection and tutelage Julia found a socially approved outlet in lower-class life for her cursing, fighting, and exploitation of men. She expected nothing good from her mother, and resisted her efforts to make her "respectable." At one time her mother had hopes of preparing Julia for middle-class status, and sent her to a private school. But Julia soon punctured these hopes and ended her mother's attempts to raise her social status. She was discovered gambling and drinking in the boys' dormitory, and was expelled for these offenses (pp. 36–37).

Julia's relationships to members of her family is summarized by Davis and Dollard as follows:

> Her mother denied her those habits which were gratifying and left her without substitutes. Her oldest sister, who had control of her during the long periods when her mother was at work, also rejected her by strictly enforcing the mother's training demands. Her brother, Earl, replaced her in the mother's favor, and there was no peace between them. Her father was away on jobs in other towns so she very seldom saw him. She valued him simply for the gifts he brought her and for the shopping "splurges" on which he took her against her mother's wishes. The only person for whom she ever expresses love and approval is her next older sister, Mary, who was too young to help the mother train Julia, and who also fought against the mother's control. . . .
>
> Toward Earl, the baby, her behavior is still revengeful. She boasts that she used to beat him and take everything she could from him, "even if I didn't want it." She also used to make faces at Earl, when the mother was whipping him. In order to harass him now, she insists that he be made to escort her home from parties or visits, even when he has just "come home from work an' be so tired." When she fights with Earl, she tries "to kick him where I can ruin him for life" (pp. 33–34).

Beyond the family are relationships with others of Julia's age. The character of these relationships, and their impact upon Julia, are also described by Davis and Dollard:

> The children from "across-the-tracks," with whom she played, maintained a continuous feud with the children from the River Side of town. They had a well-organized system of terrorizing the unlucky children from the River Side who strayed into their province. Julia helped to beat up strange girls and to blackmail them for protection. She put River Side boys "on the spot" by leading them into traps and whistling for her gang of boys. She was friendly with boys who carried knives and sometimes pistols, who broke street lights so that they could beat up "outside" boys under cover of darkness, and who "turned out" house parties by hurling bricks through the windows. This warfare continued until late adolescence. . . .
>
> Julia was not intimidated by this warfare. She did not flee from lower-class life. Instead she entered into it with such zest that she earned the honorific nickname, "Raddie," and the reputation from students and teachers alike of being "crazy" and capable of doing "anything" (pp. 37–38).

With the coming of adolescence, relationships with members of the opposite sex became an increasingly significant feature. But for Julia such relationships suggest no psychological intimacy, and there are sharp limitations on physical intimacy as well. But men are important.

> She always seeks men out in order to use them, to take from
> them. Her skill is great and her thirst unquenchable. She takes
> the lead in sexual advances, next she asks favors and presents,
> and then she repeats the process without permitting consumma-
> tion. To Julia, sex is not a reward in itself as it is to most people.
> The genuine reinforcement to Julia is to "get something"—candy,
> clothes, money. All her approaches to men are simply instru-
> mental acts toward her real goal, money, and the childish satis-
> factions which it brings. In the lower class, men are accustomed
> to giving money to girls, but they are not accustomed to having
> the sequence stop there. Here Julia's aggression comes to her aid.
> In fact, this is now the chief use which she makes of her facility
> in cursing and fighting. After she has been given her presents, she
> drives off the man by what she calls her "craziness" (pp. 40–41).

Earlier it was mentioned that Julia had been married. However,
not much significance is attached to this relationship in the original
case study. Once, when drunk, Julia had premarital intercourse. Later
when she was frightened by a stomach pain, the man involved suggested it was a baby on the way. Julia then married him, but refused
to have anything to do with her husband after she found out that she
was not pregnant after all.

SOCIAL STRUCTURE

Enclosing the relationships of family members and interpersonal relationships outside the family is the broader web of society. A set of
social institutions sets the stage for the family and community life of
Julia Wilson, and our understanding of her also requires attention to
this broader sociological perspective.

Let us note first of all that Julia is a Negro growing up in a Southern city.

> The fact that Julia was born into this severely underprivileged
> group means that the social and economic world available to her
> has been arbitrarily limited. She goes to schools which are infer-
> ior even to those which lower-class white children attend. She
> and her parents constantly face a thoroughly organized occupa-
> tional blockade which is directed against them as Negroes. Even
> the fact that her playmates and her neighbors can make a battle-
> field of "across-the-tracks" and that they can all fight without fear
> of the white law, is caste controlled. For . . . cutting and shooting
> among Negroes are not regarded as crimes by the white law. A
> Negro's fighting becomes really criminal and punishable only if
> he fights a white man (p. 41).

Although the specific facts below describing conditions of life for
blacks in New Orleans in the late 1930s may no longer precisely describe conditions of today, they well represent part of the setting for
Julia's development.

The rate of home-owning families among all Negro families (13.2 per cent) was lower in 1930 in New Orleans than in any other large southern city. More than one-third of the homes owned by Negroes were valued at less than $2,000. The average income of colored families was less than $500 a year. Today the average wage for Negroes in New Orleans is estimated to be lower than in any large southern city. Only six out of every 100 Negro men in 1930 had white-collar employment, whereas almost half of all white male workers had such positions. Even the foreign-born whites in New Orleans enjoyed a tremendously superior economic status as compared with the Negro inhabitants. Although they had been in America for a comparatively short time, seven out of ten of these whites held white-collar or skilled jobs as compared with only two out of every ten Negroes.

A major effect of the caste system upon the Negro family in New Orleans has been to force almost half of the married Negro women to work, chiefly in domestic service, whereas less than one-tenth of the married white women work out of the home. Four of every ten Negro children, aged sixteen to seventeen years in New Orleans, were at work in 1930; only seven of the eighty-three largest cities in the United States had a higher rate. In spite of the fact that colored people were only one-fourth of the population, there were as many unemployed Negro adults in 1938 as white. In the most thickly populated Negro areas, two-thirds of all colored families were receiving some form of public relief.

Illegitimacy, nurtured by slavery and still tolerated by the white society, is very high in the Negro population; in New Orleans, one-tenth of all Negro births were illegitimate in 1938. . . . The rates for both illegitimacy and juvenile delinquency were much greater for Negroes than for whites. In Louisiana as a whole, the rate of illiteracy in 1930 for Negro adults (28 per cent) was almost three times as high as that for white adults (10 per cent). The amount of money invested by this state in each Negro child's education represented only a small proportion of that expended upon the white child's (pp. xxiv–xxv).

Not only was Julia born into the disadvantages of the Negro race; she was also born into the underprivileged lower-class segment of the black community. Davis and Dollard comment:

In their efforts to teach, lower-class Negro parents punish their children with great energy and frequency and reward them seldom. They cannot offer the more effective status rewards to their children because both economic and educational privileges are class-bound and there are very few to which the child in the lower class has access. The chief reason for the relative lack of socialization of lower-class children seems to be that their incitement to learn, which means in part to renounce direct impulse gratification and to build up more complex habits and skills, is crippled by the scarcity of available rewards (p. 267).

But Julia was not only forced into, and molded by, her place within a lower-class existence. She also found here an opportunity for the active expression of dominant themes in her personality.

She was constantly reinforced in her resentful attack on life. Embracing a lower-class role, she became more aggressive and rowdy in her behavior than are most lower-class children. She had no desire to be trained by her mother into middle-class "goodness" and respectability, because she was, above all, instigated to express her animosity against her mother and against life in revenge for the frightful "injustice" which had been done to her when she was incapable of protecting herself. She flees not up but down the class ladder, therefore, because in lower-class modes of action she can shout out her grudge, her unrequited claim against the world. . . .

In the weakness of its controls upon cross-sex relations, lower-class society also provided Julia with a virtually unlimited field for her exploitative passion. In the lower class, a girl cannot depend upon her parents or upon the law to control the fighting, slashing, and promiscuous male. Only a woman's wits, her cunning in playing off one man against another—in exploiting before she is exploited—can protect her. Julia welcomed this pattern of behavior. To her, the world of men appears as a dangerous but booty-laden field of conquest and she counts her trophies proudly and often. She not only seeks a "sucker," but she "bumps his head." "He tells me that he's just a fool. I know he is, and I'm using him for one, too" (pp. 38–40).

Julia's aggressive mode of response to deprivation does not stop at the boundary of the color line. Her relations to whites are quite consistent with other features of her life.

In her relations with the white world, Julia feels the sting of systematic deprivation. She says that she wishes that she were white "because white people got all the money." She remembers that when she was a little girl she always sat in the front of the streetcar (in the section for whites), and that her mother had to bring her back to the rear of the car. White boys have called her "nigger" and once when she cursed at them they cut her leg with a stone.

But Julia is not a person to be controlled by force, or to accept rejection meekly. She fights back and returns hate for contempt. "I hate white people," she repeats many times. "I just like to beat on white people. I hate white people. They don't like us, so I don't see why we should like them." She says that she fights white girls on every occasion she can find; she was a member of a clique of girls which regularly fought white school girls until the white principal complained.

In the theater she not only is a trouble-maker in the colored gallery, but as she says, "Sometimes I lean over the banister and spit down on them ol' white people's head." On a bus, when a white girl called her "nigger," Julia began to hit her and was stopped by a colored teacher who was on the bus. On another occasion, in a crowded bus, Julia was called "nigger" by a white woman who was standing beside her. She threatened to "beat up" the white woman, and was prevented by the bus driver himself (p. 42).

Individual Case Study

Studies of individual human beings constitute one of the richest— and one of the most dangerous— sources of information for social psychology.

The study of a concrete case is always rich in information. And when the concrete case is an unusual human being, like Julia Wilson, such study is also very interesting. Many ideas about more general relationships may be suggested in dramatic form by an individual case (for example, that a combination of violent and grudgingly indulgent child-training practices is apt to produce a highly aggressive child). Or more general ideas can be applied to the particular case to see if they fit.

But individual case study also has its dangers. The very richness of potential information itself presents dangers, for the information obtained is always highly selective. It is selective in terms of what the individual wishes to tell about himself, what the individual is able to remember, what the investigator asks about, what the investigator records, and what the investigator emphasizes from his recorded data. So some degree of bias nearly always enters into the results. Not bias in the sense of dishonesty, but rather bias in the sense of selective attention.

One of the chief results of such selective attention is to reduce the complexity of the individual studied. This frequently gives us more of a sense of understanding—but sometimes this is achieved at the expense of seeing important ambiguities, which are present in every human being.

JULIA TWENTY YEARS LATER

In summing up the case of Julia, Davis and Dollard conclude:

> Essentially, Julia is a person with a grudge against life itself. It seems in the very beginning to have starved her and robbed her of gratifying and necessary habits, when she was incapable of protecting herself and unable to understand what was asked of her. Her deep animosity toward people stems from the hostile demands and the abrupt, traumatic training which she received from her mother and oldest sister. She has a just, but never to be requited, claim against the universe. Therefore, she can never expect anything good of most human beings, nor can she absolve them and her mother from having taken the good things of life away. Long ago, she learned not to expect support and guidance and love, and therefore not to move unless driven. Restitution is not to be made. She must take what will not be given. She must abstract from people, by wile or force, what was taken from her. She will love, genuinely love, only herself (p. 43).

This does not leave us with a very hopeful picture concerning Julia's prospects in adjusting to occupational or domestic roles in the adult world.

A number of the cases studied by Davis and Dollard in the late 1930s were subjected to an intensive follow-up study twenty years later (Rohrer and Edmonson, 1960). Although Julia Wilson was not among those studied in this follow-up, we are given a very few later facts about her. With some surprise, we learn that she has "achieved an enduring marriage to a sailor, who is apparently a good provider even though he is away a great deal." She lives on the West Coast, where she has become a nurse "despite the distractions and interruptions occasioned by the births of six children" (p. 296).

Although our evidence of Julia twenty years later is meager, even these few details should caution us not to be too sure of the permanence of a given pattern of youthful personality. Nor for that matter should we neglect to recognize the possibilities of development that may come in adjustment to an adult world.

6
Seeds of Aggression

What makes individuals grow up to be aggressive personalities? Are there certain kinds of childhood experiences that produce persons who especially seek to hurt other persons?

The case of Julia suggests certain possibilities. Perhaps the timing and manner of early practices, such as weaning and toilet training, are sometimes important (violent discontinuities in early childhood may set the stage for a violent personality). But other research, such as the study by Sewell, casts doubt as to the general and enduring impact of such early experience. Perhaps, rather than the specific practices, what is important is the quality of the relationships of the child to other family members. But if so, what are the qualities of such relationships that are most apt to produce aggressive children?

To answer questions like this, we need to have evidence from more than just one or two individuals. We need comparable evidence from many individuals, obtained during or shortly after the early years of child rearing.

In this chapter, we examine a study by Robert Sears, Eleanor Maccoby, and Harry Levin devoted to early child-rearing patterns and their effects upon kindergarten-aged children. Their study, reported in the book *Patterns of Child Rearing* (1957),[1] explores much more than the seeds of aggression. The authors attempt to describe generally how mothers raise their children, why they raise them the way they do, and what effects different patterns of child rearing have upon children. We shall select out of their study only those matters especially related to the development, and control, of aggressive tendencies.

THEORETICAL POINTER

Aggression

We use the term *aggression* to refer to any intentional act of hurting another person. Such hurting may be of minor or major proportions, may be physical or verbal, may be sought for its own sake or only as a means of achieving something else. In any case, though, the hurting is not mere accident.

It should be clear that in these

[1] Robert R. Sears, Eleanor E. Maccoby, and Harry Levin, *Patterns of Child Rearing*. New York: Harper & Row, 1957. Copyright © 1957 by Harper & Row, Publishers, Inc. Quotations from this source are reprinted with permission of the publisher.

early chapters the term *aggression* does not refer simply to a high energy level in applying oneself to a task, especially a competitive task. There must rather be some harm intended. Also, our focus is primarily on behavior rather than on the feelings that may accompany such behavior. It is possible to display aggression without feeling particularly aggressive; conversely, it is possible to feel aggressive without acting upon such feelings. Generally, however, we expect aggressive behavior and aggressive feelings to go together.

A glossary at the back of this book gives brief definitions of technical terms or common terms that, like aggression, may be used in a special way. It should be consulted often, particularly when there is doubt about the way a certain concept is used.

THE ORIGINAL STUDY

For their study Sears, Maccoby, and Levin did not directly observe children. Rather, the data were obtained completely through interviews with mothers. The researchers admit that, ideally, they should have obtained data separately from mothers and their children, but this did not seem feasible.

The children who, through their mothers, were the focus of the study were 379 Massachusetts kindergarten-aged children.

Sampling

METHODOLOGICAL POINTER

Strictly speaking, some kind of sampling is used whenever the individuals studied are fewer than the entire group relevant for the investigation.

There is only one way to avoid a sampling problem, and this would be to include everybody for whom the conclusions are meant to apply. In this way there would be, by definition, no sample; the whole relevant population (also called a *universe*) would be included. Thus if we are interested in studying the effects of child rearing upon childhood aggression, the whole relevant population would be all the children who have ever lived on earth. This would be a rather ambitious study.

Often a report of research will make no mention of sampling. This is most often true with case studies and in laboratory experimentation. With case studies enough information is given so that the reader can make at least a qualitative judgment of how typical the case is of other cases for which it has implications. In the case of an *experimental sample,* it is sometimes mistakenly assumed that any collection of subjects will do. This is true, however, only if no attempt is made to carry the analysis to anything beyond the subjects studied, or if there is no reason to believe that the relationship between variables being tested in the laboratory would be different for different groups. As insurance against this second possibility, the experimenter, typically, at least identifies how subjects were obtained.

Most commonly when sampling is mentioned, what is being discussed is obtaining a *representative sample* of a clearly defined population. In a truly representative sample, every individual in the population has a chance of being included in the study. This is probably best approached by a random drawing of names from a well-mixed collection. This is also approached by a master list from which every seventh (or seventieth or whatever) name may be selected for inclusion in the study. A representative sample also may be approximated by techniques of area sampling (where both the individuals within areas and the areas themselves are randomly selected) and, perhaps with somewhat less adequacy, by techniques of quota control (where a predetermined quota for different types of individuals for the sample matches their frequency in the total population). If the characteristics of a larger population are expected to be described by the sample, it is most important that it be carefully representative.

Sometimes a *homogeneous sample* is used. Then the objective is to focus on a particular type of individual. This may be a type especially relevant for the purposes of study (for example, mothers for a study of child rearing) or especially typical of the larger population (for example, suburban residents as typical of the increasingly dominant pattern of American society). Selection of a homogeneous sample of course limits the population to which the findings might be generalized.

The study conducted by Sears, Maccoby, and Levin is a mixture so far as sampling is concerned. The children were obtained from the kindergarten lists of two public school systems near Boston, with interviews being conducted with the mothers of about 60 percent of these. The analysis of data focuses largely on relations between variables within the sample, in this respect using it as an experimental sample. But, though the researchers make no claims of having a representative sample, there is reason to believe that the individuals included represent a fairly broad cross section of Americans. And, of course, their sample is quite homogeneous in limiting attention to mothers of five-year-olds.

Mothers were asked questions about all phases of child rearing. The form of the questionnaire was a compromise between a depth interview (which is used especially for individual case studies) and a completely structured interview (which is particularly useful in survey research). For example, one of the questions was: "Some people feel it is very important for a child to learn not to fight with other children, and other people feel there are times when a child has to learn to fight. How do you feel about this?" After recording the mother's response, the interviewer followed with: "Have you ever encouraged your child to fight back?" (p. 496). Full responses of the mother to such questions were encouraged.

The questionnaires were constructed to get at several main dimensions of parental behavior. In particular, central attention was given to five main child-rearing dimensions: (1) The degree to which the mother used various *disciplinary techniques;* (2) the mother's *permissiveness* for the child's behavior concerning hunger, elimination, dependency, sex, and aggression; (3) the *severity* with which the various techniques of training were applied to change behavior; (4) certain *temperamental qualities* of the mother, such as warmth and level of self-esteem; and (5) the *positive inculcation* of more mature behavior that the mother held forth.

Variable Analysis

METHODOLOGICAL
POINTER

To simplify a problem for analysis, social psychologists usually narrow their attention to certain aspects that can be measured in some way. These aspects become the *variables* that are the focus of study.

Commonly the investigator is interested in a question within a cause-and-effect framework. Thus he may think of how certain variables may produce an effect upon other variables. Those that are considered as likely to produce the effects are called *independent variables* (independent in the sense of the starting point for analysis), and those variables that measure effects produced are called *dependent variables* (dependent in the sense that their action is traced back to other variables). In the Sears-Maccoby-Levin study such aspects as permissiveness of aggression and severity of punishment for aggression are considered primarily as independent variables, and the amount of aggression shown by the child represents a dependent variable.

Of course, sometimes the cause-and-effect relationship may work either way. Then it sometimes becomes the interest of the investigator that determines what is considered as an independent or dependent variable. For example, for some purposes a child's aggression may be treated as an independent variable and the mother's response as a dependent variable, as well as the other way around. It depends primarily on whether the investigator is treating the child's or the mother's behavior as more stable or given (that is, the more naturally independent variable).

Rating scales (on which investigators made ratings from interview records) were developed to represent specific aspects of each of the dimensions mentioned above. A total of 188 rating scales were used. Some examples of the particular scales that are directly related to aggression:

1. Permissiveness for aggression toward siblings
2. Permissiveness for aggression toward parents
3. Permissiveness for aggression toward children other than siblings
4. Demands for the child to show aggression toward other children
5. Severity of punishment for aggression toward parents
6. Amount of aggression the child exhibits at home

Reliability and Validity

METHODOLOGICAL
POINTER

Reliability is a constant problem in social psychology. This is essentially a question of the dependability of an observation or set of observations. Do independent attempts to observe or measure the same thing yield the same results? If so, we say the result has high reliability.

Usually it is useful to build measures of reliability into a research design. This was done in the Sears-Maccoby-Levin study by having two "judges" make independent ratings of the interview materials. Then measures of correlation were obtained to show how similar these two ratings were. Correlations of these ratings for various measures of aggression ranged from .52 to .71—high enough to justify serious analysis but very far from perfect.

The question of validity is a much more difficult one than that of reliability. This is essentially a question of whether we are measuring what we say we are. Are we actually measuring "aggression of the child at home" when we make a rating based on interviews with mothers? Or are we partly measuring different interpretations of questions asked, different degrees of

openness to such questions, different degrees of willingness of mothers to see aggression in their children, and different abilities of mothers to keep track of their children? These are questions that touch on the matter of validity. While attempts to measure validity have sometimes been made for particular studies, the primary evaluation concerning validity is usually more qualitative than quantitative. The ultimate judgment of validity must include how well a particular study fits together to make sense and how well the study fits with the findings of other related research.

We have by now a fairly good idea of how Sears, Maccoby, and Levin went about their study. We are ready then to examine what they found out about aggression. The main dependent variable for us will be "aggression at home," for the home was the only context where an attempt was actually made to measure the amount of aggression. We will be interested in learning which child-rearing variables seem to show the strongest relationship to such a measure of aggression.

But before we examine the actual data that reflect the individual differences in aggression, let us note the background discussion the authors give concerning the normal development of aggression.

Rage, or something very like it, occurs soon after birth. For caution's sake, let us emphasize the "something very like it." One can never know what the feelings and perceptions of an infant are, whether he has the true sense of fury or whether he just flails his limbs and screams. And if he has the sense of fury, we cannot know whether he has also the feeling of blaming someone for something and wanting to hurt in retaliation. In any case, his behavior sometimes has certain qualities, when he is hungry or colicky or pricked or restrained, that look so like the rage of older children who do report their feelings that we incline to say that this is the early beginning of aggression. There are the flailing limbs, the blasting cry, the scarlet face and hoarse breathing. After such an episode there is likely to be a period during which food does not sit well on the stomach, and the child may even vomit.

Within the first year, a child learns to use his hands somewhat more manipulatively, and he begins to strike at people who are close enough to him to be hit when something arouses this hot behavior. He learns to bite, too, and to kick, as he gains more control over his movements, and to let loose ear-piercing screams.

Gradually he begins to supplement these direct attacks with other techniques that are effective not because they hurt the mother physically, but because they interfere with her efforts at child care. The baby discovers how to cry "miserably," how to turn his head away when his mother wants him to smile, how to remain rigid when she wants to cuddle him. He has discovered the invaluable principle of non-co-operation as a means of control.

By the latter part of their second year, many children have begun to add still another kind of behavior to the repertory of actions that they use for controlling other people. Throwing, smashing, dropping, spilling, pushing, knocking over—all begin to appear. At first these acts do not necessarily involve what adults interpret as destructiveness, but most children soon seem to learn that to destroy (or threaten to destroy) some valued object has a wholesome influence, on other children and adults, from the child's point of view. It secures compliance or wards off further interference. . . .

The sequence of development, then, seems to go like this. In the beginning, the child can do no more, in response to discomforting situations, than express angry emotion. However, his maturing skill for controlling his own movements soon enables him to learn other ways of reacting, ways that help to get rid of the frustrating state of affairs. Some of these acts are constructive from the mother's point of view, as when the child willingly co-operates with her wishes and thus ends his own frustration by making unnecessary his mother's pressure for compliance. Some of the child's acts are hurtful to her, however, and may be looked on as the earliest forms of aggression in the child's repertory of behavior. . . .

By the end of the child's second year, certain further developments have taken place. One of these is that the child has begun to respond aggressively to a good many frustrations in a purely automatic way. Even though his mother may be absent at the moment and his aggressive act may be quite futile as a means of removing the frustration, he will perform the act nonetheless. It is as if he had learned, in a blind sort of way, that aggressive acts were often followed by the relief of discomfort. So, without evaluating the probable effectiveness of his behavior, he simply aggresses whenever frustrated.

Children differ a great deal from one another in the extent to which this type of development occurs. Some seem to reach a point in their third and fourth years at which almost every little irritant or interference triggers off an aggressive reaction. Indeed, many situations that have no frustrating quality at all—to an outside observer—are sufficient, too. There may be many expressions of destructiveness or hitting or verbal attack which appear quite spontaneous. Other children, in contrast, have a greater propensity for reacting with some kind of dependency behavior. Every child, in other words, develops a repertory of actions to be used when he bumps up against frustrations: some children tend to use aggression as their typical reaction; others use some other type of act. . . .

The other change that becomes evident in the child's second year, and is increasingly notable the older he gets, is in the apparent satisfyingness of some of his aggressive acts. Most of his aggressive behavior continues to be a device for gratifying other needs—but occasional acts now seem to have the quality of gratifications in their own right (pp. 222–225).

While such a discussion provides important insights concerning the early development of aggression, it still does not explain why some children become much more aggressive than others. What are some of the conditions under which acts of aggression are more likely to be gratifying in their own right? And what are the conditions that are most apt to get the child what he wants through aggression?

Two variables that the authors believe should have an important bearing on the amount of aggression a child develops are his parents' *permissiveness* and *punishment.* They argue that since permissiveness is an expression of parental willingness to have the child display aggression, permissive mothers should have more aggressive children than mothers who do not permit aggression. They also suggest that punishment would appear to inhibit aggression. If punishment for aggression leads the child to fear such behavior, it would be natural to expect high parental punishment for aggression to go hand-in-hand with low aggression by children.

The logic of such a relationship of permissiveness and punishment to aggression is further supported by the authors' finding that permissiveness and punishment are negatively correlated. Those mothers who permitted much aggression also tended to be the same mothers who showed little severity in their punishment. And with this would fit our common-sense expectation: such mothers with high permissiveness and low punishment will have the children who show most aggression.

But what did Sears and his associates actually find? Table 5 gives some results in the form of coefficients of correlation, measuring how closely the aggression the child shows in the home was associated with other variables, including variables of permissiveness and punishment. These results do not quite agree with the common-sense expectation just mentioned.

TABLE 5   CORRELATIONS OF OTHER VARIABLES WITH "AMOUNT OF AGGRESSION AT HOME"

Variable	Coefficient of Correlation
Permissiveness for aggression toward siblings	.09
Permissiveness for aggression toward parents	.23
Permissiveness for aggression toward children other than siblings	.06
Demands for the child to show aggression toward other children	.04
Severity of punishment for aggression toward parents	.16
Extent of use of physical punishment in overall child training	.22
Mother's warmth toward the child	−.20

SOURCE: Adapted from Sears, Maccoby, and Levin (1957), p. 527.

METHODOLOGICAL POINTER

Correlation

A coefficient of correlation is a measure of the extent to which variables are associated. The general range of these measures is be-tween 1.00 (for perfect positive correlation) and −1.00 (for perfect negative correlation), with correlations close to .00 indicating an absence of correlation. Note that most coefficients of correlation indicate the direction (positive or negative) as well as the strength of the relationship.

For example, let us consider height and weight as two variables for which we have measures representing each member of a population. If we find a strong positive correlation between height and weight, such as a coefficient of correlation of .72, we could be confident that most of the taller persons of our population are also among the heavier persons and most shorter persons are among those lighter in weight. A correlation of .06 would indicate very little relationship between height and weight. And the unlikely coefficient of correlation of −.44 would indicate that the taller persons were in general considerably lighter than were shorter persons.

The best-known measure of correlation is Pearson's product-moment "r." This is the measure used to summarize results for the Sears-Maccoby-Levin study. But the student should know that there are other measures of correlation that may be used when r would not be appropriate.

Ordinarily we think of correlation as a measure of association between two variables. But there are also techniques for measuring the association among several variables, known as *multiple correlation.* And with *partial correlation* we may examine the association between two variables corrected to control for carry-over effects of intercorrelations with other variables.

The evaluation of a given coefficient of correlation depends partly on the number of cases studied. A correlation coefficient for a population or sample of a very few members would be meaningless. For a sample of the size included in the Sears-Maccoby-Levin study, an r of about .10 or more (either positive or negative) would be necessary to give convincing evidence (according to commonly used standards for statistical significance) that the results showed anything more than a chance variation.

One of the things we may note about the correlations in Table 5 is that they are all fairly low. Nothing stands out dramatically to suggest itself as a dominant explanation of a child's aggressive tendencies. Yet there does appear to be some relationship of aggression to parental permissiveness and punishment. High permissiveness is associated with high aggression, as had been anticipated. But severity of punishment is also positively associated with aggression, and this had not been anticipated. Apparently from the results shown in Table 5, the more severely punitive a parent, the more apt is the child to show aggression. Although these correlations are small, the authors point out that "they are significant, and they are artificially reduced by the negative correlation between the permissiveness and punitiveness scales" (p. 259).

Let us note the further discussion the authors give concerning these results:

> We interpret these findings in this way. When a mother adopts a permissive point of view about aggression, she is saying to her child, in effect, "Go ahead and express your angry emotions;

don't worry about me." She gives few signals in advance that would lead the child to fear to be aggressive. On the contrary, her attitude is one of expectancy that he will be, and that such behavior is acceptable. It is scarcely surprising that the child tends to fulfill her expectations. The non-permissive mother, however, does something quite different. She has an attitude that aggression is wrong, that it is not to be tolerated, and an expectancy (often subtly expressed) that the child will not behave in such undesirable ways. When he is aggressive, she does something to try to stop it—sometimes by punishment, sometimes by other means. He, also, fulfills his mother's expectations. This dimension of permissiveness, then, is a measure of the extent to which the mother prevents or stops aggression, the non-permissive extreme being the most common.

Punishment is apparently a somewhat different matter. It is a kind of maternal behavior that occurs after the child's aggression has been displayed. The child has already enjoyed the satisfaction of hurting or of expressing anger—and so has had a reinforcement for aggressive action. But then he gets hurt in return. He suffers from frustration. This should, and on the average does, incite him to more aggression. If the punishment is very severe, particular acts that get most repeatedly punished may be inhibited. But the total frustration is increased, and hence the total amount of aggression displayed in the home is higher. The dimension called *severity of punishment for aggression toward parents*, then, is one measure of the amount of painful frustration that is imposed on the child without direct guidance as to what would be a more acceptable form of behavior.

It is evident from this analysis that the mothers who were most permissive but also most severely punitive would have the most aggressive children; those who were most non-permissive but least punitive would have the least aggressive ones (pp. 259–260).

This pattern may be seen more fully in Table 6. In reading this table we should bear in mind that permissiveness and punishment are not ordinarily associated; therefore, most of the cases are in the middle two rows. Note also that of the two variables, permissiveness seems slightly stronger than punishment in distinguishing between highly aggressive and other children.

If we look back to Table 5 we may note again the moderate correlations shown for the variables measuring punishment. Concerning "extent of use of physical punishment" we are told further that this had an important effect in promoting aggression

... only when it occurred in association with quite severe punishment for aggression. That is, if a child was being severely punished for aggression, the high use of *physical* punishment (as distinct from other kinds of punishment) increased his aggression markedly. If his parents did not punish aggression severely, the use of physical punishment for other kinds of misdeeds had no effect on the amount of aggression the child showed (p. 262).

In considering the role of the mother's warmth, as well as the variables more specifically related to permissiveness and punishment,

TABLE 6 PERCENTAGE OF CHILDREN IN SUBGROUPS WHO WERE
HIGHLY AGGRESSIVE

	Number of Children		Percent of Children Who Were "Highly Aggressive"**	
*Subgroup**	*Boys*	*Girls*	*Boys*	*Girls*
Low permissiveness and low punishment	27	30	3.7	13.3
Low permissiveness and high punishment	51	47	20.4	19.1
High permissiveness and low punishment	81	63	25.3	20.6
High permissiveness and high punishment	36	22	41.7	38.1

* Subgroups are divided according to whether the mother was in the upper or lower half of the distribution on "permissiveness" and on "severity of punishment for aggression toward parents."
** By "highly aggressive" is meant that the child was rated by one or both raters as being in one of the two highest levels of aggression.
SOURCE: Sears, Maccoby, and Levin (1957), p. 260.

the authors point to complications of analysis caused by intercorrelations of variables. In the following discussion Sears, Maccoby, and Levin also try to cut through these intercorrelations to derive their main conclusions concerning the nurturing of aggression in children.

> One serious difficulty in pursuing the search for sources of children's aggressiveness is that the scales for measuring maternal behavior were not independent of one another. Just as the rating of physical punishment was somewhat correlated with severity of punishment for aggression, so the rating of affectional warmth was correlated with both these scales. Mothers who use physical punishment tended to be colder in their affectional interaction with their children, and coldness was also associated with severe punishment for aggression.
>
> In order to discover the relative amount of influence of each of the four dimensions discussed above [permissiveness of aggression, severity of punishment for aggression, extent of physical punishment generally, and warmth of mother], we have used partial correlations. These show that permissiveness contributed the most, punishment for aggression next most, and physical punishment and coldness the least. However, all four dimensions were influential in some degree....
>
> Our findings suggest that the way for parents to produce a non-aggressive child is to make abundantly clear that aggression is frowned upon, and to stop aggression when it occurs, but to avoid punishing the child for his aggression. Punishment seems to have complex effects. While undoubtedly it often stops a particular form of aggression, at least momentarily, it appears to generate more hostility in the child and lead to further aggressive outbursts at some other time or place. Furthermore, when the parents punish—particularly when they employ physical punishment—they are providing a living example of the use of

aggression at the very moment they are trying to teach the child
not to be aggressive. The child, who copies his parents in many
ways, is likely to learn as much from this example of successful
aggression on his parents' part as he is from the pain of punishment. Thus, the most peaceful home is one in which the mother
believes aggression is not desirable and under no circumstances
is ever to be expressed toward her, but who relies mainly on non-
punitive forms of control. The homes where the children show
angry, aggressive outbursts frequently are likely to be homes in
which the mother has a relatively tolerant (or careless!) attitude
toward such behavior, or where she administers severe punishment for it, or both (pp. 263–266).

SIX YEARS LATER

In Julia Wilson's case (in Chapter 5) we saw a personality outcome
in adulthood that was considerably different from what was expected
from our information about her childhood. This leads us to question
the necessary permanence of patterns of behavior produced in early
childhood. Might it not be the same with the aggression shown by many
of the kindergarten children of the Sears-Maccoby-Levin study?

Six years later some of these children were subjected to a follow-up
study, reported by Sears (1961).[2] He studied only those who were
then in sixth grade classrooms of schools in their original towns. The
original group of 379 children was thus reduced to a sample of 160, but
the characteristics of persons in this sample were quite comparable
to those of the original group.

Among the methods of data gathering in this follow-up study were
questionnaires, which included scales representing five forms of
aggression-related attitudes. These scales were designed to measure five
aspects of aggression:

1. Aggression anxiety—including feelings of fear, discomfort, and
   dislike of aggression
2. Projected aggression—the tendency to attribute aggression to
   sources outside the self
3. Self-aggression—including items referring to injury or punishment to the self (this scale was the only one that showed an
   unsatisfactory measure of reliability)
4. Prosocial aggression—aggression used in a socially approved
   way for purposes that are acceptable to the moral standards
   of the group
5. Antisocial aggression—including acts that are normally considered unacceptable.

Interviews with teachers were also included in the follow-up
study. But, as Sears reports, the interview items dealing with aggression failed to yield information "with sufficient clarity to provide use-

[2] Robert R. Sears, "Relation of Early Socialization Experiences to Aggression in
Middle Childhood," *Journal of Abnormal and Social Psychology*, 63 (1961), 466–
492. Copyright 1961 by the American Psychological Association. Quotations from
this source are reprinted with permission of the publisher.

ful data. . . The major difficulty stemmed from the lack of discriminable differences" (p. 467).

We are left then with the five scales of attitudes related to aggression. Of these the one that seems closest to the kind of aggression measured earlier (aggression shown in the home) is antisocial aggression. Are the same persons who showed high aggression in the home at age five also those who register high antisocial aggression six years later? This is what we would expect if aggression is a general feature of personality carrying the long-term consequences of the early years.

But no. The correlations between earlier aggression in the home and later antisocial aggression are −.03 for boys and −.08 for girls. These correlations fail to show more than random variation.

How can we explain this discrepancy? Several explanations are possible, any or all of which may be in some degree applicable.

One possibility is to doubt the validity (or at least the comparability) of the earlier or later measures of aggression. We note that neither of these was based on direct observations of behavior. One was based on the mother's report, the other on self-report; and these forms of inquiry are quite different.

Another possibility is to doubt the generality of an aggressive trait. At age five, aggressive behavior referred only to the context of the home, whereas ratings of antisocial aggression six years later referred more to persons outside the home. It is quite possible that many children adopt aggressive roles in some settings but show very little aggression otherwise.

A third possibility is to assume that aggression may be a fairly general characteristic, but that there are significant shifts over time. Persons highly aggressive at age five may not be those who show high aggression six years later.

But, in any case, the failure of correspondence between aggression at age five and a measure of antisocial aggression six years later is not the only surprise. The child-rearing practices that are related to these two measures of aggression are also different.

At age five it appeared that permissiveness and punishment were both positively associated with aggression. For the children six years later, antisocial aggression was more weakly associated with the previous measure of permissiveness for aggression ($r = .18$ for boys, $r = .02$ for girls). And earlier measures of punishment for aggression now are negatively correlated with later measures for antisocial aggression (measures of r range from −.06 to −.20, depending on sex and the particular measure of punishment). This requires some comments on the effects of punishment upon aggression that are more qualified than the earlier Sears-Maccoby-Levin report. Sears now says:

> Having only two chronological points of measurement—ages 5 and 12—one falls easily into a manner of speaking that implies the operation of one effect of punishment (facilitating) at one age and another effect (inhibiting) at the other. This is improper, of course. One can only suppose that both effects of punishment are always operative. The fact that at the earlier age the two interact in such a way as to allow the facilitative effect to be revealed in

group averages, and at a later age the inhibitory effect, probably means that with the particular levels of punishment, permissiveness and other relevant variables occurring in this culture, the facilitating effects are more pronounced in early stages of socialization and the inhibitory ones do not appear so generally until later (p. 479).

The plot further thickens when we include consideration of the other measures of aggression taken at age twelve. Most of these are not correlated with antisocial aggression but are correlated with each other. Aggression anxiety, projected aggression, self-aggression, and prosocial aggression show weak or negative r values when correlated with antisocial aggression. But when these four scales are correlated with each other, most of the measures of r are strongly positive. This clearly suggests that the other scales are measuring features different from antisocial aggression.

Furthermore, we learn that these other scales reflect the influence of child-rearing practices in a way different from antisocial aggression. Permissiveness for aggression in early childhood is negatively correlated with most of these variables (especially with aggression anxiety and prosocial aggression for girls).

"In summary," says Sears, "the influence of these two child rearing variables may be hypothesized to have been as follows: high punishment for aggression reduced antisocial aggression, but increased aggression anxiety and prosocial aggression, and high permissiveness increased antisocial aggression but reduced the other two [aggression anxiety and prosocial aggression]" (pp. 479–480).

The implication seems to be that early attempts by parents to reduce aggressive behavior may succeed in the long run, even if some of the short-run effects of punishment for aggression may backfire. But such a systematic attempt to reduce antisocial behavior often has the by-products of aggression anxiety and aggressive sentiments redirected into socially approved channels. If, on the contrary, little is done to discourage aggressive behavior, the child is apt to develop a considerable facility for antisocial aggression, while he will be spared the burden of heavy anxiety about his aggression.

This all leads to an interesting injustice: Those who most need to have anxiety about aggression will be least apt to have it.

CAUTION

Prediction

If understanding is the purpose of science, prediction may be considered the key test of understanding. However, much of the prediction in social psychology is of a very low order.

Even when research results have undoubted theoretical and statistical significance, predictive ability may still be quite low. One reason for this is the very rough kinds of measures used in much analysis. Thus a rating of a few things a mother says to an interviewer is used to represent the totality of a child's aggressive behavior in the home. To point out that this can only be a very, very rough index of aggressive behavior does not mean that it is not a suitable index. It may still be as good as any other that would be practical for the research purposes at hand.

Another reason for the low predictability of generalizations derived from research in social psychology is the complexity of the factors involved in social behavior. Seldom can single causes be identified for social behavior (except in the mythologies of folk wisdom and pseudoscience). Concrete behavior is nearly always best seen as the result of a combination of causes, of a complex fabric of events.

To turn again to the study just discussed, how dependable are the predictions if the generalizations are applied to a particular case? To help us answer this, we may note an additional feature of correlation coefficients. The square of a coefficient of correlation gives an estimate of the variation in one variable that may be attributed to the other (or to each other, if mutual causation is assumed). Thus a coefficient of correlation of .70 "explains" about 49 percent of the variance. So if early permissiveness for aggression had this high a correlation with later antisocial aggression, we could say that about half the variation shown from child to child in later antisocial aggression could be traced to early permissiveness. But, in fact, the correlations we actually find are only .18 for boys and much less for girls. This means that even for boys early permissiveness explains less than 4 percent of the variation shown in antisocial aggression. This may be enough to consider such a relationship significant (actually its statistical significance is at best borderline, for with a sample of seventy-six—the number of boys—an r of .18 would be obtained more than five times out of a hundred just by chance), especially if it fits within a consistent pattern of other findings. But this is hardly enough to merit much confidence in predicting whether a particular boy will show high antisocial aggression.

The prediction of the behavior of the human individual is always a very complicated matter. Only fools and certain others who give advice on child rearing (who are not fools, but who know that parents need assurance) may dare to have confidence that a particular feature of child rearing will have a clearly predictable effect upon adult behavior.

7
Aggression in the Laboratory

In exploring conditions that may produce more or less aggressive personalities, we have noted some apparent relationships between early training and later aggressive tendencies. But we have also noted the low predictability of such relationships. Possibly this low predictability is due to the fact that we have ignored consideration of the particular kinds of situations in which aggression occurs. In the present chapter we correct for this omission by examining two studies representing current laboratory research. These will deal not with the question of what makes aggressive personalities, but rather with the kinds of situations that lead to a greater or lesser display of aggression.

When do persons show aggression? This is the fundamental question for the present chapter. Let us start with a rather naïve answer to this question: People show aggression when they are angry. And when are they angry? Here the frustration-aggression hypothesis has at least some relevance.

THEORETICAL POINTER

The Frustration-Aggression Hypothesis

Since its formulation thirty years ago by a group of psychologists at Yale University (Dollard and associates, 1939), the frustration-aggression hypothesis has been a leading generalization for explaining aggressive behavior. Originally the hypothesis held that "occurrence of aggressive behavior always presupposes the existence of frustration and, contrariwise, the existence of frustration always leads to some form of aggression" (p. 1). In other words, frustration always leads to aggression, and aggression is always a consequence of frustration.

When frustrations are great, we then expect persons to show more aggression. But aggression may also be inhibited, and the very inhibition itself adds to the frustration. What happens then is the nurturing of an aggressive tendency, increasing the general predisposition of a person to respond aggressively even though the original object of frustration may not actually have elicited an aggressive response.

Later qualifications have been made to the frustration-aggression hypothesis. Miller (1941) has pointed to other possible consequences of frustration besides aggression. Berkowitz (1962) has given emphasis to the concept of anger in mediating between frustration and aggression and to the role of in-

terpretation in perceiving frustration and in selecting targets for
aggression. And Buss (1961) suggests that frustration is typically
less important than other causes of
aggression. But, generally, the main
idea that frustration tends to give
rise to aggression remains a key
hypothesis in contemporary social
psychology.

Even if we accept the main idea of the frustration-aggression
hypothesis, the question remains concerning how this aggression
becomes expressed. Is it truly free-floating aggression that can be
directed toward any kind of target? Or is aggression selective in terms
of degrees of association with previous aggression? Or is aggression
directed only against a person apparently responsible for the frustration? These questions set the stage for the experiment examined in the
following section.

EFFECTS OF FILM VIOLENCE

Let us turn our attention to an experiment by Leonard Berkowitz and
Russell G. Geen (1966), a part of a series of studies on the consequences of viewing filmed violence. A general finding of most of the
studies in this series is that viewing a film sequence depicting aggression tends to increase the probability of subsequent aggression by
members of the audience. These findings are directly contrary to a
fairly widespread idea concerning catharsis of aggression.

Catharsis of Aggression

THEORETICAL
POINTER

Sigmund Freud viewed aggressive
behavior as ultimately derived from
a death instinct, and he viewed the
death instinct as constituting a
relatively fixed quantity of energy.
It follows from this not only that
man is innately aggressive, but also
that aggression not expressed in
one way must be expressed in
another. Freud himself believed
that the only hope for control of
these aggressive impulses must lie
in their sublimation into culturally
controlled forms.

Much of the popular literature
inspired by Freud's writing has
given more emphasis to the necessity of expressing aggression than
to the necessity of sublimating it
(that is, modifying it into socially
acceptable forms). Thus it is sometimes held that the expression of
aggression is a necessary catharsis
of aggressive impulses, that such
aggression needs to be drained off
in one way or another. It is often
further assumed that fantasy forms
of violence (for example, television)
may provide a relatively harmless
outlet for such aggression, thus
leaving a person actually less aggressively inclined for the rest of
his everyday activities.

Research, however, has not given
consistent support to this idea of
catharsis of aggression. After reviewing the literature, Berkowitz
(1962) concludes: "In general, there
is no unequivocal evidence of a
cathartic lessening in the strength
of aggressive tendencies following
the performance of hostile acts.
Such a phenomenon may well exist,
but the studies that have been conducted to date have not been altogether convincing" (p. 219). Nor
has the evidence been any stronger
for catharsis through vicarious par-

ticipation in aggressive activities of others.

Why, then, the popularity of the idea of aggressive catharsis, especially through vicarious participation in aggression? Bandura (1965)[1] has speculated as follows:

The persistence of the belief in cathartic energy discharges through vicarious participation despite substantial, negative experimental findings, is probably supported by frequent subjectively experienced "tension" reduction following exposure to aggressive content provided in films, televised programs, and other audiovisual displays. There is no disputing the fact that a person who is in a state of heightened emotionality resulting from stressful and frustrating everyday events is apt to undergo some reduction in general arousal level as a function of observing aggressive performances. While such an outcome is generally interpreted as evidence of vicarious reduction in "pent-up" affects and impulses, a more plausible alternative explanation is in terms of stimulus-change processes.

After a person has been insulted, unjustly criticized, or otherwise thwarted, the resultant emotional arousal is typically revivified and even augmented on later occasions through symbolic reinstatement of the anger-provoking incidents. Thus, by brooding over the ill treatment and possible negative consequences of disturbing episodes, intense feelings can be reinstated long after the initial reactions to the situation have subsided. The persistence of elevated arousal, according to this social-learning view, is attributable to self-generated stimulation rather than to the existence of an undischarged reservoir of "aggressive drive." If the person should become immersed in new activities that supersede the preoccupying internal eliciting stimuli, a noticeable degree of "tension" reduction will, in all likelihood, take place. On the supposition that the diminution of emotional arousal is a consequence of *attentional shifts* rather than a cathartic effect of having experienced aggression vicariously, one would expect aroused subjects to experience equally salutary effects from getting involved in an absorbing book, a movie, a stage play, or a televised program containing few, if any, aggressive stimuli (pp. 27–28).

Since their line of research yielded results of *increased* aggressive tendency following the viewing of filmed aggression, Berkowitz and Geen could hardly point to catharsis of aggression as an explanation. Instead, they had to indicate sources of such increased aggression. In their introductory comments they point to three kinds of effects of filmed aggression that may be involved: (1) modeling effects, (2) disinhibitory effects, and (3) eliciting effects.

Bandura and Walters (1963) have emphasized both modeling and disinhibitory effects of observing another person on film. If this film model shows aggressive behavior, the viewer may also learn such aggressive behavior by watching him (modeling effects). The viewing of violent behavior may also serve to reduce the inhibitions the viewer has against expressing such behavior (disinhibitory effects), especially if the viewed violence is presented as justified.

While Berkowitz and Geen agree that such modeling and disin-' hibitory effects are important, the current study focuses on the third group of possible effects, eliciting effects. They believe that filmed

[1] Albert Bandura, "Vicarious Processes: A Case of No-trial Learning," in L. Berkowitz (ed.), *Advances in Experimental Social Psychology*, II. New York: Academic Press, 1965. Quotations from this source are reprinted by permission of the author and the publisher.

aggression may increase the probability of attacks upon some objects but not upon others, depending on the kind of associations produced by the film. There are, therefore, several variables that might be used to predict the amount of aggression following observed aggression: (1) the strength of the observer's habits of aggression; (2) the degree of association between the observed event and situations in which the observer has learned to act aggressively; (3) the degree of association between the situation in which aggression is seen and the postobservation situation; and (4) the intensity of guilt and aggression anxiety, along with aggressive tendencies, aroused by the observed violence.

Such possibilities lead Berkowitz and Geen[2] to surmise that

> the aggressiveness habits activated by witnessed hostility are often only in "low gear," so to speak. Other appropriate, aggression-evoking cues must be present before the observed violence can lead to strong aggressive responses by the observer. . . . Thus, a person who sees a brutal fight may not himself display any detectable aggression immediately afterwards, even if his inhibitions are relatively weak, unless he encounters stimuli having some association with the fight (p. 526).

So we expect that sometimes a film sequence will elicit an aggressive response while at other times it will not, depending in part on whether the film elicits the cues that may be associated with likely targets of aggression.

Let us now turn to the methods used in this particular study. Eighty-eight male undergraduates at the University of Wisconsin served as experimental subjects. They were divided randomly into eight treatment groups with eleven subjects per group. Let us follow the experimenters' description of the procedures:

> When each subject arrived at the laboratory he was met by a peer (actually the experimenter's accomplice) and the experimenter. The first experimental treatment was carried out by asking the two men what their names were. For half of the cases the accomplice identified himself as Kirk Anderson while for the remaining men he said his name was Bob Anderson.
>
> Following this, the experimenter said the experiment involved the administration of a mild electric shock and gave the subject an opportunity to withdraw from the study if he so desired. He then showed the men two rooms, one containing various sorts of apparatus which, he said, were instruments for giving and receiving electric shocks, and the second containing a motion picture projector and screen. In this latter room the experimenter described the experiment as dealing with problem-solving ability under stress. One person, and the experimenter indicated that the subject was to take this role, would have to work on a problem knowing the other person (the accomplice) would judge the quality of his solution. The accomplice would evaluate the subject's performance by giving the subject from 1 to 10 electric

---

[2] Leonard Berkowitz and Russell G. Geen, "Film Violence and the Cue Properties of Available Targets," *Journal of Personality and Social Psychology*, 3 (1966), 525–530. Copyright 1966 by the American Psychological Association. Quotations from this source are reprinted with permission of the publisher.

shocks; the poorer the solution the greater the number of shocks that the subject was to receive.

The accomplice then left to go into the room containing the electrical apparatus, and the subject was given his problem: to suggest how an automotive service station could attract new customers. Five minutes later the experimenter returned, picked up the subject's written solution, and strapped the shock electrode onto the subject's arm. He then left the room again, ostensibly to bring the subject's work to the other person for judging. One minute later the accomplice in the adjoining room administered either one shock (nonangered condition) or seven shocks (angered condition) to the subject. After waiting 30 seconds, the experimenter returned to the subject, asked him how many shocks he had received, and then administered a brief questionnaire on which the subject rated his mood on four separate scales.

While the subject was responding to this form, the experimenter recalled the accomplice. Then as soon as the subject had finished, the experimenter said he would show the two men a brief film in order to study the effects of a diversion upon problem-solving effectiveness. Half of the subjects (*aggressive movie* condition) saw the fight scene from the movie *Champion*. The experimenter introduced this 7-minute film clip by giving them the "justified aggression" synopsis. According to earlier findings, this context seems to lower inhibitions against aggression. Further, in the *aggressive movie-Kirk* condition the experimenter casually but pointedly remarked that the first name of the movie protagonist was the same as that of the other person, that is, the accomplice. This was done to make sure that there was a name-mediated connection between the experimenter's confederate and the witnessed violence when the accomplice was said to be "Kirk Anderson." The other half of the subjects were shown an equally long and exciting movie of a track race between the first two men to run the mile in less than 4 minutes.

Upon conclusion of the 7-minute film clip, the experimenter again sent the accomplice from the room with instructions to write his solution to the sale-promotion problem. The subject was informed that he would be given the other person's solution and then was to evaluate it by shocking the other person from 1 to 10 times. Five minutes later the experimenter brought the subject a written problem solution saying this was the other person's work but which was actually previously constructed to be standard for all conditions. He told the subject to shock the other person as many times as he thought appropriate. The experimenter then went to the control room to record the number and duration of the shocks supposedly being given to the accomplice. After waiting 30 seconds, the experimenter returned to the experimental room and gave the subject the final questionnaire on which the subject indicated how much he liked the accomplice. When this form was completed the experimenter explained the deceptions that had been practiced upon the subject and asked him not to discuss the experiment with anyone else for the remainder of the semester (pp. 526–527).

In summary, three differences were introduced: (1) In half the treatments the accomplice was introduced as Kirk and in half as

Bob. (2) In half the treatments this accomplice angered the subject by giving him seven shocks, and in the other half the subject was presumably not angered in receiving the minimum single shock. (3) In half the treatments an aggressive fight scene was witnessed, and in the other half a nonaggressive track race was shown. The business problem-solving exercise had nothing to do with the design of the experiment other than to give an apparent rationale for the procedures.

A subject's aggression (the dependent variable) is measured by the number of shocks that he gives the accomplice. The expectation is that this will be higher if the subject has been angered by the accomplice than if not. It is also expected that the aggressive fight film will have a greater tendency to arouse aggression than the neutral track film, at least when the accomplice is introduced as Kirk.

Laboratory Experimentation

METHODOLOGICAL POINTER

The purpose of laboratory experimentation is to create carefully controlled conditions for whatever is being studied. The key element here is the control of other variables so that the particular variables under scrutiny can be more carefully studied. In real-life situations such control is usually not possible, but in specially created experimental settings it may be.

In the typical laboratory experiment all variables are controlled except one, the dependent variable. The dependent variable is then measured, and differences in it are traced back to other variables, usually to controlled independent variables. (Note that the term *independent variable* refers to independence from the influence of the dependent variable, not to independence from experimental manipulation.)

Control of variables is accomplished in two main ways: explicit control and randomization. Some independent variables are usually explicitly manipulated. This makes it possible to trace their effects upon the dependent variable. Other variables, especially those not the primary focus of study, are assumed to be controlled by a random assignment of experimental subjects to one treatment or another. A relatively large number of subjects in an experiment enhances the likelihood that such other variables are in fact randomly controlled.

In the experiment by Berkowitz and Geen the tendency to give shocks is the dependent variable, controlled only to make it an effective measure of aggression. Three independent variables are deliberately controlled: the presence or absence of a basis of anger, the presence or absence of aggressive visual material, and the presence or absence of a verbal cue incidentally associating such aggression with the person who could be shocked. All of these are further controlled through an experimental design that allows us to examine any one of these three variables as affected by, or not affected by, the other two. Other variables that might affect a person's readiness to shock the accomplice are assumed to be randomized through chance assignment of subjects to different treatments.

Before we examine the main findings of this experiment, let us pause to consider a side question. How can we be sure that the experimental controls actually had the intended effects? The question of validity is always a sensitive issue in experimental work, considering the artificially created settings that experimentation involves. In the present experiment, two of the manipulations (using the name Kirk or Bob; and showing the fight or track film) are fairly specific and direct manipulations. But the manipulation attempting to create degrees of anger is more questionable. Is there any evidence that the presumably angered subjects (those receiving seven shocks from the accomplice) actually were more angry than those who were not supposed to be angered (receiving only the minimum single shock)? Fortunately, the investigators do have some evidence on this. It may be recalled that immediately after receiving the shock or shocks (and before viewing the film), each subject was given a questionnaire to rate his mood. Included in this questionnaire was a rating of felt anger. Table 7 gives the results of his rating, with higher scores representing lower levels of anger.

TABLE 7   MEAN RATING OF ABSENCE OF ANGER

Accomplice's Name	Aggressive Film		Track Film	
	Angered	Nonangered	Angered	Nonangered
Kirk	7.36_a	11.27_b	7.27_a	10.55_b
Bob	6.00_a	12.09_b	7.27_a	11.27_b

NOTE: The lower the score the greater the felt anger. Numbers having a subscript in common are not significantly different.
SOURCE: Berkowitz and Geen (1966), p. 528.

Table 7 includes eight treatment groups because there are eight ways that the three independent variables can be combined (with each independent variable split two ways, $2 \times 2 \times 2 = 8$). But the only variable that should make a difference here is the presence or absence of anger arousal. Thus we expect higher numbers (less anger arousal) in the second and fourth columns than in the first and third columns. Furthermore, assuming a random distribution of various treatments of subjects with different potentials for anger arousal, we do not expect any other comparisons to show a significant difference. And this, indeed, is what Table 7 shows. All groups of subjects receiving the angered treatment have greater indications of anger than any group receiving the nonangered treatment, and this is the only treatment difference showing a statistically significant difference in anger. We may, therefore, feel reassured that the anger treatment was successfully achieved in this experiment.

METHODOLOGICAL POINTER

Statistical Significance

Statistical significance refers to evidence that a given difference in research results may not simply be a result of a random distribution. In other words, the results may not be attributed to chance.

Statistical significance is measured in terms of probability, for in an infinite universe of trials *any* possible distribution would *some-*

time be obtained by chance. For example, if you toss ten coins you should expect about five heads and five tails. However, it is possible that you could get ten heads—extremely unlikely, but nevertheless involving a degree of probability that can be specified with precision. This probability is so small that we should be very suspicious of the coins used by anyone who consistently obtains heads.

A common standard of statistical significance in the social and behavioral sciences is the .05 level (or 5 percent level). This means that the probability is accepted that a difference might be a chance result up to five times out of a hundred.

A more rigorous standard for statistical significance is the .01 level, which would mean that the result could occur as a chance distribution less than one time out of a hundred. Frequently an investigator does not formally adopt a particular standard for statistical significance (realizing the arbitrary nature of such dividing lines) but simply reports the separate probability levels at which his various findings might be statistically significant.

Although we need not here consider the particular statistical procedures used by Berkowitz and Geen, we may note that the standard of statistical significance used was that of the .05 level.

But what about the main question this experiment was designed to answer: Under what conditions are subjects most likely to show aggression? An obvious expectation is that angered subjects will show more aggression (that is, send more shocks) than nonangered subjects. A second expectation, based on findings of previous research, is that the fight film treatments might be followed with greater aggression than the track film. This assumes that the fight film would serve somewhat more to arouse aggressive impulses than it would to provide a vicarious catharsis of aggression. But what of the third variable, the first name presented for the accomplice who became the potential target for aggression? What difference could it make whether the name were Kirk or Bob? Perhaps not much, but there is at least this possibility: the name Kirk is the same as that of an actor being beaten in the fight scene, Kirk Douglas. Presumably this link might facilitate a more aggressive response when present than when such a link does not occur.

Let us study the results shown in Table 8. First of all, we note the consistent pattern dividing the angered and nonangered groups. All the angered treatment groups administered more shocks than did any of the nonangered groups. This is clearly according to expectations.

TABLE 8   MEAN NUMBER OF SHOCKS GIVEN TO ACCOMPLICE

Accomplice's Name	**Aggressive Film**		**Track Film**	
	Angered	*Nonangered*	*Angered*	*Nonangered*
Kirk	6.09$_a$	1.73$_c$	4.18$_b$	1.54$_c$
Bob	4.55$_b$	1.45$_c$	4.00$_b$	1.64$_c$

NOTE: Numbers having a subscript in common are not significantly different.
SOURCE: Berkowitz and Geen (1966), p. 528.

Next we observe whether or not the two films produced a difference in subsequent aggression. Here the answer is not completely clear. Three of the four comparisons between the fight film and corresponding track film treatment groups show a greater frequency of shocks following the fight film, but in only one of these comparisons is the difference of statistical significance. This occurs only when the subject is angered and the accomplice is named Kirk (6.09 vs. 4.18 mean number of shocks). Also it may be seen that the only condition in which the name Kirk brings forth significantly more shocks than the name Bob occurs when the subject has been angered *and* has also watched the fight film.

The implication of these findings is that the effect of viewing aggression upon a viewer's own tendency to show aggression depends on other factors. It may partly depend on whether a predisposition to be sensitive to the aggressive content (either through a temporary arousal of anger or through a more permanent feature of personality) is brought to the viewing. But it also depends on whether the aggression viewed has any association with potential targets of aggression. Even a little thing like a name might make a significant difference.

But perhaps there is something about the name Kirk that in itself is responsible. Or maybe subjects didn't like Kirk Douglas, and the association with the name Kirk Anderson and the fight film simply facilitated expression for an already present hostility. Berkowitz and Geen considered these possibilities. To check on the possibility that negative attitudes toward the name Kirk were themselves responsible, they asked a comparable sample of subjects to rate "liking" or "disliking" of a number of first names. No particularly strong feelings toward the name Kirk were noted. Another check showed that the name Kirk was, in fact, often associated with Kirk Douglas, but that attitudes toward Kirk Douglas were neither particularly positive nor negative when viewed in relation to other public figures.

What we have left then is the idea of the importance of cues that help select particular targets for aggression. "Observed aggression," Berkowitz and Geen conclude, "does not necessarily lead to open aggression against anyone. Particular targets are most likely to be attacked, and these are objects having appropriate, aggression-eliciting cue properties" (p. 529). Sometimes these "aggression-eliciting cue properties" reside in the general culture, suggesting that certain kinds of persons or certain kinds of occasions are more appropriate than others for aggressive behavior. At other times these eliciting cues may stem from personal associations, and at still other times they may arise from quite incidental features of the situation.

OBEDIENT AGGRESSION

Attention to situational cues that may elicit aggression may lead to considering the impact of a total setting, as well as the impact of a specific cue, for eliciting aggressive behavior. For considering this broader picture we may take note of a recent series of experiments by Stanley Milgram.

An especially interesting thing about this research is the experimental technique. Milgram (1965)[3] has summarized it as follows:

> Two persons arrive at a campus laboratory to take part in a study of memory and learning. (One of them is a confederate of the experimenter.) Each subject is paid $4.50 upon arrival, and is told that payment is not affected in any way by performance. The experimenter provides an introductory talk on memory and learning processes and then informs the subjects that in the experiment one of them will serve as teacher and the other as learner. A rigged drawing is held so that the naïve subject is always assigned the role of teacher and the accomplice becomes the learner. The learner is taken to an adjacent room and is strapped into an electric chair.
>
> The naïve subject is told that it is his task to teach the learner a list of paired associates, to test him on the list, and to administer punishment whenever the learner errs in the test. Punishment takes the form of electric shock, delivered to the learner by means of a shock generator controlled by the naïve subject. The teacher is instructed to increase the intensity of the electric shock one step on the generator for each error. The generator contains 30 voltage levels ranging from 15 to 450 volts, and verbal designations ranging from "Slight Shock" to "Danger: Severe Shock." The learner, according to plan, provides many wrong answers, so that before long the naïve subject must give him the strongest shock on the generator. Increases in shock level are met by increasingly insistent demands from the learner that the experiment be stopped because of growing discomfort to him. However, the experimenter instructs the teacher to continue with the procedure in disregard of the learner's protests.
>
> A quantitative value is assigned to the subject's performance based on the maximum intensity shock he administered before breaking off (p. 128).

What this is supposed to measure is the length to which persons go in their obedience. We might add that obedience is obedience in aggression, for somebody is apparently getting hurt by the shocks being sent.

A few further features of the experimental procedure are described elsewhere by Milgram (1963):[4]

> In all conditions the learner gives a predetermined set of responses to the word pair test, based on a schedule of approximately three wrong answers to one correct answer. In the present experimental condition no vocal response or other sign of protest

[3] Stanley Milgram, "Liberating Effects of Group Pressure," *Journal of Personality and Social Psychology*, 1 (1965), 127–134. Copyright 1965 by the American Psychological Association. Quotations from this source are reprinted with permission of the publisher.
[4] Stanley Milgram, "Behavioral Study of Obedience," *Journal of Abnormal and Social Psychology*, 67 (1963), 371–378. Copyright 1963 by the American Psychological Association. Quotations from this source are reprinted with permission of the publisher.

is heard from the learner until Shock Level 300 is reached. When
the 300-volt shock is administered, the learner pounds on the wall
of the room in which he is bound to the electric chair. The pounding can be heard by the subject (p. 374).

If the subject turns to the experimenter for advice at this point,
he is told to treat this as a wrong answer. Subjects are told to allow
five to ten seconds for an answer, and, if none is forthcoming, they are
to punish no answer the same as a wrong answer. The learner pounds
again on the wall after the next shock. After this point there is only
silence from the learner. No more answers, no more pounding, only
silence.

When the teacher indicates an unwillingness to continue the experiment, he is told to "please continue." If he continues to object, he is
told that "the experiment requires that you continue." Further protest
is countered with the statement, "It is absolutely essential that you
continue." If protest continues after this, the reply is, "You have no
other choice, you *must* go on." Only when all four of these "prods" have
been used without effect at a given shock level is the subject allowed to
stop. The experiment is then terminated, and the last shock level
administered indicates the degree of obedience.

One of the interesting questions that arises is that of just how far
subjects will go in their obedience. Would anyone go beyond the
"Intense Shock" level of 300 volts at which time the learner stops
answering and begins pounding on the wall? Could anyone possibly go
all the way to the "XXX" level of 450 volts? Or would most subjects
refuse to give anything more than the lowest level of shock?

Before we find the answers to these questions, let us note some
further comments from Milgram (1963):

> . . . it is instructive to consider how persons predict others will
> perform when commanded to administer powerful shock to an-
> other person. Fourteen Yale seniors, all psychology majors, were
> provided with a detailed description of the experimental situa-
> tion. They were asked to reflect carefully on it, and to predict the
> behavior of 100 hypothetical subjects. More specifically, they were
> instructed to plot the distribution of obedience of "100 Americans
> of diverse occupations, and ranging in age from 20 to 50 years,"
> who were placed in the experimental situation.
>
> There was considerable agreement among the respondents on
> the expected behavior of hypothetical subjects. All respondents
> predicted that only an insignificant minority would go through to
> the end of the shock series. On the average, students believed
> that only about one per cent of subjects would continue through
> to the end. Milgram also asked some of his colleagues to make
> predictions, and they generally agreed that few if any subjects
> would go beyond the "very strong shock" level (p. 375).

What happened when the experiment was actually conducted?
Although there were several variations to test the effects of different
conditions upon the strength of obedience, we may limit our present
attention to the base-line condition used as a basis for comparing with
other variations. This experiment involved forty subjects, all adult

males from the New Haven area obtained through a newspaper advertisement or direct-mail solicitation. Occupations represented included postal clerks, salesmen, engineers, and laborers. Some had advanced postgraduate degrees, and others had not finished elementary school. All subjects were led to believe that the research at Yale that they would take part in was a study of memory and learning.

In the results of this experiment, all forty subjects administered shocks beyond the "Slight Shock" level. Most of them also proceeded beyond the level of "Intense Shock." In fact, most of the subjects continued through the "Extreme Intensity Shock" and "Danger: Severe Shock" designations all the way to the maximum designation of "XXX" at 450 volts. Twenty-six of the forty subjects went all the way.

Did the subjects have no hesitation or anxiety about this? Hesitation was usual and so was anxiety, but most remained obedient to the end. Observers watching through a one-way mirror could scarcely believe their eyes. One observer reported (Milgram, 1963):

> I observed a mature and initially poised businessman enter the laboratory smiling and confident. Within 20 minutes he was reduced to a twitching, stuttering wreck, who was rapidly approaching a point of nervous collapse. He constantly pulled on his earlobe, and twisted his hands. At one point he pushed his fist into his forehead and muttered: "Oh God, let's stop it." And yet he continued to respond to every word of the experimenter, and obeyed to the end (p. 377).

A basic question this experiment raises for us concerns why most of the subjects did not stop very early in the sequence. Why did they continue to administer such apparently near-fatal shocks? Milgram suggests some answers:

1. The experiment is sponsored by and takes place on the grounds of an institution of unimpeachable reputation, Yale University. It may be reasonably presumed that the personnel are competent and reputable. . . .
2. The experiment is, on the face of it, designed to attain a worthy purpose—advancement of knowledge about learning and memory. Obedience occurs not as an end in itself, but as an instrumental element in a situation that the subject construes as significant, and meaningful. He may not be able to see its full significance, but he may properly assume that the experimenter does.
3. The subject perceives that the victim has voluntarily submitted to the authority system of the experimenter. He is not (at first) an unwilling captive impressed for involuntary service. . . .
4. The subject, too, has entered the experiment voluntarily, and perceives himself under obligation to aid the experimenter. He has made a commitment, and to disrupt the experiment is a repudiation of this initial promise of aid (p. 377).

These and other possible factors are pointed out by Milgram, who indicates that such points "need not remain matters of speculation, but can be reduced to testable propositions to be confirmed or disproved by further experiments" (p. 378). The nature of the experimental technique makes it relatively simple to alter some of these conditions and observe the effects. Some such further experiments have already been done by Milgram.

But what does this kind of study have to do with aggression? In what sense is such obedience aggression? It is true that the subject does not send the shock on his own initiative. It is also true that he probably does not want the learner to be hurt. Still it is no accident that the current is sent, and it is the subject's hand that operates the switch. To this extent it is an intended act of hurting. True, hurting is not the main purpose of the subject's behavior. It is only a by-product of his desire to do the right thing as an experimental subject. Yet when he is given this disagreeable duty, the subject does pull the switch.

If we measure aggression in terms of actual damage done or suffering caused, far more aggression has been shown by good and reasonable men than by disturbed or chronically aggressive personalities. Most of the destruction in the world has been done by men who were simply doing their job. They do not want to hurt or kill, but in the situation in which they find themselves it seems to be the expected thing to do.

EXERCISE

Write down a basic description of procedures in Milgram's study, including the apparent voltage levels. Present this to different individuals and ask them to plot the expected distribution of obedience of one hundred Americans of diverse occupations, ranging in age from twenty to fifty.

If you have time, get different groups of individuals to respond. This will allow you to compare the expectations of males and females, younger persons and older persons, social science majors and physical science majors, or whatever.

How far do the expectations of the individuals you study depart from the results obtained by Milgram?

8
Aggression: Review and Discussion

We have examined five studies, all of which have something to do with aggression. With the case of Julia we speculated concerning the effects of early influences upon an aggressive young girl. In the two studies by Sears and associates we attempted to trace the effects of child-rearing practices upon aggressive tendencies in a somewhat larger collection of children. In the experiment by Berkowitz and Geen we noticed how particular properties of the situation may affect the degree of aggression displayed. And in Milgram's study we observed to what lengths persons will obediently aggress when they are given strong social support.

While aggression is the common theme, the way it has been studied has been quite different in these various studies. Three main methods of study have been used: (1) the case study, (2) the questionnaire study, and (3) the laboratory experiment. The case study, used by Davis and Dollard for the study of Julia, is especially useful for an examination in depth to suggest how a complex set of influences work together in a concrete case. The questionnaire study, illustrated by the work of Sears, is useful when one has more limited questions for investigation and wants the evidence of many cases to make conclusions more reliable. A laboratory experiment, such as the one conducted by Berkowitz and Geen, or the one done by Milgram, becomes useful when the question posed is very precisely limited and controls that will clarify the answer are possible. These three methods of investigation, therefore, present something of a continuum from the most general and open method of study (the case study) to the most specific and closed approach (laboratory experimentation). Knowledge in social psychology grows from all three of these approaches, though experimentation has become the most dominant approach in the research literature of recent years.

In this variety of studies the insights we have gained about aggression have also been various. Is it possible to put these insights together into a single framework? This will be the purpose of this review and discussion chapter.

In developing a common framework for our insights on aggression, several distinctions are useful. One important distinction is between *habitual aggression* (where aggression, the intentional hurting of others, becomes a way of life) and *occasional aggression* (where aggression is evidenced only in particular kinds of situations).

HABITUAL AGGRESSION

We start with the common observation that some people are meaner than others. No doubt our tendency to categorize people into good guys and bad guys (or, more euphemistically, into well-socialized versus highly aggressive or disturbed personalities) is overdone. Still, we know there are important differences in the readiness of persons to hurt others. How can we explain such differences of strength in the readiness to aggress? How do we explain the development of a strongly aggressive personality?

Our first impulse might be to say that some people are just naturally that way. Does this mean that we are speaking of something inherited? It is quite possible that there may be genetic linkages to character traits like aggression. But whatever the genetic contributions, such elements must emerge through behavioral development, and in this behavioral development learning must play a predominant role. How, then, does a person learn to become aggressive?

One way of becoming aggressive is suggested by the frustration-aggression hypothesis. A person who frequently feels deprived may develop a strong tendency to strike out as a way of responding to the world. The case of Julia would seem to fit with this idea. But there is also a more subtle kind of development suggested by the frustration-aggression hypothesis. The inhibition of aggression when frustration occurs may actually add to the frustration and eventual capacity for aggression. This may not seem to apply to Julia, whose inhibition of aggression was not great (at least in childhood), but it might help to understand certain cases where a mild exterior masks an explosive capacity for destruction.

In either case (direct frustration-aggression linkages or delayed and displaced aggression following inhibition of original aggressive tendencies), aggressive potential is assumed to reflect the amount of frustration. Incidentally, it should be kept in mind that frustration is not the same as objective deprivation. Frustration is the *feeling* of being deprived or prevented from attaining a goal, and it is the intensity of this rather than the amount of objective deprivation that builds the potential for aggression.

But a highly aggressive personality can also be developed out of a background relatively free from severe frustration. There are other roots of character besides frustration or its absence. One of the most important of these is identification with a model. Examples presented by others are extremely important to the young child, and the example presented by a parent is extraordinarily so. A child may become aggression-prone because his significant childhood models represented highly aggressive behavior. In identifying with such persons the child also copies ways of behaving and ways of thinking, including tendencies toward aggression.

Nearly all of Julia's potential models showed a high capacity for aggression, so should it be surprising to find her copying such a pattern? The relationship between parental punishment and the child's aggressive tendency, which Sears and associates found for kindergarten-aged children, can also be interpreted in this light. Punitive parents tend to provide a model for their children's aggressive behavior.

Still another way of learning to be aggressive is provided by being rewarded or reinforced for aggression. People who attain rewards for their aggressions become more prone toward further aggression.

An especially important base for such reinforcement of aggression is to be found in early childhood. Sometimes aggression may actually bring approval (for boys more often than for girls). But even if approval is not given, aggression may bring desired attention or help to achieve other goals and thus be nourished by such reinforcement. This is why the permissiveness of parents toward aggressive behavior may be an important element in fostering aggressive tendencies in children.

Even if early childhood has not provided much reinforcement for aggressive behavior, such reinforcement may be developed in later social adjustment. This is apt to be the case if one becomes a part of a group that places a high value on aggressive behavior. Even though his parents may not approve, a boy may develop strong habits of aggression through association with a tough gang of boys, and the reinforcement he receives from them may be more than enough to develop an aggressive pattern of behavior.

We see then that there are several different paths toward developing an aggressive character. They include (1) developing in response to repeatedly severe frustration, (2) identifying with aggressive models, (3) receiving reinforcement for aggression in early childhood, and (4) adjustment to groups that provide rewards for aggression. In some cases, such as that of Julia (at least into adolescence), all four of these seem to be present. But any one of them by itself might also produce a strong tendency toward aggression.

There are various ways in which a similar pattern of personality may be developed, and this is true of habitual aggression as well as of other characteristics. Aggressive personalities are not made in only one way.

OCCASIONAL AGGRESSION

Nobody is always aggressive, and even a mild man shows aggression occasionally. So we haven't explained nearly the whole story by pointing to habitual aggression. The question remains: When is aggression displayed and when is it not? What occasions are the most likely to elicit aggression, whether we're talking of a person with a high tendency or a low tendency to act aggressively?

To deal with this question, let us make one further distinction, between *angry aggression* and *strategic aggression*.

Anger is the emotional arousal that tends to occur whenever we experience frustration. The more intense the frustration, the greater the anger. Also, the more we perceive the source of frustration to be arbitrary, unwarranted, or unjust, the stronger is the feeling of anger. In brief, we may say that those situations most likely to arouse anger are also likely to bring forth aggression.

But anger need not always bring aggression. We all learn to "count to ten" and other ways of inhibiting aggression when angry. Such inhibition is usually effective, for in most kinds of social situations others will not further disturb a person who shows anger. Only when the frustration is both unwarranted and severe, and when the agent of frustration is both present and personal, is it probable that anger will lead to attack. And even then, for most human adults, the attack is much more often verbal than physical.

In order for anger to produce aggression, we need an appropriate target for aggression as well as strong feelings. It may be true that when a man is angry enough he will attack quite incidental targets, but it is still true that certain targets draw aggression better than do others. Two primary bases of the suitability of a target for aggression are (1) its degree of association with the causes of frustration (a person who directly and willfully causes frustration is more likely to receive aggression than a person who is only indirectly responsible), and (2) associations we carry with us concerning suitable targets of aggression. Some of these latter associations are cultural, such as notions about the kinds of people who are most often subject to verbal abuse. Other associations may be quite incidentally produced, like the association between the name Kirk and the fighter being beaten in the film that accentuated aggression (in the experiment by Berkowitz and Geen).

But not all aggression is done in anger. Much intentional destruction is done by men who are neither aggressive personalities nor particularly angry. We need also to consider what, for want of a better term, we call *strategic aggression*. By strategic aggression we refer to instances in which the hurting of others is not itself sought but in which others are still deliberately hurt in the process of trying to achieve certain other goals. Thus character assassination of a rival politician may not be considered desirable, but it may be considered at times a necessary part of gaining political office. Or killing people may not be considered good by a bombing crew, but they consider this as a likely achievement of a successful mission. Such hurting or destruction of others often receives full social approval. In just doing their job well certain people must sometimes hurt and destroy, and such aggression (though never called that except by enemies) also wins positive approval from associates.

The clearest example of strategic aggression in the studies we have examined is in Milgram's experiment. Subjects in this study of obedience believed they were sending extremely severe electric shocks, and yet they continued, and continued, and continued. They did not want to hurt the person strapped in the electric chair. He had done nothing to hurt or frustrate them. Nor were the subjects persons with strong character-rooted predispositions toward giving electric shocks to innocent victims. But they were motivated to take part in an experiment; they did want to do the right thing. And the right thing—the experimenter kept assuring them—was to send severe electric shocks to the poor learner.

Aggressive behavior, then, may be a result of any or all of several different influences: (1) of a person with strong aggressive predispositions (for whatever reason), (2) of a condition that arouses anger, and (3) of a social situation in which the hurting of others becomes a means to socially approved ends. In the preceding discussion these have been termed, respectively, habitual aggression, angry aggression, and strategic aggression. A combination of these of course sets the stage for the most destructive actions—especially when strategic aggression may be supported by habitual or angry aggression.

THEORIES OF BEHAVIOR

In the process of examining studies of aggression, we have also acquainted ourselves more generally with theories of behavior. We have, first of all, noted Freud's theories of early development and tried to see how these might be involved in Julia's case. We also noted his view of the instinctive roots of human aggression. But at the same time we pointed out the limitations of such theories. Neither in the case of Julia nor in the Massachusetts children studied by Sears did early experience give a very good basis for predicting later personality patterns.

Such limitations of a theory rooted in instinct and early experience must make us sensitive to the learning process. We are shaped by a learning process that includes much more than infancy. Something like a *learned-drive* model may therefore be a useful theory to supplement psychoanalytic views of early experience. In the case of aggressive tendencies, Dollard and associates (1939) suggest how this may apply. Frustration, combined with the inhibition of aggression, sets up an aggressive drive. This in turn provides a potentiality for later aggression. Other kinds of learned drives are possible to explain predispositions toward other kinds of behavior.

But even theories of learned predispositions have serious limitations. For particular kinds of behavior are not shown on just any occasion. They tend to be shown in particular ways in particular situations. A theory of behavior that neglects such situational factors, therefore, can never be more than just part of the truth. In the case of aggression, we noted in experimental studies just how much particular features of a situation may affect tendencies to show aggression.

Theories of human behavior are only partial. They explain behavior with reference to certain kinds of considerations. Usually these considerations are focused either in the person or in the situation. But behavior is always a product of both the person and the situation he is in (and always in a way that shows dynamic effects for both person and situation—never simply a summing up of static qualities of person and situation). It is hard to fashion a single theory to encompass all this; so we must be prepared to beware of the limitations of most theories of behavior.

Perhaps another way to express this idea about theories of behavior is to suggest that we may need to use a variety of theories to understand the complex field that is human behavior. At the same time, it is important to be alert for those theories that may provide the greatest opportunities for unifying our knowledge. But we must expect all theories to fall short of explaining *all* of the things in which we might be interested.

METHODOLOGICAL POINTER

Seven Methodological Questions

"How do we know it?" is the key question in any scientific field. It may be broken down into several further questions, each of which has received some attention already.

1. How do we know that what we are studying represents that which we want to study? This is the basic problem of *validity.*
2. How do we know that the data we gather actually represent the persons we want to study? This is the more specific problem of *sampling.*
3. How do we know that a similar result would be found in repeated studies (or in different attempts in the same study)? This is the problem of *reliability.*
4. How do we know that a given finding is not just a random result? This is the more specific problem of *statistical significance.*
5. How do we attempt to isolate particular causes and effects? This is usually done through *variable analysis.*
6. What statistical procedures may help us identify close relationships between different variables? This is often a matter of coefficients of *correlation.*
7. How well can we anticipate a particular result? This fundamental problem of *prediction* depends on all the above questions.

These seven questions (all of which are discussed specifically in Chapter 6) are applicable to any research in social psychology. Indeed, they all apply to any scientific investigation.

A final word of caution, however, should be made here. The questions framed above never occur in a theoretical vacuum. The question of validity, for example, depends on how the overall problem of an investigation is conceptualized. Sampling procedures depend on the kind of applications seen for theoretical variables, and the other methodological questions also have their theoretical considerations.

The basic purpose of methodological sophistication is not so much simply to do research, but rather that the research done will point toward more adequate theoretical results. Theory, in this sense, is not something seen apart from research, but something that is constantly developed and changed through research.

AGGRESSION AND AFFILIATION

At the end of Chapter 4 it was pointed out how closely affiliative and aggressive behavior may be tied together. Now the point should be better appreciated. In considering the concept of strategic aggression, we can see very clearly how much destructive behavior may be done for the sake of social ends. Rather than considering aggression as typically apart from social attachments, we must recognize that man is most fiercely aggressive when seeking to preserve or protect his basic ties to other people.

AGGRESSION AND SOCIAL INFLUENCE

One of the main reasons there is so much aggression—violent and verbal—in the world is because of the common faith in the power of such acts for influencing other people. We cannot well evaluate whether or not this faith is misplaced until we note more carefully just what is involved in social influence. This we will do in the next four chapters, which are built around the broad topic of social influence.

part three: SOCIAL INFLUENCE

A wise prince will seek means by which his subjects will always and in every possible condition of things have need of his government, and then they will always be faithful to him.

Niccolo Machiavelli

Social influence, the influence upon human beings by other human beings, is a very broad subject. It is probably too broad, in fact, for an introductory social psychology student to absorb quickly in its most general form. We start, therefore, with the study of leadership of informal groups. This allows us to begin with a relatively concrete level of analysis for Chapter 9 ("Informal Leadership").

In Chapter 10 ("Experiments in Conformity") we proceed to a somewhat more abstract level in reviewing some experimental work. Here we analyze some of the factors involved in group influence upon the individual.

That social influence may be much deeper and more enduring than simple effects upon thoughts or actions is the basic theme of Chapter 11 ("Influence and Identity"). In this chapter we concern ourselves with the influence of others upon how we define ourselves and how we interpret our inner feelings.

Chapter 12 will provide another review and discussion in which a general theory of social influence derived from the ideas discussed in the three previous chapters will be presented.

9
Informal Leadership

MOOCHIE

We begin our study of the subject of informal leadership with the case of Moochie. Moochie, a young marine captured by the Japanese early in World War II, was the subject of an essay in the *New Yorker* magazine (Nielsen, 1947),[1] and the excerpts that follow are from this account:

> He was reckless and fearless, and he had always been big—on Guam, before he was taken, he weighed two hundred and thirty-five pounds. He was friendly and cheerful by nature and he laughed easily. In prison camp, these common-place civilian virtues, which in ordinary life had brought him very little reward, became respected and admired. He made jokes at the expense of the guards and took his punishment without flinching. He devised a system by which the prisoners regularly looted the cargo they unloaded of quantities of sugar and fish. When the men fell sick, his laughter was their only medicine.

Moochie's leadership became fully confirmed after he led an uprising against the Japanese guards at their work site.

> For his leadership in this uprising Moochie was thrown into solitary confinement, and the other prisoners were locked in the compound. All of them expected to be killed. Moochie was compelled to stand at attention sixteen hours a day for nineteen days; then he was released and sent back to work. He had lost thirty pounds during his ordeal. His release was a genuine victory.

When the war was over, the former prisoners were on a train going to Yokohama, where they would embark for the United States. An eyewitness recounts:

> For several hours after we pulled out of Osaka, the men who had lived through so much with him kept lurching down the aisle to

[1] Waldemar A. Nielsen, "Moochie the Magnificent," *The New Yorker*, February 1, 1947, pp. 55–59. Copyright © 1947 The New Yorker Magazine, Inc. Reprinted with permission of Russell & Volkening, Inc.

his berth and paying awkward tribute to his leadership. Some of them sat on the edge of his berth beside him, others stood up in the aisle. There was a great quantity of Japanese beer aboard and almost unlimited amounts of American Army food. With their belt knives, the men opened bottles of beer and punched open cans of K-ration cheese and biscuits. They passed around open cans of tomatoes. Someone brought out a gasoline stove and set it in the middle of the aisle, and they made a large tin can of hot coffee.

As the men ate, they talked about the camp, and about happenings on the docks, and told jokes on one another. Moochie ruled over the group with easy, kingly grace. He was the magnetic center toward which the others pointed their conversation and in little ways they deferred to him and showed their regard. When, now and then, a man left to go to his berth, he generally gave Moochie a friendly punch on the arm or tousled his hair.

And then, along about one o'clock in the morning, Moochie's crown was lifted from him. Quietly and rather suddenly, it just disappeared. The conversation had slowed down from time to time before that, and the silent gaps between stories had begun to grow longer and longer. Finally everyone stopped talking. There was a long pause. A sailor who had been taken in the Philippines and who had spent a couple of years with Moochie in camp said, "Listen, goddam it, let's stop talking about it. From now on, I'm concentrating on getting home."

"Right!" someone added quickly. "I'm ready to knock it off. Let's change the subject to something pleasant, something natural."

Just that suddenly, the conversation turned a corner. The talk from then on concerned home, wives, and Stateside things, the camp world passed into memory and Moochie moved from the center to the periphery of the group. At first, neither he nor the others seemed to be aware of the change that had taken place. The next time I glanced across at him, Moochie was looking out of the train window at the dark, and the bull session was gradually breaking up. When I went to sleep, Moochie was still staring out of the window.

The next morning Moochie was talking with an English seaman by the name of Haines.

> "I don't know what the hell is wrong with me," Moochie told him, "but I just can't get very excited about getting to Yokohama."
>
> "Ah, you're just blue, boy, because the old gang's breaking up," Haines said.
>
> "No, it isn't that," Moochie said. "I don't know what it is." . . .
>
> "You've got to keep your spirits up. You fellows have a big day ahead of you."
>
> "Maybe my biggest days are in back of me," Moochie remarked.
>
> "That's surely no way for you to be talking, Mooch. They'll be looking to you to lead the way."
>
> "No, no more, Haines," Moochie said. "From here on in, I'm just a guy who used to work in a gas station." He looked down the aisle and smiled. "Well, it was fun while it lasted." Then he laughed and shook his head. "Can you imagine talking like that about the camp?" (pp. 55–59).

The Nature of Leadership

THEORETICAL POINTER

Leadership is social influence. More specifically, it is influence exerted in a group setting that is not based on compulsion. That is, it derives from persons following voluntarily rather than from the leader's control of formal sanctions of reward or punishment.

Leadership depends on the nature of the person who exerts influence, the needs of other persons involved, the situation in which they are together, and, above all, the particular combination of persons and situation. For example, Moochie's leadership was the product of a particular kind of personality together with a particular kind of situation. Moochie's physical stamina and cheerful extroversion were especially useful in the prison setting, but he had little to say in discussions about home. When the end of the war brought a marked change in the situation of the prisoners, then also was the basis for Moochie's leadership changed; and he "moved from the center to the periphery of the group."

It is somewhat misleading to speak of leadership *traits,* for the particular characteristic of a person that promotes his influence in one kind of situation may not in another—as the case of Moochie well illustrates. As a bare minimum, however, it has been suggested (Brown, 1936) that a leader must (1) have membership character (that is, he must be accepted by others as a part of the group) and (2) be outstanding in some abilities relevant to activities of the group. What is relevant depends on the nature of the group. Of course, some characteristics like intelligence, extroversion, and a resolute style of action are apt to provide a basis of influence in a great variety of social situations—but not in all situations.

GANGS IN CORNERVILLE

At the same time that Moochie was providing leadership for American prisoners in Japan, other young men were providing leadership for groups in a large Eastern city. William Foote Whyte studied these street corner gangs, and his book, *Street Corner Society* (1955), includes an analysis of their leadership.

Whyte made detailed studies of several gangs in "Cornerville," a slum area occupied by persons of Italian ancestry. During the period of his investigations he lived in Cornerville and participated personally in the activities of these gangs.

His entry was made through "Doc," the leader of one of these gangs, whom he had met in a local settlement house.

Tribulations of an Investigator

SIDELIGHT

William Foote Whyte (1943)[2] later recalled some of his problems in getting started with his research on Cornerville:

When I began my work, I had had no training in sociology or anthro-

---

[2] William Foote Whyte, *Street Corner Society.* Chicago: University of Chicago Press, 1943, 1955. Copyright 1943, 1955 by The University of Chicago. Quotations from this source are reprinted with permission of the publisher.

pology. I thought of myself as an economist and naturally looked first toward the matters that we had taken up in economics courses, such as economics of slum housing. At the time I was sitting in on a course in slums and housing in the Sociology Department at Harvard. As a term project I took on a study of one block in Cornerville. To legitimize this effort, I got in touch with a private agency that concerned itself in housing matters and offered to turn over to them the results of my survey. With that backing, I began knocking on doors, looking into flats, and talking to tenants about the living conditions. This brought me into contact with Cornerville people, but it would be hard now to devise a more inappropriate way of beginning a study such as I was eventually to make. I felt ill at ease at this intrusion, and I am sure so did the people. I wound up the block study as rapidly as I could and wrote it off as a total loss as far as gaining a real entry into the district.

Shortly thereafter I made another false start—if so tentative an effort may even be called a start. At the time I was completely baffled at the problem of finding my way into the district. Cornerville was right before me and yet so far away. I could walk freely up and down its streets, and I had even made my way into some of the flats, and yet I was still a stranger in a world completely unknown to me.

At this time I met a young economics instructor at Harvard who impressed me with his self-assurance and his knowledge of Eastern City. He had once been attached to a settlement house, and he talked glibly about his associations with the tough young men and women of the district. He also described how he would occasion-

ally drop in on some drinking place in the area and strike up an acquaintance with a girl, buy her a drink, and then encourage her to tell him her life-story. He claimed that the women so encountered were appreciative of this opportunity and that it involved no further obligation.

The approach seemed at least as plausible as anything I had been able to think of. I resolved to try it out. I picked on the Regal Hotel, which was on the edge of Cornerville. With some trepidation I climbed the stairs to the bar and entertainment area and looked around. There I encountered a situation for which my adviser had not prepared me. There were women present all right, but none of them was alone. Some were in couples, and there were two or three pairs of women together. I pondered this situation briefly. I had little or no confidence in my skill at picking up one female, and it seemed inadvisable to tackle two at the same time. Still, I was determined not to admit defeat without a struggle. I looked around me again and now noticed a threesome: one man and two women. It occurred to me that here was a maldistribution of females which I might be able to rectify. I approached the group and opened with something like this: "Pardon me. Would you mind if I joined you?" There was a moment of silence while the man stared at me. He then offered to throw me downstairs. I assured him that this would not be necessary and demonstrated as much by walking right out of there without any assistance.

I subsequently learned that hardly anyone from Cornerville ever went into the Regal Hotel. If my efforts there had been crowned with success, they would have no doubt led somewhere but certainly not to Cornerville.

For my next effort I sought out the local settlement houses. They were open to the public. You could walk right into them, and—though I would not have phrased it this way at that time—they were manned by middle-class people like myself. I realized even then that to study Cornerville I would have to go well beyond the settlement house, but perhaps the social workers could help me get started. . . .

As I look back on it now, the settlement house also seems a very unpromising place from which to begin such a study. . . . However that may be, the settlement house proved the right place for me at this time, for it was here that I met Doc (pp. 288–290).

Doc's gang was a group of young men who hung out along Norton Street. There were over a dozen fellows—Nutsy, Frank, Joe, Alec, Carl, Tommy, Angelo, Fred, Lou, Danny, Mike, Long John, and Doc—who were active in the group at one time or another. Most of the men were only occasionally employed, and therefore they had quite a bit of time to kill together.

As they met to joke and talk about sex and sports, play pool, or carry on other activities, this group had a characteristic pattern of influence. Although there was no formal structure of leadership, it could be observed that there were clear differences in influence.

> There were distinctions in rank among the Nortons. Doc, Danny, and Mike held the top positions. They were older than any others except Nutsy. They possessed a greater capacity for social movement. While the followers were restricted to the narrower sphere of one corner, Doc, Danny, and Mike had friends in many other groups and were well known and respected throughout a large part of Cornerville. It was one of their functions to accompany the follower when he had to move outside of his customary social sphere and needed such support. The leadership three were also respected for their intelligence and powers of self-expression. Doc in particular was noted for his skill in argument. On the infrequent occasions when he did become involved, he was usually able to outmaneuver his opponent without humiliating him. I never saw the leadership three exert their authority through physical force, but their past fighting reputations tended to support their positions.
>
> Doc was the leader of the gang. The Nortons had been Doc's gang when they had all been boys, and, although the membership had changed, they were still thought to be Doc's gang. The crap game and its social obligations prevented Danny and Mike from spending as much time with the Nortons as did Doc. They were not so intimate with the followers, and they expected him to lead (p. 12).

But how did Whyte determine that this was the leadership structure in the Norton Street gang? He admits that if members were asked if they had a leader or boss, they would reply, "No, we're all equal." Whyte (1941)[3] adds: "It is only through the observation of action that

[3] William Foote Whyte, "Corner Boys: A Study of Clique Behavior," *American Journal of Sociology*, 46 (1941), 647–664. Copyright 1941 by The University of Chicago. Quotations from this source are reprinted with permission of The University of Chicago Press.

the group structure becomes apparent. My problem was to apply methods which would produce an objective and reasonably exact picture of such structures" (p. 649).

METHODOLOGICAL
POINTER

Participant Observation

The primary approach of Whyte in his study of Cornerville may be called *participant observation.* His main source of information was firsthand observation, and his observation was made as a participant in the events he recorded. He became accepted into the activities of Doc's gang and the other groups that he studied. While participating, he also made detailed observations about what was going on around him.

The method of participant observation has both assets and liabilities. An advantage lies in the intimacy it makes possible. The investigator in this way gets a real feel for his subject matter; he is more likely to know what the behavior he is observing means to one of the participants. He is also likely to obtain a relatively complete and comprehensive picture of behavior by becoming a part of what he studies.

But there are problems as well as advantages in the method of participant observation. For one thing, it requires a rather limited focus of study; only a few groups or social settings can be thoroughly examined in this way. Also, there is sometimes a problem of objectivity. It is difficult to record the data in a form that could be verified by other observers, and the very involvement of the investigator with those he is studying may unduly bias his interpretation.

One of the methods Whyte used to record data was that of making maps of social structure. He describes how he did this in observations of another group setting, the Cornerville Social and Athletic Club:

> I sought to make a record of the groupings in which I found the members whenever I went into the club. While the men were moving around, I would be unable to retain their movements for my records, but on most occasions they would settle down in certain spatial arrangements. . . . As I looked around the room, I would count the number of men present so that I should know later how many I should have to account for. Then I would say over to myself the names of the men in each grouping and try to fix in my mind their positions in relation to one another. In the course of an evening there might be a general reshuffling of positions. I would not be able to remember every movement, but I would try to observe with which members the movements began; and, then, when another spatial arrangement had developed, I would go through the same mental process as I had with the first. As soon as I got home from the club, I would draw a map or maps of the spatial positions I had observed and add any movements between positions which I recalled (1941, pp. 649–651).

Such maps gave Whyte a fairly objective basis for identifying groupings within the informal organization.

But Whyte was interested in more than identifying groupings. He was also interested in the organization within groupings. For this he was especially interested in patterns of influence within the groups he studied. He was guided by some suggestions in the work of Chapple and Arensberg (1940), emphasizing a distinction between the origination of action and the termination of action. To originate an action is to make a proposal or suggestion, to open a sequence for interaction; to terminate an action is to follow the initiative of another in an interaction sequence.

In temporary groupings between two people Whyte typically found both persons originating and terminating action for each other. Such one-to-one relationships (*pair events*) therefore did not suggest clearcut patterns of influence. But when larger groupings were involved (*set events*, with one person initiating action for two or more others at the same time), patterns of influence could be clearly indicated. In such groupings certain individuals stood out as being the most likely to originate action, and others were most likely to terminate action. In this way, structure within the group could be identified by who was most likely to originate action for whom.

Pair Events and Set Events

THEORETICAL
POINTER

Many years ago the German philosopher and sociologist Georg Simmel, comparing the two-person group (*dyad*) with the larger groupings, observed some of the specific features of dyads. When a third party is added to a dyad, he pointed out, the group becomes something completely different. This kind of difference is not made if still additional members are added. Simmel (1950) uses the family as an example:

For instance, a marriage with one child has a character which is completely different from that of a childless marriage, but it is not significantly different from a marriage with two or more children. . . .
In an analogous way, in regard to marriage forms, the decisive difference is between monogamy and bigamy, whereas the third or twentieth wife is relatively unimportant for the marriage structure. The transition to a second wife is more consequential, at least in one sense, than is that to an even larger number (pp. 138–139).

One fundamental difference between human groupings of two members and those of more than two members, Simmel points out, is that dyads automatically disappear with the removal of any member; the existence of larger groupings is not so limited. The person in a dyad is also more vulnerable to direct influence, whereas in larger groupings the formation of coalitions and subgroups can always counter the social influence of a dominant member.

A similar recognition is present in Chapple and Arensberg's distinction between pair events and set events. Pair events tend to be characterized by mutual influence. In set events, even in informal groupings of three persons, a division of influence and an organization of action are typically noticeable. Such events thus take on a collective character absent from the more individualized pair events.

Through such an analysis of interaction even informal groups reveal a hierarchical structure. There tends to be a dominant group leader, several "lieutenants" who share in leadership but who are especially influenced by the leader, and other members with lesser degrees of influence upon group events.

The effects of such a leadership structure can be seen in the way activities of the group are carried out. Some of the consequences of the leadership structure in Doc's group are suggested by Whyte's discussion of a bowling contest.

> Doc had an idea that we should climax the season with an individual competition among the members of the clique. He persuaded the owner of the alleys to contribute ten dollars in prize money to be divided among the three highest scorers. . . .
>
> Interest in this contest ran high.' The probable performances of the various bowlers were widely discussed. Doc, Danny, and Long John each listed his predictions. They were unanimous in conceding the first five places to themselves, Mark Ciampa, and Chris Teludo, although they differed in predicting the order among the first five. The next two positions were generally conceded to Mike and to me. All the ratings gave Joe Dodge last position, and Alec, Frank, and Carl were ranked close to the bottom.
>
> The followers made no such lists, but Alec let it be known that he intended to show the boys something. Joe Dodge was annoyed to discover that he was the unanimous choice to finish last and argued that he was going to win.
>
> When Chris Teludo did not appear for the match, the field was narrowed to ten. After the first four boxes, Alec was leading by several pins. He turned to Doc and said, "I'm out to get you boys tonight." But then he began to miss, and, as mistake followed mistake, he stopped trying. Between turns, he went out for drinks, so that he was not interested in the competition. His collapse was sudden and complete; in the space of a few boxes he dropped from first place to last place. . . .
>
> There were only two upsets in the contest, according to the predictions made by Doc, Danny, and Long John: Mark bowled very poorly and I won. However, it is important to note that neither Mark nor I fitted neatly into either part of the clique. Mark associated with the boys only at the bowling alleys and had no recognized status in the group. Although I was on good terms with all the boys, I was closer to the leaders than to the followers, since Doc was my particular friend. If Mark and I are left out of consideration, the performances were almost exactly what the leaders expected and the followers feared they would be. Danny, Doc, Long John, and Mike were bunched together at the top. Joe Dodge did better than was expected of him, but even he could not break through the solid ranks of the leadership.
>
> Several days later Doc and Long John discussed the match with me.
>
> Long John: I only wanted to be sure that Alec or Joe Dodge didn't win. That wouldn't have been right.
>
> Doc: That's right. We didn't want to make it tough for you, because we all liked you, and the other fellows did too. If somebody had tried to make it tough for you, we would have protected you. . . . If Joe Dodge or Alec had been out in front, it would have been different. We would have talked them out of it. We would have made plenty of noise. We would have been really vicious. . .
> (1955, pp. 20–21).

WHYTE'S CONCLUSIONS

Based on such observations as those of Doc's gang, Whyte draws a few conclusions about the nature of leadership in such informal groups. We shall quote at length from his discussion:

> The stable composition of the group and the lack of social assurance on the part of its members contribute toward producing a very high rate of social interaction within the group. The group structure is a product of these interactions.
>
> Out of such interaction there arises a system of mutual obligations which is fundamental to group cohesion. If the men are to carry out their activities as a unit, there are many occasions when they must do favors for one another. The code of the corner boy requires him to help his friends when he can and to refrain from doing anything to harm them. When life in the group runs smoothly, the obligations binding members to one another are not explicitly recognized. . . .
>
> It is only when the relationship breaks down that the underlying obligations are brought to light. While Alec and Frank were friends, I never heard either of them discuss the service he was performing for the other, but when they had a falling-out over the group activities with the Aphrodite Club, each man complained to Doc that the other was not acting as he should in view of the services that had been done him. In other words, actions which were performed explicitly for the sake of friendship were revealed as being a part of a system of mutual obligation. . . .
>
> The leader spends more money on his followers than they on him. The farther down in the structure one looks, the fewer are the financial relations which tend to obligate the leader to a follower. This does not mean that the leader has more money than the others or even that he necessarily spends more—though he must always be a free spender. It means that the financial relations must be explained in social terms. Unconsciously, and in some cases consciously, the leader refrains from putting himself under obligation to those with low status in the group.
>
> The leader is the focal point for the organization of his group. In his absence, the members of the gang are divided into a number of small groups. There is no common activity or general conversation. When the leader appears, the situation changes strikingly. The small units form into one larger group. The conversation becomes general, and the unified action frequently follows. The leader becomes the central point in the discussion. A follower starts to say something, pauses when he notices that the leader is not listening, and begins again when he has the leader's attention. When the leader leaves the group, unity gives way to the divisions that existed before his appearance.
>
> The members do not feel that the gang is really gathered until the leader appears. They recognize an obligation to wait for him before beginning any group activity, and when he is present they expect him to make their decisions. . . .
>
> The leader is the man who acts when the situation requires action. He is more resourceful than his followers. Past events have shown that his ideas were right. In this sense "right" simply means satisfactory to the members. He is the most independent

in judgment. While his followers are undecided as to a course of action or upon the character of a newcomer, the leader makes up his mind.

When he gives his word to one of his boys, he keeps it. The followers look to him for advice and encouragement, and he receives more of their confidences than any other man. Consequently, he knows more about what is going on in the group than anyone else. . . .

The leader is respected for his fair-mindedness. Whereas there may be hard feelings among some of the followers, the leader cannot bear a grudge against any man in the group. He has close friends (men who stand next to him in position), and he is indifferent to some of the members; but, if he is to retain his reputation for impartiality, he cannot allow personal animus to override his judgment.

The leader need not be the best baseball player, bowler, or fighter, but he must have some skill in whatever pursuits are of particular interest to the group. It is natural for him to promote activities in which he excels and to discourage those in which he is not skillful; and in so far as he is thus able to influence the group, his competent performance is a natural consequence of his position. At the same time his performance supports his position.

The leader is better known and more respected outside his group than are any of his followers. His capacity for social movement is greater. One of the most important functions he performs is that of relating his group to other groups in the district. Whether the relationship is one of conflict, competition, or cooperation, he is expected to represent the interests of his fellows (1955, pp. 256–260).

THEORETICAL POINTER

Dependence and Influence

Most of the points made by Whyte about informal leadership may be summed up in the concept of *dependence.* We may conceive of a person's dependence on a relationship to be the value of such a relationship to him as compared to the value of any alternatives. The greater such dependence, the more is a person likely to be influenced or led. And the more a person provides what is valuable for others (especially when that which he provides is in short supply), the more influential is such a person.

He thus becomes a leader.

Some of the elements of informal leadership pointed out by Whyte emphasize personal qualities that followers may find of value. Others reflect a group focus, suggesting that simply to have someone mediate group activities is itself an important value. In either case, it is important to note that what makes for influence or leadership ability must be relevant to the needs of others in a particular social situation. Influence never occurs in a social vacuum.

WHO LEADS THE LADIES?

The cases of informal leadership examined so far in this chapter might be considered as special cases. At least they reflect groups that are not in the common experience of most college students. But what would we find concerning patterns of influence if we studied persons who are more firmly embedded in the common activities of middle-class society —such as housewives?

Let us take a typical American city, obtain a representative sample of the adult female population, select areas of rather frequent decision making, and find out who influences whom on these matters. Fortunately, our work has already been done for us by two sociologists, Elihu Katz and Paul F. Lazarsfeld, and the results may be found in their book, *Personal Influence* (1955).

As a reasonably typical American city, Katz and Lazarsfeld chose Decatur, Illinois, a city with a population, at the time, of about 65,000. They next selected a random sample of households and interviewed an adult female in each case possible. These women were asked questions dealing with a variety of common activities, including especially the areas of household marketing, fashions, public affairs, and movie attendance.

Two months later these same women were interviewed again to see what changes might have occurred in their behavior regarding such areas (marketing, fashions, public affairs, and movies). Where an important change was noted, intensive questioning sought to discover what social influences may have been behind the change. Interviewers especially sought information about persons who had influenced the respondents in the sample, and also about persons the respondents may have influenced. Additional interviews were then conducted with samples of both groups (persons who had influenced the original respondents, and persons the original respondents claimed to have influenced). All in all, over 750 persons were interviewed to obtain a picture of the everyday flow of influence among the ladies of Decatur.

SIDELIGHT

"The Part Played by People"

The subtitle of Katz and Lazarsfeld's book, "The Part Played by People in the Flow of Mass Communications," suggests more of a mass communications orientation for the research than our introduction has given. It is true that the study was designed to identify mass-media effects upon everyday decisions. But it is also true that their main results emphasized the effects of interpersonal relations rather than direct influences of mass media.

In each of the four areas (marketing, fashions, public affairs, and moviegoing) the authors present evidence that personal influence was far more effective in influencing decisions than was mass-media exposure. Furthermore, where mass-media influences were identified, they were frequently combined with interpersonal influences. The authors interpret this as evidence for the *two-step flow of communication* hypothesis to indicate the primary flow of mass-media influences as from the mass media to opinion leaders and from opinion leaders to the less active segments of the population. It may be noted that opinion leaders are found in all segments of the social structure. They are often otherwise quite ordinary people who happen to be more alert and influential on particular matters than most of their friends.

What do we expect to find about the pattern of person-to-person influence among the ladies of Decatur? Are there certain kinds of persons who tend to be more influential? Take, for example, age. Does age carry with it the wisdom that will be respected by younger women? Within families, according to findings of Katz and Lazarsfeld, influence does flow between different age levels—but not always in the same direction. In matters of fashion, influence tends to flow from young to old, but in public affairs the older persons influence the younger ones. Also in public affairs, primary influence within families came from men rather than other women. In marketing and moviegoing, influence tends to be exerted most by family members of similar age, though in such special·cases as breakfast cereals children appeared to exert primary influence.

Outside families, the flow of influence between age groups follows somewhat different patterns from those within families. In marketing there is evidence of a flow from older to younger women. In public affairs there is a slight tendency in the same direction, though influence here is much more apt to flow between persons of similar age levels. For extrafamily influences in fashions and moviegoing, the evidence suggests a weak tendency for the younger persons to influence the older ones.

Perhaps this is enough of Katz and Lazarsfeld's findings to indicate the relativity of generalizations that apply to influence patterns. What applies for marketing decisions may not apply for public affairs. And what applies to influences within the family may be different from what applies outside the family.

There is no single network that represents the structure of influence in Decatur. A person whose advice is important for fashions may have little or no influence in the area of public affairs. And the people who may have influence in any one area are many and various. But are there not some who exert generalized leadership, some who are influential in all areas? Perhaps, but the data of Katz and Lazarsfeld's Decatur study give little evidence of this. They conclude: "Each area, it seems, has a corps of leaders of its own" (p. 334).

10
Experiments in Conformity

Our studies in the last chapter have suggested that influence lies as much in the situation of the person to be influenced as it does in what is celebrated as leadership ability. But beyond pointing to a general concept of dependence, we have not done much to indicate just what the crucial factors are in such situations of influence. What more specific generalizations can be made? Are there certain kinds of situations in which we are much more susceptible to the influence of other people? Are there certain kinds of people who are more susceptible than others? How else might we explain variations in the amount of influence?

In this chapter we will pursue these questions by an analysis of several experiments. These experiments are usually labeled *conformity studies* because they suggest how individuals adjust to group pressures. Actually, however, these are only marginal studies of group conformity, for persons are not examined here in natural group settings. Instead, they are placed in highly artificial settings so that more selected aspects of social influence can be examined than would be possible in real life. From such studies, however, we may infer something about factors involved in conformity in more ordinary group settings. We can also obtain insights about the general topic of social influence.

Let us start with a study by Muzafer Sherif (1936), which has become one of the classics of experimental social psychology.

CONFORMITY IN DARKNESS

An experimenter leads two or three persons into a completely darkened room. After they are seated, they are told that they will soon see a point of light and that after a few moments they will see the light move. After the light disappears, subjects are to report orally their estimates of how far the light moved.

This would appear to be a simple experiment in perception. In fact the experimental setup is even simpler than it seems, for the light actually does not move at all. That it appears to move is, however, a practically universal result. This tendency to perceive motion where none exists (known as the *autokinetic effect*) is common when one focuses visually upon a specific object against an ambiguous background. And a completely darkened room is about as ambiguous a background as can be produced.

What Muzafer Sherif found in his experiments with the autokinetic effect was that judgments about how far a light moves tend to converge within a limited range during a particular series of trials. An individual tested alone tended to develop his own range of judgments, which might be quite different from those of another individual. When several individuals were tested together (with answers reported orally), the range of their estimates tended to be one that they shared. There was no demand that such a range of estimates be developed; subjects just claimed to report movement as they saw it. But the range within which they "saw" movement tended to reflect earlier judgments—made by themselves or others present.

When persons were tested first individually and then in groups of two or three, their responses tended to converge after they were tested together. Convergence was even closer, however, when subjects worked first in the group situation and then were tested as individuals. That is, their estimates as individuals strongly showed the influence of the previous group situation.

It was also found that the judgments of a subject could be influenced by direct suggestions from the experimenter or by predetermined suggestions from another subject secretly cooperating with the experimenter. In the latter case when the naïve subject was subsequently tested alone, his judgments conformed more closely to those previously suggested than when the influencing person was present—even though the subject felt he was acting with more independence.

What do such studies prove? At the very least they show that persons tend to be influenced by other people when they lack standards for making their own judgments. But Sherif believes the significance of such studies is even broader. Noting that the group influence also extended to individuals tested alone (following previous testing in the group situation), he suggests that here might be a prototype of the most far-reaching forms of social influence. Such experiments, he suggests, confirm the psychological view that "our experience is organized around or modified by frames of reference participating as factors in any given stimulus situation" (p. 106). Contact and communication between individuals lead to a convergence in these frames of reference. That is, through contact and communication with others, we develop and modify the frames of reference that also shape our private experience. Sherif goes on to suggest that "the psychological basis of the established social norms, such as stereotypes, fashions, conventions, customs, and values, is the formation of common frames of reference as a product of the contact of the individuals" (p. 106).

MAJORITY PRESSURES WITHOUT DARKNESS

But before we infer too much about social influence from studies with the autokinetic effect, we should remind ourselves of a basic feature: there is a complete absence of environmental cues to serve as a basis for judgment. Isn't this a rather rare kind of situation? Doesn't most social influence occur when there are numerous environmental cues?

Could a completely darkened room, then, provide the prototype for such influence?

At any rate, it would be useful to examine a comparable experiment done under conditions when the environmental cues are more clear. In fact, it would be interesting to see if social influences upon a person's judgment would still exist if he could easily see the facts he is to judge. Such an experiment, with several interesting variations, has been performed by Solomon Asch (1951). In his basic experimental approach, Asch gathered together about eight college students for an experiment in visual judgment. The experimenter showed sets of lines, which subjects were asked to match in terms of length. Their answers were stated publicly, subject after subject. For the first few trials everyone reported the same answers. Then came scattered trials on which the majority reported incorrect answers. They were in fact coached in advance by the experimenter to give these wrong answers to see what would be the effect upon the lone uncoached subject. Our interest is, of course, limited to this focal subject, the one who was not an accomplice of the investigator. How frequently did such a subject yield to the majority, giving the majority's response as his own?

When similar discrimination problems were posed outside the experimental context, mistakes were made less than 1 percent of the time. This may serve as a basis for comparison with the frequency of mistakes inspired by majority pressure. Under group pressure subjects yielded to the wrong estimates of the majority about one-third of the time.

There were, of course, marked individual differences. A few subjects yielded nearly all the time, most yielded some of the time, and about one-fourth maintained their independence throughout the experiment. Furthermore, among those who yielded there were important differences in the way they yielded, as revealed by follow-up questioning by Asch (1951). One group of subjects displayed only a distortion of *action*. These subjects believed that the majority was wrong, but they did not want to report answers that were different from the majority. A second group of subjects, including at one time or another most subjects, experienced a distortion of *judgment*. They "saw" the correct answer as being right, but they did not believe that it really was correct. In other words, they doubted the evidence of their own senses in favor of the evidence given by the judgment of others. A third group of subjects appeared to display distortion of *perception*. There were only a very few subjects who were influenced to this extent; but these few, according to their own reports then and following the experiment, actually came to perceive reality the way the majority reported.

Asch also reported on the effects of a number of situational variations. In one variation he had two naïve subjects rather than one. In another variation there was only one focal subject, but one of the accomplices was prepared to give all correct answers rather than go with the majority. In another case, one of the coached subjects left the majority in the middle of the sequence of estimates and began reporting correct answers. In all of these treatments the impact of the majority pressure was markedly reduced. With these variations the proportion of mistakes in the direction of the majority ranged up to about one-tenth (as compared to about one-third with a unanimous majority). However, after one of the coached subjects started giving correct answers and then deserted to the majority, the focal subject showed as much yielding as if there had been a unanimous majority throughout. In such variations we may see that independence, as well as conformity, is partly a product of the pattern of group influences.

Another set of experimental variations dealt with the size of the majority. In these variations the majority was always unanimous, but the number in this united front varied from one to two, three, four, eight, and sixteen. The remarkable finding here was that a unanimous majority of three or four produced as strong an effect as did larger majorities. Up to a majority of three or four there were sharp increases in yielding with majority size, but when the majority increased beyond four there were no significant relationships between majority size and frequency of yielding to the majority.

Still another experimental variation was of the stimulus situation. As the situation diminished in clarity, with certain answers less obviously correct, there was a stronger majority effect. Also the subjects were less disturbed in yielding under these situations of greater ambiguity. "We consider it of significance," commented Asch, "that the majority achieves its most pronounced effect when it acts most painlessly" (p. 189).

Asch also increased the discrepancy between the correct answer and the majority answers, hoping to reach a point where no one would continue to yield to the majority. "In this we regretfully did not succeed," Asch (1955) reported. "Even when the difference between the lines was seven inches, there were still some who yielded to the error of the majority" (p. 34).

A variation of Asch's technique for studying yielding to group pressure was developed by Richard S. Crutchfield (1955). The Crutchfield technique avoided the necessity for accomplices of the experimenter by placing the subjects in separate booths alongside one another. Persons in the booths could not see or talk with one another, but all could see slides projected on a wall. The slides posed problems of perception or judgment, and each person operated a switch to indicate his answers. Each subject's panel registered not only his own answers but apparently those of all the other subjects as well. Actually, the experimenter was able to manipulate these apparent answers from his master control panel. He thus could provide on any given trial whatever combination of apparent responses of the other subjects that he wished to produce.

In addition to reporting results similar to those reported by Asch, Crutchfield has used his technique to study relationships of conformity (as measured by yielding to the apparent group majority) to personality characteristics. Crutchfield has summarized some of his main findings as indicating that

> As contrasted with the high conformist, the independent man shows more intellectual effectiveness, ego strength, leadership ability and maturity of social relations, together with a conspicuous absence of inferiority feelings, rigid and excessive self-control, and authoritarian attitudes (p. 194).

CAUTION

The Ugly Face of Conformity

Conformity seems to be a bad thing. Crutchfield doesn't exactly say that conformists are bad, but he does show that they tend to be low in intelligence, low in ego strength, inclined toward feelings of inadequacy, and given to rigid and authoritarian outlooks. And over and beyond such scientific evidence is the fact that all the large, mass-circulated magazines of America have featured articles condemning conformity.

But beware of overgeneralizing under the rubric of conformity. Whether or not conformity is useful or harmful depends upon the nature of the object of conformity. Some standards of behavior are necessary for all groups in society, and such standards of behavior require at least a certain degree of conformity. Such conformity to norms of behavior need not always suggest uniformity, for often these standards apply in different ways to persons occupying different roles.

On the other hand, there are instances where conformity to prevailing views serves no useful purpose. The Asch and Crutchfield techniques are based on the study of just such useless conformity. No one, no individual and no group, is ordinarily benefited by a person agreeing with the misperceptions of others. It is small wonder that such conformity tends to have a less desirable profile of associations than would independence.

But suppose conformity were measured by the number of times a subject agreed with the majority in giving the *right* answers. Would independence then be more prized?

BUT WHERE IS THE GROUP?

The experiments of Sherif and Asch are frequently interpreted as showing group influence. But where is the group? Do subjects participate as a group? In one sense, they do. Subjects are together for the purpose of the experiment, and they are aware of the presence and behavior of one another. But in another sense there is no group. At least there is no feeling that the persons involved are together for anything beyond the experiment; and even the experiment is not presented as anything involving a common goal. It is as if all the individuals involved just happened to be there together.

Such experiments can give us insights into fundamental processes of group behavior, but we need other kinds of studies to make the link to groups outside the laboratory. An example of such a study has been reported by Lewis Carter and associates (Carter, Hill, and McLemore, 1967). The purpose of Carter's research was to study groups outside the laboratory setting and explore how well theoretical models of conformity processes developed in laboratory studies might apply to them. The groups that Carter studied were supervising nurses involved in training sessions to improve their skills in working with people. During this five-day training period, they spent a large proportion of their time in small discussion groups. A total of 371 nurses were divided into 42 small discussion groups, with each nurse continuing in the same group throughout the week. Lectures and other presentations were also included in the training program.

On the first and last day of the training period three measures were obtained to indicate attitudes toward democratic processes, authoritarianism, and tolerance for ambiguity. The main task of the investigators was to predict the pattern of final results on these scales, given the distribution of initial scores and the nature of the groups involved.

The investigators first tried a simple conformity model. They predicted that in each discussion group the variation of attitudes of group members would become less as individuals tended to converge around a common position. Results, however, did not support this model. There was no general reduction in variation of attitudes in most groups.

Other models were then tried. One of these emphasized change only for those who originally deviated most from others in their group. Another model took into account the direction of change of the group. While some results supported each of these models, they still did not give a satisfactory prediction of final attitude patterns.

Finally Carter and associates tried a model that took into account pressures outside as well as inside the discussion groups. As they expressed it: "The magnitude of change in a conforming direction is dependent upon both the pressures exerted by the group upon the members of that group and by the pressures exerted by the social context within which the group operates" (p. 12). In this particular case, the social context was the training environment, which exhorted the nurses to try to become more democratic, less authoritarian, and more tolerant of ambiguity. Taking this into account, as well as pressures toward conformity within each group, the researchers arrived at the following predictions:

1. The greatest tendency toward change would be found among those who initially deviated most from the group average in the direction that was also most opposed by the broader social context.
2. An intermediate tendency to change would be found among those initially near the group average but opposed to the broader social context, or among those deviating most from the group average in the direction that was supported by the broader social context.
3. The least tendency to change would be found among those initially near the group average but in the direction that was favored by the broader social context.

These predictions, they found, fit their data quite well.

A study such as that of Carter and associates should lead us to be cautious about applying laboratory studies of conformity directly to everyday life. Groups studied in the laboratory are not ordinary kinds of groups. One of the special ways they differ is in their isolation from ordinary contexts and from the pressures that may be found within such contexts. The laboratory technique may be useful for isolating some of the internal dynamics of groups; but for predicting the overall pattern of group conformity, we also need to know something of the context within which the group is operating. It is the combination of pressures from within the group and pressures from the context of the group that gives the best prediction of conformity pressures felt by individuals. Such, at any rate, is the implication of the work of Carter and associates on conformity in nonlaboratory groups.

11
Influence and Identity

We have seen some of the situational factors that affect the degree to which a person's behavior is influenced by other persons. So far we have looked chiefly at influences upon external behavior. In this chapter we explore the possibility that very private behavior may also be the product of social influence. How much are a person's thoughts and feelings, indeed, his very sense of identity, the result of social influence from those around him?

EFFECTS OF "SUPROXIN"

A study of the effects of vitamin supplements on vision was (falsely) indicated to subjects as the purpose of an experiment designed by Stanley Schachter and Jerome Singer (1962).[1] The subjects were told by the experimenter:

> In this experiment we would like to make various tests of your vision. We are particularly interested in how certain vitamin compounds and vitamin supplements affect the visual skills. In particular, we want to find out how the vitamin compound called "Suproxin" affects your vision.
> What we would like to do, then, if we can get your permission, is to give you a small injection of Suproxin. The injection itself is mild and harmless; however, since some people do object to being injected we don't want to talk you into anything. Would you mind receiving a Suproxin injection? (p. 382).

After the subjects agreed to have the injection, the experimenter left the room. Then a doctor entered, made similar statements about the experiment, took a reading of the subject's pulse, and then injected him with Suproxin.

In one experimental condition the Suproxin received was really epinephrine; in another condition subjects received a placebo, which had no active effects. The effects of epinephrine may be described as follows:

[1] Stanley Schachter and Jerome E. Singer, "Cognitive, Social, and Physiological Determinants of Emotional States," *Psychological Review*, 69 (1962), 379–399. Copyright 1962 by the American Psychological Association. Quotations from this source are reprinted with permission of the publisher.

Epinephrine or adrenalin is a sympathomimetic drug whose effects, with minor exceptions, are almost a perfect mimicry of a discharge of the sympathetic nervous system. Shortly after injection systolic blood pressure increases markedly, heart rate increases somewhat, cutaneous blood flow decreases, muscle and cerebral blood flow increase, blood sugar and lactic acid concentration increase, and respiration rate increases slightly. As far as the subject is concerned the major subjective symptoms are palpitation, tremor, and sometimes a feeling of flushing and accelerated breathing. With a subcutaneous injection (in the dosage administered to our subjects), such effects usually begin within 3–5 minutes of injection and last anywhere from 10 minutes to an hour. For most subjects these effects are dissipated within 15–20 minutes after injection (p. 382).

In some cases where epinephrine was to be given, the subject was well informed about what he would feel. Here the experimenter prepared him with these words:

I should also tell you that some of our subjects have experienced side effects from the Suproxin. These side effects are transitory, that is, they will only last for about 15 or 20 minutes. What will probably happen is that your hand will start to shake, your heart will start to pound, and your face may get warm and flushed. Again these are side effects, lasting about 15 or 20 minutes (p. 383).

When giving the injection, the physician also gave a similar prediction of the symptoms.

In other cases where epinephrine was given, the subjects were either given no information about the side effects or were actually misinformed.

Finally, there were the placebo cases in which the injection was simply a saline solution. These subjects were given no reason to expect feelings.

In summary, we may refer to these three treatments as (1) informed, (2) not informed (either misinformed or uninformed), and (3) placebo conditions. Let us see what happened next.

Immediately after the subject had been injected, the physician left the room and the experimenter returned with a stooge whom he introduced as another subject, then said: "Both of you have had the Suproxin shot and you'll both be taking the same tests of vision. What I ask you to do now is just to wait for 20 minutes. The reason for this is simply that we have to allow 20 minutes for the Suproxin to get from the injection site into the bloodstream. At the end of 20 minutes when we are certain that most of the Suproxin has been absorbed into the bloodstream, we'll begin the tests of vision."

The room in which this was said had been deliberately put into a state of mild disarray. As he was leaving, the experimenter apologetically added: "The only other thing I should do is to apologize for the condition of this room. I just didn't have time to clean it up. So, if you need any scratch paper or rubber bands or pencils, help yourself. I'll be back in 20 minutes to begin the vision tests."

As soon as the experimenter had left, the stooge introduced himself again, made a series of standard icebreaker comments, and then launched his routine (p. 384).

This routine is elsewhere (Schachter, 1964)[2] summarized as follows:

He reached for a piece of paper, doodled briefly, crumpled the paper, aimed for a wastebasket, threw, and missed. This led him into a game of "basketball" in which he moved about the room crumpling paper, and trying fancy basketball shots. Finished with basketball, he said, "This is one of my good days. I feel like a kid again. I think I'll make a plane." He made a paper plane, spent a few minutes flying it around the room, and then said, "Even when I was a kid, I never was much good at this." He then tore off the tail of his plane, wadded it up, and making a slingshot of a rubber band, began to shoot the paper. While shooting, he noticed a sloppy pile of manila folders. He built a tower of these folders, and then went to the opposite end of the room to shoot at the tower, and while picking up the folders he noticed a pair of hula hoops behind a portable blackboard. He took one of these for himself, put the other within the reaching distance of the subject, and began hula hooping. After a few minutes, he replaced the hula hoop and returned to his seat, at which point the experimenter returned to the room.

All through this madness an observer, through a one-way mirror, systematically recorded the subject's behavior and noted the extent to which the subject joined in with the stooge's whirl of activity (p. 57).

And what effect is this supposed to have? The expectation of the experimenters was that this show of euphoria by the stooge might lead the real subject to feel euphoric too. Especially when he has the side effects of epinephrine and does not know how to interpret them would we expect him to be influenced by the stooge in interpreting his own emotional state. When he has the side effects of epinephrine and had been told correctly what to expect, he should be less influenced by the stooge's antics—at least so far as evaluating his own feelings is concerned.

Physical Reality and Social Reality

THEORETICAL
POINTER

Leon Festinger (1950) has pointed out the importance of a distinction between physical reality and social reality. Physical reality is the reality we come to know primarily through physical cues, and social reality is the reality we come to know primarily through social cues. Social reality seems as "hard," just as certain in its impact upon us, as physical reality. We sense it as being just as real, even though its truths

[2] Stanley Schachter, "The Interaction of Cognitive and Physiological Determinants of Emotional State," in L. Berkowitz (ed.), *Advances in Experimental Social Psychology*, I. New York: Academic Press, 1964. Quotations from this source are reprinted with permission of the author and publisher.

are more matters of consensual validation (checked through the conceptions of others) than of physical validation (checked through observing actions of the physical world). Actually, what we know as reality is practically always a combination of physical and social reality.

As the studies of the previous chapter indicate, we tend to use social reality as a basis for judgments to the extent that physical cues are missing. Even when the physical cues are very much present, as in Asch's experiments, reliance upon social reality is some- times more important for behavior than is physical reality.

In the present experiment by Schachter and Singer, the design included an explicit manipulation of the extent to which a subject's interpretation of his condition might be affected by another subject's suggestions about reality. Under those conditions where he is less prepared for the feelings he experiences, then the subject is expected to be more influenced by the social reality provided by the example of the stooge.

Immediately after the experimenter returned to the room, he gave the participants a questionnaire. Included in the questionnaire were self-ratings of mood—how "happy and good" or "irritated and angry" the subject felt. Table 9 summarizes the results of these ratings. Subjects tended toward sharing the stooge's euphoria when they were injected with epinephrine and not correctly prepared for its side effects. In such cases they tended to feel especially happy. This was not the case when they were correctly prepared for the side effects of epinephrine. The difference in results is statistically significant. Somewhere between are results for those with the placebo treatment—apparently more affected by the stooge than in the informed treatment but less than in the not informed treatment.

TABLE 9 SELF-REPORT OF MOOD (WHEN STOOGE SHOWED EU-
          PHORIA)

Treatment	Happiness Self-Rating
Informed	.98
Not informed	1.84
Placebo	1.61

NOTE: Scores were obtained by subtracting each subject's rating on an "irritation" scale from his rating on a "happiness" scale.
SOURCE: Schachter and Singer (1962), p. 390.

But euphoria may be an especially likely way of interpreting an unusual internal feeling. What would have been the case if the cues of the stooge had been quite otherwise?

In another set of treatments the stooge did provide a quite different example. In these "anger" conditions:

> Immediately after the injection, the experimenter brought a stooge into the subject's room, introduced the two, and after explaining the necessity for a 20-minute delay for "the Suproxin to get from the injection site into the bloodstream," he continued, "We would like you to use these 20 minutes to answer these questionnaires." Then handing out the questionnaires, he

concluded: "I'll be back in 20 minutes to pick up the questionnaires and begin the tests of vision."

The questionnaires, five pages long, started off innocently, requesting fact sheet information and then grew increasingly personal and insulting, asking questions such as:

"With how many men (other than your father) has your mother had extra-marital relationships?"

4 and under ———: 5–9 ———: 10 and over ———.

The stooge, sitting directly opposite the subject, paced his own answers so that at all times subject and stooge were working on the same question. At regular points in the questionnaire, the stooge made a series of standardized comments about the questions. His comments started off innocently enough, grew increasingly querulous, and finally he ended up in a rage, ripping up his questionnaire, slamming it to the floor, saying "I'm not wasting any more time. I'm getting my books and leaving," and stomping out of the room (Schachter. 1964, pp. 57–58).

It is interesting to note the ratings made of the subject's behavior under these conditions. Again, there are the three treatments: informed, not informed, and placebo. Results are given in Table 10. Table 10, like Table 9, shows the strongest effects of the stooge to appear in the not informed treatment. Only this time it is anger that is shown rather than euphoria. In other words, the emotion is almost the opposite, but this treatment still has the strongest effects. Again the informed treatments shows the least effects, and the effects with the placebo treatment are intermediate. Furthermore, the anger index for the not informed treatment is statistically significant when compared to results of either of the other two treatments.

TABLE 10 BEHAVIORAL INDICATIONS OF EMOTIONAL STATE IN THE ANGER CONDITIONS

Condition	Measure of Anger
Informed	−.18
Not informed	+2.28
Placebo	+.79

NOTE: The above measures are based on combined ratings by observers who noted especially appearances of anger and agreement with the stooge's angry comments.
SOURCE: Schachter and Singer (1962), p. 392.

What general interpretation may be given to these experiments? Schachter (1964) suggests that a key idea that may be applied is that of the presence of an "evaluative need"—in this case a need to evaluate, understand, and label ambiguous body states. "Given a new, strange, or ambiguous bodily state, pressures will act on the individual to decide exactly what it is that he feels and to decide how he will label these feelings" (pp. 76-77). Only some of the cues for such an interpretation come from within him; other cues come from the situation or other persons present. Also important are the labels that people use for talking about or responding to such feelings.

It may sometimes occur that an uncommon interpretation or an inappropriate label may be attached to a feeling state through the suggestions of other people. As Schachter (1964) points out:

Where such is the case, we may anticipate bizarre and pathological behavior. As an example of this possibility, consider the state of hunger. We are so accustomed to think of hunger as a primary motive, innate, and wired into the animal, unmistakable in its cues, that even the possibility that an organism would be incapable of correctly labeling the state seems too far fetched to credit. The physiological changes accompanying food deprivation seem distinct, identifiable, and invariant. Yet even a moment's consideration will make it clear that attaching the label "hunger" to this set of bodily feelings and behaving accordingly, is a learned, socially determined, cognitive act.

Consider the neonate. Wholly at the mercy of its feelings, when uncomfortable, in pain, frightened, hungry, or thirsty, it screams. Whether it is comforted, soothed, clucked at, fondled, or fed has little to do with the state of its own feelings, but depends entirely on the ability and willingness of its mother or nurse to recognize the proper cues. If she is experienced, she will comfort when the baby is frightened, soothe him when he is chafed, feed him when he is hungry, and so on. If inexperienced, her behavior may be completely inappropriate to the child's state. Most commonly, perhaps, the compassionate but bewildered mother will feed her child at any sign of distress.

It is precisely this state of affairs that the analyst Hilde Bruch (1961) suggests is at the heart of chronic obesity. She describes such cases as characterized by a confusion between intense emotional states and hunger. During childhood these patients have not been taught to discriminate between hunger and such states as fear, anger, and anxiety. If correct, these people are, in effect, labeling a state of sympathetic activation as hunger. Small wonder that they are both fat and jolly (p. 79).

SOCIAL INFLUENCE AND THE SELF

If the implications just drawn from the experiment with Suproxin are correct, we are not always able to decide how we feel all by ourselves. In addition to the internal physiological cues are verbal habits from past experience and cues from the immediate social situation. How we feel normally represents a composite of all of these influences.

A similar analysis can be made concerning other forms of self-definition. In fact, most matters of self-definition are less dependent on physiological cues than are feelings or emotional states. We would, therefore, expect the social cues to be even more important in such cases.

To begin with, the newborn infant has no sense of self. His actions are without meanings, in the sense of self-conscious purpose. But his actions do have meanings to other persons, who respond to him in terms of these meanings. The infant, utterly dependent upon others for the satisfaction of his needs, begins to organize his behavior around the reactions of others. And inherent in these reactions are the meanings the infant will come to apply to his own behavior. These are not only meanings for specific situations; they also become generalized to provide a continuity of interpretation from situation to situation. And so a sense of self begins to emerge.

The "Looking-glass Self"

THEORETICAL
POINTER

Charles H. Cooley's description (1922)[3] of the "looking-glass self" gives a vivid figure of speech for describing how self-concepts may be developed.

As we see our face, figure, and dress in the glass, and are interested in them because they are ours, and pleased or otherwise with them according as they do or do not answer to what we should like them to be; so in imagination we perceive in another's mind some thought of our appearance, manners, aims, deeds, character, friends, and so on, and are variously affected by it.

A self-idea of this sort seems to have three principal elements: the imagination of our appearance to the other person; the imagination of his judgment of that appearance; and some sort of self-feeling, such as pride or mortification.

Cooley goes on to qualify the looking-glass idea:

The comparison with a looking-glass hardly suggests the second element, the imagined judgment, which is quite essential. The thing that moves us to pride or shame is not the mere mechanical reflection of ourselves, but an imputed sentiment, the imagined effect of this reflection upon another's mind. This is evident from the fact that the character and weight of that other, in whose mind we see ourselves, makes all the difference with our feeling. We are ashamed to seem evasive in the presence of a brave one, gross in the eyes of a refined one, and so on. We always imagine, and in imagining share, the judgments of the other mind (pp. 184–185).

Closely linked with a development of the sense of self is the development of a sense of social structure. The meanings we learn to apply to our own behavior imply related meanings for other people. Thus a sense of social roles emerges side by side with a sense of selfhood. Many social psychologists, following especially the ideas of George Herbert Mead, would in fact emphasize the developmental precedence of a primitive sense of social roles over the development of a sense of self. According to Mead, we become aware that our acts have meanings only as we learn to "take the role of the other."

G. H. Mead on Role-taking

THEORETICAL
POINTER

George H. Mead (1863–1931) was for many years a philosopher at the University of Chicago, where he had a strong influence upon social scientists trained there. In his lifetime he published no books, but his students compiled several volumes, largely from classroom notes, which were published after his death. *Mind, Self and Society* (1934) presents most fully his social psychological interpretations. The following quotations are from this work:[4]

[3] Charles H. Cooley, *Human Nature and the Social Order*. New York: Charles Scribner's Sons, 1922. Quotations from this source are reprinted with permission of the publisher.

[4] George Herbert Mead, *Mind, Self and Society*, edited by C. W. Morris. Chicago: The University of Chicago Press, 1934. Copyright 1934 by The University of Chicago. Copyright renewed 1962 by Charles W. Morris. Quotations from this source are reprinted with permission of the publisher.

. . . there are two general stages in the full development of the self. At the first of these stages, the individual's self is constituted simply by an organization of the particular attitudes of other individuals toward himself and toward one another in the specific social acts in which he participates with them. But at the second stage in the full development of the individual's self that self is constituted not only by an organization of these particular individual attitudes, but also by an organization of the social attitudes of the generalized other or the social group as a whole to which he belongs. . . .

Such is the process by which a personality arises. I have spoken of this as a process in which a child takes the role of the other, and said that it takes place essentially through the use of language. Language is predominantly based on the vocal gesture by means of which co-operative activities in a community are carried out. Language in its significant sense is that vocal gesture which tends to arouse in the individual the attitude which it arouses in others, and it is this perfecting of the self by the gesture which mediates the social activities that gives rise to the process of taking the role of the other. . . .

After all, what we mean by self-consciousness is an awakening in ourselves of the group of attitudes which we are arousing in others, especially when it is an important set of responses which go to make up the members of the community. . . .

Selves can only exist in definite relationships to other selves. No hard-and-fast line can be drawn between our own selves and the selves of others, since our own selves exist and enter as such into our experience only in so far as the selves of others exist and enter as such into our experience also. The individual possesses a self only in relation to the selves of the other members of his social group . . . (pp. 158–164).

This, of course, should not suggest that personal identities are simply passively acquired collections of expectations of others. There is nothing more original and creative than the way a person weaves the meanings of his experiences into the fabric of a personal identity. A personal identity—the sense a person develops of who he is and the purposes that will guide the continuity of his actions—is a complex product of experience. And as it becomes developed, it becomes a filter for the interpretation of all subsequent experience. This involves resistance to, as well as acceptance of, the influences of other persons.

But we do not form a sense of personal identity in a social vacuum. The main import of what we have been discussing is that relationships with other people present the ground upon which is built a sense of identity, the soil in which a sense of self is nurtured. And this is the most profound form of social influence, the social influence that reaches the very roots of our sense of selfhood.

ROLE, SELF, AND FACE

The concept of *role* refers to the pattern of behavior expected of a person by others in a given social context. Usually the social context for a role is a particular group or organization (for example, husband, daughter, chairman of the board, or jokester for the gang). In some cases the context for a role may be broader, even as broad as society itself (for example, the roles of a man, woman, citizen, or decent human being). Roles may be formal or informal, temporary or permanent, deeply involving or superficial—depending primarily on the kind of social context in which they occur.

The concept of *self* refers to a person's organization of ideas that have primary reference to his own behavior, especially those ideas considered most central and enduring in his behavior. Such an organization of ideas tends to be relatively enduring and provides a continuity between different kinds of social situations. The self system includes expectations of others, but only as they become filtered to fit consistently with other self-images.

Situation (especially the roles indicated for a given situation) and self, then, are two frameworks into which behavior becomes organized. But these are not independent of each other. The self is used for purposes of the situation as the person shapes his thoughts and feelings to fit a particular role. And the situation is used for purposes of the self as the person carries out a role with the mark of his own personality and with the intention of winning attention or approval from others by doing so.

Erving Goffman (1955) has pointed to a third concept, *face*, as an appropriate bridge between the concepts of role and self. Face represents the accepted claims a person makes for himself through social interaction. To point out that these claims must be accepted by others is to indicate that cooperation from others is needed for an individual to carry out a successful face in a given encounter. "While it may be true that the individual has a unique self all his own," states Goffman (1956), "evidence of this possession is thoroughly a product of joint ceremonial labor." For "the individual must rely on others to complete the picture of him of which he himself is allowed to paint only certain parts" (p. 493).

The concept of face is a particularly vivid way of pointing out how situation and self may be involved in each other at one and the same time. The person is not just passively playing out a social role; he is actively trying to achieve enhancement for his ego. But this requires regard for the particular situation, especially for the expressed feelings and expectations of others.

The way in which the concept of face is different from those of role and self is in its duration. Face tends to be transitory, reflecting the self in a given social encounter (and alternatively, reflecting a given social encounter in the self). In contrast, role and self are linked respectively to the more stable systems of group and personality.

At any given time, only part of a person's self or role is presented to other people. Nevertheless, the face he presents in social interaction necessarily depends both on his sense of self and the social role he is playing—and in the process, role and self become so intertwined that even theoretically it is almost impossible to separate them.

Effects of Drastic Situational Change

SIDELIGHT

A continuity in our sense of identity tends to be nurtured by a continuity of social roles. We move in the same groups time after time, we have experiences similar to what we have known before, we continue in contact with many of the same persons, and these persons expect similar actions from us.

But what would happen if an individual's social setting were drastically changed, if old roles could be made obsolete as a person became engulfed by a completely new situation? Would a sense of personal identity then continue without notable change, or would there be a marked reorganization of personal meanings and values?

Rarely does it happen that there is a really drastic change of a total social world. When it does occur, it is usually not entered into voluntarily, for we avoid situations that would totally disrupt those patterns to which we are accustomed. But there have been forced changes in social environments, and observations of what happens in extreme instances of this sort may be instructive for understanding the relationship of personal identities to social surroundings.

An extreme example was provided by Nazi concentration camps. Bruno Bettelheim, a psychologist and himself a prisoner, made observations about differences between typical old prisoners and new prisoners. These differences indicate something of the nature of the personal adjustment to the camp situation, with the old prisoners showing more complete adjustment. Bettelheim (1943)[5] describes this adjustment as follows:

. . . the main concern of the new prisoners seemed to be to remain intact as a personality and to return to the outer world as the same persons who left it; all their emotional efforts were directed towards this goal. Old prisoners seemed mainly concerned with the problem of how to live as well as possible within the camp. . . . Once this stage was reached . . . [they] were afraid of returning to the outer world. They did not admit it directly, but from their talk it was clear that they hardly believed they would ever return to [it]. . . . They real-ized that they had adapted themselves to the life in the camp and that this process was coexistent with a basic change in their personality. . . .

Old prisoners did not like to be reminded of their families and former friends. When they spoke about them, it was in a very detached way. . . .

The prisoners found themselves in an impossible situation due to the steady interference with their privacy on the part of the guards and other prisoners. So a great amount of aggression accumulated. In new prisoners it vented itself in the way it might have done in the world outside the camp. But slowly prisoners accepted, as expression of their verbal aggression, terms which definitely were taken over from the vocabulary of the Gestapo. From copying the verbal aggressions of the Gestapo to copying their form of bodily aggressions was one more step, but it took several years to make this step. It was not unusual to find old prisoners, when in charge of others, behaving worse than the Gestapo . . . because they considered this the best way to behave toward prisoners in the camp. . . .

Old prisoners who seemed to have a tendency to identify themselves with the Gestapo did so not only in respect to aggressive behavior. They would try to arrogate to themselves old pieces of Gestapo uniforms. If that was not possible, they tried to sew and mend their uniforms so that they would resemble those of the guards. . . . When asked why they did it they admitted that they loved to look like one of the guards. . . . The satisfaction with which some old prisoners enjoyed the fact that, during the twice daily counting of the prisoners, they really had stood well at attention can be explained only by the fact that they had entirely accepted the values of the Gestapo as their own. Prisoners prided themselves of being as tough as the Gestapo members. This identification with their torturers went so far as copying their leisure-time activities. One of

[5] Bruno Bettelheim, "Individual and Mass Behavior in Extreme Situations," *Journal of Abnormal Psychology*, 38 (1943), 417–452. Copyright 1943 by the American Psychological Association. Quotations from this source are reprinted with permission of the publisher.

the games played by the guards was to find out who could stand to be hit longest without uttering a complaint. This game was copied by the old prisoners. . . .

Often the Gestapo would enforce nonsensical rules, originating in the whims of one of the guards. They were usually forgotten as soon as formulated, but there were always some old prisoners who would continue to follow these rules and try to enforce them on others long after the Gestapo had forgotten about them. . . . These prisoners firmly believed that rules set down by the Gestapo were desirable standards of human behavior, at least in the camp situation (pp. 437–450).

12
Social Influence: Review and Discussion

There are two sides to every instance of social influence: (1) the ability to influence and (2) the susceptibility to be influenced. Let us focus first on the susceptibility to be influenced.

KINDS OF DEPENDENCE

We are the servants of whatever we have come to value. Therefore, another person can influence us to the extent that he affects what we value. He may affect what we value in an immediate way, or the influence may be a more long-term matter. What is influenced may be simple actions, or it may involve very complex and long-term commitments.

Something of the range of social influence may be indicated by the following breakdown of the kinds of dependence.

1. *Instrumental dependence:* Another person may be in a position to help us obtain whatever we want. We thus come under this influence in the process of realizing our goals. This is especially apparent when our goals are clearly defined objectives, for which another person's help may also be clearly identified.

2. *Orientational dependence:* Other persons do more than just help us achieve the objects of our wants. They also help us to determine the meanings of these objects and to give shape to our wants. When we refer to such internal influences upon thought and judgment, we may use the concept of orientational dependence, to contrast this with the more externally focused instrumental dependence.

3. *Ego dependence:* Sometimes the very nature of the self is involved in the influence of others. Other persons influence the orientations we have toward our own self by the cues, intended and unintended, that they give off. Such influences may be considered the most internal of all—striking at the very heart of commitments that direct our life. (Logically, ego dependence may be considered as a special kind of orientational dependence, but it is here listed separately for purposes of special emphasis.)

After making such a classification, we must immediately point out that seldom is one of these kinds of dependence found without some degree of another also being present. Instrumental dependence has a

134

tendency to grow into orientational dependence and, if continued for long, into ego dependence as well. And orientational dependence and ego dependence are not apt to be found without some instrumental dependence.

Chapter 9 dealt primarily with social influence stemming from instrumental dependence. Moochie was a leader because he was instrumental in securing the day-to-day satisfactions of his fellow prisoners. Likewise with the street corner groups studied by Whyte, it was out of a fabric of everyday activities that the influence of a person such as Doc came to be exerted. And in the Decatur ladies' choices of fashions or movies, or in marketing or public-affairs preferences, influences were based on quite instrumental foundations. Still, in spite of the instrumental base, generalized leadership shown by a man like Moochie or Doc took on an orientational character as well—to help supply meanings for activities as well as means for goals.

Chapter 10 dealt primarily with influence stemming from orientational dependence. When we are with other people, we depend on them for cues in interpreting what is going on. Sometimes these social cues become the principal elements in judgments of reality, as in the study by Sherif. Even when cues other than social cues may be present—as in studies by Asch, Crutchfield, and Carter and associates—social cues may still exert a significant influence. Of course, such social cues are more impelling under certain conditions than they are under others. Asch showed that the majority effect was strongest (and least felt) when the stimulus situation was most ambiguous. He also showed that the power of a majority was far stronger when united than when divided. And Crutchfield showed that certain kinds of persons are more vulnerable than others to such majority pressures.

Chapter 11 dealt primarily with influence stemming from ego dependence. The cues about reality that we get from others include cues as to the reality of our own selves. Among these are judgments about our own feelings, as the experimental work of Schachter and Singer indicates. These also include the development of a more general concept of self (as suggested by Cooley and Mead) and the sustaining of our self-concept in particular situations (as suggested by Goffman's concept of face).

The most far-reaching social influence is one that becomes part of the self system. But of course we no longer usually recognize this as social influence; rather, it is seen as simply a natural expression of the person. And that it is too. For in a normally socialized person the desires of the individual become merged with the influences of persons around him. And so it is also true that the most common, and the most effective, kind of social influence and control is one that is also self-control.

ALTERNATIVES

The amount of dependence on a social relationship may be formally conceived as a function of the ratio of the total value of the relationship to the value of alternative states of affairs. The value of the relationship (or of alternatives to the relationship) may include instrumental, orientational, and/or ego-supportive bases. Alternatives to a social relationship may include comparable relationships with other persons, but they may also include simply the absence of such a relationship.

From this it is clear that we are influenced by a social relationship not only to the extent that we find it valuable, but also to the extent that alternatives are less valuable.

SIDELIGHT ➤ **The Battle of the Sexes**

Consider the matter of courtship. The more a person is attracted to a relationship, the more he or she will be influenced by it. And the fewer the alternatives available, the greater will be the influence of the loved one. This leads to what Waller and Hill (1951) have called the "principle of least interest," namely: "That person is able to dictate the conditions of association whose interest in the continuation of the affair is least" (p. 191). As they point out, on the subject of falling in love:

If there is too pronounced a difference in the tempo of involvement, there is an abnormally great chance that the relation will be arrested on a level of exploitation, or at least at some point at which the person less involved takes the other person very much for granted. According to the conventional notions of courtship, the man should first become involved and should take the lead in furthering the affair. If the woman is first involved, she should hide this fact from the man in order to prevent him from exploiting her and also to avoid destroying his interest in her as an unsolved problem (pp. 190–191).

But with marriage, this pattern of influence may be drastically changed. If the marriage vows mean anything, they mean that alternatives to the relationship are sharply reduced. This is supposed to create greater mutual dependence, which,

though never the same as romantic love, may mature into another kind of love. But this mutual absence of alternatives also sets the stage for strategies of power that would never work in courtship. In fact, Waller and Hill suggest, power within a marital relationship might often be described according to the "principle of control," namely: "That person controls who is most ruthless." They go on to say that:

In marriage, control often goes to the person who steadily, ruthlessly, and without insight adheres to his own purposes. One dominates by being willing to quarrel before outsiders, by threatening to break up the marriage, by being willing to shatter the rapport and to resist the temptation to be the first to make up . . . (p. 312).

Such ruthless control, however, also has its limitations—even in marriage! For one thing, the value of such a marriage for the dominating spouse is apt to decline with the increasing coolness of the other partner. And for another, not even marriage can eliminate all other social relationships. Imagination (or failing that, perhaps television) can create all kinds of alternatives that, while not a direct challenge to the marriage, may lessen dependence on a dominant spouse. And if things get too bad, a more public kind of disengagement is ultimately possible.

PROMISES AND THREATS

Among mature human beings, social influence very largely occurs through what is said. Often such verbal influence is a matter of deliberate intent. When this is the case, it takes (explicitly or implicitly) two main forms: promises and threats.

A few comments about the advantages and liabilities of these two main forms of deliberate verbal influence should help us to understand the frequency of their use in different kinds of settings.

Threats have one key advantage over promises. When a threat is successfully made, the person making the threat need do no more. If, on the other hand, he tries to exert influence by making a promise, then something will have to be done to fulfill the promise. Therefore, threats are much easier to give than promises—so long as both are effective in creating compliance. When a person is fully in control of a situation, this greater ease in the use of threats yields clear advantages. Under these conditions, threats—whether made explicitly or implicitly —are apt to be used with high frequency.

But there are also liabilities in the use of threats. For one thing, a threat must be believed to be effective. And in order to be believed, threats must be carried out when compliance is not forthcoming. This can be distasteful for all concerned. When a person is in a situation of uncertain authority, a continual need to prove threats may make threatening a very costly matter. (Nations also sometimes experience this problem.)

A second liability of the use of threats is the amount of surveillance they require. When people are threatened, they have to be carefully watched, for they will usually try to hide any degree of noncompliance. With promises it is quite different, for persons ordinarily are only too happy to volunteer evidence of their compliance when important rewards may be so gained. The supervision problem is therefore easier with promises than with threats.

A third liability of the use of threats is that they drive people away. People tend to withdraw from situations in which they are threatened. When such withdrawal is possible, not only may threats prove ineffective, but the person may not be around for less threatening kinds of influence either.

These liabilities of threats may be considerably lessened under certain circumstances. A stable authority structure accepted by all concerned may make it unnecessary for threats to be constantly made or proved (and when made, they can be proved more easily). Concentrating persons into restricted physical settings may make problems of surveillance less difficult. And bars against withdrawal, especially when supported by a general consensus, may help keep persons available to be threatened. These, then, are the three main foundations needed for an effective system of threats (stable authority, convenient surveillance, and bars against withdrawal), and each neutralizes one of the key problems in the use of threats (reliability of the threat, obtaining evidence of compliance, and keeping persons in the threat system).

Examples of settings that have fairly effectively lessened all three of these problems of threats may be seen in prisons, mental hospitals, the army, and traditional schoolrooms. In each of these settings the authority structure is made quite clear, persons are restricted in their movements to maintain maximum surveillance, and there are bars against withdrawal.

The principal work settings of peasant societies also had all of these main characteristics, and modern work settings have tended to maintain two of the three conditions for the effective use of threats. The main change for modern work settings is in the greater ease of movement (persons are not stuck forever with an unsatisfactory work setting), but the authority structure and physical concentration for surveillance remain even today as key ingredients of most places of work.

At one time in the Western world marriage also had all the ingredients for effective control through a threat system. But, alas for would-be patriarchs, the authority structure of the modern family is no longer a clear matter of general social consensus. Also, with the advent of the automobile and mass media of communication, both physical and psychological withdrawal are more possible. But the bars against complete withdrawal and the amount of surveillance still possible within a modern home continue conditions where threats may have greater utility with family members than with persons outside the family—if not so much any more with a spouse, still at least with the children.

Theoretically, the conditions for the effective use of threats can be summed up very briefly as the conditions of high dependence. When the dependence of a person is high—when he has much of value at stake and few if any alternatives—then he is most vulnerable to threats. When dependence is low, then effective influence may require promises in order to create the temporary dependence needed as leverage for social influence.

ABILITY AND VARIABILITY

We have identified one of the three key ingredients of social power: that is, the dependence of a person to be influenced. Two other ingredients are needed to complete the picture of interpersonal power: the resources of the one who exerts influence, and the range of behavior that it is possible for the person influenced to perform.

Resources may be anything that a person has, represents, or is able to give that may be useful to another person. A resource for social influence may be property or other forms of wealth. It may be the control that goes with a position of formal authority. It may consist of special skills. It may be knowledge or access to knowledge. It may be the symbolic representation a person gives of truth, goodness, beauty, power, or prestige. It may be a pleasant appearance, a winning smile, or a willingness to pay attention to others. All of these are resources that at one time or another become useful to others and therefore can be used to exert influence.

Whether or not a particular possession or attribute constitutes a resource for power and influence depends on the particular situation.

Superior physical prowess may be an important basis of influence among Doc's Norton Street gang and in Moochie's prison camp situation, but it would hardly be a resource for influence at a meeting of a corporation's board of directors. Wealth and general social recognition may be more important in such a corporate setting, as well as thorough knowledge about the particular corporation. Thus whether or not a resource creates power for a person depends upon whether or not it is useful to others in that particular setting. If the setting changes so that other things become useful, a person's influence in a group may also change—as Moochie found out on the train to Yokohama.

If resources are to promote power, they must not only be useful; they must also be scarce. If human veracity, charity, and loveliness were all present in this world in unlimited degree, qualities of truth, goodness, and beauty would not add to a person's influence upon others. Rather, like oxygen, these would simply be taken for granted. Only scarce resources (that is, scarce in the sense of being in shorter supply than people would like to make use of) serve as bases of interpersonal power. In this context it is worth noting that certain resources, like wealth and authority, are by their essential nature always scarce; and this makes them likely to contribute to a person's power in a great variety of situations.

Resources, then, create social power when they are both useful to others and in scarce supply. In considering such usefulness and scarcity we must take note of the characteristics not only of the person exerting influence but also of the persons to be influenced and the social setting in which attempts at influencing others may occur. So we come back again to dependence as the natural complement of resources for influence. If an individual's resources are to create influence, others must be dependent on these resources.

A final general factor in social influence is the variability in behavior that it is possible to perform. The greater the range of behavior open to a person, the greater the scope of influence that may be exerted through such a person. Note that we are speaking of the variability of a *person to be influenced* as a factor in the influence to be exerted through him. Variability in the behavior of the person originating the influence may also be a factor in his resources, but that is another matter.

It may be obvious that a person can have greater influence by influencing people who can do more than those who can do less. What is less obvious is that sometimes an individual's own power may be increased by becoming able to do less. This, indeed, sounds contradictory, but it may be seen as a special case of the same general principle.

If a person wants to create the conditions where others will make necessary efforts on his behalf, it is sometimes useful *not* to be able to perform such actions for himself. The variability in behavior of others may thus be used at the same time that the individual's may be restricted. This applies especially when the parties involved are highly interdependent. In such circumstances a person may actually choose to commit himself in such a way as to become unable to perform a needed act, leaving to others responsibility for seeing that it gets done. This

may be present in a young child's frequent protest of "I can't do it."
Thomas C. Schelling (1956) gives an example of a somewhat more
sophisticated use of this principle:

> . . . it has not been uncommon for union officials to stir up ex-
> citement and determination on the part of the membership dur-
> ing or prior to a wage negotiation. If the union is going to insist
> on $2 and expects the management to counter with $1.60, an
> effort is made to persuade the membership not only that the
> management pay $2 but even perhaps that the negotiators them-
> selves are incompetent if they fail to obtain close to the $2. The
> purpose—or rather, a plausible purpose suggested by our analy-
> sis—is to make it clear to the management that the negotiators
> could not accept less than $2 *even if they wished to* because they
> no longer control the members or because they would lose their
> own positions if they tried. In other words, the negotiators re-
> duce the scope of their own authority, and confront the manage-
> ment with the threat of a strike that the union itself cannot
> avert, even though it was the union's own action that eliminated
> its power to prevent the strike (p. 286).

By thus limiting the range of their own behavior, union leaders are
limiting the range of influence that management may exert.

This principle of variability (the more variable one's behavior, the
more one is apt to be influenced by others; and, conversely, the less
variable one's behavior, the more another person's influence may be
neutralized) may also help us understand certain instances of general
disability. If school is a very unsatisfactory place and a young student
wishes to remove himself as much as possible from the influences of
such persons as teachers, a very reasonable solution is to become
dumb. Demands upon a dull student will ordinarily be relaxed. And
when interaction with human beings is threatening and an individual
wishes to withdraw from the influence of other people, then the adoption of rigid and unvarying behavior routines may be very useful. An
extreme case may be seen in the catatonic patient who spends the full
day on his mental hospital ward in the same location and with the
same body position. He presents the rare case of a person who successfully neutralizes essentially all social influence, albeit at a high
personal cost.

IN SUMMARY

To summarize briefly the central principles of social influence presented thus far in this chapter, we may say that a person's influence
upon another increases with (1) his own resources and (2) the other
person's dependence on these resources. Ability to exert influence by
means of other persons also increases with (3) the variability in the
behavior such others can perform. All other points discussed in this
chapter have been built around these three central principles.

A final point should be emphasized that may have been only implicit
in the preceding discussion: social influence is never a one-way street.
It is practically always mutual. A leader does not influence group mem-

bers without at the same time finding his behavior molded by them. A mother does not control her child without in some degree being manipulated in turn. And not even a prison guard is free from the influence of his inmates. If we have seemed to suggest that different persons exert and receive influence, this is only a simplification introduced for purposes of analysis. In real life we are practically always recipients of social influence at the very moment (indeed, perhaps especially at the moment) that we try to work our influence upon others.

AGGRESSION AND INFLUENCE

At least one kind of aggression discussed in Chapter 8 would seem to have important implications for social influence. This is strategic aggression, in which the hurting of others is not in itself an end but is only a means to an end. Most commonly the aim of strategic aggression is social influence. We are now in a better position to analyze the circumstances in which such aggression may actually facilitate influence.

Aggressive behavior will be most likely to exert effective influence when two conditions apply to the target of aggression: (1) he cannot get away, and (2) he is not in a position to return the aggression. Under these conditions an individual's influence may be strengthened by aggressive acts, at least in the short run. Acts of aggression here may serve primarily to demonstrate superior power and to enhance this power, reminding the individual as well as the target of such power. But if either of the two basic conditions is absent, aggression may be self-defeating. If the target can get away, an attempt at aggression may simply drive him further from the aggressor's influence and make him less apt to comply with demands in the future. In other words, he will become less dependent on the relationship and thus less susceptible to its influence. If the target has the strength and will to return the aggression, aggression may be self-defeating as a strategy of influence. Even when the target of aggression may not be able to escape and even if his relative power is less, he may still fight back in one way or another and cause considerable inconvenience for an aggressor—as children have often demonstrated to punitive parents.

Also, it should be kept in mind that disengagement may be psychological as well as physical. Even when a person may not withdraw from the presence of a person who may hurt him, he will be apt to move away in terms of attention and affections. Thus slaves have reacted to heavy authority systems more frequently with laziness than by showing open rebellion. And even in the patriarchal family system, where, by common agreement, the husband was boss and the relationship was not to be broken, husbands who relied too much on force found their wives less willing helpmates than the wives of men who used more gentle persuasion.

From these considerations it would appear that strategic aggression isn't very reliable for stable social influence. Even within a stable authority system where threats may be a common feature, things run most smoothly—as every bureaucrat knows—when force is used sparingly.

Why then is there so much aggression? Much aggression, of course, arises from anger rather than from a careful calculation of outcomes. But aggression is also suggested as a rational recourse. When? Primarily when it is felt that such aggression might drive a person into an authority system in which he might be better influenced. Strategic aggression is most common at the fringes of an authority system (for example, in international conflict), or in an authority system that isn't very effective (for example, in upheavals within a nation, or in their repression).

Here the purpose of the aggression is to drive a person into an authority system where more moderate threats may suffice. In some cases (such as revolutions) the attempt may be made to replace one authority system with another; here the ultimate purpose is the creation of a new authority. In any event, persons caught up in a conflict between rival claims of authority are those who are most apt to suffer from strategic aggression.

SOCIAL INFLUENCE AND ATTITUDES

In the last several chapters it has been emphasized that the most effective social influence concerns whatever a person to be influenced is most dependent upon. Where influence is most significant this includes orientational dependence and ego dependence as well as instrumental dependence. This clearly involves thoughts and feelings, and instances of significant social influence must, therefore, often include changes in thoughts and feelings. This may also be considered under the category of attitude change.

How, more specifically, can we describe the processes of such attitude change? This question will be the general focus of the next four chapters. In our discussion we will not limit attitude change to occasions of direct social influence; it should be apparent that all key generalizations about attitude change can also be applied to identify possibilities for social influence.

part four: ATTITUDES

You tell me whar a man gits his corn pone, and I'll tell you what his 'pinions is.

Mark Twain

Rather dramatic changes in attitudes sometimes do occur. In Chapter 13 ("Conversion") we examine instances of such attitude change as a means of introducing the study of attitudes.

What basic psychological processes may be involved in attitude development and change? Chapter 14 ("Studies of Learning and Association") deals with experimental studies of conditioning and of cognitive consistency that aid in the exploration of this question.

In Chapter 14, however, the role of the person is quite passive. A more active role of the individual in the process of attitude change is explored in Chapter 15 ("Decisions and Dissonance"). We end this chapter with a special emphasis upon the role of commitment in the dynamics of attitudinal adjustments.

Finally, in Chapter 16 ("Attitude Change: Review and Discussion") we integrate what has been learned about attitudes and attitude change. The final theme here will be that of the importance of attitudes in mediating between inner needs and external demands.

13

Conversion

MINNIE MAE[1]

> She was one of 11 children, began dating at 12, and married at 15, having completed only rural elementary school. She and her young husband left Arkansas for lack of jobs and settled in Northwest Town. Her husband took a job as a laborer in a plywood factory. Although the young couple did not join a church, they came from a religious background (Minnie Mae's mother was a Pentecostal lay preacher), and they began attending tent meetings near Northwest Town. During one of these Minnie Mae began speaking in "tongues" and fell into a several-hour trance. After this her husband discouraged church activities. The couple had three children at roughly two-year intervals, and until 1960 Minnie Mae seems to have spent most of her time caring for these children and watching television. She reported tuning in a local channel when she got up in the morning and keeping it on until sign-off at night. In 1958 the couple built a small house in Elm Knoll. Here, in her behavior and conversations with neighbors, she began to reveal severe dissatisfactions in her marriage. She repeatedly complained that her husband only had intercourse with her about once a month, but she also reported being very afraid of getting pregnant again. Furthermore, she wanted to get out and have some fun, go dancing, etc., but her husband only wanted to watch TV and to fish. She wondered if she had let life pass her by because she had been married too young. And, often, she complained about her husband's opposition to fundamentalist religious activities (p. 866).

In her late twenties Minnie Mae came into contact with a group of religious seekers. These were followers of the Divine Precepts, and Minnie Mae became one of them.

THE DIVINE PRECEPTS

The Divine Precepts originated in Korea, where a man named Chang proclaimed himself to be "Lord of the Second Advent." Within a decade

[1] John Lofland and Rodney Stark, "Becoming a World-Saver: A Theory of Conversion to a Deviant Perspective," *American Sociological Review*, 30 (1965), 862–875. Quotations from this source are reprinted with permission of the authors and the American Sociological Association.

and a half he had attracted a following of over five thousand converts in Korea. According to the Divine Precepts, the name by which his teachings came to be known, there was soon to be a great "Restoration of the World" to the conditions of the Garden of Eden.

Chang's teachings were brought to the United States by Miss Yoon-Sook Lee.

> Miss Lee was born and raised in Korea and converted to Chang's cult in 1954 when she was 39. During her early teens she was subject to fits of depression and used to sit on a secluded hilltop and seek spirit contacts. Shortly she began receiving visions and hearing voices—a hallucinatory pattern she was to maintain thereafter. Her adolescent mystical experience convinced her she had a special mission to perform for God and at the age of 19 she entered a Methodist seminary in Japan. She was immediately disenchanted by the "worldly concern" of the seminarians and the training she received, although she stuck out the five-year course. Prior to entering the seminary she had become engrossed in the Spiritualistic writings of Emanuel Swedenborg, who soon began to appear to her in visions. Her estrangement from conventional religious roles was so great that upon graduating from seminary she, alone among her classmates, refused ordination. She returned to Korea at the start of World War II, and by 1945 was professor of social welfare at a denominational university of Seoul. In 1949 the Methodist Board of Missions sent her to a Canadian university for further theological training. There she wrote her thesis on Swedenborg, who continued to visit her in spirit form. In Canada, as in Japan, she was bitterly disappointed by the "neglect of things of the spirit," caused concern among the faculty by constantly hiding to pray and seek visions, and occasionally stole away to Swedenborgian services. Her spirits continued to tell her that she was a religious figure of great importance. Returning to her academic life in Korea, she fell ill with chronic diarrhea and eventually nephritis, both of which resisted all medical treatment. After two years of this, her health was broken and she was completely bedridden. At this time her servant took her to see Chang (p. 865).

Miss Lee became dramatically cured of her afflictions and a follower of the Divine Precepts immediately thereafter. A few years later, in 1959, she arrived in a city in America's Pacific Northwest. Within two years she had gathered five fully committed converts, including Minnie Mae. This group lived together with daily interaction; three converts moved into the same house with Miss Lee, and the other two took up residence in neighboring houses. Soon, however, local opposition led the group to move to another city.

In this other West Coast city the group grew to a following of well over a hundred. Most converts lived in houses and apartments and contributed their wages and salaries to a common treasury. Miss Lee was their full-time leader, and converts gave as much time as possible to enlist further converts and to prepare themselves for the new age, which they believed was soon to dawn.

It is here also that the followers of the Divine Precepts came under the observation of sociologists John Lofland and Rodney Stark. These men professed a personal interest in the faith (but without pretending commitment) and participated in the group for over a year in order to obtain information about it. In the process they also formed conclusions concerning how and why people became caught up in this movement.

CAUSES OF CONVERSION

In their analysis of the process of conversion to the Divine Precepts, Lofland and Stark (1965) divide the conditions for conversion into two main categories: (1) predisposing conditions and (2) situational conditions. The predisposing conditions are those that help to explain an individual's motivation to take a serious interest in such a cause. Given such motivation, the situational conditions are seen as determining whether or not full commitment to the faith actually takes place. Let us examine in some detail the main elements Lofland and Stark saw in each of these two categories.

Primary among the predisposing conditions is the experience of considerable psychic tension. This tension could be derived from many possible sources. Among the sources Lofland and Stark identified in members of this cult were the longing for wealth and prestige, sexual and marital frustrations, disturbing hallucinations, and disfigured personal appearances. These authors further comment:

> From the point of view of an outside observer, however, their circumstances were not extraordinarily oppressive: in the general population, many persons undoubtedly labor under tensions considerably more acute and prolonged. Perhaps the strongest qualitative generalization supported by the data is that pre-converts felt themselves frustrated in their rather diverse aspirations. Most people probably have some type of frustrated aspirations, but pre-converts experienced the tension rather more acutely and over longer periods than most people do (p. 867).

But psychic tension alone was not a sufficient basis for identifying when a person would be predisposed to listen to the message of the Divine Precepts. Those who became converts also had a primarily religious problem-solving orientation in response to their tensions.

Most people do not make a religious orientation this basic. Much more characteristic in the modern world is a psychiatric orientation (in the broad sense that problems are seen as residing in the nature of a self, which may be improved through treatment) or a political orientation (in the broad sense that problems are seen as residing in the organization of society, which may be changed through collective action). Even many people recognized as being religious adopt largely such orientations for problem solving. But for some people an appeal to the supernatural is the central response for personal problem solving. This appeal may be that of a doctrine about external events that will resolve their difficulties (a religious parallel of a political solution) or that of internal spiritual forces that will enable them to overcome personal difficulties (a religious parallel of a psychiatric solution), or a combination of both kinds of faith.

Among those who became converts to the Divine Precepts, as we have said, a religious orientation to solving personal problems was predominant. Other solutions were attempted, but the problems remained. Particular religious answers were tried, but these typically failed to meet their needs fully either. Thus they became religious seekers, vaguely unsatisfied with the religious answers they had obtained. For example:

> I was reared in a Pentecostal church and as a child was a very ardent follower of Christianity. Because of family situations, I began to fall away and search for other meanings in life. This began . . . when I was about 12 years old. From that time on, my life was most of the time an odious existence, with a great deal of mental anguish. These last two years have brought me from church to church trying to find some fusion among them. I ended up going to Religious Science in the morning and fundamentalist in the evening (p. 869).

It was in such a state of "seekership" that most converts had made contact with the Divine Precepts. Typically this occurred simultaneously with a turning point in a life career, such as a change of employment or failure in school. At such turning points both the awareness of past difficulties and the opportunity for a new start were increased. At such turning points in their life careers, converts usually heard the message of the Divine Precepts. Typically they also developed close interpersonal bonds with one or more members of the cult. As one member testifies:

> Early in 1960, after a desperate prayer, which was nothing more than the words, "Father if there is any truth in this world, please reveal it to me," I met [Miss Lee]. This day I desire to never forget. Although I didn't fully understand yet, I desired to unite with her . . . (p. 872).

As Lofland and Stark express this general point:

> The development or presence of some positive, emotional interpersonal response seems necessary to bridge the gap between first exposure to the Divine Precepts message and accepting its truth. That is, persons developed affective ties with the group or some of its members while they still regarded the Divine Precepts perspective as problematic, or even "way out." In a manner of speaking, final conversion was coming to accept the opinions of one's friends (p. 871).

At the same time, extracult attachments are for some reason or other minimized. Most were away from their home communities, with few acquaintances near at hand. When converts were acquainted with nearby persons, none was usually close enough to intervene in such a way as to actively oppose the conversion process.

With all of the above features present, a seeker would become a convert. Sometimes, however, his conversion couldn't be fully trusted. There seemed to be a difference between those who were "total converts," that is, fully accepted as among the faithful, and those who may be considered as only "verbal converts." How might a verbal convert become a total convert and put his life fully at the disposal of the cult? According to Lofland and Stark:

> Such transformations in commitment took place, we suggest, as a result of intensive interaction with Divine Precepts members, and failed to result when such interaction was absent.
>
> Intensive interaction means concrete, daily, and even hourly accessibility to Divine Precepts members, which implies physical proximity to total converts. Intensive exposure offers an opportunity to reinforce and elaborate an initial, tentative assent to the Divine Precepts world view, and in prolonged association the perspective "comes alive" as a device for interpreting the moment-to-moment events in the convert's life.
>
> The Divine Precepts doctrine has a variety of resources for explicating the most minor everyday events in terms of a cosmic battle between good and evil spirits, in a way that placed the convert at the center of this war. Since all Divine Precepts interpretations pointed to the imminence of the end, to participate in these explications of daily life was to come more and more to see the necessity of one's personal participation as a totally committed agent in this cosmic struggle.
>
> Reminders and discussion of the need to make other converts, and the necessity of supporting the cause in every way, were the main themes of verbal exchanges among the tentatively accepting and the total converts, and, indeed, among the total converts themselves. Away from this close association with those already totally committed, one failed to "appreciate" the need for one's transformation into a total convert.
>
> In recognition of this fact, the Divine Precepts members gave highest priority to attempts to persuade verbal converts (even the merely interested) to move into the cult's communal dwellings. . . .
>
> Thus, verbal conversion and even a resolution to reorganize one's life for the Divine Precepts is not automatically translated into total conversion. One must be intensively exposed to the group supporting these new standards of conduct. Divine Precepts members did not find proselytizing, the primary task of total converts, very easy, but in the presence of persons who reciprocally supported each other, such a transformation of one's life became possible. Persons who accepted the truth of the doctrine, but lacked intensive interaction with the core group, remained partisan spectators, who played no active part in the battle to usher in God's kingdom (pp. 873–874).

In summary, we may review the main conditions for conversion to the Divine Precepts and total dedication to them. Lofland and Stark identify three predisposing conditions and four situational contingencies. Where all of these were present, conversion was accomplished. Where any one of these was absent, conversion was never complete. These seven necessary and (when taken together) sufficient conditions may be summarized as follows (following closely Lofland and Stark, p. 874).

For conversion a person must: (1) experience enduring, acutely felt tensions, (2) within a religious problem-solving perspective, (3) which combine to lead him to define himself as a religious seeker. (These are the three main predisposing conditions of conversion. The characteristic situational conditions follow.) (4) Encountering the Divine Precepts at a turning point in his life, (5) the potential convert forms (or already has) an affective personal bond with one or more converts, (6) under conditions where extracult attachments are absent or neutralized, and (7) if he is to become a total convert, he is exposed to intensive interaction with faithful followers of the cult.

POLITICAL PERSUASION AT BENNINGTON

Conversion to a faith such as that of the Divine Precepts is rather rare. One of the reasons it is rare is the ultimacy of such a commitment. It is a commitment to this gospel as the absolute truth and, for a total convert, a surrender of all of one's life to this cause. Rarely is attitude change so drastic.

Much more common are changes in the degrees of our commitments to certain viewpoints. This probably applies to most changes in religious views for people whose religious seeking is less intense than those converts characterized above. And in political attitudes, perhaps even more than religious views, such gradual change is characteristic. In this section we will examine a study of political attitude change in a college setting. The college is Bennington College, a girls' school in New England. The time is the 1930s. And the investigator is Theodore Newcomb (1943).[2]

Bennington College was opened shortly before as a college for very carefully selected female students. It was geared to what was considered at the time to be a progressive educational philosophy, and its 250 students had to pass rigorous entrance requirements. Most students were from relatively wealthy families; however, about one-fourth of them worked to help pay for their education.

The college was located on a hilltop four miles from Bennington, Vermont, then a town of ten thousand. As most needs were supplied at the college itself, students seldom went to town. They lived in houses of about twenty students, all ate in a common dining room, and nearly all took part in the same extracurricular activities. Especially interesting at Bennington were the extent of student-faculty relationships and the degree of responsibility given students. Reports Newcomb:

> Student-faculty relationships are, in general, friendly and informal. Most classroom groups include only six or eight students. Classes are conducted as workshops, studios, laboratories, or as discussion groups far more frequently than by the lecture method. Every student does part of her work, and often a considerable part, in individual conference with an instructor. Other community arrangements, mentioned later, tend to further an atmosphere of camaraderie. The total community numbers only

[2] Theodore M. Newcomb, *Personality and Social Change: Attitude Formation in a Student Community.* New York: Holt, Rinehart and Winston, 1943. Copyright 1943 by Theodore M. Newcomb. Quotations from this source are adapted and reprinted with permission of the publisher.

about 300 individuals, and since most of them spend most of their time in very limited environs, formal sorts of arrangements would be difficult to maintain, even if they seemed desirable.

Community government is the responsibility of student-faculty committees. Faculty members, however, are greatly outnumbered; while their advice is apt to count heavily, they hold no veto powers, and decisions are made by majority vote. Several decisions of which faculty members disapproved are on record. General policies were laid down by these committees, early in the history of the college, according to which a maximum amount of responsibility was allotted to each student for her own conduct. It was not found necessary, for example, to limit the number of evenings in a week on which a student might leave the college grounds, or to state a fixed hour at which she must return, but it was found necessary to devise a rigorous system of signing out, so that the whereabouts of each student were known (p. 7).

It is here that Theodore Newcomb came as a teacher in 1935, and he proceeded to use the student population for several years of attitude research. It should be noted that this was during the middle of America's New Deal period.

The Nature of Attitudes

THEORETICAL POINTER

An attitude is a relatively enduring evaluative orientation toward some object of experience.

Attitudes typically have three components: (1) cognitions, (2) feelings, and (3) action tendencies. Cognitions and feelings are the internal expressions of an attitude; action tendencies are the external expressions.

Attitudes always include evaluations of positive or negative character. These pro or con tendencies are present in cognitions, in feelings, and in action tendencies. Although there are other features of an attitude that might be measured, this positive or negative character is what is most often measured in attitude research.

Attitudes have direction. They are always toward something—toward a specific thing or toward a class of objects. Objects of attitudes may be persons, physical objects, or abstract ideas. These typically are objects of experience with some recurring importance to the person concerned.

Persons tend toward a consistency between the various components of an attitude, especially between internal and external expressions. This means that a person selects behavior, insofar as the structure of the situation allows, that fits his internal attitudes. It also means that when his external behavior is at variance with the internal expression of an attitude, the internal thoughts and feelings tend to change to fit what he does.

Attitudes may be broadly conceived as basic tools of adjustment whereby a person organizes his behavior, both internal and external, to meet the recurrent features of his environment.

One of the attitude scales used by Newcomb was a scale to measure a tendency toward liberalism or conservatism in political and economic attitudes. Liberalism was generally expressed in terms favorable to innovations along New Deal lines, and conservatism was viewed as a tendency to resist such measures and to defend the status quo. This scale was called the P.E.P. scale (after "Political and Economic Progressivism"); however, it should be kept in mind that a high score represents conservatism rather than liberalism.

METHODOLOGICAL POINTER

Attitude Scales

An attitude scale is more than just a set of questions. It is rather a set of questions designed to give a measure of attitudes. Usually the purpose is to measure a *single dimension* of attitudes.

One question that is immediately raised in such an attempt is that of the unit of measurement. How can we devise units of measurement that form meaningful intervals on an attitude scale? Without having standard intervals on the scale there can be little meaning in comparing attitude scores.

There are two main ways that persons who develop attitude scales attempt to standardize the intervals they measure. One of these, the Thurstone-type scale, is constructed by judges attempting to give an objective assessment of the degree to which various possible items express favorable or unfavorable attitudes toward the subject in question. A large number of judges is given a great variety of attitude statements on the subject. They are asked to rate each item. They give not their own attitude, but rather how favorable or unfavorable is the view expressed by the item. After the judges have made their ratings, the investigator then puts together his attitude scale. An item's scale value is based on the judges' ratings. The investigator is careful to include items for which there is wide agreement among judges concerning location on the scale. He also is careful to select items representing various points on the scale.

A somewhat different procedure is that of the Likert-type scale, and the P.E.P. scale used by Newcomb was this kind of scale. In the Likert procedure a large number of items are given to judges to indicate their own attitudes. A typical procedure in this type of scale construction is for judges to choose a response from the following alternatives: strongly agree, agree, undecided, disagree, and strongly disagree. Answers are weighted 5, 4, 3, 2, and 1, respectively, and scores are obtained for each judge on each item, and also a combined score is obtained for all items. A small number of these items that show a high degree of consistency with total scores are then finally selected. In the final form these items are presented, and respondents are asked to choose one of these responses: strongly agree, agree, uncertain, disagree, or strongly disagree. These are counted 5, 4, 3, 2, and 1 (or 1, 2, 3, 4, and 5, for items expressing the negative form of the attitude), and these weights constitute the intervals for attitude measurement.

Although attitude scales produced by the Thurstone and Likert procedures do not produce standardized intervals as precise as those we are accustomed to for physical measurements such as weight or distance, they do provide at least rough units of comparative measurement on a particular attitudinal dimension.

Not only is it important to have an

attitude scale reflect meaningful intervals for measurement, it is also desirable to have evidence that the various items are in fact measuring the same attitude. We call this a measure of the unidimensionality of the scale. An attitude scale that has a clear meaning is ordinarily assumed to be of a single dimension. Guttman (1950) has pioneered in techniques for scale analysis, known as the scalogram method, designed to measure whether or not a scale is actually unidimensional. According to Guttman's technique, a measure is obtained of the extent to which an entire pattern of responses may be predicted from knowledge of only the scale score. A very high degree of such prediction indicates that the scale approaches measuring a single dimension.

One of the most interesting patterns in Newcomb's data is the change that tended to occur for Bennington students during their college years. Consider the class of 1939. As Table 11 indicates, this class became more progressive in political and economic attitudes with each year of college.

TABLE 11   THE INCREASING PROGRESSIVISM OF THE CLASS OF 1939

	Mean Scores, P.E.P. Scale, for Class of 1939, Bennington College
Fall 1935	74.5
Fall 1936	68.5
Fall 1937	64.1
Fall 1938	63.2

NOTE: A high score represents conservative attitudes and a low score represents progressivism.
SOURCE: Newcomb (1943), p. 23.

Another measure of this shift is indicated by different attitudes of freshmen and seniors during the same year. A dramatic example of this came in a poll of preferences for presidential candidates in the fall of 1936. The preferences of a sample of fifty-two freshmen are given in Table 12.

TABLE 12   PERCENT PREFERENCE BY FRESHMEN AND THEIR PARENTS FOR PRESIDENTIAL CANDIDATES, 1936

	Students	*Parents*
Landon (Republican)	62	66
Roosevelt (Democrat)	29	26
Thomas (Socialist) or Browder (Communist)	9	7

SOURCE: Newcomb (1943), p. 28.

Figures are also given to indicate students' reports of the preferences of their parents. It can be seen in Table 12 that freshmen had a pattern of preferences very close to those of their parents. It may also be noted that both freshmen and their parents were predominantly Republican.

However, the pattern for upper-class students was rather different. This is given for fifty-two juniors and seniors in Table 13. Parents of upper-class women (shown by Table 13) represent a range of preferences not much different from parents of freshmen (Table 12). It is unlikely that precollege political attitudes differed much between the freshmen and the upperclassmen. But figures shown for these two groups of students (Tables 12 and 13) certainly do show differences. Most freshmen supported Landon, whereas most juniors and seniors preferred Roosevelt. The decline of pro-Landon sentiment with year in college (62 percent to 15 percent) is especially dramatic, as is the increase in Socialist or Communist sentiment (9 percent to 30 percent).

TABLE 13   PERCENT PREFERENCE BY JUNIORS AND SENIORS AND
             THEIR PARENTS FOR PRESIDENTIAL CANDIDATES, 1936

	Students	*Parents*
Landon (Republican)	15	60
Roosevelt (Democrat)	54	35
Thomas (Socialist) or Browder (Communist)	30	4

SOURCE: Newcomb (1943), p. 28.

Such evidence would appear to indicate rather strongly that students became more liberal during their years at Bennington College (at least during the 1930s). But how permanent was this attitude change? In 1939 Newcomb made a follow-up study of those who had graduated or withdrawn from Bennington. Selected results are given in Table 14.

TABLE 14   MEAN P.E.P. SCORES OF FORMER STUDENTS

	Last Score in College	*1939 Score*
Students with 1 or 2 years at Bennington	70.0	76.4
Students with 3 or 4 years at Bennington	62.6	61.9

SOURCE: Adapted from Newcomb (1943), p. 77.

Two things seem to be shown by Table 14. One apparent result is that the students who left Bennington earlier tended to be more conservative. Another feature of Table 14 is the difference in stability of attitudes of the two groups. Those who went through college at Bennington tended to maintain about the same degree of liberalism after they left, whereas those who dropped out after one or two years became increasingly conservative after leaving.

That the liberalizing tendency of Bennington lasted for many years has also been shown by a follow-up study (Newcomb, Koenig, Flacks, and Warwick, 1967). Twenty-five years later the women who had been Bennington students in the 1930s still maintained relatively liberal political attitudes.

We have seen enough evidence to suggest that Bennington College in the 1930s had a predominantly liberalizing influence upon students' political and economic attitudes. But why? Was it a matter of faculty influence? Was it an adolescent reaction against parental views? Was it the particular spirit of the 1930s? Or what?

WHY THE CHANGE AT BENNINGTON?

Although the particular conditions of attitude change at Bennington College in the 1930s are quite different from those of the converts to the Divine Precepts, we may again identify among the factors of attitude change both predisposing conditions and situational conditions. Newcomb's analysis makes clear that the particular situations to be found at Bennington were especially productive of attitude change but also that predispositions of different persons led them to be affected in different ways by these conditions.

What was it about the college that gave Bennington such a potential for attitude change? First, it may be noted that attitude change had little to do with academic courses of study. Reports Newcomb:

> There was a slight tendency for those initially least conservative to choose their major work in Social Studies, and for those initially most conservative to major in Science or Music. These initial differences increased slightly during three or four years of college experience. But the important influences making for attitude change were clearly of a community-wide rather than of an academic-major sort (p. 148).

We may recall the relative isolation of the college and the high degree of interaction within it. "It was," as Newcomb has pointed out, "not only a highly integrated community, but its members always referred to it by precisely that term. No phrase was more constantly on our lips than 'the college community'" (p. 8). It is in the nature of this community that the primary basis of attitude change could be found. Newcomb's main conclusion was that "nonconservative attitudes are developed at Bennington primarily by those who are both capable and desirous of cordial relations with their fellow community members" (pp. 148–149). He goes on to summarize the evidence for this:

> The most substantial evidence for this conclusion is the close relationship between attitude scores and prestige, whether the latter is measured in terms of desirability as a friend or of worthiness to be considered a college representative. In two successive years, and in each of four college classes, the group chosen most frequently had least conservative attitudes; those not chosen at all had most conservative attitudes; and the conservatism of those classified as intermediate increased directly with decrease in prestige. It is also of considerable interest that this same relationship is found, though in lesser degree, between prestige as juniors or seniors and attitudes as freshmen. Thus we see that those who are later to achieve considerable prestige have less conservative attitudes, as just-entered freshmen, than those who are later to achieve little or no prestige....

A study of friendship groupings reveals that those chosen as friends tend to be less conservative than those who choose them; the hierarchy of friendship-desirability is directly related to nonconservatism. The nonconservatives are a more cohesive group than the conservatives; the former tend to choose each other, and to be chosen by the latter. It is also of considerable interest that the only freshmen who have much prestige are extremely nonconservative. Altogether, the evidence clearly suggests that social attitudes are an important component of whatever bonds there are that make for friendships in this community.

Reputation for active community participation is also closely related to less conservative attitudes, while reputation for critical or negativistic attitudes toward the community is commonly associated with greater conservatism. The latter finding is of particular significance in view of the common assumption, in many colleges, that it is the "liberals" or "radicals" who are most community-negativistic. Lesser conservatism is also associated with reputation for energy and enthusiasm, while greater conservatism is associated with reputation for absorption in extra-college social life. Most significant of all, perhaps, is the fact that nearly all of those reputedly much interested in public affairs turn out to be those whose attitude scores are highly nonconservative. Such an interest, in this community, is apparently assumed to be identified with the holding of nonconservative attitudes (pp. 149–150).

That the impact of Bennington College was not the same for all students is well illustrated by two students whom we shall call Mary and Jane. Mary is typical of many who showed a clear change in political attitudes during college, and Jane represents those who showed little change. Their attitude scores on entrance were about the same, but during four years at Bennington, Mary became considerably more liberal while Jane remained conservative. During their senior year both these girls were interviewed. Mary responded, in part, as follows:

I've changed a lot since coming here, but I'm not revolutionized. A year or two ago I was pretty scared at how much I had changed, but now I guess I've swung part way back, or else I've become more used to myself. I've developed an attitude toward attitudes. I believe in acting on your present attitudes, but realizing that they are tentative. I met a whole body of new information my sophomore year. I took a deep breath and plunged. I became much less conservative, then swung part way back, then found more evidence for the new opinions, and am more liberal again. I was teased and criticized at home for my extreme opinions. My father criticizes me for lack of experience, and I him for the limited nature of his experience. . . . When I came here I decided to make up for the shortcomings of my previous school life. I had put sports and work above personal contacts. I had put leadership above group membership. I always wanted to be head, though I tried not to dominate. In previous schools I wanted terribly to be prominent, and I wasn't too successful. I didn't make a secret club that was very important to me. This was partly because I wouldn't play up to people.

On coming here I wanted to make good socially, whether I was leader or not, and I decided that the way to do it was to be nice to people whether you really like them or not, and that this wasn't really hypocritical . . . (pp. 98–99).

In contrast we have these comments from Jane:

I'm more to the side of not changing at all since I came here. My biggest change, I guess, is realizing how conventional my family is. I spent my first two years trying to fit Bennington to my pattern, and now I realize you can't do it. Now I can see my teacher's point of view at least part of the time. When I was on the ———— Committee I discovered how extreme my views were, but I still think Progressive Education needs more external discipline. . . . As to public affairs, I'm just as uninterested as ever, and really less well informed than when I came, because then I could at least echo my family. What opinions I had before have been neutralized. I'm still as conservative as my family, who think Roosevelt is *really* insane, but I haven't their strength of conviction. I think I'm a pretty typical student that way: most students lose what opinions they had and don't replace them with anything. But I wasn't typical in one respect: I was one of a group of about 20 freshmen who were wild—we smoked, drank, swore, and everything. About half of us, including me, got over it. . . . I guess, after seeing my scores, that I'm not so typical after all. Probably I was judging from my own crowd, who just aren't interested. My lack of change you'll have to put down to lack of interest. It couldn't be a general resistance to what is new, because after a while I got to like modern art and modern music which are so prevalent around here. That makes it look as if I had built up some sort of resistance to the political ideas you get around here, but that isn't the case; it's just laziness. I read enormously as a child; then at 13 or 14 I got intellectual and attacked learned tomes. Then I reacted against it. Now I hate textbooks, and never read voluntarily except fiction, and little of that . . . (p. 99).

It is also interesting to note how Mary and Jane were thought of by other students. When other students selected phrases that they believed described Mary, two or more selected the following: "absorbed in community affairs," "absorbed in public affairs," "anxious for college positions," "influenced by community codes," "influenced by crowd enthusiasms," "influenced by faculty authority," and "enthusiastic college supporter." Corresponding selections describing Jane were: "resists faculty authority," "absorbed in college work," "critical of educational policies," "critical of faculty," and "critical of student committees."

By and large, Newcomb found the strongest liberalizing tendencies of college upon persons who had personality patterns predisposing them to be sensitive to participation in social life and to work cooperatively with other people. Those who did not become more liberal in their attitudes tended to be either much more self-absorbed and less aware of the social world around them, or else aware of this broader community but reacting against its pressures.

HOW TYPICAL?

How typical is Newcomb's Bennington College study of the impact of college upon social attitudes? Does it show essentially what goes on at all colleges? Or is Bennington no more typical of most colleges than the Divine Precepts is typical of most religious groups?

Bennington was in many ways not a typical college at all. It was a small school, physically isolated, with an unusual degree of both student power and faculty-student interaction. Students expected a nontraditional education, and faculty members were nearly all progressive in their attitudes toward public issues. All of these factors provided an unusually favorable climate for political liberalization.

When Newcomb did the study at Bennington in the late 1930s, he also collected comparable data from two other colleges. In both schools he found a greater tendency for upperclassmen to be more liberal than freshmen, but the differences were not nearly so great as at Bennington.

But that was in the 1930s. By the late 1950s Newcomb's evidence concerning Bennington had begun to look much more unusual. After his review of the literature on the impact of college upon student attitudes and values, Jacob (1957) found that most colleges do not have a general liberalizing effect. "When all is said and done," Jacob concluded, "the value changes which seem to occur in college and set the college alumni apart from others are not very great, at least for most students at most institutions" (p. 20).

By the 1970s there was a much stronger impression of fundamental attitude change at American colleges. Yankelovich (1972) examined survey data and concluded that a great cultural revolution was indeed taking place on campus. A "new naturalism" was seen in the making among the present generation of college students. Perhaps. But it is also likely that colleges generally only reflect and, sometimes, accentuate the cultural trends already apparent in the larger society. If the late 1970s should be dominated generally by a more conservative mood than that characterizing the start of the decade, we can expect that colleges too will be less noted for producing fundamental attitude change.

14
Learning and Association

We saw in the previous chapter that people sometimes show a rather profound attitude change within a few months or years. In the study of Lofland and Stark it was a reorganization of religious attitudes to allow commitment to the Divine Precepts. In the study by Newcomb it was a reorganization of political attitudes to support New Deal measures. In both cases, furthermore, we can identify some common influences behind attitude change.

Both the religious converts and the Bennington students were influenced by information received. People did not become followers of the Divine Precepts who did not receive information about these teachings, and Bennington students would not have changed political attitudes without hearing and reading about the events of the 1930s. But such attitude change was not simply a result of receiving new information. Other influences were also at work.

Most significant among these other influences were the immediate social situation and the personality of the person concerned. The people received their information in a particular social setting. First let us note the situation of the individuals who became religious converts. If their social situation was ambiguous, if they were temporarily removed from groups of past influence, and/or if friendship with a follower of the Divine Precepts seemed to be developing—under such situations they were much more likely to accept the Divine Precepts. Likewise, Bennington students who had a strong involvement in the college community were most apt to show marked change toward more progressive political attitudes. But personality predispositions were also involved as filters for attitude change. The Divine Precepts were not accepted if a person did not already have a religious problem-solving orientation; and political liberalization appeared most apt to occur in those Bennington students with strong interests in social participation.

But what exactly goes on when a person with a strong potential for attitude change is exposed to new information? Granted that his personality and his social situation may be key determinants, how precisely do they have their impact on the way he receives a message?

A preliminary answer would be to say that attitudes are learned responses. And, likewise, attitude change is a matter of new learning. Personality and social situation are key factors determining the general drift of such new learning. But precisely how does this new learning take place? What are the fundamental psychological principles in this process?

ATTITUDES AS CONDITIONED RESPONSES

If attitudes are learned responses, presumably the processes of attitude development and attitude change reflect basic laws of learning. If this is so, experimental evidence should be easy to obtain. Let us examine a study by Staats, Staats, and Heard (1960) to search for such evidence. They present their research as an examination of the process through which adoption of ready-made attitudes occurs, and their basic hypothesis is that attitudes are conditioned responses.

THEORETICAL POINTER

The Conditioned Response

Ivan Pavlov (1849–1936), Russian physiologist and psychologist, pioneered in the study of conditioned responses (or, as he called them, *conditioned reflexes*). According to Pavlov, learning takes place because of the contiguity of stimulus and response. It is because of previous associations connecting stimulus and response that an animal makes the kind of responses that he does. The nature of these previous associations may be summarized in terms of the concepts of unconditioned stimulus (US), unconditioned response (UR), conditioned stimulus (CS), and conditioned response (CR).

The original response an animal makes to a particular kind of stimulus is an unconditioned response. If, however, another stimulus becomes associated with this "natural" stimulus-response connection, the animal will tend to generalize his original response (UR) to the new stimulus. Then with the new stimulus, and in the absence of the old stimulus, the same or similar response may be elicited (now CR).

This may be illustrated by a typical Pavlovian experiment. A hungry dog naturally salivates (UR) when food is presented. This may be used as the basis for conditioning. The dog is presented with food and at the same time a buzzer sounds. After a number of times with the food and buzzer associated together, the buzzer alone is presented. Now with only the buzzer as a stimulus (CS), the dog salivates (CR). We may say that the dog has now been conditioned to give the response of salivation to the stimulus of the buzzer.

The process can be continued into *higher-order conditioning*. Once the dog has been conditioned to respond to the buzzer with salivation, a bell may be sounded at the same time as the buzzer. After the bell is sounded with the buzzer a number of times, the bell may be sounded alone. Then the bell, which previously brought forth no such response, now (as a CS) brings forth salivation (CR).

What we have described so far is sometimes called *classical conditioning* to distinguish it from the *operant (or instrumental) conditioning* that has more recently become a popular subject of experimentation. In classical conditioning the linkage of stimuli with each other preceding the response is emphasized, whereas in operant conditioning the emphasis is upon the linkage of a response with associated reinforcement. These two approaches represent different experimental traditions. One is symbolized by Pavlov and his hungry dogs, and the other by B. F. Skinner and his "Skinner box" in which the supply of a reward such as food is made automatically contingent on particular behaviors of the animal. In one tradition (classical conditioning) the focus of experimental attention is largely on the stimulus side of the stimulus-response connection, whereas in the other tradition (operant conditioning) the focus is on the response side. For giving a full explanation of the formation of conditioned responses, however, these two traditions are probably more complementary than competing. Both emphasize an automatic association of stimuli and responses as the basis of conditioning.

But how can we test the idea that attitudes develop as conditioned responses? Let us see how this was attempted by Staats, Staats, and Heard in their report titled "Attitude Development and Ratio of Reinforcement."

One hundred and fourteen subjects were used, thirty-eight for each of three planned treatments. Treatments planned were those of (1) 100 percent reinforcement, (2) 50 percent reinforcement, and (3) 0 percent reinforcement. The use of the term reinforcement may be a bit misleading, since there is no specific reward involved in the experimental design. The study actually represents a classical conditioning design, not an operant conditioning model (as might be inferred by the different reinforcement treatments). The reinforcement, as we shall immediately see, is simply a matter of the pairing of stimuli.

Two types of stimuli were used: words presented orally by the experimenter (with the meanings of these words assumed to be conditioned by past experience), and nonsense syllables presented visually by slide projector. Each word was presented only once by the experimenter, and subjects were asked to repeat each word immediately after the experimenter pronounced it. A nonsense syllable was shown on the screen for five seconds during the period that the spoken word was presented and repeated. Four nonsense syllables, presented in random order, were each used several times. The nonsense syllables were YOF, XEH, LAJ, and QUG. In this design the nonsense syllables are to be the conditioned stimuli, to be conditioned by their association with the words presented orally.

In the treatment identified as 100 percent reinforcement, YOF was always paired with words of positive evaluative meaning and XEH was always paired with negative words. For the 50 percent reinforcement treatment, this was done for only half the trials, with neutral words used on the other trials. For the 0 percent reinforcement treatment, neutral words were used for all pairings with YOF and XEH. For all treatments the other two nonsense syllables (LAJ and QUG) were paired with words of nonsystematic meaning.

When these conditioning trials were over, subjects were given a questionnaire that included requests for rating the pleasantness or unpleasantness of the nonsense syllables used.

If the assumptions of conditioning are to hold true, what do we expect to be the results of this experiment? Which of the nonsense

syllables would be given pleasant ratings, and which unpleasant ratings? In the reinforcement groups YOF was associated with positive
words, and XEH was associated with negative words. We would therefore expect YOF to build up more pleasant associations than XEH. We
would not expect this from the 0 percent reinforcement group, for
here YOF and XEH (as well as QUG and LAJ) were associated with
evaluatively neutral words. A further expectation would be that the
100 percent reinforcement subjects would show a stronger conditioning effect than the 50 percent reinforcement subjects.

   This is exactly the pattern of results obtained by Staats, Staats,
and Heard. Both 50 percent and 100 percent reinforcement treatments
showed significant conditioning effects, with the 100 percent group
showing the strongest effect. This led the investigators to conclude
that this

> supports the conception that attitudes are responses by showing
> that attitudes possess another of the functional properties of a
> response. The conditioning of attitudes was consistent with basic
> research on acquisition of responses: there was stronger atti-
> tudinal response acquisition under continuous reinforcement
> than under partial reinforcement (p. 345).

   Although not studied in this particular experiment, there is another
point worth making about the difference between continuous reinforcement (here at least suggested by the 100 percent treatment) and partial
reinforcement (here represented by the 50 percent treatment). Once
developed, learning under partial reinforcement tends to persist longer
than learning under continuous reinforcement. In the terms of learning theorists, learning with partial reinforcement shows greater "resistance to extinction"—even though it may be more slowly learned
than learning under continuous reinforcement. Ease of learning is not
always accompanied by persistence of learning.

   From their theory of attitudes as conditioned responses these
investigators also infer differences in effectiveness between one-sided
communications and two-sided arguments. This is a question frequently
faced by communicators in planning a persuasive message. Should they
make a single-minded plea, or should the message make some attempt
to incorporate opposing arguments? Staats, Staats, and Heard consider
one-sided communications to be instances of continuous reinforcement,
with all the good images associated with the conclusions of the message.
On the other hand, two-sided communications represent an instance of
partial reinforcement, with only some of the good images associated
with the conclusions intended for the message. They therefore reason
that one-sided communications should generally (other things equal)
have a stronger initial effect than two-sided arguments due to the more
continuous reinforcement of one-sided messages. But two-sided arguments, by carrying the more durable impact of partial reinforcement,
should be more resistant to change once they are learned. Experimental
evidence and field studies can both be cited to support these generalizations.

   A final point may be raised about this study. In their results,

Staats, Staats, and Heard found that females generally showed stronger conditioning effects than did males. But why? The investigators do not know. They suggest it is possible that the words used as the unconditioned stimuli (words such as *gift, love,* and *honest* as opposed to *trouble, criminal,* and *sour*) may have had different meanings for males than they did for females. Or perhaps females generally show more facility for verbal learning than do males. Does the reader have another hypothesis?

THE FRAGILE REPUTATION OF PROFESSOR SAMUELS

There is at least one major objection that might be raised against the procedures of Staats, Staats, and Heard. They used meaningless nonsense syllables as stimuli to be associated with words. They saw this as an advantage; such nonsense syllables would not have previous meanings to bias the results. But critics would say that it is precisely such other meanings that are the crucial features of attitude development. Attitudes are developed not about utterly meaningless things, but about things that have meanings. To show that laws of simple conditioning apply to emerging meanings about essentially meaningless objects may tell us very little about attitude dynamics more generally. What if the conditioning treatments dealt with more meaningful social objects? Would the same kind of conditioning through automatic generalization then apply?

To help us explore these questions, let us examine an experiment by Percy H. Tannenbaum (1966). For this experiment two hundred subjects were obtained among male high school students taking a series of tests at a summer military camp. In the course of their program they read materials regarding a number of subjects, including a report of an ostensible symposium at the 1963 convention of the American Psychological Association dealing with "new educational procedures." The views of a fictitious person, Professor Walter E. Samuels of the University of California, were here represented. Professor Samuels commented separately about two subjects: teaching machines and Spence learning theory. Half an hour later (following other unrelated testing), subjects were given another message about teaching machines. This was represented as an Associated Press article dealing with "a comprehensive report on teaching machines from the U.S. Office of Education." Still later, measurements were made of attitudes toward teaching machines, Spence learning theory, and Professor Samuels.

The two hundred subjects were divided into eight treatment groups, based on all of the various possible combinations of positive or negative messages. In half of these treatment groups Professor Samuels was represented as favorable to teaching machines. Subjects read that

> Professor Samuels, a strong proponent of teaching machines, praised the use of teaching machines for instructional purposes in no uncertain terms. He hailed teaching machines as "the most significant single contribution of the behavioral sciences in the field of education" (p. 494).

In the other treatments, in contrast, Professor Samuels was presented as a strong opponent of teaching machines, attacking them as a "most pernicious influence on the entire educational system and a source of shame for behavioral sciences."

This symposium, which "caused quite a stir" and contained "considerable debate," also represented Professor Samuels's views on Spence learning theory. In half of the treatments (varied to include treatments both favorable and unfavorable toward teaching machines) Professor Samuels applauded the theory:

> At the same time, Professor Samuels also expressed himself as strongly in favor of the Spence Learning Theory. Known as a vigorous supporter of the Spence Theory, he called it "the most compelling explanation of the learning process yet presented" (pp. 494–495).

In the other half of the treatments Professor Samuels expressed himself against this theory, which he called "a veritable hodgepodge of unfounded notions with no meaningful basis."

Finally, the article ostensibly reporting the U.S. Office of Education's conclusions about teaching machines had two forms. One form was predominantly favorable toward teaching machines, and the other was largely unfavorable. The favorable form was given to half the treatment groups (including groups representing all combinations of Professor Samuels's reported views), and the unfavorable form was given to the other half.

The various possible treatment combinations are presented in Table 15. All of these eight treatments were used in Tannenbaum's study.

TABLE 15 EXPERIMENTAL DESIGN OF TANNENBAUM'S STUDY

Professor Samuels's Attitude		Later Communication Regarding Teaching Machines
Toward Teaching Machines	Toward Spence Theory	
positive	positive	positive
positive	negative	positive
negative	positive	positive
negative	negative	positive
positive	positive	negative
positive	negative	negative
negative	positive	negative
negative	negative	negative

SOURCE: Adapted from Tannenbaum (1966).

Later a series of attitude measures captured final impressions, which, when compared with measures taken before the experiment, gave an indication of attitude change. Let us examine in turn the results for (1) attitudes toward teaching machines, (2) attitudes toward Professor Samuels, and (3) attitudes toward Spence learning theory.

We would expect that the strongest experimental influence upon attitudes toward teaching machines would come from the U.S. Office of

Education report. Not only was it the most authoritative, but it also had much more to say about teaching machines than did Professor Samuels. We expect then that in Table 16 the results of the fourth column could best be predicted from the treatments indicated by the third column. And this is in fact confirmed by the experimental results; the pattern of these two columns is precisely the same. Positive change in attitudes toward teaching machines was registered in those treatments where the Office of Education report was favorable, and negative change was registered where the report was unfavorable. Furthermore, the statistical results for this relationship were the strongest results in the experiment. This is precisely what Tannenbaum wanted, for his object was to see if manipulating subjects' attitudes toward teaching machines would affect their attitudes toward things previously associated with teaching machines. For this a prerequisite would be the successful manipulation of attitudes toward teaching machines. This did indeed occur, and in precisely the way planned.

TABLE 16 EXPECTED RESULTS FOR TANNENBAUM'S STUDY

Professor Samuels's Attitude		Later Communication Regarding Teaching Machines	Direction of Final Attitude Change		
Toward Teaching Machines	Toward Spence Theory		Toward Teaching Machines	Toward Professor Samuels	Toward Spence Theory
positive	positive	positive	positive	?	?
positive	negative	positive	positive	?	?
negative	positive	positive	positive	?	?
negative	negative	positive	positive	?	?
positive	positive	negative	negative	?	?
positive	negative	negative	negative	?	?
negative	positive	negative	negative	?	?
negative	negative	negative	negative	?	?

SOURCE: Adapted from Tannenbaum (1966).

Now we come to a more interesting question. What effect did this have on attitudes toward Professor Samuels? Remember that he too had had something to say about teaching machines. What effect would this association have upon attitudes toward him? There are two different predictions that might be made. If it is simply the presence of an association between Professor Samuels and teaching machines that is the important thing, we would expect attitude change toward Professor Samuels to show exactly the same pattern as attitude change toward teaching machines. In other words, column 5 of Table 16 should show a pattern identical with column 4. This would be true if Professor Samuels is simply and uncritically associated together with teaching machines.

But there is another prediction that might be made if we take into account the meaningfulness of the communications. Remember that in some treatments Professor Samuels had spoken in favor of teaching machines and in others he had opposed them. What difference would this make? None, if Professor Samuels's words registered like so many nonsense syllables. But if they were taken at face value there would be something incongruous between Professor Samuels's support of teaching machines and the Office of Education's criticism of them, or between Samuels's criticism and the Office of Education's support. In these cases, if the Office of Education report is to be the main influence, then it would be reasonable to believe that attitudes toward Professor Samuels would decline. This would make the associations of Samuels and teaching machines more congruous. On the other hand, where Professor Samuels and the Office of Education had similar attitudes toward teaching machines, influence toward the Office of Education view should be accompanied by more favorable views of Samuels. If psychological congruity of attitudes, then, is the key, we would expect column 5 of Table 16 to be positive when, and only when, entries of column 1 and column 3 are the same (either both positive or both negative).

THEORETICAL
POINTER

Congruity and Balance

The congruity model of attitude change was first developed by Charles E. Osgood and Percy Tannenbaum (1955) as an extension of research to measure meanings in communication materials. Their original framework was built around the communication of a message. Key elements in this analysis were those of *source* (who or what gives the message), *concept* (what the message is about), and *assertion* (the particular communication made by the source about the concept). In each case primary attention was given to evaluative meanings involved; in analyzing attitudes, in fact, Osgood and Tannenbaum limited their attention to the evaluative aspects.

Congruity is considered to be a condition of evaluative consistency. Congruity would be considered to obtain when a person has a favorable evaluation of both a source and a concept and, in addition, the assertion shows a positive association between source and concept. Congruity would also obtain if evaluation toward source and concept were opposed (one positive and the other negative), so long as the assertion showed negative association between the two. For example, a Republican who dislikes ideas he considers socialistic would find nothing incongruent in hearing a Republican denounce socialism (or in hearing a Socialist denounce the Republican party).

Attitude change is not produced by conditions of congruity. Rather, it is a condition of incongruity that is most apt to bring attitude change. The basic assumption here is that our attitudes tend toward simplicity in their organization of evaluations. And a condition of perfect congruity is one of maximum simplicity.

To take the previous example of our Republican partisan, suppose he hears a respected Republican leader praise ideas he himself had always condemned as socialistic. Here is incongruity, and consequently the potential for attitude change. And Osgood and Tannenbaum's framework suggests three places where such attitude change might be focused: source (for example, to wonder if this leader is really a good Republican, or if perhaps Republicans may be subject at times to serious error), concept (for example, to wonder if all socialistic ideas are really so bad after all), or assertion (for example, to doubt if the Republican really said that, or if he really meant what he appeared to say). By adjustments at any of these three points, incongruity can be reshaped into attitudes with congruous evaluations.

Osgood and Tannenbaum also present a model for identifying the amount of change needed to produce perfect congruity (given a set of relationships with some degree of incongruity), and the proportion of such change that might be predicted to come from different parts of the attitude system. For example, they suggest that the more extreme an evaluation, the less susceptible it is to being modified—therefore, the adjustment would be more likely to be made through other elements of the incongruous system.

A formulation somewhat different from that of Osgood and Tannenbaum, but based on essentially similar ideas, is the theory of cognitive balance. Cognitive balance is associated especially with the work of Fritz Heider (1958), who developed this theory largely out of an interest in perception.

In Heider's terms, cognitions associated together are seen as having *unit relations,* whereas different degrees of positive or negative attachment felt toward elements of thought represent *sentiment relations.* The basic idea of balance theory is that unit relations tend to harmonize with sentiment relations so that we have similar sentiments toward elements of the same cognitive unit. Or, what amounts to the same thing, we create groupings of ideas in such a way that the dissimilar sentiments will not be closely associated.

Heider's formulation is somewhat more general than that of Osgood and Tannenbaum, especially because Heider's concepts were derived from more general cognitive theory. Also, Osgood and Tannenbaum make more specific predictions concerning how incongruity is to be reduced than Heider does for the reduction of imbalance. Still, the central idea is the same for both formulations: human nature abhors cognitive inconsistency, and so we tend to reorganize attitudes toward a condition of maximum evaluative consistency.

Which of these two predictions, simple association or congruous association, best fits the results regarding attitudes toward Professor Samuels? As column 5 of Table 17 shows, the congruency interpretation appears to give the correct prediction. Attitudes toward teaching machines generalized to affect attitudes toward Professor Samuels—not indiscriminately, but in a manner that took account of the meaning of what Samuels had said. Professor Samuels was more highly regarded if his views agreed with the direction of a subject's attitude change (whether positive or negative); when Samuels's views were in the other direction his reputation declined. This suggests, more generally, that we tend to think more favorably of people who have correct attitudes (that is, attitudes like those we develop), and we think unfavorably of those with the wrong attitudes (that is, unlike our own).

Still another attitude studied by Tannenbaum concerned the Spence learning theory. This was never presented as having anything to do with teaching machines. Furthermore, the only information we are

TABLE 17   SUMMARY OF RESULTS OF TANNENBAUM'S STUDY

Professor Samuels's Attitude		Later Communication Regarding Teaching Machines	Direction of Final Attitude Change		
Toward Teaching Machines	Toward Spence Theory		Toward Teaching Machines	Toward Professor Samuels	Toward Spence Theory
positive	positive	positive	positive	positive	positive
positive	negative	positive	positive	positive	negative
negative	positive	positive	positive	negative	negative
negative	negative	positive	positive	negative	positive
positive	positive	negative	negative	negative	negative
positive	negative	negative	negative	negative	positive
negative	positive	negative	negative	positive	positive
negative	negative	negative	negative	positive	negative

SOURCE: Adapted from Tannenbaum (1966).

given about Spence learning theory was whether Professor Samuels was for or against it. Should this make any difference? Maybe it should and maybe it shouldn't. The tie is sufficiently weak that one shouldn't be too surprised if no clear-cut pattern emerges. But Tannenbaum believes the principle of congruity has implications even here. If Professor Samuels has the "right" views about teaching machines, what he says about Spence learning theory will tend to be accepted. In contrast, if his views on teaching machines tend to be "wrong" (that is, opposed to the views found more persuasive by subjects), then what he says about Spence learning theory would be subject to doubt. To generalize, people who have the wrong attitudes on some subjects are suspected of having wrong attitudes on other matters as well.

To specify what this predicts in the present experiment, the last column of Table 17 should be positive when, and only when, the second and fifth columns represent the same direction of attitude. One approves of Spence theory when one approves of Samuels *and* Samuels approves of Spence theory, or when one disapproves of Samuels *and* Samuels disapproves of Spence theory. Spence theory loses approval when Samuels is approved but doesn't approve of Spence theory, or when Samuels is disapproved and in turn approves Spence theory.

In the results of Table 17 we see a perfect fit with these predictions of congruity theory. Apparently it is the psychologically congruous associations, rather than just any associations, that have the main influence upon attitude change.

But this is not to say that incidental conditioning has no effect in such attitude change. In fact, in the present experiment there is evidence of such automatic and undiscriminating generalization. There was a slight overall tendency for a positive message from the Office of Education about teaching machines to yield a slightly more favorable evaluation about whatever Professor Samuels said than would a negative message from the Office of Education. This affected only overall averages and was not strong enough to affect the pattern of results of Table 17, but Tannenbaum reports that some of these secondary effects are still statistically significant. We can conclude therefore that there is some evidence of automatic stimulus-response conditioning in this study, but it is overshadowed by the stronger relationships that generalized from meaningful associations.

FRUITS OF HYPNOSIS

In Tannenbaum's study, attitude change was primarily a product of the relationship of different cognitions. The persons had rather limited impressions of three subjects: teaching machines, Spence learning theory, and Professor Samuels. There is no evidence that either feelings or behavior were much affected by the cognitive impact of attitude change in this experiment.

Other approaches that emphasize the role of consistency in attitude change emphasize consistency between cognitions and feelings, between cognitions and behavior, and between feelings and behavior—as well as between cognitions and cognitions. In the next chapter we will look at several studies in which behavior is an important part of attitude change. In the remaining paragraphs of the present chapter we will take note of a study in which the focus is upon the relationship between cognitions and feelings.

The usual way in which we think of cognitions and feelings being involved in attitude change is that we first learn something new (change our cognitions) and then change our feelings (to make them more consistent with our cognitions). For example, after we understand that race prejudice is damaging to ourselves and others, we may come to feel less antagonism toward persons of other races.

Precisely the reverse of this process is explored in an experiment by Milton Rosenberg (1960).[1] In this experiment the subjects were made to *feel* different about an object of attitudes, then examined to see if the difference in feelings led to changes in cognitions.

Rosenberg used twenty-two subjects. Eleven of these served as a control group, and eleven constituted the experimental group. The subjects in the experimental group were hypnotized, then told that they were going to have strong feelings about two subjects (one for, and one against) when they awoke from hypnosis. The following is an example of the hypnotic instructions given one subject:

> When you awake you will be very much in favor of Negroes moving into white neighborhoods. The mere idea of Negroes moving into white neighborhoods will give you a happy, exhilarated feeling. Although you will not remember this suggestion having been made, it will strongly influence your feelings after you have awakened.
>
> Also, when you awake you will be very opposed to the city-manager plan. The mere idea of the city-manager plan will give you a feeling of loathing and disgust. Although you will not re-

[1] Milton J. Rosenberg, "Cognitive Reorganization in Response to the Hypnotic Reversal of Attitudinal Affect," *Journal of Personality*, 28 (1960), 39–63. Copyright 1960 by the Duke University Press. Quotations from this source are reprinted with permission of the publisher.

member this suggestion having been made, it will strongly
influence your feelings after you have awakened.

Only when the signal to remember is given will you remember these suggestions and only then will your feelings revert to
normal (p. 43).

The hypnosis was successful. The subjects did display the suggested
feelings toward blacks moving into white neighborhoods and toward
the city-manager plan. Furthermore, they were not aware that these
were not their normal feelings. But what is more to the point, the
persons in the hypnotized group also changed their cognitions about
these subjects. If their feelings were made more favorable, their beliefs
about the subject also became more favorable than in a pretest. For
example, one might believe that integrated housing would make for a
more effective local school system. And if their feelings were to be
unfavorable, their beliefs about the subject (for example, the city-
manager plan) also tended to become more unfavorable—at least until
the posthypnotic suggestion was removed.

Consistency, then, appears to apply to relationships between feelings and beliefs, as well as to relationships among beliefs. Attitude
change is most likely when it will promote such consistency, and least
likely when consistency is already present.

15
Decisions and Dissonance

In the studies examined in the previous chapter, the role of persons undergoing attitude change has been quite passive. They have been given experiences that lead them to make certain associations. These associations then yield certain changes in attitude.

But human beings are not just passive recipients of experience. Experience is also actively sought. People choose to have one kind of experience rather than another; they decide to behave one way rather than another. In this chapter we will be concerned especially with the role of such active elements of behavior in attitude change. We will pay particular attention to the impact of choices and commitments.

ATTITUDE CHANGE AS DISSONANCE REDUCTION

Let us suppose that a person finds himself in a situation where he must choose between two things that are equally desirable (or equally undesirable). He has to choose, yet whatever he chooses, he is bound to feel some doubt about the correctness of his choice.

Or suppose a person finds himself in a situation where he behaves in a way he would not ordinarily approve. Surely he must feel some doubt about the correctness of his behavior.

In both of these cases we may make use of the theory of cognitive dissonance, developed by Leon Festinger (1957). According to this theory, when there is a discrepancy between two cognitions held at the same time (or between cognitions and behavior), a force is created that tends to bring about change. Such pressure toward change continues until a cognitive state of greater consonance is achieved.

Consonance and Dissonance

THEORETICAL
POINTER

Cognitive elements that fit together psychologically are, in Festinger's words, *consonant*. And two cognitions are in *dissonant* relation if "considering those two alone, the obverse of one element would follow from the other" (p. 13). Such consonance and dissonance is psycho- logical rather than logical. Whatever seems to fit together in a person's mind constitutes consonance, and whatever does not represents dissonance.

When dissonance occurs, it is uncomfortable; and the individual seeks to reduce it. The more elements of thought in dissonant relationship to each other, the greater will be the pressure to reduce the dissonance, thus the greater the potential for attitude change.

When a choice is made between two things that are almost equally desirable, dissonance is created to the extent that what was not chosen still appears attractive. But such dissonance may be lessened by exaggerating the value of what was actually chosen, devaluing the rejected alternative, or denying personal responsibility for the choice— or some combination of these modes of dissonance reducton.

In similar manner, when a person finds himself engaging in behavior of questionable value, there is dissonance. And such dissonance may be reduced by reevaluating such behavior to make it more justified, devaluing the alternatives to such behavior, or denying any personal responsibility for what one is doing. A still more drastic mode of reducing such dissonance would be to stop the behavior.

Festinger's concept of consonance has much in common with Osgood's notion of congruity and Heider's theory of balance. All three approaches are based on the assumption that people are motivated to seek maximum consistency in their cognitions. The main difference is Festinger's somewhat broader and less explicit formulation. This has made the status of Festinger's theory more pointedly criticized (for example, by Chapanis and Chapanis, 1964) than the other theories of cognitive consistency. But the very looseness of its theoretical structure has also made dissonance theory easy to relate to behavior. A person's own behavior presents cognitions that are either consonant or dissonant with other cognitive elements. If consonant, his behavior reinforces his previous attitudes. If dissonant, there is the basis of a change of some kind or another.

When there is dissonance about what we've done or what we've chosen, we do what we can to lessen the dissonance. Sometimes we might change our behavior—to keep it consistent with our previous attitudes. Other times we might try to revoke our choice—to concede our mistake and try to make up for it. But more often than not such actions are very difficult or impossible. The time for choice is past, and we know the choice has been made. Or we are so obviously behaving in a certain manner that it is impossible to deny that these actions are ours. Then another possibility occurs: to change our attitudes to support us. When we have made an explicit choice, we may change our attitudes to give stronger value to whatever is chosen. And when we have made the implicit choice of a particular kind of behavior, we may adopt whatever attitudes will best justify our acts.

Under some conditions dissonance theory leads us to predictions that would be quite opposite from common sense. Consider, for example, an experiment by Festinger and Carlsmith (1959).[1] In this ex-

---

[1] Leon Festinger and J. Merrill Carlsmith, "Cognitive Consequences of Forced Compliance," *Journal of Abnormal and Social Psychology*, 58 (1959), 203–210. Copyright 1959 by the American Psychological Association. Quotations from this source are reprinted with permission of the publisher.

periment sixty subjects were required to perform exceedingly dull and repetitive tasks. There were three experimental treatments. Twenty subjects were individually given a payment of one dollar each to tell the next person (who he thought was the next subject but who was actually an accomplice of the experimenter) that the task was indeed very interesting. Twenty other subjects were given twenty dollars each for the same request. And the remaining subjects did only the monotonous task, thus serving as a control group.

Later an interview was conducted, ostensibly for a different study, to find out under which condition, if any, subjects had shown attitude change. Attitude change, in this case, would be indicated by a tendency to look favorably upon their own participation in the experiment and to consider the task interesting. (With random assignment of subjects to treatments, it could be assumed that initial attitudes were randomly distributed between treatments. Differences between treatment groups in later attitudes toward the experiment can therefore be assumed to show attitude change.)

We may pause to note two different theories that would suggest different results. A simple reinforcement theory would suggest that the twenty-dollar payment condition would produce the greatest tendency to evaluate the experiment positively. This much reward should create a stronger positive association with the experimental task than either of the other conditions. This prediction also seems to fit with common sense.

But Festinger and Carlsmith had another prediction, based on dissonance theory. They reasoned as follows:

1. If a person is induced to do or say something which is contrary to his private opinion, there will be a tendency for him to change his opinion so as to bring it into correspondence with what he has done or said.
2. The larger the pressure used to elicit the overt behavior (beyond the minimum needed to elicit it) the weaker will be the above-mentioned tendency (pp. 209–210).

Specifically, what they expected was that dissonance, and therefore pressure for attitude change, would be greatest with the one-dollar treatment. Here the reward wasn't enough to free them from the sense of freely choosing to tell a lie (namely, to say that the task was interesting). If they could believe that it was for the sake of science, this would undoubtedly help them to overcome their doubts, but not so much so as where payment is also large. But the one-dollar subjects could compensate by a greater reevaluation of the experiment and their role in it.

The results are indicated in Table 18. Here we see that the predictions of Festinger and Carlsmith were indeed correct. Those subjects who were paid one dollar to tell the experimental lie showed the greatest tendency toward favorable reevaluation. The twenty-dollar treatment did not differ significantly from the control group.

TABLE 18 AVERAGE RATINGS OF INTERVIEW RESPONSES

| | **Treatment** | | |
Question	$20	$1	Control
How enjoyable were tasks?	−.05	1.35	−.45
How much estimate of scientific importance?	5.18	6.45	5.60
Willing to participate in similar experiment?	−.25	1.20	−.62

NOTE: The above average ratings are each based upon a ten-point scale. The estimate of scientific importance had a scale ranging from 0 to 10, while the other two scales ranged from −5 to +5.
SOURCE: Festinger and Carlsmith (1959), p. 207.

CAUTION

Dissonance vs. Reinforcement

In the study by Festinger and Carlsmith, dissonance theory yielded results in direct contrast to what would be predicted by a simple reinforcement theory. This does not disprove reinforcement theory; but it does suggest that dissonance may be another, and in some instances a stronger, influence.

Other studies have not always yielded results to confirm a dissonance prediction. For example, Rosenberg (1965), in an experiment similar to that of Festinger and Carlsmith, found evidence that would support either a reinforcement theory or an extension of balance theory (which Rosenberg preferred), but not dissonance theory. Another study by Carlsmith, Collins, and Helmreich (1966) found that under certain conditions (especially when subjects are involved in face-to-face interaction) small amounts of reward are most effective in producing attitude change—as would be predicted by dissonance theory—whereas under other conditions (for example, writing an essay contrary to one's previous beliefs), larger amounts of reward are more productive of attitude change—as reinforcement theory would predict. This suggests that the more personal the involvement, the more likely will dissonance theory predict the pattern of results.

More recently Sherman (1970) designed an experiment to determine under what conditions dissonance theory or incentive theory would be the better predictor of attitude change. His results led him to conclude that "incentive relates inversely to attitude change when there is initial behavioral commitment to the discrepant act, but relates positively in the absence of such commitment" (p. 249). In other words, dissonance theory predicts best under conditions of personal commitment; otherwise, incentive theory predicts best.

Such studies should remind us that dissonance reduction is seldom the *only* significant force involved in attitude change. They also indicate those conditions under which the dissonance predictions are most likely to hold: when individuals are personally involved or strongly committed to behavior they ordinarily would not approve.

Another study predicting results in apparent contrast to common sense was made by Aronson and Mills (1959).[2] The specific hypothesis

[2] Elliot Aronson and Judson Mills, "The Effect of Initiation on Liking for a Group," *Journal of Abnormal and Social Psychology*, 59 (1959), 177–181. Copyright 1959 by the American Psychological Association. Quotations from this source are reprinted with permission of the publisher.

they tested was that "individuals who undergo an unpleasant initiation to become members of a group increase their liking for the group; that is, they find the group more attractive than do persons who become members without going through a severe initiation."

Aronson and Mills describe their basic method as follows:

> In designing the experiment it was necessary to have people join groups that were similar in every respect except for the severity of the initiation required for admission—and then to measure each individual's evaluation of the group. It was also necessary to randomize the initial motivation of subjects to gain admission to the various groups in order to eliminate systematic effects of differences in motivation. These requirements were met in the following manner: Volunteers were obtained to participate in group discussions. They were assigned randomly to one of three experimental conditions: A *Severe* initiation condition, a *Mild* initiation condition, and a *Control* condition. In the Severe condition, subjects were required to read some embarrassing material before joining the group; in the Mild condition, the material they read in order to join the group was not very embarrassing; in the Control condition, subjects were not required to read any material before becoming group members. Each participant listened to the same tape recording which was ostensibly an ongoing discussion by the members of the group that he had just joined. Subjects then evaluated the discussion (pp. 177–178).

The subjects were sixty-three college women. Each participant was individually scheduled to meet with a group to discuss the "psychology of sex." When the subject arrived, the experimenter explained that she was to take the place of another person in a group already formed. The study was presented as one investigating "the dynamics of the group discussion process" with sex chosen as a subject that should provide interesting discussion material. The experimenter further commented:

> But the fact that the discussions are concerned with sex has one major drawback. Although most people are interested in sex, they tend to be a little shy when it comes to discussing it. This is very bad from the point of view of the experiment; if one or two people in a group do not participate as much as they usually do in group discussions because they are embarrassed about sex, the picture we get of the group discussion process is distorted. Therefore, it is extremely important to arrange things so that the members of the discussion group can talk as freely and frankly as possible. We found that the major inhibiting factor in the discussion was the presence of the other people in the room. Somehow, it's easier to talk about embarrassing things if other people aren't staring at you. To get around this, we hit upon an idea which has proved very successful. Each member of the group is placed in a separate room, and the participants communicate through an intercom system using head-

phones and a microphone. In this way, we've helped people relax, and have succeeded in bringing about an increase in individual participation (p. 178).

All this was to set the stage for the subject to listen to a tape recording, believing that she was hearing a live discussion.

> The experimenter then mentioned that, in spite of this precaution, occasionally some persons were still too embarrassed to engage in the discussions and had to be asked to withdraw from the discussion group. The subject was asked if she thought she could discuss sex freely. She invariably answered affirmatively. In the Control condition the subject was told, at this point, that she would be a member of the group.
>
> In the other two conditions, the experimenter went on to say that it was difficult for him to ask people to leave the group once they had become members. Therefore, he had recently decided to screen new people before admitting them to the discussion groups. The screening device was described as an "embarrassment test" which consists of reading aloud some sexually oriented material in the presence of the experimenter. . . .
>
> In the Severe condition, the "embarrassment test" consisted of having subjects read aloud, from 3 × 5 cards, 12 obscene words . . . [and] two vivid descriptions of sexual activity from contemporary novels. In the Mild condition, subjects read aloud five words that were related to sex but not obscene. . . . In both the Severe and the Mild conditions, after each subject finished reading the material, she was told that she had performed satisfactorily and was, therefore, a member of the group and could join the meeting that was now in progress (p. 178).

In order that the subject would not actually enter into the discussion, it was explained that the group was focusing the discussion on an assignment in a book, *Sexual Behavior in Animals,* and that

> Because the presence of a participant who isn't contributing optimally would result in an inaccurate picture of the dynamics of the group discussion process, it would be best if you wouldn't participate at all today, so that we may get an undistorted picture of the dynamics of the other three members of this group. Meanwhile, you can simply listen to the discussion, and get an idea of how the group operates. For the next meeting, you can do the reading and join in the discussion (p. 179).

The recording that each subject actually heard was a discussion by three undergraduates designed to be "as dull and banal as possible." At the close of the "meeting" the investigator explained that each member was to fill out a questionnaire giving reactions to the meeting. In this way responses were obtained from each subject evaluating the discussion just heard.

We recall that the basic prediction was that those undergoing a most severe initiation would have the highest evaluation of the group. For them the dissonance would be greatest between the thought of joining the group and the realization that it was a very stupid group. Therefore, it was expected that this dissonance would be reduced by developing a higher evaluation of the group.

TABLE 19   RATINGS FOR THE DIFFERENT EXPERIMENTAL CONDI-
TIONS

	Total of Mean Ratings	*Significantly (p < .05) Different From*
Severe	195.3	Mild, control
Mild	171.1	Severe
Control	166.7	Severe

NOTE: Figures are based on a sum of ratings of seventeen different scales dealing with the discussion group and its participants.
SOURCE: Adapted from Aronson and Mills (1959), p. 179.

Did this actually occur? Some results are given by Table 19. We can see that those undergoing the severe initiation did indeed show a higher evaluation of the discussion and its participants than did subjects in the other two treatments.

Could we generalize from this study and the Festinger-Carlsmith experiment to say that we come to like more the things for which we have to suffer?

COMMITMENT AT YALE

The past two studies both suggested that participation in a rather boring experience could be made more attractive by retrospectively re-evaluating the experience. Furthermore, this reevaluation would show strongest impact when dissonance is greatest (for example, through telling a lie with the least cause or engaging in the greatest discomfort to enter a group). But perhaps we have failed to point yet to a critically important feature of these situations. That is, perhaps the crucial factor that creates the dissonance is the commitment of the person involved. In the Festinger-Carlsmith experiment it may be that the sense of commitment (to tell an experimental lie) is what is most strengthened for those receiving minimal payment. And in the Aronson-Mills study we may doubt if any effects would have been found had there not been a felt commitment on the part of subjects to join the sex discussion group. The more they suffered in the embarrassment test, the stronger they must have sensed that commitment.

Jack W. Brehm and Arthur R. Cohen in *Explorations in Cognitive Dissonance* (1962)[3] have given special emphasis to the concept of commitment for understanding the effects of cognitive dissonance. We will give attention to two of their reports of examples from the experi-

[3] Jack W. Brehm and Arthur R. Cohen, *Explorations in Cognitive Dissonance.* New York: John Wiley & Sons, 1962. Copyright © 1962 by John Wiley & Sons, Inc. Quotations from this source are reprinted with permission of the authors and publisher.

mental work of the late Arthur R. Cohen done while he was at Yale University.

In one experiment by Cohen and Bibb Latané, sixty Yale undergraduates were chosen at random and given an attitude questionnaire concerning campus matters, which included an item about the establishment of a compulsory course in religion. Only the fifty-one students who opposed the idea of compulsory religion at Yale were included in the experiment proper. These were approached by the experimenter, who introduced himself as a student working for the Yale News Bureau. He explained that an alumni group was interested in the idea of a compulsory course in religion and that they wanted to hear some ideas from students on this issue. The News Bureau representative said he was therefore collecting student statements both for and against the idea of a compulsory religion course. However, he reported to the subjects, "We have many statements against the compulsory religion course, and now we need some ideas on the other side of the issue— a strong convincing argument *in favor of* the compulsory religion course at Yale" (p. 89).

But before their responses were recorded, the subjects were presented with the crucial experimental variable. In half of the cases the subjects were given the low choice condition, and the other half received the high choice condition. In the low choice condition "The microphone was practically pushed into their hands, and they were given no chance to decline or to have any say in the matter" (p. 89).

In the high choice condition the subjects were told that "We need some people to speak in favor of the proposal, but, of course, the matter is entirely up to you." Although he made it clear that the subject was free to refuse, the experimenter nevertheless provided reasons why it was important for him to cooperate. These were argued with just enough force to persuade the subject to take part. After he decided to take part, "the experimenter emphasized that he did not want to force the subject into anything he did not want to do, and he made certain the decision was again seen by the subject as his own decision" (p. 89).

In all, twenty-six subjects were given the low choice condition and twenty-five were given the high choice condition. Then, quoting further from Brehm and Cohen:

> The subject was again told that it was necessary to take a strong stand for compulsory religion at Yale; he gave his name, address, and class at Yale; he spoke into a tape recorder which was apparently taking down everything he said; and he assumed that his speech, identified as his statement, would be played before an important group of Yale alumni. Thus subjects in this experiment who varied in the amount of choice given them *took a strong public stand on an issue they opposed, producing a situation in which differential dissonance and attitude change could be expected.*
>
> After finishing his speech, the subject filled out the postquestionnaire. He was asked for "some of his reactions to this business, before continuing." The subject first filled out an opinion

scale identical with the premeasure. The subjects also answered
an item checking on the choice manipulation. They were asked:
Considering that you agreed to participate in the survey, how
much choice do you feel you really had in choosing which side
of the issue to speak on (pp. 89–90)?

Before we examine the main results, let us check to see whether the
choice treatment was actually successful. We are told that "The mean
perceived choice for the Low Choice condition was 3.71, for the High
Choice condition, 8.54; these differences are significant at well beyond
the .001 level" (p. 90). Therefore, it would appear that Cohen and
Latané were successful in their experimental treatments.

In noting the main results, it is of interest that practically all subjects showed at least a slight attitude change toward less complete
rejection of a compulsory religion course after they had argued for it.
In other words, they were to some degree affected by their own contrived arguments. But our central interest is in a comparison of the
two groups, those with the sense of choice and those with little choice.
Table 20 shows a comparison between these two groups. As can be

TABLE 20 DISTRIBUTION OF SUBJECTS BY ATTITUDE CHANGE
SCORE AND CHOICE CONDITION

Condition	Number of Subjects With	
	Low Attitude Change	*High Attitude Change*
Low choice	18	8
High choice	8	17

SOURCE: Adapted from Brehm and Cohen (1962), p. 91.

seen, most of the persons in the low choice condition showed only
moderate attitude change. But in the high choice condition more subjects showed a high degree of attitude change toward the position they
presented. Those persons in the high choice condition had apparently
been more influenced by their arguments for a compulsory religion
course than those who perceived they had little choice.

Finally, let us examine another study done at Yale, this one using a
less contrived situation. As Christmas was approaching, Arthur Cohen
identified thirty Yale students who were considering becoming engaged
during Christmas vacation. A questionnaire was given to these men
that included the following questions:

1. How many girls are you dating now while taking out your
   intended fiancée?
2. How important an issue is loss of freedom to you in considering engagement?
3. How much of a financial discrepancy is there between her
   family and yours?
4. How much religious disagreement is there between you and
   your fiancée?

5. How much difference in "social levels" would you say there is between you and your fiancée?
6. Being as honest as you can, how much difficulty have you had in making the decision to marry her (pp. 78–79)?

These questions were intended to measure relatively objective indications of difficulty between members of the couple. From answers to these questions was obtained an index of overall preengagement conflict.

A somewhat different order of phenomena was that of subjective feelings of need for, and devotion toward, the loved one. These are not so clearly tied to objective reality but, for Cohen's purposes, were equally significant. So both before and after Christmas vacation the following three questions were asked:

1. How much does your future seem empty without your fiancée?
2. In general, being as frank as possible, how much would you say you love your girl?
3. How much do you feel you were "meant for each other" (p. 79)?

Only twenty of the thirty students actually became engaged during the vacation. The rest of the study therefore deals with only these twenty men. They were divided into two halves: those ten with the higher scores for realistic preengagement conflict and those ten with lower scores for preengagement conflict.

What particular prediction would dissonance theory contribute to such a study? Where a commitment is made amid great difficulties, the consequent cognitive impact should be greater than where the difficulties are less. Therefore the expectation was that

the less positive was an objective aspect of the engagement prior to the actual decision, the greater would be the dissonance afterward. Since the dissonance would be difficult to reduce by distortion of the objective differences, it would more likely be reduced by magnification of the subjective need to love. Hence it was expected that, for all subjects who actually became engaged, the more negative the measure of objective conditions prior to engagement, the greater would be the amount of increase in need and devotion from before to after engagement (p. 79).

In Table 21 we find that this was indeed the case. The felt need for

TABLE 21   CHANGES IN NEED AND DEVOTION AS A FUNCTION OF OBJECTIVE PREENGAGEMENT DIFFICULTIES

| | Overall Index of Need and Devotion | | |
	Before	*After*	*Change*
High preengagement conflict	4.93	5.72	+.79
Low preengagement conflict	5.23	5.10	−.13

SOURCE: Brehm and Cohen (1962), p. 80.

the sweetheart and devotion toward her before engagement was somewhat higher where there was less realistic difficulty about deciding to become engaged. Where there was more preengagement conflict, however, there was a higher estimation of need and devotion *after* engagement. Those with realistic difficulties become more devoted through engagement, and those without such difficulties did not. The differences between the change scores of these two groups are statistically significant at the .001 level.

May the reader proceed with caution as he attempts to relate results of this study to events in his own life.

16
Attitudes: Review and Discussion

An attitude is a relatively enduring orientation toward some object of experience. To say that attitudes are relatively enduring is to say that they persist over time to give continuity to behavior. But we also know that attitudes change, and it is upon attitude change that our attention has been especially focused in the last three chapters.

Dramatic attitude change may be present in religious conversion, as was noted in Lofland and Stark's study of followers of the Divine Precepts. Fundamental shifts in political attitudes may also occur, as was seen in Newcomb's Bennington College study. Such marked changes in attitudes may not be common, but they well serve to pose the question of why attitudes change.

The analyses of Newcomb and Lofland and Stark suggest two general bases of attitude change. One of these is in the person, and the other is in the social situation. From his past experience a person carries with him characteristics that may predispose him to be receptive to certain kinds of influence while resistant to others. Only persons with certain characteristics were likely to become converts to the Divine Precepts, and rather different characteristics of students facilitated political liberalization at Bennington College. But at least equally important are the situational conditions. Conversion to the Divine Precepts required satisfying relationships with followers of the Precepts, and political attitude change at Bennington was facilitated especially by social relationships of the college community.

Attitudes, then, are products of persons in situations, and changes in attitudes also reflect the nature of persons and their situations. Furthermore, it is not just an adding up of personal and situational factors that produces attitude change; rather it is the dynamic interplay of personality with situational conditions.

To speak of attitude change as a "dynamic interplay of personality with situational conditions" may be true enough, but we would like to know more about this. What generalizations may we make to indicate more precisely the nature of this dynamic interplay by which situational conditions become intertwined with predispositions?

THE LEARNING OF ATTITUDES

Very broadly, attitude change may be seen as a matter of learning; for *learning* is the name we give to any modifications of response tendencies that follow experiences with new situations. To view attitudes as matters of learning suggests that some of the most common and basic principles of psychology might be applied to this subject of attitude change, for much of twentieth-century psychology has been focused upon the study of learning.

Two sets of psychological principles may be especially important for explaining attitude development and change. These are (1) principles of conditioning and (2) principles of cognitive organization.

One of the basic principles of conditioning is that of *stimulus generalization*. When a particular response habitually follows a particular stimulus, elements similar to, or closely associated with, this stimulus also show a tendency to elicit a similar response. This has been well known since Pavlov's early studies. But do such conditioned reflexes have anything to do with complex orientations such as attitudes? It is at least conceivable that attitudes might themselves be viewed as conditioned responses. To see how the principle of stimulus generalization might then apply, imagine a strong attitude toward a particular group (say, for example, Negroes or Presbyterians). Then as Joe Doe happens to be associated in some way (perhaps even accidentally) with this group in a situation, his attitude toward the group will tend to color the attitude toward other associated objects of experience.

The same basic pattern should apply to all possible sorts of objects of attitudes—from socialism to dill pickles. Furthermore, these conditioning tendencies should occur even when a person gives no conscious thought to these associations. Thus in the unlikely event that a person regularly finds himself eating dill pickles whenever the subject of socialism comes up, we would expect him to show some generalization of his attitude toward socialism to dill pickles—or vice versa.

Another key psychological generalization is that of *response reinforcement*. Responses are more clearly fixed the more they are associated with reward. To apply this basic idea of operant conditioning to attitudes, we need only note that attitudes that are rewarded are more likely to be developed. If a favorable attitude toward a particular church is more apt to bring us rewards from people important to us (or, for example, if unfavorable attitudes toward another nation's government are more apt to be approved by our friends) then we will tend to develop the attitudes associated with such reinforcement. Nor does this require much thought. Quite automatically we tend to form those attitudes that have been associated in our experience with positive reinforcement.

One way, then, to view attitudes is to see them as conditioned responses. And as conditioned responses, they reflect the same principles of stimulus generalization and response reinforcement as do other responses. Undoubtedly these principles help us to understand how attitudes are formed and how they change, as was indicated by the experimental study of Staats, Staats, and Heard examined in Chapter 14.

But a primary emphasis upon such a conditioning approach to attitude analysis may neglect other key points about attitudes. One of these is that attitudes are largely composed of meanings. How some attitudes relate to others depends on their meaningful content. This is not simply a matter of associations between physical stimuli; it is at least equally a matter of the organization of meanings within systems of symbols. These symbolic systems are learned as organizations that include a combination of all the elements in an orientation toward an object, and these elements must be seen in their combination and not simply as discrete responses.

All this suggests that principles of cognitive organization as well as principles of conditioning need to be considered for understanding the learning of attitudes. We shall mention two principles of cognitive organization that we shall call (1) the principle of simplicity and (2) the principle of evaluative consistency.

In order to use ideas and impressions, we must simplify the information available to us. The principle of *simplicity* is, quite simply, that our cognitions tend to become organized into a framework of maximum uniformity and regularity. This basic idea was presented some years ago by psychologists of the Gestalt school in the form of the law of *prägnanz*, that our perceptions tend toward as "good a figure" (that is, as simple and clear) as the stimulus pattern will permit. Applying this general idea more broadly to cognitions, and not only to perception, we may suggest that all cognitive fields tend toward simplicity. For example, in perceiving another person, we tend to organize our impressions into a simplified general impression—often taking a single feature (for example, ability, appearance, occupation, or group membership) as an anchor around which other impressions are fitted. These impressions then tend to be merged into each other—what social psychologists have sometimes called an *assimilation effect*.

Of course, sometimes cognitive elements obviously do not fit together. Then simplicity demands that they be set apart into separate organizations. Once it is clear that impressions are to be divided and set apart from each other, then to simplify this dualism we tend to exaggerate the differences—what has been called a *contrast effect*.

Consider, for example, an American's attitude toward foreign aid. For most Americans foreign aid is all one thing—whether to Britain or Botswana, whether by grant or loan, whether involving emergency food relief or military support. For a person who sees his need limited to a very general view of American foreign policies, it may be most convenient to assimilate all aspects of foreign aid into a central image of a generous, perhaps overly generous, Uncle Sam. However, a little more acquaintance with the subject of foreign assistance will force a person to make important distinctions. He may come to see a grant program as quite different from development loans, perhaps in so doing minimizing the subsidies involved in loans or reciprocal responsibilities tied to grants. Or his predilection for seeing international relations in terms of groupings of nations may lead him to see a development loan to Brazil as far different from a similar loan to Bulgaria. In this any aid to Brazil might be assimilated into one category in contrast to all aid to Bulgaria. An experienced foreign-service officer may decry the ignorance in such oversimplified images of foreign aid, but even he will have to use some of these simplified categorizations in his own thinking—at least those categorizations enacted into laws by Congress.

Closely related to a tendency to simplify our impressions and thoughts is a tendency toward an *evaluative consistency*. In order to use ideas and impressions we must relate them to our wants and values. This provides an evaluative component for practically all cognitions. Some ideas or impressions have a more favorable value than others, and some have a negative value. The principle of evaluative consistency holds that we tend to have similar evaluations of cognitive elements that are associated together. That is, if we closely associate two things in our thinking, we will tend to have similar evaluations, pro or con, in regard to them. And, conversely, if we have similar evaluations of two objects, we will be more apt to organize them together.

The theories of congruity and balance discussed in Chapter 14 may be seen as two formulations based on the principle of evaluative consistency. This principle is not quite so explicitly central in Festinger's concept of consonance, though it is clearly one of the main processes involved in consonant relations between cognitions.

Consistency vs. Novelty

CAUTION

Theories about cognitive congruity or balance and about dissonance reduction all assume that the tendency of human beings is to promote maximum consistency in thought—even though it sometimes may be at the expense of a realistic view of the world. And we have fairly good evidence that people in fact often behave in ways predicted by these theories.

But do they always? Is not some behavior quite otherwise? What about the artist who seeks out subtle ambiguities to express in his work? What about the millions of persons who plan vacations for places they have never seen, or children who seem to possess overwhelming energy for new experience? Certainly more than motives for cognitive simplicity and consistency give organization to such purposive creativity and novelty.

So side by side with a tendency toward simplicity in our thought processes, there is also often a tendency to complicate these processes. The popularity of chess or crossword puzzles bears witness that the simplest level of imagination is not always the most satisfying.

And side by side with a tendency toward evaluative consistency is a tendency to seek out new ways for seeing and evaluating experiences. Even a rather bad detective story may have an appeal partly because readers enjoy the uncertainty—at least until near the end of the story—concerning who are the good guys and who are the bad guys.

It is possible that the predictions of theories based on the principles of cognitive simplicity and evaluative consistency may prove generally true without the central principles being universally valid. What we may find is a statistical tendency toward such consistency that masks those occasions where novelty may be sought. Or, what may amount to the same thing, in our everyday adjustment the demands to simplify and make our experience more consistent may be far more dominant than our demands for elaboration and novelty. But this is not to say that the principles of simplicity and evaluative consistency apply absolutely.

It is interesting to speculate that for any person in a given situation there may be a kind of optimum he seeks—a midpoint or level between perfect order in cognitive organization and the disorder of variety or novelty. This optimum, we specu- late, must be different for different people and different for the same person in different situations.

ATTITUDES AS ADJUSTMENTS

We have tried to indicate some of the specific psychological principles that guide the learning and relearning of attitudes. But we also need to say something more about the broader context in which attitudes function. Very broadly, we may do this by saying that attitudes are adjustments, ways in which a person has learned to cope with his world by forming relatively stable orientations toward common objects of his experience.

Viewing attitudes in this broad fashion, we may identify three basic determinants of attitudes, each of which constitutes a basic function of attitudes for human adjustment. Attitudes are determined by (1) the external world of physical reality, which we come to know through our senses, (2) the social world of other people, whom we know through contact and communication with them, and (3) the world of our own inner personality, which manifests itself through our thought and action. The functions that attitudes fulfill are thus respectively (1) to aid in our adjustment to reality by giving us a useful way of organizing the information from our senses, (2) to aid in our adjustment to other people through attitudes that facilitate communication and agreement, and (3) to express and achieve our inner personality needs in developing orientations toward things around us. And attitudes typically function in all these ways at one and the same time.

Sometimes one or another of the three determinants may appear to be the primary base for an attitude—information, social conformity, or psychic needs—but nearly always all of these are involved to some degree. For attitudes are ways by which we mediate between the information our senses bring us and the needs we have within, between the needs we have within and the social pressures without, between the pressures of social conformity and the demands of objective reality. Through our attitudes these forces may cushion each other's impact, yielding an emergent unity in behavior that would not be present without such mediation.

Once we recognize what attitudes are based upon, we can see more clearly what is involved in attitude change. If we want to change someone's attitude, it is important to make a judgment roughly as to what extent it is based on information about objective reality, as to what extent it is rooted in social conformity, and as to what extent it is the expression of deep-seated personality needs.

An attitude may be changed through new information to the extent to which it is based upon a person's knowledge about reality. For example, an American may have attitudes toward Buddhism that are based on an incorrect understanding of the tenets of the faith. If so, further information about Buddhism may produce a considerable change in attitude.

In order for attitude change to occur as a result of the introduction of new information, two basic processes are necessary. The information must be received, and the information must be accepted. Just giving information does not necessarily mean that it is received, as any teacher can testify. And even when the information is received, there is still the matter of acceptance. The new information must be related to the rest of what a person knows, or at least thinks he knows. If it doesn't fit it may be rejected—like what Professor Samuels said about teaching machines when it conflicted with what was "known" from the Office of Education report.

An attitude may be changed through new social relationships to the extent to which it is based upon social adjustment. For example, if a person is a Republican because all his family and friends are Republicans, he is likely to remain a Republican as long as he maintains these group relationships. But if he moves into new groups, or if some of the members of his groups shift their political allegiance (say, in the face of a war or depression), then we would expect him also to show changes in political attitudes. Apparently this was precisely what occurred for many of the students Newcomb studied at Bennington College.

An attitude is less subject to external influence to the extent to which it expresses inner personality needs. New facts and new social relationships may leave the basic attitude unchanged. However, a reworking of some inner personality patterns, perhaps through psychotherapy, may produce a change in attitudes. Or, more frequently, there may be a shift in the object toward which the inner needs express themselves. A person with a strong pattern of authoritarianism, rooted in an early childhood mixture of respect and resentment toward dominating parents, may have the need to identify with a world view in which his weakness can be ultimately explained and justified. He may shift from, say, communism to Calvinism (or vice versa) as a focus for expressing these needs; but although such a conversion may show drastic change on certain attitude scales, the way he holds such attitudes may be little changed.

ATTITUDES AND THE SELF

So far we have looked at attitude change as the result of a relatively passive process. The individual receives new information or adjusts to new social relationships. Even if his attitudes reflect inner personality needs, the picture is still that of being largely determined by forces beyond conscious control. We automatically adjust to our own personality needs, the discussion thus far would suggest, in ways somewhat parallel to those in which we adjust to group needs.

But we have not yet given much consideration to the kind of attitude change in which the individual shows his most active individuality. This occurs in attitude change that is related to self-conceptions.

The self, that organization of attitudes that has primary reference to the persons's own behavior, is not just a passive product of experience. It is also an active molder of experience, and with this a molder of other attitudes. The studies of Chapter 15 can all be interpreted as showing that attitude change is likely to occur when self-conceptions are dissonant with some aspect of experience.

Whenever a person makes a conscious act, whenever a choice is clearly made, his self-conception is involved. And it is for this reason that it becomes necessary to see the result as consistent with the self-conception. Thus it is that if there begins to be evidence that a wrong choice was made, we tend to reorganize our attitudes to shield us from, to resist, or to explain away such evidence. And if there is a discrepancy between our behavior and our attitudes, at least much of the time it is the attitudes that must give. For when the self has been committed to a course of action, the cognitive dissonance of disturbing evidence makes it well worth our best efforts to reduce such dissonance—even if some restructuring of attitudes is necessary.

In general, we have a tendency to change attitudes when such change will provide support for us in that to which we have become committed—whether the commitment was made by an explicit choice or not. We may also make several generalizations concerning situational conditions that may affect the strength of this tendency toward self-supportive attitudes. Let us briefly mention three factors: difficulty of choice, amount of effort, and degree of public commitment.

Choices are sometimes easy and sometimes difficult. The more difficult choices are those that, once made, are most apt to have an impact upon attitudes. For when a choice is difficult, we tend to become more involved in the process of deciding; and we therefore have a stronger need for attitudinal support for whatever is the final decision. An illustration of this may be seen in Cohen's study of Yale Christmas engagements discussed in Chapter 15. Those men who appeared to have a more difficult time deciding whether or not to become engaged also, once engaged, were most apt to show attitude change in support of their commitment.

Usually related to the difficulty of a choice, though theoretically distinct, is the amount of effort that goes into the formation of a commitment. Some commitments are practically forced upon us with very little activity on our part, whereas other commitments require our concentrated efforts. The greater the amount of effort involved in the process, the greater will be the need to have the final product supported by appropriate attitudes. An illustration of this may be seen in the study by Aronson and Mills of the effects of the severity of initiation (Chapter 15). We may conclude that when initiation conditions were more severe, experimental subjects expended more effort in getting into the group; therefore they required greater attitudinal support for this commitment. This tended to produce a higher evaluation of the group than where conditions of initiation were less demanding.

A third variable that affects the amount of self-supportive change is that of the degree of public commitment. Some commitments are made without being noticed by others, whereas other commitments may be the focus of much interest of other people. In general, as at least one experiment (Deutsch and Gerard, 1955) has indicated, the more public the process of commitment, the greater the tendency for attitudes to support the commitment.

All three of these factors—difficulty of choice, amount of effort, and degree of public commitment—have in common a tendency to increase the salience of a commitment. They, so to speak, have the effect of underlining the commitment, thus making a stronger impact upon attitudes than otherwise would have been the case.

RECAPITULATION

So far in this chapter we have reviewed the subject of attitude change from three main perspectives.

One perspective is that of students wanting to know where to look for causes of attitude change. For an introductory orientation it was suggested that neither the person alone nor his social situation alone determines the precise result. Rather, both situation and person, in dynamic interplay, determine the outcome.

The other two perspectives are ways of conceiving this dynamic interplay: one on the level of specific response tendencies and one on a broader level of adjustment.

On an elementary level, attitude change may be seen as learning. As such it involves basic psychological principles of conditioning (such as stimulus generalization and response reinforcement) and of cognitive organization (guided by principles of simplicity and evaluative consistency).

On a broader level, we may conceive of attitudes as adjustments— adjustments that must be made to bring into working relationship our (1) information about the external world, (2) social relationships to other people, and (3) inner personality needs. And all of these must in some way be related to the self-conception, a hard master that constantly forces a restructuring of attitudes to fit commitments made.

ATTITUDES AND SOCIAL INFLUENCE

The most fundamental forms of social influence, we concluded in Chapter 12, are not simply matters of external pressure. Rather, we become influenced as we come to see ourselves as the kind of person for which a given behavior is appropriate. This is fundamentally a matter of attitude change—changes in attitudes toward other things as related to the self. Such social influence very much involves the principles of attitude change that have been discussed in the past several chapters and were summarized in the previous section of this chapter.

However, this is not to say that all social influence involves significant attitude change. Influence upon a person's acts through external pressure is apt to produce little attitude change; but here the social influence is also apt to be quite temporary.

ATTITUDES AND GROUPS

Attitudes, we have learned, are in part a function of social adjustment. Changing group relationships are apt to give rise to changed attitudes. In the following four chapters we examine more fully the nature of group relationships.

part five: GROUPS

Society is not a mere sum of individuals. Rather, the system formed by their association represents a specific reality which has its own characteristics.

Émile Durkheim

In the following four chapters we deal with selected topics concerning groups, all of which have received particular attention from social psychologists.

The role of groups within work organizations is the subject of Chapter 17 ("Productivity in Organizations"). Here the interest in productivity provides a vehicle for studying the impact of some of the more social psychological factors of a work setting, such as the effects of worker participation in decision making.

Not only in established settings of organizations but also apart from these, may we find group behavior emerging. Such group behavior includes the fascinating phenomena of crowds. Chapter 18 ("The Madness (?) of Crowds") deals with selected features of crowd behavior.

Certain groups are important especially for the extent of personal involvement we may find therein. Such primary groups are discussed in Chapter 19 ("The Ubiquity of Primary Relationships").

Part Five closes with Chapter 20 ("Groups: Review and Discussion") in which we attempt to present a more general explanation of group behavior.

17

Productivity in Organizations

THE RELAY ASSEMBLY STUDY

Back in 1927 the Western Electric Company, at its Hawthorne plant near Chicago, was involved in a series of studies dealing with the effects of various working conditions. They had just finished some inconclusive research on the effects of different levels of illumination and were planning another small study of the effect of variations in working conditions upon work output. For this, six girls were selected to work in a room where special observations might be made. These girls were average workers, and their work was to be the relatively routine task of assembling telephone relays. Since it took only about a minute to put together the coil, armature, and other parts to make a telephone relay, the number of relays assembled could be used as a fairly simple and clear index of productivity. An automatic recording device indicated the completion of each telephone relay when it was placed in the chute for finished work. Rather detailed observations were also made of their work and anything that might influence it (including the amount of sleep and dietary habits of the girls, as well as the temperature and humidity of the test room).

The basic purpose of the series of experiments, which continued for five years, was to try out different types of working conditions to see which provided for maximum productivity. At the start of the experiment, and whenever any new experimental conditions were subsequently initiated, the girls were called in for a conference concerning the planned changes. The purpose of the new conditions was explained, their reactions were sought (and sometimes used as a basis for further changes in plans), and they were cautioned to work only at a natural speed.

For five weeks after the girls were put into the test room, working conditions were kept as much as possible as they had been before. The only differences were their new location and the careful, though unobtrusive, observations made of their work.

Then began a series of planned changes. A new system for computing piecework pay rates was introduced. After another eight weeks two rest periods of five minutes each were introduced. Later these were lengthened to ten minutes each. Then there were six five-minute rest periods. Later the company added light lunches for the girls in the middle of the morning and afternoon. Then the workday was ended earlier at 4:30 P.M. Then 4 P.M. Then back to 5 P.M. Then the workweek was changed from six days to five days.

Each of these new conditions continued for several weeks before the next variation was introduced, and during all this time productivity was very carefully measured. What happened to productivity? The general pattern of work output appeared to be up, no matter what experimental conditions were created. Thus, after about a year of experimentation, there were important increases in productivity but no clear indication of the working conditions that specifically led to these increases. At this point it was decided to return to the original working conditions; and with these conditions work output increased to its highest level yet. Then a return to conditions of another previous period was arranged and continued for thirty-one weeks— and output rose steadily to all-time highs.

What was going on here? Apparently nearly every new experimental condition facilitated work better than the previous condition—even when the new condition was a return to an earlier condition. A report made by the company at this time (quoted by Mayo, 1960) concluded that a "better mental attitude and greater enjoyment of work" was a key factor in the increased productivity. "The operators have no clear idea as to why they are able to produce more in the test room; but as shown in the replies to questionnaires . . . there is the feeling that better output is in some way related to the distinctly pleasanter, freer, and happier working conditions" (pp. 65–67).

An example of the kind of happier working conditions may be seen in the freedom of conversation. In theory, conversation was not allowed for this job under regular working conditions, though it was often tolerated in practice. In the test-room situation conversation was very common, and the company did not interfere.

The greater freedom of conversation, the special attention of management, and the special test room in which they worked together all produced the effect of a strong sense of group identity. The girls became good friends on the job and continued social contacts after hours. A common goal developed for the group: to keep a high output. They knew that their output records were given special attention by the supervising investigators, and they did their best to oblige.

In summary, Homans (1958a) concludes that "the increase in the output of the girls in the Relay Assembly Test Room could not be related to any changes in their physical conditions of work, whether experimentally induced or not. It could, however, be related to what only can be spoken of as the development of an organized social group in a peculiar and effective relation with its supervisors" (p. 587).

The effects of informal work groups are not always so happy, especially from the point of view of management. This was made clear in further studies of the Western Electric Company, especially that of the Bank Wiring Room (Roethlisberger and Dickson, 1939; Homans, 1950; Homans, 1958a). In this case the experimental group used group influence to keep potential rate boosters in line and to maintain production at a minimally adequate level. This is probably more common than the enthusiasm for production shown by the girls of the Relay Assembly Test Room. In the factory setting the informal organization of the work group is often a counterweight to the influence of management. Only rarely are the objectives of the informal organization and the official organization fully harmonious.

Human Relations in Industry

SIDELIGHT

The Western Electric studies just cited represent the beginnings of a major shift in the attentions of industrial management. Largely through the participation and interest in these studies by men such as Elton Mayo and F. J. Roethlisberger at the Harvard Business School, the Western Electric studies became required reading in the training of industrial managers. In such training these studies served to emphasize the role of the social organization of industry as distinct from the specifically technical organization. Those who emphasized the importance of such social organization, especially when informal work groups and interpersonal relationships were the focus of attention, sometimes labeled this interest the *human relations approach.* In the years since the Western Electric studies, such a human relations approach has become one of the key ingredients in the training of modern management.

The human relations approach is of course a form of applied social science. Applied to what ends? To the ends of management, many critics say and some supporters agree. A strong emphasis in the management literature is upon the use of the informal organization of workers to realize objectives of production. Whether or not this works for management's goals, the human relations approach is often considered overly paternalistic by spokesmen for organized labor.

For many years the Western Electric studies have been cited in textbooks as "proving" that human relationships are more important in the motivation of workers than either physical working conditions or economic incentives. Recently several industrial sociologists have urged a reconsideration of this evidence. Not only is it suggested that some of the claims for the Western Electric studies have been too sweeping, but Carey (1967)[1] goes so far as to assert that the original data are nearly meaningless from a scientific point of view. In a very critical reexamination of the procedure of the Relay Assembly Test Room study, he suggests that changes of personnel (two of the girls were dropped, and two new ones, including the one who was to become the informal leader, were added in the middle of the study) and changes in economic incentives may have actually been highly significant factors in productivity change. However, he complains that even here the data are not sufficiently clear to test alternative hypotheses. Carey concludes:

> The results of these studies, far from supporting the various components of the "human relations approach," are surprisingly consistent with a rather old-world view about the value of monetary incentives, driving leadership, and discipline. It is only by

[1] Alex Carey, "The Hawthorne Studies: A Radical Criticism," *American Sociological Review*, 32 (1967), 403–416. Quotations from this source are reprinted with permission of the author and the American Sociological Association.

massive and relentless reinterpretation that the evidence is made
to yield contrary conclusions. To make these points is not to
claim that the Hawthorne studies can provide serious support
for any such old-world view. The limitations of the Hawthorne
studies clearly render them incapable of yielding serious support
for any sort of generalization whatever (p. 416).

METHODOLOGICAL POINTER

Verification in Social Psychology

A chief purpose of publication in any field of science is to make the results of investigation available for others to verify. For this it is important that methods of investigation be spelled out in detail, so that another investigator could do a similar study and compare results.

Seldom is an exact replication of an experiment attempted. More commonly, some differences in technique are used; but so long as differences are not too great, results can still be compared. Especially when there is some theoretical point at issue can we expect such replication of experimental work—and then the debate goes on concerning differences in results and methods.

Verification of field experiments, such as those represented by the Western Electric researches, is much more difficult than is verification of laboratory studies. Much more time and effort usually go into a field experiment, and entry into a comparable setting is frequently difficult or impossible to achieve. As a result of the enormous obstacles posed by restudy, verification is primarily a matter of comparison with whatever studies are most similar.

In the case of the Western Electric researches, there were for many years no other studies nearly so comprehensive. Thus the conclusions of those originally reporting these investigations, especially Mayo and Roethlisberger and Dickson, were generally accepted. Besides, they fit the new climate of thought in industrial management, then becoming disenchanted with the hard-driving ideology and practices of Frederick W. Taylor's so-called scientific management. Informal organization was being "discovered" by management, and growing unionization, if nothing else, was enough of a spur to examine morale problems of workers. Such extrascientific climates of opinion have their influence even in scientific circles, and what is accepted often must fit the prevailing or emerging views as well as rest on sound empirical evidence.

But there is also the matter of empirical evidence. In the years since 1928, the standards of evidence in social science have become more demanding. Hence it is perhaps inevitable that later studies will stimulate a reevaluation of earlier work on the basis of its evidence. One challenging study may be comfortably forgotten; but as more and more evidence accumulates, the foundations of earlier knowledge must again be reexamined. This is how the process of verification works out in practice.

PARTICIPATION AND PRODUCTIVITY

One of the main hypotheses of the Western Electric studies was that motivation to work will increase as participation in determining the conditions of work increases. Even if one agrees with Carey's criticism that personnel changes and wage incentives are not ruled out as factors of increased productivity in the original studies, the attitude that the Relay Assembly girls had toward their work also seemed to be an important part of the picture. And for this it is important to note that they were taken into special confidence by management. Furthermore, they had a chance to react to planned changes before they were instituted, and in some cases to change the plans. One member of management commented (cited by Mayo, 1960):

> A relationship of confidence and friendliness has been established with these girls to such an extent that practically no supervision is required. In the absence of any drive or urge whatsoever they can be depended upon to do their best. . . . They have ceased to regard the man in charge as a "boss" (pp. 74–75).

Certainly one of the points that stands out is the absence of any sense of the arbitrary authority of management. Their job may have been defined by management, but the decision governing how they were going to do it on an hour-to-hour basis was sensed by the workers as being primarily their own responsibility.

That increased motivation for work might be a feature of increased involvement in a work setting should be no surprise. It is very much in line with social psychological principles discussed earlier in this book (especially Chapter 15). The more active initiative a person takes in a work situation, the more will he see such work as an extension of his self—thus, the greater will be his motivation to perform well.

This is in line also with the thought of a group of psychologists led by Kurt Lewin, who were especially influential in the 1940s and 1950s. One very famous study by Lewin, Lippitt, and White (1939; also Lewin, 1930; Lippitt, 1939) explored the effects of leadership styles upon performance in children's play groups. Three kinds of groups—"democratic," "autocratic," and "laissez faire"—were created through different styles of adult leadership. The most impressive results were obtained under the conditions of "democracy," which of course fit very well with the ideological climate of the 1940s. This experiment became justly famous as an early example of experimental research on the group level; great effort and imagination were shown in planning these experiments and in observing and recording the behavior of the groups created. But some interpreters were perhaps too free in applying the findings directly to settings of formal organizations. Is the same kind of democracy—that is, major decision making determined through a group process—applicable to school or factory as readily as it is to a children's play group? This can by no means be concluded without further evidence.

Two of Lewin's students, Lester Coch and John French, did test the consequences of participation upon productivity in a factory setting (Coch and French, 1948). They were conducting studies at a Virginia pajama plant, of worker resistance to changes in working conditions. They noted that job turnover and absenteeism frequently increased following the introduction of new procedures; furthermore, production also declined and did not return to a normal level as rapidly as even a generous allowance for relearning would suggest. It did not take long for the investigators to discover that group factors were involved in this resistance to change. Restriction of output frequently became a group pattern after a change in procedures. But would this be the case if the workers themselves had a hand in planning the changes? To answer this question, a field experiment was set up. There were four groups doing comparable jobs. One of these was to serve as a kind of control group, receiving orders for work changes in the usual "no participation" manner. In contrast, two groups were brought fully into "total participation"—the whole group being brought into the process of planning work changes. In one other group there was participation through representatives of the group.

The effects upon productivity following work changes were quite marked. The total participation groups were very soon producing considerably *above* previous levels. The participation through representatives group took longer to return to a normal production level but also finally surpassed that level. The no participation group, however, when given orders for comparable changes, did not return to a normal production level. They maintained a depressed production level until the end of the experiment.

Could this low performance by the control group be due to the nature of the individuals who happened to be in the group? To test this notion, these workers in the control group were later brought together for a new change in work procedures, only this time they were given a total participation treatment. Production soon rose above normal levels.

This would seem like very good news. Here is a way to combine democratic ideals with industrial efficiency. But before we get carried away with the productive prospects of such participation in organizational decision making, let us look at some further evidence. First we may note that an attempt to replicate the Coch and French study in a Norwegian setting failed to produce significant differences between experimental (participation) and control (no participation) groups (French, Israel, and Ås, 1960). This suggests at least the possibility of cultural differences in the impact of participation upon productivity.

Another piece of evidence to consider has been provided by Victor Vroom (1959). He studied supervisors in a parcel delivery company. Most supervisors did indeed show positive correlations between felt participation in decision making and job performance. That is, most supervisors who had a stronger sense of participation in decision making were rated higher in job performance; also they themselves showed more favorable attitudes toward their job. However, this pattern did not apply to all supervisors studied. Those supervisors who had very high scores on a measure of "authoritarianism" did not show this pattern at all. In fact, the high-authoritarianism group showed a slightly *negative* correlation between felt participation in decision making and job performance. This suggests that whatever general relationship may apply between participation and productivity might not be true for all individuals. Personality is another variable that is likely to be relevant.

Another line of evidence that is relevant here is provided by Fred Fiedler's studies (1964) of conditions of effective leadership. Although not directly dealing with participation, he did concern himself with a related dimension: the extent to which leaders identified themselves with those under them. To be more precise, Fiedler's work dealt with measures of "assumed similarity," and one of these measures that appeared especially interesting was that of a leader's "assumed similarity of opposites" (ASo). A leader with a high ASo was one who did not make great distinctions in his evaluation of the men under him, and this was seen as a manifestation of a degree of psychological identification with these men. Since the ASo concept may be a difficult one to grasp, let us give an oversimplified summary of its meaning:

High ASo—perceives others in the group with little differentiation, implies low psychological distance

Low ASo—perceives others in the group with considerable differentiation, implies high psychological distance

After developing the techniques for measuring such evaluations as the ASo, Fiedler investigated the relationship these measures may have to group productivity. High school basketball teams and student surveying groups were the first groups studied; and, much to Fiedler's surprise, he found a strong *negative* correlation between ASo scores of leaders and measures of group productivity (winning basketball games or accuracy in surveying). It appeared that psychological distance in a team captain was correlated with team success. Further studies of bomber crews, tank crews, infantry squads, and artillery crews produced a more complicated picture. It appeared to depend on the sociometric pattern of the group whether the leader's measure of ASo was positively or negatively related to group productivity. If the leader was widely popular, his ASo and group productivity tended to be negatively correlated. On the other hand, where the leader and his key man were especially close, the leader's ASo and measures of group productivity tended to be positively correlated. In a study of a group of farm supply companies it was further demonstrated that patterns of both social relationships and task conditions affected the relationship between ASo scores of leaders and group effectiveness. As Fiedler here found, "the effective executive group performed better under an accepted, low ASo leader, while the policy- and decision-making groups operated more effectively under permissive, nondirective, and considerate, high ASo leaders" (p. 157).

This may all sound a bit confusing, and Fiedler himself was confused by some of the complications until he developed a *contingency model* to explain leadership effectiveness. He called his theory a contingency model because he held that the effects upon group productivity of one variable (such as a leader's ASo) were contingent or dependent on the operation of other variables. In this theory three situational features were given special consideration as variables that might affect whether a permissive and considerate leader or a managing and controlling leader would be more effective in obtaining group productivity. These variables were (1) the leader's personal relations with members of his group, (2) the amount of authority in the position he occupied, and (3) the degree of structure in the task to be performed. For example, a permissive and considerate style of leadership is predicted to be most effective when either (1) leader-member social relations are good, the leader's authority position is weak, and the task is unstructured *or* (2) leader-member social relations are moderately poor, the leader's authority is strong, and the task is well structured. On the other hand, a managing and controlling style of leadership is apt to be most effective when either (1) leader-member social relations are good and the task is well structured *or* (2) leader-member relations are poor and the task is unstructured (when the leader apparently has to be mean to get anything done!). These are some of the predictions from Fiedler's contingency theory of leadership effectiveness, and he cites evidence from studies of other investigators, as well as his own studies, in support of such generalizations.

Although the debate continues as to the validity of Fiedler's specific conclusions—for critical evidence see Graen and associates (1970), and for supporting evidence see Chemers and Skrzypek (1972)—we can at least recognize that the general idea of the contingency model is a useful one; whether or not a particular style of leadership leads to greater group productivity depends upon the nature of the task, organizational structure, and group relationships.

The contingency theory of leadership effectiveness takes us some distance beyond the simple notion that sociability boosts production, which we may have received from a first glance at the Western Electric studies. Of course it isn't that simple. The nature of the task and the structure of authority are factors that must be taken into account in considering whether fostering an atmosphere of permissiveness or encouraging wide participation in decision making may yield greater productivity for the organization.

A distinction that might be useful here is that between *consideration* and *initiation* as basic categories of leadership behaviors. A study by Halpin and Winer used these terms to identify the two main factors of leadership behavior, and other studies have pointed to similar divisions (see Bass, 1960, pp. 96–105). Somewhat similar are also Bales's distinction between social-emotional and task areas of group activity (Bales and Slater, 1955; Bales, 1958) and Thibaut and Kelley's distinction between maintenance and task functions in groups (1959, pp. 274–276). While a leader in an organization may be called upon to perform both group maintenance (through consideration) and task functions (initiation), under certain conditions one of these will be more critical than another. Fiedler's findings may then make sense as indicating that when group maintenance functions are already well served without special attentions from the leader, then group effectiveness is apt to be tied especially to the leader's concentration on task functions. On the other hand, if the social solidarity of the group or organization is a critical issue, then task specialization at the expense of consideration may actually have adverse effects on productivity.

EXPERIMENTS WITH COMMUNICATION NETWORKS

Studies cited so far in this chapter have been chiefly those that were conducted in actual organizational settings. It seems reasonable to expect that organizational behavior can be studied only in organizational settings; thus the relative absence of laboratory studies in this chapter should be no surprise. But the chapter is not yet finished. There are several lines of laboratory research that are related, one of which we may single out for special mention. This is the investigation, first inspired by Alex Bavelas (1948; 1950), of the consequences of different communication networks.

An early study by Harold Leavitt (1951) provides a good example of this work. Subjects were arranged into groups of five, and each group was seated at a special apparatus and given a task for collective problem solving. The apparatus was such that subjects were partitioned from one another's view, but the experimenter could open channels for sending messages between any combinations of positions he desired. The task required the locating of a common symbol on cards that were presented to the five subjects, each subject being given a slightly different card. When all five subjects guessed the common symbol, a "trial" was completed, and another set of cards was presented. This went on for fifteen trials for each of twenty groups, involving a total of one hundred subjects in all.

Leavitt selected four specific patterns of communication networks for his experiment. These were called the "circle," the "chain," the "Y," and the "wheel"; each pattern was used for five groups of subjects. In the circle each position was connected for communication with each of two other positions. In the chain all positions except two had two channels each, with these two positions having only one channel each. In the Y one position had three channels open, one position had two channels, and the other three positions had one channel each. And in the wheel one position was connected to all other positions, and the other positions were connected only to the central position. These four networks may be presented as indicated below.

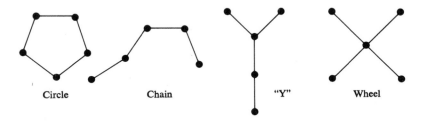

| Circle | Chain | "Y" | Wheel |

It should be made clear that these represent only four out of a great variety of communication networks possible for five-person groups. Furthermore, the only structure given to the group by the experimenter consisted in the task and in the particular arrangement of communication channels left open. There was no designation of any leader, nor were subjects told to whom they should send messages. Each subject knew that they would have to exchange messages (in this study written messages were used) to obtain one solution to their common problem, and each was given a set of numbered cards for writing and sending messages, but the rest was up to him.

One reason for the selection of the particular networks (the circle, chain, Y, and wheel) was that they represented different degrees of centralization. The wheel represented maximal centralization, the circle had no position more central than any others, and the chain and Y were intermediate in the degree of centralization inherent in their structures (with the Y somewhat more centralized than the chain).

We shall not go into a detailed analysis of Leavitt's results, the general pattern of which can be seen in Table 22. Here we note that the more centralized networks generally performed with greater efficiency than the less centralized networks. There is, however, one criterion for which the less centralized networks showed superiority; but this is a criterion of satisfaction, not of performance. On all criteria of problem-solving performance, the more centralized networks tended to be better than those that were less centralized.

Perhaps it is now apparent why we relate this experiment to the study of organizations. The focus is upon organizational forms. There is really no recognition at all of individual behavior in these results. There are, of course, individuals behaving in the experimental setting, but the critical variables being examined are those of group organization.

Communication structure is only one aspect of group organization. There are also other aspects; for example, authority structure (the pattern of legitimate power) or affect structure (the pattern of personal liking of group members for one another). These were not studied in

TABLE 22   COMPARATIVE PERFORMANCE OF DIFFERENT COMMUNICATION NETWORKS IN LEAVITT'S STUDY

Criterion	*Rank Order of Networks*
Fewest messages needed for correct trial	1. Wheel 2. Y 3. Chain 4. Circle
Fastest single correct trial	1. Wheel 2. Y 3. Circle 4. Chain
Fewest errors on final trials	1. Y 2. Wheel 3. Chain 4. Circle
Average rating of success of group	1. Wheel 2. Y 3. Chain 4. Circle
Average personal satisfaction with task	1. Circle 2. Chain 3. Y 4. Wheel

SOURCE: Adapted from Leavitt (1951).

Leavitt's experiment. Still, communication structure is enough to be interesting in its own right and to suggest implications that might apply to organizations beyond the laboratory.

Is not the main pattern of Leavitt's results one that every good manager in an organization would recognize as valid: group effectiveness is correlated with the degree of centralization for the coordination of task activity? Of course, people are not always most happy with such a system. Therefore, morale considerations sometimes require some relaxation of centralization. But if we focus only upon factors of task efficiency, then the advantages of centralization must be recognized.

However, such a set of conclusions is premature. We have examined only one of the first of a long line of studies of the effects of various communication networks that followed from Bavelas's suggestions of the late 1940s. When we take into account the later studies, we are forced to alter some of the conclusions suggested above.

Not all the studies of communication networks have been primarily concerned with the effects of the degree of centralization, but this has been repeated often enough to provide one of the main questions for subsequent research. Shaw (1964), in reviewing this research, points out that many studies have *not* confirmed that the more centralized networks provide most efficient problem solving. In fact, as is indicated by Table 23, there is no unanimity that centralized networks are either faster in coming to solutions or more free from errors.

Table 23 represents a tabulation based on all comparisons showing a difference between more centralized and less centralized networks reported for eighteen different experiments. Some experiments provided for several comparisons on a given criterion, and other experiments provided for none; this is why the number of comparisons reported for different criteria in Table 23 varies from sixteen to thirty-six. While there is not a universal pattern of results for any criterion, the trend indicated by Shaw's review is clearly that the more decentralized networks generally sent more messages than centralized networks and also that persons in decentralized networks showed greater satisfaction. But on criteria more precisely related to efficiency—speed and accuracy— the pattern is less clear. In only ten out of sixteen comparisons did the decentralized networks produce more errors, and in twenty-two out of thirty-six comparisons decentralized networks were actually faster than centralized networks.

TABLE 23 COMPARISONS OF RESULTS WITH CENTRALIZED AND DECENTRALIZED COMMUNICATION NETWORKS

	Number of Comparisons Showing Higher Ratings for Networks That Are	
Criterion	*Centralized*	*Decentralized*
Number of messages sent	1	35
Speed of solution	14	22
Frequency of errors	6	10
Satisfaction	2	17

SOURCE: Adapted from Shaw (1964), p. 123.

Shaw suggests that some of the ambiguity of these results can be reduced if we take into account the degree of complexity of experimental tasks. In some cases, such as Leavitt's experiment, a very simple task was used. Here the activity of the group is mostly limited to a fairly simple exchange of information—such as the symbols they had on cards given by the experimenter. In other experiments more complex problem-solving tasks were presented, such as constructing sentences or solving mathematical problems. By classifying comparisons according to the amount of task complexity, Shaw obtained the results reported in Table 24.

TABLE 24   COMPARISONS OF RESULTS WITH CENTRALIZED AND DECENTRALIZED COMMUNICATION NETWORKS, TAKING ACCOUNT OF TASK COMPLEXITY

Criterion	Task Complexity	Number of Comparisons Showing Higher Ratings for Networks That Are	
		Centralized	Decentralized
Number of messages sent	Simple	0	18
	Complex	1	17
Speed of solution	Simple	14	4
	Complex	0	18
Frequency of errors	Simple	0	9
	Complex	6	1
Satisfaction	Simple	1	7
	Complex	1	10

SOURCE: Shaw (1964), p. 123.

Table 24 represents a further breakdown of results shown previously in Table 23. The general patterns of decentralized networks sending more messages and having higher satisfaction are seen in Table 24 as holding for both simple and complex tasks. On the other two criteria indicated, however, task complexity appears to be a very critical factor. On simple probems the more centralized networks produce solutions more quickly but on complex problems the decentralized networks are more likely to show the advantage of speed. Also, on simple problems more errors are made in decentralized networks, but on complex problems the centralized networks show more mistakes. From such evidence Shaw concludes: "Centralized networks are generally more efficient when the task requires merely the collection of information in one place. Decentralized networks are more efficient when the task requires, in addition to the information collection process, that further operations must be performed on the information before the task can be repeated" (p. 144).

It would be misleading if we suggested that these experiments with communication networks *prove* anything about behavior in ordinary organizations. They do, however, point to some relationships between

certain variables in laboratory settings, and there is good reason to believe that variables such as communication centralization and task
complexity are also relevant to organizational settings. But to prove
anything about ordinary organizations we must study the organizations
themselves.

Still, we would be missing an important point if we did not comment upon a basic similarity between the results of studies of the effects of centralization of communication networks and the conclusions
of the previous section of this chapter. Just as we cannot say flatly that
more centralized networks provide greater efficiency, neither could we
previously conclude that wide participation of workers either necessarily promotes or inhibits production. Both in laboratory studies and
in research in real-life settings, we have come to recognize the importance of other contingencies in affecting such relationships. And chief
among these other contingencies must be considered the nature of the
task. Centralization and problem-solving efficiency may be correlated—
when the task to be performed is quite simple (and also assuming satisfaction is reasonably high). But when the task is more complex, this
simple relationship vanishes—or may even be reversed.

18

The Madness (?) of Crowds

STORMING THE BASTILLE

It was a long, hot summer. Discontent was brewing throughout the French countryside and especially in the streets of Paris. In Versailles the Estates General was meeting, with the Third Estate shaking the foundations of the nation by forming themselves into a National Assembly. King Louis XVI was known to disapprove, but what could he do? There were rumors, well founded, that he intended to do something; it was said that he was about to make several moves designed to strengthen royal authority. These moves might include the strengthening of foreign regiments stationed in Paris, the firing of his finance chief, Necker, who had promoted the calling of the Estates General, and an order to dissolve the National Assembly.

On July 12 at noon Paris received the news of Necker's dismissal. Crowds formed and public protest meetings were held. Uncertain of safety on the Paris streets, the royal troops withdrew to fortified positions, and more and more the crowd took over the city. First most of the hated customs posts, where taxes were collected on food and wine coming into Paris, were destroyed. Then the search was on for grain and arms. Alarmed both at the intensity of the riots and at the possibility of extreme countermeasures by royal military forces, the Paris members of the Third Estate formed themselves into a provisional city government and organized a citizen's militia to restore order.

However, order was not restored immediately, and on July 14 the insurgency continued with growing force. "To the Bastille!" became the cry of an armed throng. The Bastille, the prison-fortress that had long housed political prisoners, was for Paris citizens a symbol of royal oppression. Its guns could do great damage to the surrounding neighborhood, and, above all, it was known to have recently received stocks of ammunition, which were now much in demand by the insurgents. The people gathered at the Bastille and attempted to storm the armed fortress. Guns were fired back into the crowd, killing scores and wounding many more. But the mob, aided by several small cannons, continued to attack. Finally, two detachments of the French guard who had defected and joined with the insurgents marched up to the main gate. The drawbridge was lowered, the fortress surrendered, and the mob surged inside. The following day the citizens began the systematic destruction of this great and gloomy edifice. The Bastille was soon removed from the sight of Parisians, while ever more indelibly marked upon French memories.

As a military event, the fall of the Bastille was of little significance. However, the political consequences were far-reaching, as this event dramatized the momentum of events that soon would sweep away the old order of French power. Almost immediately the king recognized the legitimacy of the National Assembly and of the new government of the city of Paris. But the revolution did not stop there. A process had begun that was not to stop until all vestiges of royal and noble power were swept away in France.

RETRIBUTION IN QUITO

Listeners to a radio station at Quito, Ecuador, on February 12, 1949, heard a rather strange series of reports. The music was interrupted with the announcement of an "urgent piece of late news." An enemy in the shape of a cloud was approaching Quito after destroying a neighboring town. A "governmental minister" went on the air to urge calm. Then the "mayor" came on to promote the defense of the city against the unknown peril—and urged the evacuation of women and children. Then came the report that a monster surrounded by fire and smoke had been seen at the northern edge of the city.

This was all meant to be only a radio program. It was an adaptation to local conditions of H. G. Wells's novel, *The War of the Worlds.* Perhaps those who produced the program should have anticipated that many listeners would be overly impressed by the realism of the program. There was a precedent from a decade earlier when a similar broadcast had caused mass panic in the United States (Cantril, Gaudet, and Herzog, 1940). But apparently nobody at Radio Quito anticipated the events that actually followed that evening in Quito.

Most of the people of Quito were in the streets before the broadcasters were aware of the effectiveness of their presentation. Then the station earnestly pleaded for the people to be calm, pointing out that the invasion had all been fiction. But the crowds were not easily calmed. They began to gather around the building that housed the radio station. An Associated Press report (Britt, 1950) indicates what happened next:

> Groups set fire to the building at various points, and some of the occupants leaped from the third-story windows as the flames trapped them.
>
> Witnesses said about a hundred persons were in the building when the mob formed in front, crashing in windows with stones. A number of the occupants escaped through a rear door, but others were forced upstairs by the rampaging mob.
>
> As the flames cut off escape, occupants formed a human chain from balconies and windows. Some were dashed to the ground when the "chain" broke. Others leaped (p. 305).

In all, fifteen persons were reported killed in this riot. Over a dozen others were injured. The building, also housing the city's oldest newspaper, was almost completely destroyed. Police aid was slow to arrive, for many of the police had been out to investigate the reported invasion. Finally, army troops with tear gas had to be called on to restore order.

Here again, as in the storming of the Bastille, an attack upon a building became the objective of an aroused mob. Both of these cases, the storming of the Bastille in 1789 and of Radio Quito in 1949, are here presented to give examples of extreme actions taken by crowds. How can we make sense out of such behavior?

THEORETICAL POINTER

Crowds and Collective Behavior

The crowd is a temporary group based upon a common object of attention. The characterization of a crowd usually emphasizes the extent to which behavior grows out of mutual stimulation among crowd members. This mutual stimulation may develop through the random milling of persons in close physical contact, through the collective excitement of some unusual event, and through the rapid social contagion of a mood or action from one member to another. Some authors suggest that milling, collective excitement, and social contagion form a natural sequence in the development of crowds.

Blumer (1951) distinguishes between four main kinds of crowds:

1. Casual crowds—momentary organizations around objects of common attention
2. Conventionalized crowds—in which persons are unified by witnessing a common event and by the rather standard patterns of behavior they display in so doing
3. Expressive crowds—in which physical movement serves primarily for the expression of a common mood and the release of individual tensions
4. Acting crowds—in which the group comes to focus upon performing a particular common deed

Examples of these respective types may be seen in persons on the street observing a minor accident, spectators at a typical basketball game, participants in an unusually spirited religious revival, and members of a lynching mob. It is the acting crowd, illustrated also by the storming of the Bastille or of Radio Quito, which has received the special attention of social scientists. Therefore, unless specified otherwise, crowd behavior usually means the behavior of persons in an acting crowd.

The crowd is one of several main forms of what is usually called collective behavior—a category that emphasizes the fluidity of behavior rather than the presence of established customs or institutions. Other main forms of collective behavior are the mass and the public.

The mass is distinguished from the crowd by its dispersal, its more indirect communication, the anonymity of its members from each other, and its inability to carry out concerted action. It is illustrated by the consumers of a particular product or the viewers of a particular television show.

The public is distinguished from both the crowd and the mass by its focus upon a particular issue and the presence of discussion on that issue. Like the mass, the public is dispersed; but like the crowd, the participants are involved in direct influence upon one another.

ARE CROWDS INSANE?

We opened this chapter with two historical cases of crowd action as a background for considering the social psychology of crowd behavior. We wonder how crowds could be formed to assume such an unlikely task as the storming of the Bastille or the destruction of Radio Quito. Perhaps people must be more than a little mad, in more ways than one, to attempt such undertakings.

The Frenchman Gustave LeBon (1841–1931), the first systematic student of crowd behavior, emphasized the irrationality and impulsiveness of crowds. When persons come together in crowds, he suggested, they lose their power of critical judgment. Instead they get carried away by the sentiments of the crowd, itself a kind of common denominator of unconscious impulses. As LeBon (1895) expresses it, "The heterogeneous is swamped by the homogeneous, and the unconscious qualities obtain the upper hand" (p. 29). Crowd behavior also has a temporary and immediate character.

> Any display of premeditation by crowds is in consequence out of the question. They may be animated in succession by the most contrary sentiments, but they will always be under the influence of the exciting causes of the moment. They are like leaves which a tempest whirls up and scatters in every direction and then allows to fall (p. 37).

With such a susceptibility to immediate impulses, crowds may do rather extreme things. Quoting again from the sometimes quaint but always lucid discussion of LeBon:

> The simplicity and exaggeration of the sentiments of crowds have for result that a throng knows neither doubt nor uncertainty. . . . A suspicion transforms itself as soon as announced into incontrovertible evidence. A commencement of antipathy or disapprobation, which in the case of an isolated individual would not gain strength, becomes at once furious hatred in the case of an individual in a crowd.
>
> The violence of the feelings of crowds is also increased, especially in heterogeneous crowds, by the absence of all sense of responsibility. The certainty of impunity, a certainty the stronger as the crowd is more numerous, and the notion of a considerable momentary force due to number, make possible in the case of crowds sentiments and acts impossible for the isolated individual. In crowds the foolish, ignorant, and envious persons are freed from the sense of their insignificance and powerlessness, and are possessed instead by the notion of brutal and temporary but immense strength.
>
> Unfortunately, this tendency of crowds towards exaggeration is often brought to bear upon bad sentiments. These sentiments are atavistic residuum of the instincts of the primitive man, which the fear of punishment obliges the isolated and responsible individual to curb. Thus it is that crowds are so easily led into the worst excesses (pp. 50–51).

This does not mean, LeBon hastens to add, that crowd behavior is necessarily always bad. Crowds may also perform very noble and heroic deeds. But whether bad or good, the deeds of a crowd always tend to be carried out in exaggerated form.

The writings of LeBon, and of many others since his time, characterize crowd behavior as highly spontaneous and variable, tending toward extreme violence and destructiveness, and displaying gross irrationality. Other scholars have emphasized that such a picture is overdrawn. An example of a more qualified interpretation may be seen in recent work of the historian George Rudé.

In his survey of seventeenth- and early eighteenth-century riots of England and France, Rudé (1964) grants that unexpected events may sometimes change the focus of a crowd. However, he concludes that in most cases the riots were directed toward precise objects and that rioters "rarely engaged in indiscriminate attacks on either properties or persons" (p. 254). These crowds usually limited their efforts quite systematically to the business at hand.

On the matter of violence, Rudé recognizes that destruction of property was frequently the objective of crowd action. In fact, there were particular techniques that became almost traditional: machine breaking, "pulling down" houses, and setting things afire—the latter apparently as characteristically a British technique as throwing up barricades was a favorite among French mobs. But seldom were rioters very destructive of human life. As Table 25 indicates, death was much more apt to come from the reactions of authorities to English riots than from the direct actions of rioters. The same could be said about the actions of French mobs, even including most of the action in the French Revolution. For example, those who stormed the Bastille did kill the governor of the fortress and 7 or 8 other defenders; but the guns from the fortress had already killed or wounded 150 of the crowd. So, according to Rudé, in the most typical cases "it was authority

TABLE 25   YE OLDE ENGLISH RIOTS

	Persons Killed by Rioters	Persons Killed by Authorities
Food riots of 1766	0	31
Wilkite riots of 1768	0	11
Gordon riots of 1780	0	310
Luddite riots of 1811–1813	1	30
"Swing" riots of 1830	0	9

SOURCE: Adapted from Rudé (1964), p. 255.

TABLE 26   DEATHS IN DETROIT

	Persons Killed in the 1967 Detroit Riots
By police, National Guard, or army	At least 28
By rioters	2 or 3
Other deaths	12 or 13
TOTAL	43

SOURCE: Adapted from Kerner (1968), p. 107.

rather than the crowd that was conspicuous for its violence to life and limb" (p. 256). Could the same thing be said about recent American riots?

Rudé also believes that conclusions about crowd irrationality have been overdrawn. He suggests (p. 254) that, from the point of view of crowd members, its purposes were generally rational and that it chose "not only the targets but the means most appropriate to the occasion" (p. 254). Rudé concludes:

> In short, the crowd was violent, impulsive, easily stirred by rumor, and quick to panic; but it was not fickle, peculiarly irra-tional, or generally given to bloody attacks on persons. The con-ventional picture of the crowd painted by LeBon and inherited by later writers is not lacking in shrewd and imaginative in-sight; but it ignores the facts of history and is, in consequence, overdrawn, tendentious, and misleading (p. 275).

But Rudé is an historian whose studies have been primarily of prein-dustrial or early industrial periods. Would the same generalizations apply to, say, American race riots of the twentieth century?

American race riots provide many illustrations of apparently wild and irrational behavior. A small incident may quickly explode into a full-scale riot. Usually there is little about the particular incident to explain such a response, though it is interesting to note that incidents between black men and white policemen have been rather frequent sparks of riots (see Table 27).

But behind the incidents are the underlying conditions. Can we iden-tify the conditions that have led to race riots? In a general way, we can. Race relations in urban America have a number of features (in-cluding extreme patterns of residential segregation and limited job op-portunities for Negroes, combined with the presence of conspicuous wealth and power on the part of others in the community) that in a general way enhance the likelihood of riots. But we must also be care-ful not to be too confident about our understanding of the causes of riots on the basis of such generalizations about American race rela-tions.

One line of argument is that recent American riots represent wild, irrational outbreaks on the part of the lowest and most miserable seg-ment of American society. It is the poorest blacks, those without hope of improvement, who are simply expressing their collective rage. There may be some truth in this analysis, but there are also real problems in

TABLE 27 IMMEDIATE PRECIPITANTS OF 76 AMERICAN RACE RIOTS, 1913–1963

Arrest, injury, or interference of Negro men by white policemen	15
Attack or holdup of white women by Negro men	10
Other interracial fights	27
Friction over specific public issue (segregation, housing, etc.)	14
Job-based conflicts	5
Other	5
TOTAL	76

SOURCE: Lieberson and Silverman (1965), p. 889.

trying to relate this interpretation to empirical propositions that can be proven. If this revolt-of-the-miserables interpretation is correct, we should expect to find a definite pattern in the incidence of riots. They ought to occur in those cities where the lot of the black man is poorest, and the participants should be overwhelmingly of the lowest social classes. However, an attempt by Lieberson and Silverman (1965) to identify background conditions of riots by comparing cities with race riots between 1913 and 1963 with cities of similar size but without riots showed few indications that cities with riots had poorer conditions. In surveying more recent evidence, Spilerman (1970) also found little relationship between economic conditions and the riot potential of a city.

In a related prediction, we would expect that rioting would be focused primarily in the poorest slums. There is of course ample evidence to associate the occurrence of race riots with Negro slum areas (Grimshaw, 1960). However, in a study of the Watts section of Los Angeles after the 1965 riots, Raymond Murphy and James Watson failed to find very dramatic differences between middle-class and lower-class blacks in regard to their attitudes toward or participation in the riot (Samuelson, 1967).

TABLE 28   RESPONSE TO THE WATTS RIOT, BY ECONOMIC AREAS
           OF WATTS

	Poorest Neighborhood	*Richest Neighborhood*
Took some part in the riot	25.6%	17.9%
Felt highly or moderately favorable toward the riot	50.0%	41.2%

SOURCE: Adapted from Samuelson (1967), p. 664.

Often related to the interpretation that contemporary American riots are the reaction of the very poor is the assumption that they are completely irrational outbursts representing at most only very few persons. But the complete irrationality is certainly put into question by the fact that more Watts residents believed in retrospect that their riot had helped the Negro cause than believed it hurt that cause (Samuelson, 1967). Many thought such a riot served effectively to call attention to their problems. If so, could it be considered totally irrational? And as for the point that only a very few were actually involved in the riots, the question becomes, How few are "very few"? Is the quarter of the Watts population that took part to some degree in the 1965 riots to be considered a very small minority?

In reviewing recent studies of riot participation, McPhail (1971) found few consistent relationships between the characteristics of individuals and participation in a riot. This led him to suggest that the critical features for producing riots might be simply the availability of large numbers of persons with free time who can come together at the same place when events capture their attention. That young black males have been most frequent riot participants can be understood largely in terms of such situational factors; in American cities today they are most apt to be highly concentrated in numbers, to have free time, and to be ready to congregate on the street when attention is aroused.

We are now at a point of confusion in our interpretation of race riots and similar forms of crowd behavior. Are they simply spontaneous and irrational outbursts; or do they carry out a rational, even if largely unorganized, strategy? Are they symptoms of despair or of rising aspirations? Are they completely free of customary restraints of behavior, or do they embody forms that themselves become customary?

As is so often the case, the above questions tend to force an either-or kind of response when a more qualified answer is needed. Crowd behavior is characterized by suggestibility and irrationality, but this does not mean that crowds do not pursue primary objectives that might have some rational justification. They may be relatively unrestrained by conventional forms of behavior, but never completely so. And of course the crowd itself may give rise to the formation of new conventions.

Probably our greatest cause of confusion is our inability to predict the emergence or to explain the behavior of particular crowds. Crowds do not show the predictability of behavior that may be seen in most groups, where an established system of positions and roles regulates the behavior of members. This makes group behavior ordinarily quite predictable, and this predictability goes a long way toward commending such behavior to us as being rational rather than irrational.

Crowds, however, are not established groups. They are always only groups in the process of organization. If they evolve into established groups, we no longer consider them to be crowds. Usually, the crowd does not become anything other than a crowd, existing only temporarily and then vanishing with the dispersal of its individual members.

While crowds are not without standards of behavior—crowd members are of course typically influenced by a common cultural background as well as by one another—the standards tend to be redefined and altered within the immediate situation. Thus the main features that give predictability to group behavior—established role systems and conventionalized norms—are present in only a shadowy form in crowds. This makes the concrete behavior of crowds far less predictable than that of most groups.

This lack of predictability of crowd behavior makes us more likely to brand it as "crazy." But the things we brand as insane are no less the products of cause and effect than the events we see as normal and natural. They are, however, more elusive in terms of our ability to predict and control—and thus they are more likely to be causes of anxiety and objects of emotional labeling.

Ideal Types and Operational Definitions

METHODOLOGICAL
AND THEORETICAL
POINTER

Many years ago Max Weber (1864–1920) characterized the work of social scientists as typically dealing with basic concepts that are *ideal types* (Weber, 1949). *Ideal* here carries no value connotation; it refers rather to the simplified and purified nature of such concepts. These concepts are constructed by the investigator, not directly given by reality. And in the construction of such concepts, the ambiguities of reality are sifted out, leaving the investigator free to organize his discussion around pure verbal forms.

The crowd is certainly an example of an ideal type. It gives us a picture of a certain kind of behavior, but not all crowds perfectly represent this behavior. In fact, none does completely. Persons in a crowd never completely lose all sense of the habits that constrain them in other group settings, and their very presence in the crowd probably is influenced by their important social roles (for example, sex or occupational roles). What the concept allows is for us to focus attention upon the *relatively* large degree to which behavior sometimes grows out of the immediate mutual stimulation of an otherwise unorganized group. Where this is noteworthy we may talk about crowd behavior.

As a science develops, experimentation tends to replace naturalistic observation as the most common way of seeking evidence. As this occurs there is a desire to achieve much more precision in the concepts used. The older taxonomies no longer seem precise enough to describe what emerges from experimental manipulation. Thus the demand is for concepts more clearly related to actual experimentation. In the twentieth century this has produced a movement sometimes called *operationism.* Stimulated especially by Percy W. Bridgman's *The Logic of Modern Physics* (1928), experimental psychologists have often been persuaded that scientific concepts must be defined in terms of the operations that produce them.

Thus concepts come to be tied to the particular experimental procedures that allow their measurement. This provides a precision which is lacking in more general conceptualizations.

However, such *operational definitions* never completely replace the need for more general concepts. Indeed, it is often the more general concepts that suggest the experimental activity in which operational concepts find their place. Experiments are not just performed at random, but along lines suggested by ideas of what is important. And what is important to observe or study is not necessarily identified by what is most measurable or capable of being expressed through precise operational definitions.

So it is that the main concepts of social psychology are not themselves usually presented in terms of operational definitions. However, as we try to clarify the research literature under any one of the main topics, operational definitions do become important. Thus it is with collective behavior. The main labels we use—*expressive crowd, mass,* even *race riot*—are clearly ideal types. There is no sense of the exact operations by which an investigator produces or identifies such forms. His concepts point to general classes of events more than they help him to measure precise variables. However, within a particular line of experimental study (more characteristic of other areas of social psychology than that of crowd behavior), more and more attention is given to the concepts that are tied to actual experimental operations.

THE PSYCHOLOGY OF MUTUAL STIMULATION

Are crowds insane? This question cannot be fully answered as a scientific one because it involves other issues besides matters of fact. Do we like to be in crowds? Do we like the results of crowds? Such questions are suggested by the introduction of the concept of insanity to apply possibly to the group level of crowd behavior.

However, if our purpose is not so much to either approve or condemn crowd behavior as to see it as a part of nature, we must acknowledge two points: (1) crowd behavior is purposeful, not accidental, and (2) the particular behavior shown by crowds emerges out of mutual stimulation.

The first point tends to negate a "madness" interpretation, or at least to point out that there is method in the madness. That is, given the goals adopted by a crowd, temporary though they may be, the behavior of a crowd in pursuing these goals may be quite effective. The crowd that stormed the Bastille, for example, carried out its purpose quite effectively, as did the mob that destroyed the building housing Radio Quito. Whether or not the objectives of a crowd are rational is of course another question. Here we must include in our judgment the kind of long-range perspective that is difficult to bring to any immediate situation, whether involving crowds or involving conventional organizations. In retrospect we see the storming of the Bastille as an incident in a purposeful revolutionary movement and the events at Quito as simply an unruly incident; but this demands a perspective beyond that of the participants. The Quito rioters undoubtedly felt at the time that their retribution upon Radio Quito was well deserved, just as the Paris mob felt that they had good reasons for wanting to destroy the Bastille.

But to go on to the second point, there is a difference between the way a crowd finds its goals and the way goals are pursued in more established settings. The mutual stimulation in the immediate situation is a major ingredient in developing the goals of crowd behavior, while it is much less so in other settings. This is really the crux of the difference, the role of mutual stimulation. And recognition of the role of mutual stimulation in the genesis of crowd behavior should help us understand behavior that otherwise would defy comprehension.

In this final section of the chapter we will focus on the psychology of mutual stimulation. This is really the central characteristic of crowd behavior. However, in the remaining discussion we will no longer be dealing with crowds as such. We will rather take this central feature, mutual stimulation, and try to identify the psychological dynamics involved.

Some years ago Floyd Allport (1920) performed some experiments on *social facilitation*. These, incidentally, were some of the earliest laboratory experiments in social psychology. Allport's studies presented subjects with various mental tasks, such as producing free chain associations (that is, subjects were given an initial word and then asked to write below it other word associations). They did this in one of two basic conditions: "together" or "alone." The task was the same; but sometimes it was done in the presence of others with the same task, while in the alone condition only a single individual performed at one time.

The most general conclusion from these studies was that more associations were produced in a given time in the together condition than in the alone condition. This was especially true with experimental variations that made the process of association simple and almost mechanical; in more highly mental tasks the greater productivity in a group setting was not so marked. In fact, mental productions of the highest quality tended to come from alone rather than together treatments.

These experiments were of course in no way a study of crowds. We mention them here simply for the idea of social facilitation that they suggest. The presence of other persons does commonly exert something of a stimulating effect upon an individual. We have only to add that under certain conditions the stimulating effect of the presence of others is greater than under other conditions, and we begin to see one of the important strands in the psychology of crowd behavior.

But what are the conditions under which the presence of others is more stimulating? Some further evidence may come from studies of rumors by Gordon Allport and Leo Postman. In their book, *The Basic Psychology of Rumor* (1947), they suggest that there are two basic conditions for the spread of a rumor: (1) the theme of the rumor must have some importance to the persons involved, and (2) the true facts must be ambiguous. Let us quote from some of Allport and Postman's discussion of these points:[1]

> The two essential conditions of importance and ambiguity seem to be related to rumor transmission in a roughly quantitative manner. A formula for the intensity of rumor might be written as follows:
>
> $$R = i \times a$$
>
> In words this formula means that the amount of rumor in circulation will vary with the importance of the subject to the individuals concerned *times* the ambiguity of the evidence pertaining to the topic at issue. The relation between importance and ambiguity is not additive but multiplicative, for if either importance or ambiguity is zero, there is *no* rumor. For instance, an American citizen is not likely to spread rumors concerning the market price for camels in Afghanistan because the subject has no importance for him, ambiguous though it certainly is. He is not disposed to spread gossip concerning the doings of the people in Swaziland, because he doesn't care about them. Ambiguity alone does not launch or sustain rumor.
>
> Nor does importance. Although an automobile accident in which I lose my leg is of calamitous significance to me, I am not susceptible to rumors concerning the extent of my injury because I know the facts. If I receive a legacy and know the amount involved, I am resistant to rumors that exaggerate its amount. Officers in the higher echelons of the army were less susceptible to rumor than was G. I. Joe, not because coming events were less important to them, but because, as a rule, the plans and strategies were better known to them. Where there is no ambiguity, there can be no rumor (pp. 33–34).

[1] Gordon W. Allport and Leo Postman, *The Basic Psychology of Rumor*. New York: Holt, Rinehart and Winston, 1947. Quotations from this source are reprinted with permission of the publisher.

Let us now put together these three threads: (1) the generally activating effect of the presence of other people, (2) an event or series of events of considerable importance to persons involved, and (3) a general ambiguity about how these events are to be interpreted or what action would constitute an appropriate response. Combine these three, and the potential for mutual stimulation is very great.

Crowd behavior is of course not the only form mutual stimulation may take. Falling in love may provide another example of the combination of (1) social stimulation (2) creating meaning and reducing ambiguity on (3) issues of supreme importance for the persons involved. But when more than a small handful of persons are involved at the same time and place, the results of these characteristics of mutual stimulation are usually recognized as crowd behavior.

19
The Ubiquity of Primary Relationships

ARE FAMILIES NECESSARY?

In his fictional, we hope, view of the future of modern civilization, Aldous Huxley (1953) describes the future "brave new world" as existing without the presence of human families. Human fertilization, incubation, and early education are all managed in large centers of mass production, like the Central London Hatchery and Conditioning Centre, which Huxley describes in great detail. Sexual behavior is widely and freely engaged in, but it has nothing to do with families.

In such a hypothetical world it may appear that the family is functionally unnecessary. But would this be possible in any known society? Before we decide too quickly, let us note what main functions families fulfill in human society and discover whether they always serve these functions.

Murdock (1949), in his extensive cross-cultural survey of kinship systems, arrived at the conclusion that the nuclear family is indeed universal. That is, all societies studied make an important grouping of parents-with-children—though it is true that many societies consider the larger extended family, which includes other relatives of the blood line, as even more important. Furthermore, in all societies the nuclear family seems to have four basic kinds of functions: sexual, reproductive, economic, and educational.

While not doubting the general application of Murdock's summary of the functions of the nuclear family, some anthropologists have pointed to societies that appear to offer exceptions. LaBarre (1954), for example, points to the extreme case of the Nayar of India. In this society it is customary that girls experience both marriage and divorce before puberty. They are then left to entertain lovers after they are grown, but they may not remarry. This leaves the male lovers without clear responsibility for either their mates or their biological children. This does not, however, allow Nayar men to escape paternal responsibilities; they have economic and educational responsibilities for their sisters' children. But of course these "parental" responsibilities have nothing to do with biological parenthood. The Nayars thus put into three separate social systems (marriage, a system of sex and reproduction, and a system of child rearing) what in other societies is all in one system, the nuclear family. Still, it is interesting to note that all the

218

basic functions of the nuclear family, at least according to Murdock's list, are well supplied.

The Israeli kibbutz has also been cited as an example of a society without the family. Spiro (1954) points to the collectivistic community as a case in which marriage is practically meaningless and in which parents do not supervise their own children. A man and woman may become a couple and live together in the same room, but their children are from the beginning cared for by established institutions of the community—hospital, nursery, and school. The children do not live with their parents, and the parents do not have any economic obligations toward their children—nor toward each other, for that matter. All economic obligations are organized for the community as a whole; families are not economic units. Still, Spiro points to ways in which the whole community itself becomes psychologically like a family. He suggests that "only in a 'familial' society, such as the kibbutz, is it possible to dispense with the family" (p. 846).

Even in these extreme cases, we can see the basic functions of the nuclear family being fulfilled. Adults mate and reproduce; children are cared for and educated; and economic cooperation is in some way managed. Perhaps these extreme cases also make us sensitive to some of the more psychological functions of the human family. Nuclear families provide care and affection no less than sex and economic needs. Young children require close attention, psychological as well as physical; and adults have needs for intimate acceptance, which is not simply sexual. In the kibbutzim (plural of kibbutz) studied by Spiro it is clear that a couple is not simply a pair of lovers. They would not be granted a room together if they only wanted a sexual union. Their life together is assumed to cover a much broader range of intimacy. Furthermore, parents do recognize particular children as their own. In fact, despite the lack of specific economic and educational obligations, Spiro tells us that parents serve the child "as the objects of his most important identifications, and they provide him with a certain security and love that he obtains from no one else. If anything, the attachment of the young children to their parents is greater than it is in our own society" (p. 844).

We may therefore conclude that the family, or something like it, satisfies basic human needs in all societies, and that among these needs is the sense of belonging or acceptance in a small, intimate group. Psychological security no less than economic security is rooted in families, and psychological identification no less than the learning of basic skills is acquired by children from parents. A person may be close to persons outside his family, but usually his most primary social relationship is within the family. And the family is generally the most primary of primary groups.

Charles H. Cooley on Primary Groups

THEORETICAL POINTER

The concept of the primary group was introduced over half a century ago by the sociologist Charles H. Cooley. Certain groups, such as the family, may be identified as primary determinants both for the human nature of individuals and for the continuity of society. Let us note how he presents these ideas in his book *Social Organization* (1909):[1]

By primary groups I mean those characterized by intimate face-to-face association and cooperation. They are primary in several senses, but chiefly in that they are fundamental in forming the social nature and ideals of the individual. The result of intimate association, psychologically, is a certain fusion of individualities in a common whole, so that one's very self, for many purposes at least, is the common life and purpose of the group. Perhaps the simplest way of describing this wholeness is by saying that it is a "we"; it involves the sort of sympathy and mutual identification for which "we" is the natural expression. One lives in the feeling of the whole and finds the chief aims of his will in that feeling.

It is not to be supposed that the unity of the primary group is one of mere harmony and love. It is always a differentiated and usually a competitive unity, admitting of self-assertion and various appropriative passions; but these passions are socialized by sympathy, and come, or tend to come, under the discipline of a common spirit. The individual will be ambitious, but the chief object of his ambition will be some desired place in the thought of the others, and he will feel allegiance to common standards of service and fair play. So the boy will dispute with his fellows a place on the team, but above such disputes will place the common glory of his class and school.

The most important spheres of this intimate association and cooperation—though by no means the only ones—are the family, the play-group of children, and the neighborhood or community group of elders. These are practically universal, belonging to all times and all stages of development; and are accordingly a chief basis of what is universal in human nature and human ideals. . . .

Primary groups are primary in the sense that they give the individual his earliest and completest experience of social unity, and also in the sense that they do not change in the same degree as more elaborate relations, but form a comparatively permanent source out of which the latter are ever springing. Of course they are not independent of the larger society, but to some extent reflect its spirit; as the German family and the German school bear somewhat distinctly the print of German militarism. But this, after all, is like the tide setting back into creeks, and does not commonly go very far . . .

These groups, then, are springs of life, not only for the individual but for social institutions. They are only in part moulded by special traditions, and, in larger degree, express a universal nature. The religion or government of other civilizations may seem alien to us, but the children or the family group wear the common life, and with them we can always make ourselves at home. . . .

. . . the view here maintained is that human nature is not something existing separately in the individual, but a *group-nature or primary phase of society,* a relatively simple and general condition of the social mind. It is something more, on the one hand, than the mere instinct that is born in us—though that enters into it—and something less, on the other, than the more elaborate development of ideas and sentiments that makes up institutions. It is the nature which is developed and expressed in those simple, face-to-face groups that are somewhat alike in all societies; groups of the family, the playground, and the neighborhood. In the essential similarity of these is to be found the basis, in experience, for similar ideas and sentiments in the human mind. In these, everywhere, human nature comes into existence. Man does not have it at birth; he cannot acquire it except through fellowship, and it decays in isolation (pp. 22–30).

---

[1] Charles H. Cooley, *Social Organization.* New York: Charles Scribner's Sons, 1909. Quotations from this source are reprinted with permission of the publisher.

Although Cooley talks about primary groups, with the family as perhaps the best illustration, it is relevant to suggest that not all families are fully primary. The crucial ingredient of primary groups, that is, psychological intimacy in person-to-person relationships, may be absent in a particular family, even though families usually show such intimacy more than do other groups. A distinction may therefore be made between primary groups and primary relationships. In this chapter we are especially concerned with the qualities of the latter, typically found in those groups Cooley has described as primary.

PRIMARY RELATIONSHIPS IN FORMAL ORGANIZATIONS

Cooley spoke of primary groups as those groups in which intimate, face-to-face exchange takes place. But intimate exchange is not limited to groups like the family or peer groups. Such exchange also goes on in the context of formal organizations. As we saw in Chapter 17, there is an informal as well as a formal organization of relationships in such settings; and primary relationships are embedded in the informal organization. Thus we can recognize the presence of primary relationships even in groups that seem furthest from Cooley's ideal type of the primary group.

Take, for example, the army. No other organization is more formally structured than the army. Persons do not usually enter the army for purposes of making friends, and friendship is not typically the basis of assignments to army duties. However, friendships do form in all parts of the army structure. And more and more military leaders are considering dealing with these primary-group patterns as a crucial feature of their job.

This interest in primary groups by leaders of formal organizations does not arise just out of curiosity. Very practical questions of organizational effectiveness are involved. Thus, as was suggested in Chapter 17, a factory's productivity may vary with features of informal organization. And even the very survival of the larger organization may depend on the network of primary relationships. For example, Shils and Janowitz (1948) report that this was the crucial factor in holding the German *Wehrmacht* together in the face of certain defeat in World War II. Not because of ideological passions nor even so much out of national loyalty did German troops continue as effective fighting units, but, Shils and Janowitz suggest, more out of interpersonal loyalties. Their fighting morale was not broken until their smallest units were disrupted. Shils and Janowitz conclude:

> It must be recognized that on the moral plane most men are members of the larger society by virtue of identifications which are mediated through the human beings with whom they are in personal relationships. Many are bound into the larger society only by primary group identifications (p. 315).

SPONTANEITY AND SOCIAL ORDER

A spontaneous network of primary-group relationships, we have just suggested, may be seen as constituting a substructure within more formal kinds of social structure. Bonds of fellow feeling develop psychological ties between associates as such informal structure takes shape. An early student of spontaneous forms of human affiliation, J. L. Moreno (1934), used the term *tele* to represent these bonds. His suggestion was that most forms of social organization would be much more effective if they took account of, and perhaps even restructured themselves according to, the tele expressed in such person-to-person relationships. Moreno not only pointed to the importance of these emotionally rooted bonds; he also indicated how they might be identified. He thus was not only the father of a sociometric movement (suggesting how identification of spontaneous psychological relationships may be used to facilitate better group adjustments), but also the father of the sociometric test.

In the early days of the sociometric movement it was suggested that such spontaneous forms of choice would present a single basic pattern of the psychological geography within a group. Jennings (1947; 1950), however, pointed out that the patterns of social choice varied quite systematically according to the criterion of choice. She thus distinguished between the *psychegroup*, in which the criterion of attraction is private and personal (for example, for leisure-time association), and the *sociogroup*, in which the criterion of choice reflects activity that is more collective in nature (for example, the choice of a work partner). Not only may the individuals chosen be different, but the whole pattern of social choices in a group may take a different shape under the two conditions. From this Jennings came to realize that there could not be just a single psychological structure within a group, but rather there exist multiple substructures (or at least two) reflecting different kinds of social choice.

METHODOLOGICAL POINTER

The Sociometric Test

The sociometric test developed by Moreno and associates is in essence an application of the idea of asking persons what they think of other persons. Moreno's use was to ask persons to indicate choices of other individuals in the group according to a particular criterion of choice (for example, sharing the same living area or spending leisure time together); then these responses would be used to restructure group arrangements or activities. Most investigators who have used sociometric tests, however, have used them as a research tool, rather than for purposes of social engineering.

By asking persons which other individuals they would choose (often allowing first and second choices, but sometimes requesting a rank order of the whole group), investigators can identify what cliques or subgroups may be present in the larger group. Also, they can identify psychological leaders (or *stars*) and those who, in contrast, are the psychological *isolates*. This is often done by making a sociometric matrix with a list of persons in the group presented in rows (as persons choosing) and also in columns (as persons chosen). A simple illustration may be given by Abe and Joe (who each choose Pete as a best friend), Pete and Stan (who choose each other), and George (who chooses Abe). This can be put into the following matrix form (using an X to indicate the single choice expressed by each):

Person Choosing	Person Chosen *Abe*	*Joe*	*Pete*	*Stan*	*George*
Abe		X			
Joe			X		
Pete				X	
Stan			X		
George	X				

This can also be expressed more pictorially in a sociogram with arrows used to represent positive attraction. In this imaginary little group, Pete is obviously something of a psychological star, while Joe and George appear to be isolates:

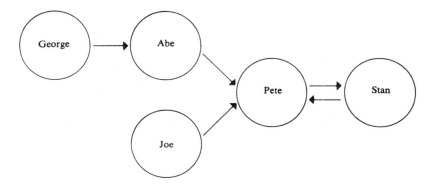

What does this have to do with the title of this section, "Spontaneity and Social Order"? We started with Moreno's suggestion that the spontaneous affective bonds might be identified and used as a basis for revamping larger structures. Now we see that the larger structures themselves may produce the basis of social choices, especially in sociogroup choice. This suggests that social organization and interpersonal spontaneity may be correlated without either being reducible simply to the other. Indeed, is not a degree of social order—including common purposes, similar attitudes, and some agreements on rules—required for close interpersonal bonds to thrive? And is not a large degree of such interpersonal spontaneity often found even within formal organizations? To shed some further light on this last question, we shall next take note of a study by Peter Blau.

INVESTIGATING THE INVESTIGATORS

Peter Blau (1963) observed sixteen agents in a law-enforcement agency of the United States government. These agents' work involved special investigative assignments into possible violations of federal laws. Much of their time was spent in the field carrying out investigations, and slightly less than half was spent in the office where the all-important reports were written and discussed. Each agent was in theory on his own in a case, and there were actually regulations against consultation with fellow agents (who had their own jobs to do). As a matter of fact, however, Blau observed a considerable amount of informal consultation. We shall follow Blau's analysis of this informal consultation for clues concerning the causes and consequences of such informal association in a bureaucracy.

One possible factor that Blau considered for explaining the patterns of informal consultation was that of competence. Especially in a professionally oriented group such as Blau studied, one might expect that the more competent persons would be most sought for purposes of informal consultation. This is indeed what Blau found.

Blau also developed measures of sociability, derived primarily from observations of who ate lunch with whom. From such records it was determined which agents had an extensive network of informal relationships and which moved in a more limited informal circle. In general the pattern was that those with more varied social contacts when off duty also tended to receive more informal consultation in the office.

Let us now attempt to tie these two patterns together. Contacts at work tended to be received by persons regarded as high in competence and by persons high in sociability. But do competence and sociability go together? No. Blau informs us that he found these to be negatively correlated. Agents with lower competence tended to be those with more extensive informal relations. The recognition that the two variables that correlate closely with contacts received at work are not correlated with each other makes it evident that these may be treated as separate influences upon informal consultation. It also makes us aware that rather different kinds of motives may be combined in seeking such contacts. We may call these motives help and acceptance. Help is primarily a job-related motive, and acceptance sought is primarily of a personal sort. Only a person capable of giving both would be especially sought after for consultations by his colleagues at work.

However, there are also costs involved in these informal consultations. Because of this, most of the more expert agents preferred to limit their informal contacts. We must therefore also note some of the ways that informal consultation was limited in the group of federal agents studied by Blau.

In our attention to the compromise process (Chapter 2) we suggested that a kind of exchange system might be seen at work in determining the outcome of relationships involving personal acceptance. In his discussion of informal work consultation among these agents, Blau (1963)[2] suggests that a somewhat parallel attention to an exchange process may be relevant—though of course the nature of what is exchanged here may be somewhat different.

> A consultation can be considered an exchange of values; both participants gain something, and both have to pay a price. The questioning agent is enabled to perform better than he could otherwise have done, without exposing his difficulties to the supervisor. By asking for advice, he implicitly pays his respect to the superior proficiency of his colleague. This acknowledgment of inferiority is the cost of receiving assistance. The consultant gains prestige, in return for which he is willing to devote some time to the consultation and permit it to disrupt his own work. The following remark of an agent illustrates this: "I like

[2] Peter M. Blau, *The Dynamics of Bureaucracy,* 2nd edition. Chicago: The University of Chicago Press, 1963. Copyright 1963 by The University of Chicago. Quotations from this source are reprinted with permission of the publisher.

giving advice. It's flattering, I suppose, if you feel that the others come to you for advice." . . .

The role of the agent who frequently solicited advice was less enviable, even though he benefited most directly from ·this un-official practice. Asking a colleague for guidance was less threatening than asking the supervisor, but the repeated admis-sion by an agent of his inability to solve his own problems also undermined his self-confidence and his standing in the group. The cost of advice became prohibitive if the consultant, after the questioner had subordinated himself by asking for help, was in the least discouraging—by postponing a discussion or by re-vealing his impatience during one. To avoid such rejections, agents usually consulted a colleague with whom they were friendly, even if he was not an expert. One agent explained, when asked whether he ever consults a colleague whom he con-siders outstandingly competent: "I sometimes would like to, but I'm hesitant. I always have the feeling that I don't have the right to pick his brain. I ask the ones I know well because I don't feel any reluctance about asking them."

The establishment of partnerships of mutual consultation virtually eliminated the danger of rejections as well as the status threat implicit in asking for help, since the roles of questioner and consultant were intermittently reversed. These partner-ships also enabled agents to reserve their consultations with an expert whom they did not know very well for their most com-plicated problems (pp. 130–131).

Did all this help to make for a more effective agency? Probably. But in this chapter we are not so much concerned with the operation of an office as with showing how personal relations become woven into such presumably impersonal operations. Even the federal bureauc-racy is not immune to the widespread development of informal re-lationships.

INTIMACY AND RESTRAINT

Primary relationships have another side in addition to that of friend-ship and intimacy. This is the development of boundaries, of barriers, and of restraints against too much intimacy. Some of these are barriers around a relationship—to prevent intimacy from being spread too far. Other barriers are also found within an intimate relationship, even here restricting the range of personal intimacy.

Writing about soldiers in World War II, the cartoonist Bill Mauldin (1945) observed that wartime friendships, especially at the fighting front, are closer than friendships in peacetime. Why? "You depend upon friends in war much more" (p. 55).

Such intimacy of informal relationships, however, cannot be ex-tended too widely. It also requires boundaries. To help preserve the identity of intimate relationships, many languages provide separate forms for intimate and for more formal communications. This is often done by using different verbs and pronouns for addressing close friends than the forms otherwise used. Thus German distinguishes the familiar pronoun *du* from the formal *Sie*; French distinguishes between *tu* and *vous*; and Spanish distinguishes between *tú* and *usted*. In English the distinction between *thou* and *you* is now essentially obsolete, but use of last names or first names—or beyond that, of nicknames—presents a somewhat similar means of recognizing the distinction between the familiar and the more formal relationships. It provides a way of keeping the circle of intimates verbally distinguished from more impersonal relationships. Although foreign visitors sometimes feel Americans overdo the generosity of such first-name designation, it still serves at least as one of the tools by which Americans signal the acceptance of a personal relationship.

There is also another side of the picture. Not only must a way be found to preserve the identity of personal relationships, separating them from more polite or formal patterns; the less primary relationships (secondary relationships, as sociologists often call them) must be protected against the inroads of too great familiarity. Brotherhood makes fine rhetoric, and the image of a society of brotherly love may provide a useful ideal. But much of the work of the world must be done through relatively impersonal social relationships. Only in a most metaphorical sense can such relationships bear a familial mark—at least in modern civilization as distinct from tribal societies. Indeed, most modern organizations encourage the separation of work and family. And words like *cronyism* or *nepotism* carry a negative or pejorative meaning in most formal organizations.

Some theorists even go so far as to suggest that a major thrust of human society and culture is to *prevent* the free expression of intimate relationships. Thus Freud (1930) considered that a primary achievement of human culture is to check the spontaneous impulses of the pleasure-seeking force he calls libido. And chief among these impulses is that of intimate love.

Following the lead of Freud, Slater (1963)[3] also sees an inherent conflict between an individual's attachment to society (that is, the broader web of relationships and obligations) and his attachment to more intimate relationships. Slater discusses three main forms of what he calls *social regression* (that is, the withdrawal of emotional attachment from broader social forms in favor of a more limited and intimate concentration of affections), and he suggests how society organizes its forces to resist each of these. These forms he labels as *familial withdrawal, dyadic withdrawal*, and *narcissistic withdrawal*—depending on whether the focus of affections comes to be the family, another individual, or one's own self.

Slater's discussion of marriage illustrates his conception of the cross-currents competing for a person's emotional allegiance. He calls the marriage ceremony an "intrusion ritual," which asserts demands that the wedding pair identify themselves with broader social purposes at the same time that they give themselves to each other. The very details surrounding a typical wedding show this, as Slater points out:

[3] Philip E. Slater, "On Social Regression," *American Sociological Review*, 28 (1963), 339–364. Quotations from this source are reprinted with permission of the author and the American Sociological Association.

As the time for the wedding draws near, the forces drawing the couple apart become more intense. It is often believed to be "bad luck" for the groom to see the bride in her wedding dress before the ceremony, and, in general, contact between the couple on the day of the wedding is considered bad form. When they enter the church it is from opposite ends, as leaders of separate hosts of followers. Prior to the wedding day there are showers or a bridal supper for the bride and a "bachelor's dinner" for the groom, in which peer group ties are very strongly underlined. This tends to create the impression that in some way the couple *owe* their relationship to these groups, who are preparing them ceremonially for their marriage. Often this is made explicit, with family and friends vying with one another in claiming responsibility for having "brought them together" in the first place. This impression of societal initiative is augmented by the fact that the bride's father "gives the bride away." The retention of this ancient custom in modern times serves explicitly to deny the possibility that the couple might unite quite on their own. In other words, the marriage ritual is designed to make it appear as if somehow the idea of the dyadic union sprang from the community, and not from the dyad itself (p. 355).

Primary relations are ubiquitous; that is, they are found almost everywhere. But they are also embedded in institutionalized forms. And always in interpersonal behavior there is the potentiality for tension between the spontaneous and the institutional, between intimacy and restraint from intimacy.

20
Groups: Review and Discussion

The materials in the past three chapters have been quite varied. Chapter 17 focused upon behavior in organizations, emphasizing especially the role of group factors in the productivity of organizations. An initial suggestion of the role of group factors in productivity was given by a review of research at the Western Electric Company. Some doubt about this evidence and some evidence from other settings were then prsented. Finally, the conclusion was suggested that such features as the strength of informal organization, the amount of participation in decision making, and the degree of organizational centralization may be variously related to productivity in organizations—depending upon what other factors were involved (such as the kind of task or the general acceptance of those in authority). This is not a very neat conclusion, but the evidence does not point to a very simple formulation.

Chapter 18 focused upon crowd behavior, especially the reputed irrationality and extremism of crowds. Here, too, the conclusions were not simple. After examining evidence from a variety of sources—from the storming of the Bastille to contemporary American race riots—we concluded that the dynamics of mutual stimulation does indeed exaggerate certain forms of behavior in crowd situations. At the same time it was suggested that wholesale indictments of the irrationality, unconventionality, and violence of crowds have been considerably overdrawn—both in the popular mind and in the literature of social science. The role of mutual stimulation was finally considered not so much as a process that directly produced violence or extreme behavior, but rather as a process that reduced the ambiguity about how one might behave in the situation at hand. If the immediate situation is of an extreme sort for which past conventions do not seem to apply, then the crowd behavior resulting may also be extreme.

Chapter 19 focused upon the extensiveness of primary relationships in society. We early concluded that the family—or something like it—was universal, in the sense that it may be found in all societies. Furthermore, close personal relationships form a key ingredient for many of the more presumably impersonal organizations (such as the German army in World War II or an agency of the American federal bureaucracy). Finally, however, it was suggested that personal intimacy always carries with it a note of restraint—restraint in the way such intimacy is handled for the sake of established social institutions, as well as other forms of restraint that may be demanded for the sake of the relationship.

A common general theme in these last three chapters has been the study of groups, but we certainly have not presented an exhaustive survey of human social groups. In fact, readers should recognize by now that this book does not present an exhaustive survey of any topic; the tendency throughout is to be selective. In the last three chapters this selectivity has been shown by moving to a group level of analysis, by examining some of the main forms of group life, and by emphasizing certain themes of particular interest to social psychologists.

The behavior of individuals in groups has been a constant frame of reference in this book. In earlier chapters the main framework was that of individual behavior. The group setting was an important consideration for understanding this behavior, but the behavior under investigation was primarily that of individuals. In the past three chapters the focus has shifted to group behavior. In doing this we do not wish to grind any ideological ax—for example, by suggesting that the ultimate social reality resides in groups rather than individuals. We simply want to show that social psychology is interested in the study of groups as well as the study of individuals.

Psychology, Sociology, and Social Psychology

THEORETICAL POINTER

Early in this book we suggested that although there are no precise boundaries to separate social psychology from psychology (or, if you prefer, from the rest of psychology), there has developed at least a partial consensus and division of labor for these fields. Social psychology focuses primarily upon the effects of social variables and only incidentally upon the form of behavior as such or its organization in individual personalities.

Now a similar point may be made about the relationship between social psychology and sociology. There are no precise boundaries to separate social psychology from sociology (or, if you prefer, from the rest of sociology—for, in our view, social psychology can be viewed either as a discipline in its own right or as a subdiscipline shared by both psychology and sociology). There are, however, differences in focus between social psychology and sociology. Sociology is primarily the study of the behavior of groups and of the interrelationships of groups in society. Social psychology is interested in groups too—but primarily for the light they shed upon person-to-person behavior. Also, there seem to be particular questions that have captured the attention of social psychologists even though they are focused more on group life as such than on interpersonal behavior. One of these is that of conditions for morale in organizations. Another topic of special interest to social psychologists has been crowd behavior. These topics have also been included in this book, in Chapters 17 and 18 respectively.

The reader should be reminded that the distinctions between the subject matters of social science disciplines are due more to accidents of historical development than to logic. So also is it with psychology, sociology, and social psychology. We might say that, theoretically, they have their respective points of focus upon individual organisms, groups, and interpersonal behavior; and this would be generally true. But we must also recognize that human behavior at any one of these levels requires, for adequate understanding, some consideration of the other two. So, in truth, the fields of psychology, sociology, and social psychology are very much mixed up with one another, in spite of whatever textbook definitions we may make to separate them.

KINDS OF GROUPS

There are many ways of classifying the varieties of human groups. On the basis of size, we may distinguish between small groups and larger groups and organizations. On the basis of the degree of intimacy of members, we may distinguish between primary groups and secondary groups. On the basis of the degree of formalization of activities, we may distinguish between informal groups and formal organizations.

While all these, and other, bases of classification have their uses, we would like to suggest another that will tie into a central theme of this book. At several points we have suggested the usefulness of distinguishing between instrumental dependence, orientational dependence, and ego dependence. Groups may also be classified on the basis of the kind of dependence needs that they serve most directly.

Some groups are based primarily upon instrumental dependence. When people come together to work, they do not need to love each other. Nor do persons engaged in buying and selling need to make deep personal commitments to one another. It is enough that there be goods or services, real or symbolic, that they may obtain through such groups.

Other groups are based primarily upon orientational dependence. There are times when other people are needed primarily for the cues they give to guide one's own behavior. This is especially the case when one faces a situation for which past guides no longer seem to fit. A person may then come to depend primarily upon others in the immediate situation for orientation, temporary though such an immediate group may be.

Finally, we must recognize that there are groups that serve largely to provide a sense of identity for their members. They provide a home, so to speak, for his ego dependence by providing social relationships of both intimacy and permanence.

It now may be seen that the kinds of groups discussed in Chapters 17, 18, and 19 fit at least roughly with these three forms of dependence. Work organizations and other groups mentioned in Chapter 17 serve primarily instrumental needs. Crowds, discussed in Chapter 18, function primarily to provide orientation for persons in situations of ambiguity. And primary groups, our chief concern in Chapter 19, may be seen as prime providers of ego dependence.

This said, we must immediately caution against making too much of this kind of classification. Practically all groups serve at least some degree of instrumental dependence, orientational dependence, and ego dependence for members at the same time. Primary groups serve some very basic instrumental needs—the preparation and consumption of food by families, for example. Crowds also may provide for achievement of instrumental goals—such as new members added to churches through revival meetings. And even impersonal organizations may provide both general orientation and a sense of identity for millions of persons—witness the loyalty displayed by most citizens toward their national governments.

Groups as Persons?

SIDELIGHT

One of the more fascinating features of group life is the extent to which groups sometimes take on attributes of personality. A corporation, the courts tell us, may be legally considered to be a person. We talk of Great Britain as "she," the United States becomes personified as Uncle Sam, and an elusive enemy may be characterized as "Charlie." Are these only legal fictions and simply figures of speech?

Part of our tendency to personalize groups may stem from the integrated nature of much group action. Groups may act just as surely as individuals may act; or at least similar properties of evaluation and coordination can be observed on a group level as can be seen on the level of individual behavior. So it is natural to carry over analogies of individual behavior to apply to the behavior of groups.

A second basis for attributing personality to groups stems from the personal leadership found in many groups. The United States presidency, for example, encourages a combination of personal authority for executive decisions and symbolic leadership for the nation; and many other presidencies (of other countries, of corporations, of universities, or even of a local League of Women Voters) do likewise.

Sometimes the leadership may be quite informal and still leave institutions that are, in the words of Emerson, the "lengthened shadow of a man." Jesus, Muhammad, and Gautama Buddha all provide rather powerful examples of this phenomenon.

Finally, and supporting the two tendencies just mentioned, is the tendency of individuals to find a large degree of their own identity in groups. We see groups as having personality partly because they do indeed constitute parts of our own personalities. They are, in part, extensions of our own egos; just as our egos are, in part, woven out of the fabric of group life. So our family, our community, or our nation may become an extension of a sense of self, imbued with properties of personality in this way.

There are of course real dangers in this personification of groups. The greatest danger is that we will so uncritically give ourselves to serving group objectives that we may support actions that are to the gross disadvantage of millions of human beings. When we treat group goals as substitutes for the needs of human beings, we are partly living a myth. But, of course, many men are much moved by myths of this sort.

GROUP BEHAVIOR AS EXCHANGE

In this section we will explore fundamental social psychological processes that underlie group behavior. Much of the discussion is based on an exchange model of social behavior.

Several times previously in this book we have made use of an exchange model of behavior. The most recent citation has been in Blau's study of consultation in a bureaucracy (Chapter 19), where he suggested that seeking or giving advice had both rewards and costs. Blau also suggested that the particular pattern of on-the-job association is a product of such exchange processes—that rewards in relation to costs are usually maximized in associations between equals.

More formal aspects of group life may also be seen in terms of an exchange model. A worker gives a certain amount of time to a company in exchange for money. A student gives attention and effort to a class in exchange for credit hours, grades, and knowledge. A politician may present legislation in exchange for votes in his past election or prospective reelection. Even in sacred rituals we may see an exchange model providing the basic structure; for example, note the following summary of the meaning of the traditional Catholic Mass:

> The Mass is an interchange of gifts; we give to God and God gives to us. This double motive is the basis of the entire Mass-structure. It determines the division into two parts of both the Mass of the Catechumens and the Mass of the Faithful. In the Mass of the Catechumens we first give to God, in the prayer-part, and then God gives to us, in the instruction-part. Likewise in the Mass of the Faithful, the sacrifice-oblation is our gift to God, while the sacrifice-banquet is God's gift to us (Michel, 1937; quoted by Warner, 1961, p. 321).

Some writers have recently used an exchange model as a basic form for explaining essentially all social behavior. Work by Homans (1958b; 1961), Blau (1964), and Thibaut and Kelley (1959) may be specifically mentioned, and these have become among the most influential works in recent social psychology.

Basic notions about dependence are also susceptible of being cast into an exchange model. Elsewhere (Schellenberg, 1965) this has been attempted in the form of five basic propositions about behavior toward another person:

1. The tendency toward *collaboration* with the other varies directly with a party's dependence on the relationship.
2. The tendency toward *disengagement* from the other varies inversely with a party's dependence on the relationship.
3. The tendency toward *exploitation* by one person of the other varies (a) directly with the dependence of the other, and (b) inversely with one's own dependence (p. 159).

Supplementing, and somewhat modifying, these relatively static propositions are the following two propositions regarding interaction effects.

4. The tendency toward *collaboration* with the other varies directly with the amount of collaboration from the other.
5. The tendency toward *disengagement* from the other varies directly with the exploitation of the other (p. 160).

In these propositions collaboration, exploitation, and disengagement are defined, respectively, as processes in which one attempts (1) to increase values for the other as well as oneself, (2) to increase one's own values at the expense of the other, and (3) to withdraw from a relationship or avoid its consequences.

From such propositions we may derive patterns of group structure based fundamentally on the interpersonal dependencies members have on one another. Leadership is based fundamentally on the dependence of other members. Group solidarity is based on mutual dependencies and on a process of interaction where there is mutual collaboration. And group divisions are produced by the relative absence of mutual dependence or by exploitative behavior that weakens whatever dependence there may be.

In this view, exchange processes are based on fundamental conditions of interpersonal dependence. Patterns of group organization are in turn based on processes of exchange (whether the exchange be called an exchange of goods and bads or collaboration and exploitation).

George C. Homans on Social Exchange

THEORETICAL
POINTER

To give a further summary of the exchange perspective for viewing group behavior, we quote briefly from an article by George Homans.[1]

Social behavior is an exchange of goods, material goods but also nonmaterial ones, such as the symbols of approval or prestige. Persons that give much to others try to get much from them, and persons that get much from others are under pressure to give much to them. This process of influence tends to work out at equilibrium to a balance in the exchanges. For a person engaged in exchange, what he gives may be a cost to him, just as what he gets may be a reward, and his behavior changes less as profit, that is reward less cost, tends to a maximum. Not only does he seek a maximum for himself, but he tries to see to it that no one in his group makes more profit than he does. The cost and the value of what he gives and of what he gets vary with the quantity of what he gives and gets. It is surprising how familiar these propositions are; it is surprising, too, how propositions about the dynamics of exchange can begin to generate the static thing we call "group structure" and, in so doing, generate also some of the propositions about group structure that students of real-life groups have stated (p. 606).

INTIMATE EXCHANGE

It may be easiest to see the application of an exchange model in fomal group settings, where the expectations of what a person is to give and what he gets may be generally known. This is less clearly applicable to more intimate exchanges. Therefore, let us take up the subject of intimate exchange as a means of further examining the uses of an exchange model of social behavior.

Intimate social relationships may also be seen as typically involving an exchange of goods. By goods we mean anything that has positive value. This might involve basic material goods—such as a father's provision, or mother's preparation, of food, clothing, or shelter—but it

[1] George C. Homans, "Social Behavior as Exchange," *American Journal of Sociology*, 62 (1958), 606. Copyright 1958 by The University of Chicago. Quotations from this source are reprinted with permission of The University of Chicago Press.

may also involve nonmaterial services and symbolic goods. In fact, gifts of material things are sometimes more important as symbolic gestures than they are physically useful—as the reader may recall from some of the gifts received last Christmas.

The main kinds of goods that may be obtained through social exchange include at least the following: (1) material goods, (2) services, (3) information, (4) attention, and (5) approval. Of these, the last two are especially prominent among the goods received in intimate exchange. While attention and approval may also be received in relatively impersonal settings, their value is much enhanced by a setting in which the individual is more personally involved. For most material goods and services this involvement is not required, and these thus may become elements traded in economic routines where money provides a measure.

When we refer to attention and approval as distinctively personal goods of intimate exchange, we should not neglect the extent to which even intimate exchange tends to follow set routines. Not all intimate acts are fully individualized; and many acts that are fully individualized may nevertheless be habitual in a given social relationship. So we develop intimate routines as well as impersonal routines. A smile, a wink, a handshake, a gentle embrace—these too may become routines, even when used to give highly personalized attention or approval.

In providing goods for other persons we expect also that goods will be provided in return. There is no formal requirement that this be the case (at least for noneconomic relationships, which typically mean those where acts are not measured by monetary values), but such reciprocity is generally anticipated. If one provides the attention of saying hello, the other person is not formally obligated to respond, but he ordinarily will. In other cases the reciprocity may be less clearly a matching response, but it is still assumed that goods presented will bring goods in return.

Would we invest our time and efforts in other persons without the expectation of rewards in return? In some cases, perhaps. But the usual expectation is that those persons to whom we give much will be those from whom we also receive much. For we must not forget that there are costs as well as rewards in social relationships, especially in intimate relationships. Would we suffer our friends if they did not reward us by being friends?

Such an "economic" view of social behavior may strike some students as carrying over a crassly materialistic view into all phases of social relationships. However, this is not necessarily the intention of exchange theorists. Rather, what they wish to point out is that nonmaterial as well as material values may be important features of human give and take. Viewed in this way, exchange theory is no more materialistic than is the biblical golden rule.

CAUTION

The Limitations of Exchange

In pointing to the personalized nature of intimate exchange, we acknowledged that such exchanges had no recognized coin, no readily transferable standard of measure. This is also true, to a lesser extent, in more formal group settings. This lack of an objective measure of value represents one of the chief limitations of extending an economic exchange model to social behavior generally.

Not only is there an absence of an objective unit for measuring social goods, but there may also frequently be a deficiency in subjective assessment as well. How can a person really compare with accuracy the pleasures and pains of various friendships, or the pleasures of success in business with those of religious fulfillment. To say that people do make such assessments in a rough way in everyday decisions may still not completely justify an exchange model, for the model of exchange perhaps overstates the extent to which different values are even subjectively measurable by a common standard.

Another limitation of an exchange model is that exchange applies more to what one has than to what one is. Identities are not normally matters of exchange. Central elements of a self-concept and of group identifications are not easily given and received. These may change with experience, but not on a quid pro quo basis.

Finally, the routines of social behavior carry a great baggage of automatically produced habit and convention. These features of behavior occur without much critical evaluation as to whether they represent goods or bads to other persons. Many things are just done—without much sense of purpose or much awareness of how they affect other people. A clever social psychologist may still point out how they fit models of implicit exchange, but even he would probably have to stop his analysis at some bedrock of social custom and biological activity.

THE ORGANIZATION OF GROUPS

The view of social behavior as a process of exchange gives at least a partial explanation of the structure of group behavior. Group structure is in part the product of social exchange between individuals. Some individuals with more to offer than others take on leadership roles. Other persons take on the kind of roles that allow them to specialize in their distinctive contributions. All this can be conceived in terms of an exchange model of social behavior.

Group structure, however, is rooted in more than an interchange between individuals. Or, perhaps more accurately, we should say that the conditions of social exchange and the content of such exchange are not themselves easily explained by exchange notions. In addition to social exchange between individuals, we may see the social structure of groups as being formed by (1) the distinctive activity and goals of the group and (2) the norms of the broader social order.

Groups may be seen as being organized into roles. The roles of group members partly grow out of their interaction together. At the same time, however, the role structure grows out of the nature of the task or the objectives that the group is trying to achieve. A basketball team has a different role structure from a team of salesmen, and a street corner gang is different from a construction gang. Particularly important is the way the central purpose or activity of the group sets the framework for roles in work groups (where positions may be formally defined), but even informal groups (like the street corner groups discussed in Chapter 9) are structured by their dominant purposes and activities. If a group's dominant purpose is informal social support, roles will become differentiated around the establishment of such support. If an informal group serves primarily recreational aims, roles will tend to develop around the particular skills or particular games chosen as activities.

More than anything else, it is the common goal shared by the members that typically sets off the group as a distinct entity. The division of labor in response to group goals is not simply reducible to the characteristics of individuals or their person-to-person relationships.

The role structure of a group also reflects the larger cultural world. In few, if any, groups does the role of being a male or female lose all significance—even if sex differences may be apparently irrelevant to the goal at hand. Nor do many groups ignore age differences, even though no formal distinctions are made. Age and sex are examples of broad cultural roles that find their way into the role definitions of most groups. Other cultural norms from beyond the group also help to structure the expectations within groups; and the evaluations applied in a group tend to reflect broader cultural values as well as the more narrow interests of the particular group.

In viewing some of the factors that give shape to group structure (interpersonal exchange, group goals, and broader social norms), it may appear that structure is a simple property distinguishing groups from nongroups. But group structure is far from a simple all-or-nothing matter. Qualities of social structure differ from group to group, and the degree of structuring may itself be one of the important variables distinguishing one group from another.

The extent to which the behavior of a group is structured may in turn be broken down into several more specific variables. Some of these may be arrived at by pursuing the following questions:

1. To what degree is there consensus concerning group roles?
2. How detailed are the prescriptions for role behavior?
3. How effective are the mechanisms of surveillance (which are employed to make sure that appropriate behavior is actually being carried out)?
4. How consistent is the application of sanctions (rewards for proper role behavior and/or punishments for inappropriate behavior)?

Note that we are not here talking about structure in the sense of an organization chart, but rather in the sense of the extent to which behavior is firmly patterned. Some organizations show highly structured group behavior and others, with equally detailed written codes, may be much less structured in the way behavior is actually organized.

Attention to the extent to which behavior is structured also should give us insight into situational roots of the variability of behavior. In some situations an individual is more free to plot his behavior in his own way; indeed, he may be practically required to respond in terms of self-originated guides. When? With reference to the questions posed above, we can suggest that such self-direction will be much in evidence in group behavior when (1) there is little agreement about appropriate behavior, (2) the prescriptions for behavior are not very detailed, (3) the mechanisms of surveillance are not very effective, and (4) there is little consistency in the application of sanctions.

ATTITUDES AND GROUPS

Persons develop and express attitudes primarily in groups. Their attitudes are rooted in affiliations with other humans, and these affiliations are tied together in groups. In the present chapter we have discussed the way in which groups give structure to human affiliations, thereby serving as points of anchorage for attitudes.

GROUPS AND NORMS

However, as we suggested in the section on "The Organization of Groups," there is something very much one-sided in viewing groups simply in terms of interpersonal affiliations. Groups take on a structure from the nature of the task or activity in which they are involved and from the kind of larger organization of which they may be a part. Also mentioned was the fact that the broader culture may have norms that structure group behavior. This leads us at last to the very central topic of social norms, those patterns of expected behavior that guide human thoughts and actions. Some norms, to be sure, emerge out of a particular group context. But there are also norms that have a broader base than any particular group. It is such broader social norms that will receive primary attention in the next four chapters.

part six: SOCIAL NORMS

How can you tell a free person—a person who can do what he likes when he likes and where he likes, or do nothing at all as he chooses? Well, there is no such person, and there never can be any such person.

George Bernard Shaw

Social norms provide structure for practically all social behavior. In the following chapters, three kinds of norms are singled out for special discussion. Chapter 21 ("Language") covers those of language, Chapter 22 ("Roles") treats social roles, and Chapter 23 ("Morality") discusses moral standards.

Chapter 24 ("Social Norms: Review and Discussion") brings the materials of the previous three chapters together in a general discussion of social norms, pointing out how norms function at one and the same time to organize individual behavior and to organize the larger social order.

21
Language

THE EDUCATION OF HELEN

In 1880 Helen was born in a little town in northern Alabama. The first year of her life was quite normal, but then came an illness that left her completely blind and deaf.

Five years later her parents arranged for a special teacher from Boston, Anne Sullivan, to come and take charge of Helen's education. Miss Sullivan's first letter to a friend in Boston described Helen as "large, strong, and ruddy, and as unrestrained in her movements as a young colt" (Keller, 1954, p. 245).

The first problem for Miss Sullivan was that of obedience. Helen was used to having her own way in whatever desires she could make known to her family; and to restrain such impulsive demands Miss Sullivan had to remove Helen to a small house where the family would not interfere with the training. Here Helen learned both obedience and affection toward her new teacher, and Miss Sullivan began teaching Helen words, which were spelled out in her hand.

April 5, 1887, was an especially important day for Helen. Later, in her autobiography, she recounted events of this day:

> One day, while I was playing with my new doll, Miss Sullivan put my big rag doll into my lap also, spelled "d-o-l-l" and tried to make me understand that "d-o-l-l" applied to both. Earlier in the day we had had a tussle over the words "m-u-g" and "w-a-t-e-r." Miss Sullivan had tried to impress it upon me that "m-u-g" is mug and that "w-a-t-e-r" is water, but I persisted in confounding the two. In despair she had dropped the subject for the time, only to renew it at the first opportunity. I became impatient at her repeated attempts and, seizing the new doll, I dashed it upon the floor. I was keenly delighted when I felt the fragments of the broken doll at my feet. Neither sorrow nor regret followed my passionate outburst. I had not loved the doll. In the still, dark world in which I lived there was no strong sentiment or tenderness. I felt my teacher sweep the fragments to one side of the hearth, and I had a sense of satisfaction that the cause of my discomfort was removed. She brought me my hat, and I knew I was going out into the warm sunshine. This thought, if a wordless sensation may be called a thought, made me hop and skip with pleasure.

We walked down the path to the well-house, attracted by the fragrance of the honeysuckle with which it was covered. Some one was drawing water and my teacher placed my hand under the spout. As the cool stream gushed over one hand she spelled into the other the word water, first slowly, then rapidly. I stood still, my whole attention fixed upon the motions of her fingers. Suddenly I felt a misty consciousness as of something forgotten—a thrill of returning thought; and somehow the mystery of language was revealed to me. I knew then that "w-a-t-e-r" meant the wonderful cool something that was flowing over my hand. That living word awakened my soul, gave it light, hope, joy, set it free! There were barriers still, it is true, but barriers that could in time be swept away.

I left the well-house eager to learn. Everything had a name, and each name gave birth to a new thought. As we returned to the house every object which I touched seemed to quiver with life. That was because I saw everything with the strange, new sight that had come to me. On entering the door I remembered the doll I had broken. I felt my way to the hearth and picked up the pieces. I tried vainly to put them together. Then my eyes filled with tears; for I realized what I had done, and for the first time I felt repentance and sorrow.

I learned a great many new words that day. I do not remember what they all were; but I do know that mother, father, sister, teacher were among them—words that were to make the world blossom for me, "like Aaron's rod, with flowers." It would have been difficult to find a happier child than I was as I lay in my crib at the close of that eventful day and lived over the joys it had brought me, and for the first time longed for a new day to come (pp. 35–37).

A few days after these events her teacher, Miss Sullivan, wrote in a letter dated April 10, 1887:

I see an improvement in Helen day to day, almost from hour to hour. Everything must have a name now. Wherever we go, she asks eagerly for the names of things she has not learned at home. She is anxious for her friends to spell, and eager to teach the letters to every one she meets. She drops the signs and pantomime she used before, as soon as she has words to supply their place, and the acquirement of a new word affords her the liveliest pleasure. And we notice that her face grows more expressive each day.

I have decided not to try to have regular lessons for the present. I am going to treat Helen exactly like a two-year-old child. It occurred to me the other day that it is absurd to require a child to come to a certain place at a certain time and recite certain lessons, when he has not yet acquired a working vocabulary. I sent Helen away and sat down to think. I asked myself, "How does a normal child learn language?" The answer was simple, "By imitation." The child comes into the world with the ability to learn, and he learns of himself, provided he is supplied with sufficient outward stimulus. He sees people do things and he tries to do them. He hears others speak, and he tries to speak. But long before he utters his first word, he understands what is said to him. I have been observing Helen's little cousin lately. She is about fifteen months old, and already understands a great deal. In response to questions she points out prettily her nose, mouth, eye, chin, cheek, ear. If I hand her a flower, and say, "Give it to mamma," she takes it to her mother. If I say, "Where is the little rogue?" she hides behind her mother's chair, or covers her face with her hands and peeps out at me with an expression of genuine roguishness. She obeys many commands like these: "Come," "Kiss," "Go to papa," "Shut the door," "Give me the biscuit." But I have not heard her try to say any of these words, although they have been repeated hundreds of times in her hearing, and it is perfectly evident that she understands them. These observations have given me a clue to the method to be followed in teaching Helen language. I shall talk into her hand as we talk into the baby's ears. I shall assume that she has the normal child's capacity of assimilation and imitation. I shall use complete sentences in talking to her, and fill out the meaning with gestures and her descriptive signs when necessity requires it; but I shall not try to keep her mind fixed on any one thing. I shall do all I can to interest and stimulate it, and wait for results (pp. 257–258).

This plan for teaching language to Helen apparently worked very well indeed, as the later history of Helen Keller bears witness.

LEARNING TO TALK

Most people learn to talk by use of ears, mouth, and throat. In contrast, Helen Keller learned to talk through feeling with her hands. Although the means of learning language was for her fundamentally different than for most Americans, the language she learned was the same. And through her form of the English language she came rapidly to share in the civilization of those around her.

Not only did language come in a different sensory form for Helen Keller, but she learned it both later and more rapidly than most children. Therefore, in her case we see in concentrated form what is developed gradually in the normal case. Though the acquisition of language may be less dramatic in the typical case, the learning of human language remains a remarkable achievement for anyone. By mastering the abstractions required for a spoken language, we enter into significant participation in the human community. Without language, our humanity can be no more than marginal.

The normal process of language learning may be roughly divided into four main parts: (1) early vocalization, (2) imitative babbling, (3) the learning of meanings, and (4) the learning of language structure.

Vocalization begins for most infants a few moments after birth. The first sounds are usually cries of discomfort, though comfort sounds also may be heard within the first few days. In spite of their stridency and their systematic selectivity of vowel sounds (tight-throated and nasalized for discomfort cries, and more relaxed variations of "a," "o," and "u" for comfort sounds), these early sounds are without meaning. That is, they have no meaning to the child. To the mother the meaning of these sounds may be considerable, even overwhelming, but that is another matter. They may be *signs* that communicate to the mother, but they are not *symbols*, carriers of shared meanings from one person to another.

After a few weeks sounds of consonants become more pronounced, especially as sucking and swallowing actions become mixed with cries and gurgles. But though these sounds may become more differentiated (and thus clearer signals to the mother), the infant remains uncomprehending. How can he comprehend when he has no words to organize his perceptions? Though by chance the word *mama* may come from his lips, it only indicates his vowel cries are interrupted by sucking actions. Real words must wait till later.

During his second or third month the child will usually begin babbling. Babbling is different from the earlier vocalization in the apparent preoccupation with making sounds. Sounds are no longer just expressive noises to be given off automatically, but they become worthy of attention for their own sake. The infant appears to derive pleasure from just lying there making sounds—sound after sound after sound.

While the nervous system, necessary to coordinate his arms and legs, is still in the process of development, the infant explores the enormous potential of his vocal cords. The sound possibilities he tries out in his first year of life are many times greater than the sounds of the phonetic system of the language he will use for the rest of his years. But most of the infant's sounds are only sounds; only those associated with the phonetic system of his language have the possibility of carrying meaning. What an arbitrary limitation upon the realization of the full potential of the individual!

Before long the babbling turns quite noticeably toward the imitation of speech sounds of persons around the child. Perhaps babbling in general was rooted in pleasurable associations with these human sound-makers, but now it becomes clear that a more precise selectivity is involved. Certain experiences with other people become associated with certain sounds. As the child comes to make these sounds more clearly, he also carries more clear associations with the related experiences. And he has then reached the time of the dawning of symbolic meanings.

Before the child has finished his first year, he usually has used a few words. These may not be words of adult speech (mother and father are tremendously eager to compromise in getting those first words), and parental and infant meanings may be far apart. Still there is a continuity in the associations of the same sound for the infant, and at least something in common between the associations of the child and those that a parent can imagine. And this is how meaning begins.

Let us note two examples from responses of a nine-month-old boy (Lewis, 1963) to explore how meaning may be developing.

> (A) The child is sitting alone in his play pen. His ball rolls out of his reach. He stretches towards it, but unsuccessfully.

After several efforts he begins to say *mamama* while still reaching for the ball.

(B) He says *mammam* in a very contended tone, while lying in his mother's arms and looking up at her (p. 31).

Pushing toward an adult conception, we say the child is demonstrating his ability to use the word *mama*, even though he hasn't fully mastered its pronunciation. But this would be misleading. The child probably does not yet have a clear meaning of *mama* as related to a particular human being. The similarity to the word *mama* for these two cases may still be largely a coincidence, but the odds that it will remain sheer coincidence will decrease rapidly as the mother responds to provide meanings. This she does by her actions. In the case of example A, she senses a demand, and this becomes associated for both mother and child with the word *mama* (the beginnings of common symbolization) by the way the mother helps the child get what he wants (in this case his ball). In example B, a primitive notion of reference may be developed as the mother provides a tentative meaning for *mama* by giving a smile.

From these examples we begin to understand that the process of shaping symbolic meanings depends a great deal upon (1) a continuity of experiences with the same persons, upon whom the child is highly dependent, and (2) the way the reactions of others carry out the exploratory soundings of the child. Incidentally, in these examples we also see that ingredients of manipulative (example A) and referential (example B) functions of speech may have their origins quite early in a child's development.

But the child of nine months can scarcely be said to have a vocabulary (save perhaps in the biased judgment of his parents). Even when he is eighteen months old and older, words he uses will differ a great deal in both pronunciation and meaning from the words of his parents. He will by then probably have the naming habit, considering everything he can point to as fitting under some kind of name. But some names will be, by parental standards, too widely applied and others will be too restricted. He will slowly learn to limit more and more the application of some words, and broaden more and more the application of others, until he can communicate more effectively with adults. For example, for a child just under two *kitty* may include all kinds of pets, whereas *doggie* might mean only one particular animal. With time, however, the conception of the two classes named dogs and cats will gradually form—if parents maintain the conventional distinctions in their conversation.

The child learns not only meanings of specific words but also how to put words together into more or less appropriate forms. Formally speaking, we say that he learns morphology (the elementary structural units of meaning, consisting of words and parts of words) and syntax (the sequence of morphemes and words into conventional patterns, especially sentences). Together, morphology and syntax constitute the linguistic structure of a language; in other words, its grammar. We may not think of a two-year-old as learning grammar, but he does. As he first learns to talk, the child learns far more grammar than he will ever learn in school. He learns to shape the pattern of his speech into the patterns of those who speak to him. By the end of the second year, this process is usually noticeably under way.

For an example of the early process of learning grammar, let us note a record of a conversation between little Adam, aged two, and his mother (presented by Brown, 1965):[1]

> Adam: See truck, Mommy. See truck.
> Mother: Did you see the truck?
> Adam: No, I see truck.
> Mother: No, you didn't see it? There goes one.
> Adam: There go one.
> Mother: Yes, there goes one.
> Adam: See a truck. See truck, Mommy. See truck. Truck. Put truck, Mommy.
> Mother: Put the truck where?
> Adam: Put truck window.
> Mother: I think that one's too large to go in the window (p. 287).

Here Adam is already using sentences. The sentences are short and, by adult standards, somewhat incomplete; but they serve Adam's purposes. None of Adam's sentences has more than three words, but they already contain or imply subject and predicate forms. Every one of Adam's sentences contains a noun that serves either as the subject or object of a verb. Objects are placed after verbs; subjects are before verbs in statements but are omitted or attached to the end in commands. All this, little Adam seems to have already grasped. He is, of course, unsophisticated in details like adjusting verbs to singular or plural subjects ("there go one"), using prepositional phrases ("put truck window"), or clarifying meanings with appropriate adjectives and adverbs. But this will come with time.

Notice also in the example the language of the mother. Whether she plans it or not, she is being a good teacher of grammar. As a good teacher, she is both following and leading. In following Adam's sentences, she often recasts them into more mature form; and in so doing, she also provides models for him to follow. She suggests what she imagines he wants to say, providing word structure for his thoughts.

Such a sequence of conversation requires the close attention of each person to what the other is saying. And in this close attention there is much imitation of one form or another. The child tends to imitate the mother, reducing the form to what is somewhat more manageable for the child (for example, "put the truck" becomes "put truck"). In contrast to the child's imitation-with-reduction is the mother's imitation-with-expansion as she strives to put the child's sentences into slightly more adequate form. Little by little, the child is thus led to form his words into the kind of sentences his language uses.

From early babbling on, imitation is a leading feature of the learning of language. A child first makes the sounds adults make, then he

[1] Roger Brown, *Social Psychology*. New York: Free Press, 1965. Copyright © 1965 by The Free Press. Quotations from this source are reprinted with permission of the Macmillan Publishing Co., Inc.

comes to take on meanings from his adult associates, and finally his structure of putting words together imitates that of adult speakers. Imitation at each of these steps in the development of language ability is so common that we take it for granted, but as social scientists we must be more than a little puzzled by the scope of such imitation. Children imitate in minute detail the sound and form of speech of those around them, so much so that such highly abstract entities as parts of speech are distinguished effectively by practically every child before he starts kindergarten. This is probably a greater educational achievement than he will ever realize in all his years of schooling, and it comes without any formal teaching whatsoever. The key requirements simply seem to be adults who talk and little children who imitate. But why do little children imitate so much, and with such skillful imagination?

There is no single cause we can point to in explanation for the child's early and energetic imitation of adult vocalization, but some key features of early childhood are undoubtedly involved. Central among these are the enormous dependency of the infant, the predominant role of his oral apparatus in his earliest interpersonal pleasures, the consistency in the behavior of others who minister to these pleasures, and the sensitivity and plasticity of his nervous system.

Mowrer's Autism Theory of Early Speech

THEORETICAL POINTER

From studies of birds who have learned usage of human language, O. H. Mowrer (1952; 1960)[2] concluded that a bird learns to talk only when a human has become a love object. When the bird is strongly attached to a human being, the bird becomes susceptible to the conditioning effects of the human's sounds. As Mowrer describes this:

As one cares for and plays with these creatures, one makes certain characteristic noises. These may or may not be parts of conventional speech; any kind of a noise will do—be it a word or phrase, a whistled or sung fragment of a tune, a nonsense vocalization, or even a mechanical sound like the creaking of a door or the opening of a food box—anything so long as it is intimately and consistently associated with the trainer and his care-taking activities. As a result of the association of these sounds with basic satisfactions for the bird, they become positively conditioned, i.e., they become *good sounds;* and in the course of its own, at first largely random vocalizations, the bird will eventually make somewhat *similar* sounds. By the principle of generalization, some of the derived satisfaction or pleasure which has become attached to the trainer's sounds will now be experienced when the bird itself makes and hears like sounds; and when this begins to happen the stage is set for the bird's learning to "talk" (1952; quoted in 1960, p. 79).

Mowrer believes that a similar process occurs in the emergence of speech in human children. What basically happens is that originally neutral stimuli, the sounds made by a mother, become associated with pleasure for the child. Because of such association with an object of pleasure and affection, the mother's

---

[2] O. Hobart Mowrer, "The Autism Theory of Speech Development and Some Clinical Applications," *Journal of Speech and Hearing Disorders,* 17 (1952), 263–368. Quotations from this source are reprinted with permission of the author and the American Speech and Hearing Association.

words take on properties of positive reinforcement. In learning theory terms, we can say that words, through generalization from objects of primary reinforcement, themselves take on properties of secondary reinforcement. The child is now rewarded by words alone. As soon as he is able to produce words, or wordlike sounds, he does so with great enthusiasm, thus providing himself with these rewarding sounds at will.

Mowrer calls this an *autism* theory of early speech development because he holds that the child's first development of words is simply for his own pleasure. The more his sounds are similar to those of the object of affection (usually the mother), the greater the pleasure. Thus, the enthusiastic quality of imitation.

Later on comes the use of words for instrumental purposes. Still later is the putting of words together for descriptive or representational speech. But in the beginning, according to Mowrer, is only the subjective satisfaction and comfort that words tend to bring through association with objects of emotional attachment.

CAN ANIMALS TALK?

Animals, other than humans, communicate quite effectively with their own kind, but without language. The signals with which they communicate to each other are not primarily symbolic. This is not to say that such communication may not be highly sensitive and show significant learning. But the sensitivity and learning are directed to dealing with natural reactions rather than the artificial and conventional system of representations that we call language. So far humans are apparently the only animals who have clearly developed language systems.

Granted that other animals have not invested their intelligence into symbolic systems to the extent that humans have, does this mean that they are unable to use symbols? Does their preference for more concrete communication mean that they never use symbols? Here our answer must be a qualified one. Our knowledge of the communication systems of most species is not great enough to allow us the certainty of knowing that no symbols are ever used. Perhaps some of the callings, nuzzlings, and body gestures of various higher mammals approach the artificial and conventional nature of symbols. But if so, they probably remain borderline instances that are not incorporated into an organized system of symbols; that is, they do not develop into language. We say "probably remain" because there is still some doubt about certain species that some investigators believe may possess true languages. Dolphins, for example, have been nominated for this honor by at least one enthusiastic investigator (Lilly, 1967), but others have doubted this claim.

But what about the parrot, which so closely mimics human speech —is he not using language? Certainly such birds show great skill in imitation, but it is mostly just that, imitation, without meaningful content. However, Lorenz (1952), in a chapter on the language of animals, points to a few occasions where birds have used human speech in a manner that at least approaches symbolic meaning. But these are rare occasions even for rare birds.

One of the best chances to learn a language that any nonhuman has had was realized by Viki, a chimpanzee adopted by human parents at the age of three days and raised as much as possible as a human child would be (Hayes, 1951). Keith and Cathy Hayes, the psychologists who adopted Viki, gave her every opportunity and encouragement to learn language. They did teach her to pronounce approximations of several words (like *mama* and *cup*, which were used in a sometimes confused manner) and to respond selectively to several dozen words and phrases (which also were sometimes confused). Their general interpretation of her progress at age three was that Viki was developing remarkably in adaptation to human culture in all respects except language. No amount of training could make up for what appeared to be an innate deficiency for language.

But perhaps there are better ways for chimps to learn language than through speaking. Another approach was used by Allen and Beatrice Gardner with a chimpanzee named Washoe. The Gardners, working at the University of Nevada, began teaching Washoe in 1966 with American sign language, the system of symbolic gestures used by many deaf persons. They worked with Washoe for five years and reported notable success. During this time Washoe acquired a vocabulary of over a hundred words. In 1971 Washoe joined the research program of William Lemmon in Oklahoma, where American sign language was used with a number of chimps, some of which seemed to be learning even more rapidly than Washoe (Hahn, 1971).

Using still another approach, by inventing an artificial language represented by plastic chips with different shapes and colors, David Premack (1971) taught this language to a chimp named Sarah. He has reported impressive evidence of creative use of these symbols by Sarah, who showed awareness of grammatical structure as well as acquisition of a basic vocabulary.

These experiments, though still in process, have nevertheless progressed far enough to refute the idea that humans are the only animals who can make practical and effective use of language. The studies have shown that chimpanzees can be taught languages with which they can simply but effectively communicate with humans. Still unsettled is the extent to which such languages may be used by chimpanzees in communicating with other chimps. Is it possible that one chimp might be able to teach another, thus establishing a symbolic base for a chimpanzee culture? This we still do not know.

LANGUAGE AS AN INSTITUTION

So far in this chapter, we have examined language as something that is learned. As a central part of our early association with other human beings we learn language; and, without the learning of language, most human reality would remain foreign to us—just how foreign may be surmised from cases like those of Anna and Isabelle mentioned in Chapter 3.

But language may be seen as a part of society and culture as well as a feature of individual learning. Social life exists in terms of established patterns, ways of thinking and doing that evolve slowly in the course of many generations. Sets of such established patterns are often called social institutions.

Language is the social institution that makes all other institutions possible. The anthropologist Leslie A. White (1940)[3] expresses this idea quite clearly in his essay on the symbol:

> All culture (civilization) depends upon the symbol. It was the exercise of the symbolic faculty that brought culture into existence and it is the use of symbols that makes the perpetuation of culture possible. Without the symbol there would be no culture, and man would be merely an animal, not a human being.
>
> Articulate speech is the most important form of symbolic expression. Remove speech from culture and what would remain? Let us see.
>
> Without articulate speech we would have no human social organization. Families we might have, but this form of organization is not peculiar to man; it is not, per se, human. But we would have no prohibitions of incest, no rules prescribing exogamy and endogamy, polygamy or monogamy. How could marriage with a cross cousin be prescribed, marriage with a parallel cousin proscribed, without articulate speech? How could rules which prohibit plural mates possessed simultaneously but permit them if possessed one at a time, exist without speech?
>
> Without speech we would have no political, economic, ecclesiastic, or military organization; no codes of etiquette or ethics; no laws; no science, theology, or literature; no games or music, except on an ape level. Rituals and ceremonial paraphernalia would be meaningless without articulate speech. Indeed, without articulate speech we would be all but toolless: we would have only the occasional and insignificant use of the tool such as we find today among the higher apes, for it was articulate speech that transformed the non-progressive tool-using of the ape into the progressive, cumulative tool-using of man, the human being.
>
> In short, without symbolic communication in some form, we would have no culture. "In the Word was the beginning" of culture—and its perpetuation also (p. 460).

Such statements can be made for humanity in general because they pertain to all human societies of which we have any knowledge. All human groups have had language, and for all societies the system of symbols has been the means by which they imagined and practiced the forms of other social institutions.

Of course, the forms of language have been quite different from society to society. The differences are great in phonology (the sounds used), morphology (the ways in which words are put together), vocabulary (the meanings attached to words), and syntax (the way words are arranged into sentences). Even closely related languages have gross differences in all these respects, as every English-speaking student of German or French becomes painfully aware.

[3] Leslie A. White, "The Symbol: The Origin and Basis of Human Behavior," *Philosophy of Science*, 7 (1940), 451–463. © 1940 The Williams & Wilkins Co. Quotations from this source are reprinted with permission of the author and publisher. This essay is also available in Leslie A. White, *The Science of Culture*, 2nd edition. New York: Farrar, Straus & Giroux, 1969.

There appear to be no universal rules for phonology, morphology, vocabulary, and syntax—no rules that apply to all languages. Still, each language community has rules aplenty for its own language: what kinds of sounds are to be used with what kinds of combinations and emphases, what elements may be combined into words with what patterns of meaning, etc. In English, for instance, the rules dictate that an adjective ordinarily precedes a noun; whereas in Spanish, except for special cases, an adjective follows a noun. In ancient Chinese, in contrast, the practice was not to use adjectives at all. A sense of the type of thing and its qualifying meanings were built together by the Chinese into a single character. For example, there were seventeen Chinese words for mountain—one word expressed the idea of a bare mountain, another was used for a high mountain covered with vegetation, another meant a high and vast mountain, etc.

The basic rules of a language are learned early and persist tenaciously. A child in the United States or England, for example, will put adjectives in front of nouns long before he goes to school to study grammar, and the habit will persist throughout life. Even basic elements of the vocabulary will seem natural, almost innate, so firmly implanted are they in our habits of consciousness.

King Frederick's Experiment

SIDELIGHT

Frederick II, king of the Holy Roman Empire in the thirteenth century, provides an illustration of the dangers of being ignorant of the artificiality of language forms. Scientific soul that he was, Frederick wanted to discover which language was the most natural, so he planned an experiment to see which language children would speak who had never heard anyone speak. Infants were selected and reared under conditions in which no one was allowed to speak to them. Unfortunately, Frederick never found an answer to his question, for the children all died before they learned to speak any language.

Language, of course, must be learned by individuals and is institutionalized by society. Its rules are so obligatory that we seldom are aware of the obligations to use them. We feel we are speaking freely, choosing what we want to say; and, in a way, this is so. But isn't it also remarkable how we use the sounds only in our limited system of phonetics, we use the same words found in those detailed works of verbal etiquette known as dictionaries, and we put words together in the ways dictated by our grammar! The linguistic system is so much a part of our life that we are seldom aware just how artificial and conventional its forms are.

Glottochronology

SIDELIGHT

The relative stability of basic forms of a language makes it possible for anthropologists to use indices of language differentiation as one means of time measurement. Such measurement is known as *glottochronology* or *lexicostatistics* (Gudschinsky, 1956; Swadish, 1951; Swadish, 1955).

Basic structural features of a language change very little over a period of centuries. So also is it with central features of a vocabulary. Selecting two hundred basic items for which nearly all languages must have distinctive words (common pronouns, body parts, central features of the natural environment, distinctive actions, etc.), Morris Swadish and others have measured how much change has occurred in historical languages. Results indicate that about 80 percent of these words will remain relatively unchanged in pronunciation over a period of ten centuries. This retention rate of 80 percent does not seem to vary much from language to language, though, of course, for all languages it is much higher than the retention rates of the less basic vocabulary. Using an even more highly selected list of one hundred basic items, Swadish calculated a retention rate of 86 percent for a thousand years.

If we assume such a retention rate as a constant, we can estimate the time of divergence of two cultural groups with related languages. By measuring the proportion of basic vocabulary (out of the two hundred or one hundred basic items) that the two languages still have in common, one can estimate about how many centuries ago the two language forms would have been one common language (assuming a constant retention rate for such basic items). For example, Tlingit and Athabaskan Indian groups show correspondence in about 40 percent of their basic vocabulary, so Swadish (1951) estimates that the Tlingit and Athabaskan groups must have had separate languages for about four thousand years. Therefore, prior to about 2000 B.C. they must have been parts of the same culture.

LANGUAGE AND THOUGHT

Language reflects culture. The values of a people, their characteristic activities and ways of thinking about the world, are reflected in their language.

But language not only reflects other institutions, it also helps mold them. It does this primarily by the basic structure it imposes upon how human beings communicate with one another. And by imposing a structure for communicating with others, language also gives a structure for communicating with ourselves—in other words, for thinking.

One of the current issues for intellectual debate is that of the linguistic relativity of human thought. Just how much is our thought determined by the linguistic forms that enter into it?

The anthropologist Edward Sapir emphasized the role of language in conditioning how we think. Meanings, he said, are "not so much discovered in experience as imposed upon it, because of the tyrannical hold that linguistic form has upon our orientation in the world" (quoted by Hertzler, 1965, p. 122).

Sapir's student Benjamin Whorf states the position of the linguistic relativity of thought even more forcefully:[4]

> We dissect nature along lines laid down by our native languages. The categories and types that we isolate from the world of phenomena we do not find there because they stare every ob-

[4] John B. Carroll (ed.), *Language, Thought and Reality: Selected Writings of Benjamin Lee Whorf.* Cambridge, Mass.: Technology Press, 1956. Copyright © 1956, by The Massachusetts Institute of Technology. Quotations from this source are reprinted with permission of the publisher.

server in the face; on the contrary, the world is presented in a kaleidoscopic flux of impressions which has to be organized by our minds—and this means largely by the linguistic systems in our minds. We cut nature up, organize it into concepts, and ascribe significances as we do, largely because we are parties to an agreement to organize it in this way—an agreement that holds throughout our speech community and is codified in the patterns of our language. The agreement is, of course, an implicit and unstated one, *but its terms are absolutely obligatory;* we cannot talk at all except by subscribing to the organization and classification of data which the agreement decrees (Carroll, 1956, pp. 213–214).

As evidence, Whorf points to Indian languages, which represent modes of thought different from those of European languages. His contention is that these languages condition the whole cultural edifice by the way in which they induce people to organize concepts. The principal European languages, he points out, analyze the world in terms of things. Even nonspatial qualities are treated as though they had features of form and extension as do physical objects. This makes Europeans orient themselves toward life in a universe dominated by discrete objects. Quite in contrast is the case of Hopi language and culture. The habitual universe of thought used by the Hopi, according to Whorf,

. . . seems to have analyzed reality largely in terms of *events* (or better "eventing"), referred to in two ways, objective and subjective. Objectively, and only if perceptible physical experience, events are expressed mainly as outlines, colors, movements, and other perceptive reports. Subjectively, for both the physical and nonphysical, events are considered the expression of invisible intensity factors, on which depend their stability and persistence, or their fugitiveness and proclivities. It implies that existents do not "become later and later" all in the same way; but some do so by growing like plants, some by diffusing and vanishing, some by a procession of metamorphoses, some by enduring in one shape till affected by violent forces. In the nature of each existent able to manifest as a definite whole is the power of its own mode of duration: its growth, decline, stability, cyclicity, or creativeness. Everything is thus already "prepared" for the way it now manifests by earlier phases, and what it will be later, partly has been, and partly is in the act of being so "prepared." An emphasis and importance rests on this preparing or being prepared aspect of the world that may to the Hopi correspond to that "quality of reality" that "matter" or "stuff" has for us (Carroll, 1956, pp. 147–148).

So, according to Whorf, Hopi culture is different from European culture largely because language forces these human groups to think in different modes.

Whorf's thesis of linguistic relativity assumes that thought is necessarily shaped by linguistic cues. This seems a reasonable assumption, but it is also reasonable to see thought as being shaped more directly by experience, with the form thoughts assume being influenced by other things as well. For example, Furth (1966) has argued, with supporting evidence from studies of the deaf, that basic forms of both thought and symbolization may occur without language. While Furth agrees that language facilitates and shapes conceptualizations, he does not agree that language is necessary for human thought.

Because of the variety of influences upon human thought, it is impossible for a theory like linguistic relativity to be either proved or disproved. It is easy to muster evidence showing that linguistic forms are used for conceptual thought. But it is also easy to argue that non-linguistic features also shape our thought processes. What is needed, therefore, is some way of pointing to the *scope* (rather than the truth or falsity) of linguistic relativity; just how far can we say that linguistic cues do in fact condition our thought processes?

One way of pointing to the range of application of linguistic relativity is to take items that can clearly be experienced without linguistic tags, then see whether judgments about these are affected by the linguistic tags used. Take, for instance, judgments of color. Are our judgments about color affected by the words we use to name colors?

In one simple experiment Brown and Horowitz (Brown, 1956) used eight similar reddish-violet colors (with each of the adjacent colors equally spaced on the color continuum). These were presented individually with variations of a nonsense syllable to two sets of experimental subjects: Navaho Indians and Harvard students. The nonsense syllables associated with particular colors were alike for the two sets of subjects except for two differences: one difference recognized phonetically in both the English and Navaho languages (in English recognized as the difference between an "a" and an "o" sound), and the other difference recognized phonetically only in the Navaho language (a short appearance of the vowel or a longer continuation of the same vowel sound). As predicted, most of the Navaho subjects divided the colors into four categories (reflecting the four linguistic cues they recognized), whereas most Harvard subjects divided them into only two categories. In each case, subjects used the phonetic cues that their language system had prepared them to use.

In another study Brown and Lenneberg (1954) studied the effects of color *codability*. Some colors are more commonly and easily named than others. Brown and Lenneberg were able to measure this by the variable they called codability. The next question was whether the colors that are highest in codability are also more easily recognized. In an experiment with English-speaking subjects, four colors (with known codability scores) were presented at the same time, then subjects were asked to point to these same four colors in a chart of 120 colors. The results showed a significant postive correlation between color codability and recognition scores. That is, colors most easily named were also more apt to be correctly identified on the larger color chart.

From such studies we can conclude not only that linguistic cues affect how we think about words but also that they affect how we perceive and store more direct sensory information. In the two experiments just cited, we have been concerned with color perception (largely because color variations can be subjected to precise measurement and standardization), but it is likely that similar relationships might be found with any kind of sensory data. We do tend to see our world in terms of the cues of our language system.

But at the same time, linguistic relativity hardly begins to give a full description of the process of thought. There are other, more personal habits of interpretation as well as those that are standardized into linguistic form. There are also matters of mood and emotional state, not to mention variations in sensory stimuli. All of these must influence the form of thought. Still, insofar as thought is an inherently organizing process, the importance of language in giving shape to this process can hardly be minimized.

LANGUAGE AND THE SELF

At the beginning of this chapter we noted how Helen Keller learned to use language. That such learning, in her words, "awakened my soul" suggests that more is involved than superficial behavior. Language seems to have provided Helen Keller with a central means of organizing her conception of herself and her world.

Is it not thus with every child? Usually the process is more gradual, without a dramatic experience such as Helen's at the well. But as language is learned, a child also develops a way of viewing himself through these new-found tools of self-conceptualization.

Several features of language provide especially important tools for the formation and organization of self-conceptions. One is the naming habit, which was so dramatically illustrated by the case of Helen Keller. Without the habit of naming, the differentiation of the environment, including the differentiation of persons around the child, would be difficult. Nor could the child be so confident in his learning to separate himself from his environment. And his sense of identity is centered in the name provided to him by his parents.

Simple nouns may assist a child to sort out identities, but pronouns may be even more important in sorting out relationships between identities. The child is not just a thing, but he is an identity in relationship to significant others. Pronouns such as *I*, *me*, and *you* help to focus upon these relationships as expressed through interaction. Once a child has learned the proper use of these pronouns, for purposes of hearing as well as speaking, his ability to take the role of the other is well under way. The distinction between *me* and *you* requires a close attention to relative perspectives, which in turn prepares the way for a child's sense of self in relationship to others.

Grammar also appears to impose a certain pattern upon self-conceptions. The sentence structure of Western languages emphasizes subjects and predicates, which are organized around nouns and verbs, respectively. Is it not therefore inevitable that our self-conceptions will also tend to show a dichotomy between the self as actor (I) and the self as the object of action (me)? The same dichotomy applies to the way we tend to think of ourselves as involving both mind (the subjective form) and body (the objective form). It is interesting to speculate (and it should be emphasized that all of these remarks on language and the self are highly speculative) how much the philosophical issues of free will versus determinism and the clash in perspectives between the humanities and the sciences might evaporate if we had a different characteristic sentence structure. All of these matters may be largely reflections of the same subject-predicate dichotomy that our conception of ourselves in particular and of human nature in general takes on from our basic structure of language.

22
Roles

In this chapter we examine briefly four different topics, all dealing with the broader topic of social roles. At the end of the chapter the reasons for the examination of these particular topics will be made clear.

HYPNOTIC EFFECTS

Probably the first person to make systematic medical use of hypnotism was Franz Anton Mesmer. Back in the eighteenth century, Mesmer, a medical doctor, was convinced that magnetic forces exert a determining effect upon human behavior, including the curing of certain ills. Some of these magnetic forces may be produced by other people, Mesmer believed, and thus a skillful practitioner could apply them to techniques for curing diseases. Mesmer's techniques of "magnetism" (what we would now call hypnotism) were colorful and had a very dramatic effect. Theodore R. Sarbin (1963)[1] quotes a contemporary of Mesmer, who described his procedure as follows:

> Mesmer, wearing a coat of lilac silk, walked up and down amid this palpitating crowd. Mesmer carried a long iron wand, with which he touched the bodies of the patients, and especially those parts which were diseased; often, laying aside the wand, he magnetized them with his eyes, fixing his gaze on theirs, or applying his hands to the hypochondriac [abdominal] region and to the lower part of the abdomen. This application was often continued for hours, and at other times the master made use of passes. He began by placing himself *en rapport* with his subject. Seated opposite to him, foot against foot, knee against knee, he laid his fingers on the hypochondriac region, and moved them to and fro, lightly touching the ribs. Magnetization with strong currents was substituted for these manipulations when more energetic results were to be produced. The master, erecting his fingers in a pyramid, passed his hands all over the patient's body, beginning with the head, and going down over the shoul-

[1] Theodore R. Sarbin, "Attempts to Understand Hypnotic Phenomena," in L. Postman (ed.), *Psychology in the Making: Histories of Selected Research Problems.* New York: Alfred A. Knopf, 1963. Quotations from this source are reprinted with permission of the publisher.

ders to the feet. He then returned again, to the head, both back and front to the belly and the back; he renewed the process again and again, until the magnetized person was saturated with the healing fluid, and was transported with pain or pleasure, both sensations being equally salutary. Young women were so much gratified by the crisis, that they begged to be thrown into it anew; they followed Mesmer through the hall, and confessed that it was impossible not to be warmly attached to the magnetizer's person (753–754).

Sometimes the effects of so-called mesmerism were even more pronounced than such "warm attachment." Many of Mesmer's patients experienced wild convulsions. Sarbin quotes the same eighteenth-century observer for a description of this phenomena:

These convulsions are remarkable for their number, duration, and force, and have been known to persist for more than three hours. They are characterized by involuntary, jerking movements in all the limbs, and in the whole body, by contraction of the throat, by twitchings in the hypochondriac and epigastric [stomach] regions, by dimness and rolling of the eyes, by piercing cries, tears, hiccough, and immoderate laughter. They are preceded or followed by a state of languor or dreaminess, by a series of digressions, and even by stupor. Patients are seen to be absorbed in the search for one another, rushing together, smiling, talking affectionately, and endeavouring to modify their crises. They are all so submissive to the magnetizer that even when they appear to be in a stupor, his voice, a glance, or sign will rouse them from it. It is impossible not to admit, from all these results, that some great force acts upon and masters the patients, and that this force appears to reside in the magnetizer. This convulsive state is termed the crisis. It has been observed that many women and few men are subject to such crises; that they are only established after the lapse of two or three hours, and that when one is established, others soon and successively begin (p. 753).

We no longer believe that magnetism had anything to do with producing such results, and we recognize them as hypnotic phenomena. But we also know that hypnotism need not have such dramatic results. Much more typical of the use to which hypnotism has been put in modern medicine were the procedures used by A. A. Liebeault and his associates at Nancy, France, a century ago. A firsthand observer described this therapy as follows:

The patients told to go to sleep apparently fell at once into a quiet slumber, then received their dose of curative suggestions, and when told to awake, either walked quietly away or sat for a little to chat with their friends; the whole process rarely lasting longer than ten minutes. The negation of all morbid symptoms was suggested; also the maintenance of the conditions upon which general health depends, i.e., sleep, digestion, etc. I noticed that in some instances curative suggestions appeared to be perfectly successful, even when the state produced was only one of somnolence. . . . Liebeault took especial pains to explain to his patients that he neither exercised nor possessed any mysterious power, and that all he did was simple and capable of scientific explanation (quoted by Sarbin, 1963, p. 764).

This is of course quite in contrast with Mesmer's "therapy." But such different effects of hypnotism are no longer surprising, for today we recognize that many very different behaviors can be induced by hypnosis. In his survey of hypnotic phenomena, Sarbin concludes that hypnotic behavior is variable in much the same way that the behavior of an actor in a stage play is variable.

> The subject acts in relation to the hypnotist as the actor does in relation to the stage director. Each has a conception of his own role and each of these conceptions may be modified through social interaction. Both the hypnotist and the director instruct the occupant of the reciprocal position how to behave. The success of the subject's or actor's performance depends upon his preconception of the role, the degree of favorable motivation, and the amount and quality of role-taking aptitude or skill. In short, the hypnotic subject, like the actor, strives to fill a specified social position, to enact a given role (pp. 778–779).

That the similarity of a hypnotized person to an actor in a drama may be more than just an analogy is suggested by an experiment by Orne (1959). The purpose of this experiment was to distinguish the essence of hypnotic effects from role effects. This was done by having two groups of hypnotized subjects: (1) easily hypnotizable subjects and (2) other subjects who were instructed to only pretend to be hypnotized. The hypnotist did not know which of the subjects were in which group. Nor could the differences in the two groups be discovered in their behavior, whether real or feigned. According to the data that could be obtained, the results for these two groups were essentially the same. Both groups were apparently equally adept at playing the role of a person under hypnosis.

SIBLINGS AND SEX ROLES[2]

> One learns the behavior appropriate to his position in a group through interaction with others who hold normative beliefs about what his role should be and who are able to reward and punish him for correct and incorrect actions. As part of the same learning process, one acquires expectations of how others in the group will behave. The latter knowledge is indispensable to the actor, in that he must be able to predict what others expect of him, and how they will react to him, in order to guide his own role performance successfully. Accurate or erroneous understanding and prediction are respectively rewarding and punishing to the actor, and learning proceeds systematically through the elimination of incorrect responses and the strengthening of correct ones (Brim, 1958, p. 1).

[2] Orville G. Brim, Jr., "Family Structure and Sex Role Learning by Children: A Further Analysis of Helen Koch's Data," *Sociometry*, 21 (1958), 1–16. Quotations from this source are reprinted with permission of the author and the American Sociological Association.

With such a background of assumptions, Orville Brim set out to investigate the assimilation of roles within the family. His basic hypothesis was that "interaction between two persons leads to assimilation of roles, to the incorporation of elements of the role of the other in the actor's role" (p. 2). Applying this to the family, we would expect that a husband and wife would become more alike through time, and that brothers and sisters would come to share characteristics through continued interaction. Brim specifically focused on the latter question, the similarity of siblings, making use of data previously gathered by Helen Koch. Koch had gathered data in the form of personality ratings by teachers for 384 five- and six-year-old children, each of whom had a single sibling. Brim shows a breakdown of those personality traits most commonly found in children with each type of sibling (older or younger, male or female). He also distinguishes between personality traits that are more instrumental, and, therefore, more commonly related to masculine characteristics, and those that are more expressive, and, therefore, considered more related to feminine characteristics.

At least the following three generalizations appear to be supported by Brim's analysis:

1. Girls with brothers are more likely to have high masculinity ratings than girls with sisters.
2. Boys with sisters are more likely to have high femininity ratings than boys with brothers.
3. Younger children (with older siblings of the opposite sex) are more apt to show characteristics of the opposite sex than are older children (with younger siblings of the opposite sex).

Brim suggests that these results follow from the way personalities develop through role-taking. When the only sibling present is of the opposite sex, a child is more apt to take on and assimilate such a role through interaction than when this is not the case. Also, the younger the child (compared to his sibling), the stronger should be this effect, for younger children tend to have less power and thus must make greater adjustments in interaction than their older siblings.

The Case of Frankie

SIDELIGHT

We ordinarily conceive of male and female roles as rooted in biology, and so they are. But they also involve learning, as Brim's study suggests. Much of the social learning is so pervasive that we are hardly aware that it is going on. The importance of such social learning of sex roles can be seen by the sharp contrast of a case where an inappropriate role was learned.

Such a case was that of Frankie, reported by Lindesmith and Strauss (1968).[3] Her abnormal clitoris led to pronouncing her a boy at birth. She had been treated like a boy until a surgical examination at the age of five proved that she was in fact a

[3] Alfred R. Lindesmith and Anselm L. Strauss, *Social Psychology*, 3rd edition. New York: Holt, Rinehart and Winston, 1968. Quotations from this source are reprinted with permission of the publisher.

girl. Now Frankie, for that was the child's name, was to be treated as a girl. One of the nurses in the hospital at the time the true sex was determined describes the difficulties of the situation:

This didn't sound too difficult—until we tried it. Frankie simply didn't give the right cues. It is amazing how much your response to a child depends on that child's behavior toward you. It was extremely difficult to keep from responding to Frankie's typically little boy behavior in the same way that I responded to other boys in the ward. And to treat Frankie as a girl was jarringly out of key. It was something we all had to continually remind ourselves to do. Yet the doing of it left all of us feeling vaguely uneasy as if we had committed an error. Even remembering to say "her" instead of "him" was difficult. One of the internes just flatly stated that he couldn't do it and referred to Frankie either by name or as "it." After the surgical examination Frankie was in bed and for a few days was satisfied with the more peaceful entertainment which we furnished and in which we vainly hoped she would become interested. But after a few days she began to demand trains, wagons and guns. About the same time Frankie became increasingly aware of the change in our attitude toward her. She seemed to realize that behavior which had always before brought forth approval was no longer approved. It must have been far more confusing to her than it was to us and certainly it was bad enough for us. Her reaction was strong and violent. She became extremely belligerent and even less willing to accept crayons, color books and games which she simply called "sissy" and threw on the floor.. She talked constantly of the wagon she had been promised for Christmas and what she and the other little boys with whom she played would do when she was well and home again. She also objected strenuously to the hospital gown she wore insisting that it was too "sissy" and that she would wear pajamas or nothing. Her departure from the hospital created a disturbance: her mother had brought a dress and Frankie took one look and sent up a howl. Her mother finally got her dressed, stepped out of the room to the nurses' station and went back to find a completely nude Frankie. Frankie went home in a pair of hospital coveralls (p. 339).

EMERGENT GROUP ROLES

The very nature of group organization seems to impose certain patterns on the differentiation of roles within the group. At any rate, this is what research by Robert F. Bales and Philip E. Slater seems to show. Let us note one study by Slater (1955) as an example.

Twenty groups of male undergraduate students (from three to seven per group) each met four times. At each meeting, the subjects were given an administrative problem to discuss for forty minutes. No attempt was made to structure the activities of the groups in any other manner.

Data obtained included controlled observation of the groups through a one-way window and questionnaires given at the end of each meeting. All acts observed were classified and recorded as belonging in one or another of twelve categories (such as "shows solidarity," "gives suggestions," "shows tension," etc.) developed by Bales for such *interaction process analysis*. From such records could also be determined the total amount of talking done by each person and the amount of discussion directed toward each person (receiving).

Questionnaires given after each meeting asked for comparative evaluations of group members on such questions as: Who contributed the best ideas? Who did most to guide the discussion? Who does the subject feel he likes most? Results of these questions may be referred to as applying to the criteria of best ideas, guidance, and liking, respectively. Results of observations may be seen as indicating amounts of talking and receiving of each group member.

The most outstanding finding of the study was the relative independence of liking ratings from those of the other criteria. A person given top rank on liking seldom received the top rank on some other criterion, whereas a person was much more apt to receive top rank in any two of the other criteria (talking, receiving, best ideas, and guidance). Furthermore, the tendency of the best liked man to rank high in another category decreased with successive meetings of the group. Ratings of leadership were also obtained after the final session, and leadership coincided less often with liking than with the other criteria (with guidance, receiving, best ideas, and talking most closely associated with leadership, in that order).

Among the questionnaire results, the lowest correlations were between liking and best ideas. Nevertheless, there was sometimes a very high rate of interaction between the best liked man and the top idea man in a group. They tended to like each other more than other group members, and their relationship often seemed to be a focal point in the group. The idea man tended to initiate more interaction in problem-solving attempts, concentrating on the task and playing a more aggressive role. The best liked man appeared to concentrate more on sociability, playing a more passive role but still receiving more suggestions and opinions from other group members than the idea man.

Slater concludes that "the most fundamental type of role differentiation in small experimental groups is the divorcing of task functions from social-emotional functions" (1955, p. 308; see also Bales and Slater, 1955). Slater sees this as reflecting the twofold nature of problems facing any group: (1) difficulties of group goal achievement and adaptation to external demands (adaptive-instrumental problems) and (2) difficulties involving internal integration and the expression of emotional tension (integrative-expressive problems).

Are these tendencies toward role differentiation also present in groups outside the laboratory? More recent research (Verba, 1961; Leik, 1963; Burke, 1967) suggests that such role differentiation may apply most clearly to situations involving relative strangers and/or where no clear pattern for leadership is accepted in advance. For example, Leik (1963) indicates that, in continued family interaction, the tendency for role differentiation becomes less rather than more marked.

Interaction Process Analysis

METHODOLOGICAL POINTER

Robert F. Bales (1950) has pioneered in techniques for the observation of interaction in small groups. His methods have become known as interaction process analysis.

In a typical group observation, several observers watch behind a one-way window and record every distinct act. These are transferred by code onto a moving paper tape, indicating both who gives a particular communication and to whom it is directed. Most of the recorded acts (about fifteen to twenty per minute) consist of talk, though such events as yawns and nods are also recorded.

While there are other sets of categories devised by other scholars, in Bales's system of analysis acts are recorded according to the following classification (note the reverse symmetry between the first six and the last six categories):

Positive Reactions:
  1. Shows solidarity, raises status of others, jokes, gives help, reward
  2. Shows tension release, shows satisfaction, laughs
  3. Agrees, shows passive acceptance, understands, concurs, complies

Problem-Solving Attempts:
  4. Gives suggestion, direction, implying autonomy for other
  5. Gives opinion, evaluation, analysis, expresses feeling, wish
  6. Gives orientation, information, repeats, clarifies, confirms

Questions:
  7. Asks for orientation, information, repetition, confirmation
  8. Asks for opinion, evaluation, analysis, expression of feeling
  9. Asks for suggestion, direction, possible ways of action

Negative Reactions:
  10. Disagrees, shows passive rejection, formality, withholds help
  11. Shows tension increase, asks for help, withdraws
  12. Shows antagonism, deflates status of others, defends or asserts self

Bales believes that the above categories can provide meaningful classification for all acts in a group setting. Note, however, that what is focused upon is the function of an act in the process of interaction—not the particular content of the act.

ARE FAMILIES LITTLE STATES?

William N. Stephens, an anthropologist, was concerned with the problem of explaining some of the different patterns of families in different cultures. His book *The Family in Cross-Cultural Perspective* (1963) reports a number of interesting patterns of relationship between family forms and other cultural features. We shall select for particular attention his analysis of the relationship between patterns of deference in family relationships and patterns of political organization.

Stephens suspected that there was some correspondence between the amount of deference shown within a family and the form of political organization of the larger society. From the anthropological literature he obtained a sample of fifty-one different cultures. In each case he attempted to obtain ratings of the degree of son-to-father deference and of the degree of wife-to-husband deference. For five cultures information was not sufficient to make reliable ratings on both variables, so only forty-six cultures remained in the sample.

In categorizing the political systems of these forty-six societies, thirteen could be identified as tribal societies, that is, as being without a state. Tribes are without cities, and social stratification does not appear in very rigid form. Tribes are the earliest known forms of political organization, and those tribal societies still existing are the simple societies that anthropologists most eagerly study.

A kingdom, in contrast, is characterized by a state with coercive power, centralized in a hereditary office, which it exerts over its population. Kingdoms are also characterized by rigid social stratification, which is also based on hereditary factors. Nobles typically own the land in these agrarian societies, and commoners provide the work. Stephens identified most of the rest of his sample of cultures as presently or formerly parts of kingdoms.

In five of the forty-six cultures it was not clear whether the political form was properly classed with tribes or with kingdoms. Eliminating these, we are left with forty-one cultures. Also, five of the cultures sampled (in France, Italy, and Canada) hardly could be considered to be any longer in traditional kingdoms. For these examples from Western democratic systems, a special designation of *modern* will be used. Altogether, the forty-one remaining cultures may be divided into thirteen tribal societies, twenty-three kingdom societies, and five modern societies.

Does this breakdown of political forms have anything to do with patterns of family relationships? Table 29 suggests rather strongly that it does. As can be seen in this table, tribal societies all have a low or intermediate degree of deference within families, whereas the deference patterns of kingdoms are much more marked. Finally, the modern societies, even though formerly or still nominally parts of kingdoms, tend to show very low degrees of deference in family relationships.

High patterns of intrafamily deference tend, then, to be found particularly in kingdom societies. Does this mean that the family form sets the conditions for the political form, or vice versa? Do families with high deference create the conditions for political kingdoms, or do political kingdoms create the conditions for role relationships of high deference within families?

Stephens places the primary emphasis upon the political form

TABLE 29 POLITICAL FORMS AND DEFERENCE IN FAMILY RELATIONSHIPS

	Number of Societies with Different Degrees of Deference in Family Relationships*		
	High	*Intermediate*	*Low*
Tribal societies (13)	0	6	7
Kingdom societies (23)	7	16	0
Modern societies (5)	0	0	5

SOURCE: Adapted from Stephens (1963), pp. 332–333.

* Societies rated either 5 or 4 by Stephens on both son-to-father and wife-to-husband deference are considered as ranking high in deference. Those rated 0, 1, or 2 on both are considered to be low. All other societies are classed as intermediate.

determining the family form, rather than vice versa. He enumerates two reasons for this conclusion.

> First, in the light of my historical reconstruction—the picture of expanding, conquering kingdoms subduing and assimilating neighboring tribes—it seems reasonable to assume that the kingdom "came first" (was the antecedent) and that family deference "came afterward" (was a consequence, or result, of subjugation by a kingdom). Second, there is the suggestion in the data that when the kingdom disappears (in lieu of a democratic state) the extreme family deference customs also disappear (p. 334).

This interpretation is of course not very hopeful for would-be patriarchs in modern families. A restoration of monarchy, with all its glorious trappings to distract from the accompanying exploitation, may be a way to get family members to show more respect for the old man; but this is hardly the kind of revolution that can inspire popular enthusiasm today.

FOUR PROPOSITIONS

Back in Chapter 11 we introduced the concept of social roles, pointing out how important the expectations of others were for the development of self-conceptions.

In the present chapter we have built the basis for several additional insights concerning social roles. These may now be presented in the form of the following four propositions:

1. Other persons provide guides concerning the detailed form of behavior in particular situations.
2. In presenting guides concerning the form of behavior, others affect not only immediate behavior but long-term personality patterns as well.
3. Expectations of others become patterned according to the requirements of group activity.
4. The patterns of expected behavior to be found in particular groups reflect the broader cultural setting as well as the immediate situation in which a person acts.

These are of course all very general propositions. They are too general to be considered proved by evidence presented in this chapter Nevertheless, some evidence has been presented to make these propositions at least seem reasonable. The first proposition is supported by our observations about hypnotic effects. The second is supported by Brim's analysis of siblings and sex roles. The third is supported by Slater's study of role differentiation. And the fourth proposition is supported by Stephens's evidence concerning the association of patterns of deference within families to broader patterns of political organization.

Roles and Staging

The concept of role came out of the language of the theater. In fact, sociologists are apt to quote with approval Shakespeare's assertion that "all the world's a stage" with its inhabitants "merely players." In view of the popularity of such a stage analogy, a few cautionary points may be in order.

First, the plans for most role behavior are not as precisely detailed as are roles set forth in the script of a drama. Behavior in social roles is seldom as fully preplanned as the stage analogy suggests—though the analogy still may be useful in pointing out that some predetermination is involved.

Second, the stage analogy suggests that each actor only plays a single role. In reality we often are playing several roles at the same time. It is as though an actor had several characters to play in the same scene. This makes real life so much richer (and more troublesome) in its possibilities than the theater.

Finally, the stage analogy suggests a deliberate act of pretending what otherwise is not real. Most roles in real life are not performed in this manner. We almost always take our roles quite seriously, even when we do rather silly things. Most role playing is thus "for real"— even though the reality may be socially created. Seldom do we simply play at a role (and when we do we usually clearly set it off by a joking manner).

23
Morality

CONCERNING FREUDIANISM, TOTEMISM, AND INCEST TABOOS

How do we account for morality? Why have humans developed such numerous moral prohibitions and taboos? And how it is that individuals come to feel guilty about breaking these standards of propriety?

Sigmund Freud once told a story that implied answers to these questions. Freud borrowed from Charles Darwin the assumption of a *primal horde.* This implied for Freud that in its early dawn of development, human social organization was built around bands of females and children dominated in each case by a powerful old male. The old man kept all the females for himself, and the younger rivals—sons and all—were driven off. Such a band is the setting for Freud's story.[1]

> One day the expelled brothers joined forces, slew and ate the father, and thus put an end to the father horde. Together they dared and accomplished what would have remained impossible for them singly. Perhaps some advance in culture, like the use of a new weapon, had given them the feeling of superiority. Of course, these cannibalistic savages ate their victim. This violent primal father had surely been the envied and feared model for each of the brothers. Now they accomplished their identification with him by devouring him and each acquired a part of his strength. The totem feast, which is perhaps mankind's first celebration, would be the repetition and commemoration of this memorable, criminal act with which so many many things began, social organization, moral restrictions and religion. . . .
>
> After they had satisfied their hate by his removal and had carried out their wish for identification with him, the suppressed tender impulses had to assert themselves. This took place in the form of remorse, a sense of guilt was formed which coincided here with the remorse generally felt. The dead now became stronger than the living had been, even as we observe it today in the destinies of men. What the father's presence had formerly prevented, they themselves now prohibited in the psychic situation of "subsequent obedience" which we know so well from

[1] Sigmund Freud, "Totem and Taboo," in A. A. Brill (ed.), *The Basic Writings of Sigmund Freud.* New York: Random House, 1938. Copyright 1938 by Random House, Inc. Copyright © renewed 1965 by Gioia B. Bernheim and Edmund R. Brill. Quotations from this source are reprinted with permission of Edmund R. Brill.

psychoanalysis. They undid their deed by declaring that the killing of the father substitute, the totem, was not allowed, and renounced the fruits of their deed by denying themselves the liberated women. Thus, they created two fundamental taboos of totemism out of the *sense of guilt of the son*, and for this very reason these had to correspond with the two repressed wishes of the Oedipus complex. Whoever disobeyed, became guilty of the two only crimes [murder and incest] which troubled primitive society (pp. 915–917).

This is, of course, an outrageous story, and it may amuse us that Freud took seriously the notion that something of this sort probably did actually happen way back in the mists of time. But questions of historical details aside, what are the main ideas that we may derive from this story? Let us list them in the form of three propositions that all repeat a central Freudian theme:

1. The original form of human religion, totemism, emerged out of the ambivalence of sons toward fathers.
2. Primitive morality reflected at its core these same ambivalences, including the guilty consciences developed as a result.
3. Morality ever since has been supported by the same forms of ambivalence and feelings of guilt.

Let us examine these ideas further to consider what merit they may have.

Along with several other scholars of his time, Freud assumed that all religions emerged out of totemism, a form of primitive religion in which a natural object (usually a particular species of animal) was revered as representative of the clan. Freud also believed that totemism everywhere included not only an identification of the family, tribe, or clan with an animal symbol but also a recognition of this animal as the group's ancestor, rituals for participating in the spiritual power of the totem, and taboos against killing this animal except for the special ceremony of the totemic feast. Assuming such features to be universal experiences of early humanity, Freud sought their roots in a common human theme. The theme he pointed to was the rivalry of sons with fathers. Everywhere sons have resented the power and privilege of their fathers, and how much more must this have been the case when the human family was based (or at least as Freud imagined it was based) more simply on the brute strength of dominant males. But sons have also always admired their fathers and thus felt guilty about their acts of rebellion. In totemism we have the collective expression of this guilt projected toward an animal who symbolizes paternity. The moral taboos against murder and incest are a part of the same complex, developed to express respect for these parental spirits, for whose sake sex and aggression must be controlled.

Freud had a magnificently generalizing mind. He put many pieces together to come up with a bold theory into which they all fit. But, alas, many of the assumptions he made about totemism were premature. We now know that totemism is not always accompanied by taboos in regard to the totemic animals, that a totemic feast is not always present, and that not all totemic groups claim descent from the totem. Furthermore, there is no longer the general assumption that totemism was universal, or even that it was specifically religious. As the anthropologist Alexander Goldenweiser (1931) has pointed out in his review of totemism, "the intensity of the religious *attitude* toward the totem is scarcely ever pronounced" and "totemism, in *no* instance, constitutes the whole or even the center of the religious aspect of a tribal culture" (p. 374).

With our later anthropological knowledge of the varieties of totemic forms, part of what Freud attempted to explain has evaporated. We no longer need to explain why features of totemism were universal once we understand that they were really quite rare, and even where found they often were only incidental features of tribal cultures. So let us pass on from the task of explaining totemism to the more general question of primitive morality.

Freud's general explanation for the taboos against sex and aggression may still apply: that they arise out of inhibitions of actions toward parents. More specifically, Freud saw morality in primitive society as emerging out of the following pattern of what he considered to be basic human facts:

1. Young boys are sexually attracted to their mothers.
2. They, therefore, feel hostility and envy toward their fathers.
3. Since they cannot defeat their fathers to win their mothers, they suppress their hostility—at least so far as conscious feelings are concerned.
4. As a result of the same defeated aspirations, they suppress sexual desires—at least toward those closely associated with their mothers.

This pattern became tagged by Freud as the *Oedipus complex*, reminding us of the tragic fate in Greek drama of Oedipus, who unwittingly married his own mother. But what is the evidence for the universality of such a complex? Do we really have any evidence that it applies to other societies besides the late-Victorian Europe that Freud observed?

It is hard to test ideas of the Oedipus complex directly in different cultures because there is marked cultural variation in the expression of such themes as father-son rivalry. Certainly such rivalry should not be expected to be the same in societies where the father is the chief disciplinarian as in societies where the father has little power. But such variation in cultural roles may nevertheless provide a means of testing the validity of the basic ideas of the Oedipus complex. If cultures that create conditions for greater father-son rivalry are also the cultures with more sexual inhibitions, general support for the Oedipus complex could be assumed.

William N. Stephens (1962) has made cross-cultural analyses of precisely such phenomena. For example, he tested the prediction that societies with long post-partum sex taboos (for example, prohibition of sex relations between husband and wife for at least a year after the birth of a child), presumably a condition productive of father-son rivalry, will also be societies with other features suggestive of oedipal themes (for example, severe brother-sister avoidance, extensive menstrual taboos, and generalized sex anxiety). After a comparative study of such variables in one hundred cultures, Stephens concluded that the cross-cultural evidence supports the basic assumptions of an oedipal complex.

It is one thing to find supporting evidence for an early rivalry between sons and fathers being followed by certain inhibitions; it is quite another thing, however, to use this as the general explanation for the moral systems of primitive man. Does the Oedipus complex give all the main clues for explaining primitive morality?

Consider, for example, patterns of incest avoidance. Incest avoidance is not only one of the basic forms of morality in Freudian theory, but it also happens to be one of the few themes found in all forms of human culture. All societies have incest taboos, though what is defined as incest may vary somewhat from society to society. How adequate is the Freudian explanation that these are residues of the basic resolution of the oedipal problem (that is, by the son's repression of sexuality toward the mother, or a daughter's repression of sexuality toward the father)?

In a very thorough study of incest patterns in 250 cultures, Murdock (1949) concludes that some common features do show a significant harmony with Freudian theories. Freud's theory, he believes, helps to explain the peculiar emotional quality of incest taboos, the universal occurrence of incest avoidance within the nuclear family, the diminished intensity of taboos outside the nuclear family, and the occurrence of violations in spite of the taboos. But Murdock believes that Freud's psychological theories must be supplemented by sociological considerations for a full understanding of the phenomena of incest. Incest taboos serve group needs as well as psychic purposes. Such taboos provide one means of limiting conflict within the family group. They also avoid the cultural stagnation that would occur if family groups were not forced to go beyond themselves for mates. Presumably, therefore, those societies with weak or absent incest taboos were not successful enough culturally to survive until anthropologists could arrive on the scene to study them.

But such psychological and sociological theories, Murdock believes, still do not explain the patterns of incest avoidance beyond the nuclear family. For this, one must take account of the particular cultural configurations of different cultures. This does not mean that there are not cross-cultural regularities in such patterns, but rather that such patterns have to be seen within the logic of other cultural relationships.

For example, some societies extend incest taboos beyond the nuclear family primarily to cover relatives on the mother's side of the family. With very few exceptions, these turn out to be societies with matrilineal kinship groups. Other societies extend incest taboos primarily to cover the paternal side of the family, and almost all of these are societies with patrilineal kinship groups. Also, Murdock points to some evidence that suggests that the distance to which incest taboos are extended among relatives may be primarily a function of the time that has elapsed since the establishment of the kinship group.

This brief excursion into the cross-cultural vagaries of incest taboos suggests the usefulness of Freudian insights for understanding certain deeply rooted moral prohibitions. But it has also pointed out that psychological explanations are not enough to account for the particular patterns that these prohibitions take. There is also the logic of social and cultural systems expressed in the system of taboos. These precede the individual with patterns that are ready-made before his birth. These standards he must absorb in some way as he grows into his full moral manhood.

STUDIES OF CONSCIENCE

After considering matters of primitive morality, let us go on to discuss more fully what was earlier presented as a third proposition of Freud's interpretation of morality, namely, that feelings of guilt and of ambivalence have continued as the key supports for morality ever since the days of primitive society. In considering this we move away from primary concern with collective moral systems to a concern with the psychology of moral feelings and behavior. Here perhaps Freud's theory of morality will be more directly applicable than in explaining collective moral systems.

In brief, Freud's view was that adult morality is built around a sense of guilt, and that this guilt is in turn the product of the oedipal situation. When the family structure provides inevitable defeat for the child's early aggressive and sexual urges, he develops the capacity to suppress these impulses. The agency of such suppression is the superego, that internalization of the demands and prohibitions of society that becomes built into his personality to guard against misbehavior. When the impulses of the id bring their temptations, the response of guilt from the superego tends to inhibit such behavior.

It is hard to make a direct empirical test of this picture of the dynamics of individual morality. If true, however, several predictions may be made that can be tested. One is that persons who feel the most guilt (that is, who have the strongest superegos) will tend to be those who show the least misbehavior. As Freud (1930) expressed it, "the more righteous a man is, the stricter and more suspicious will his conscience be, so that ultimately it is precisely those people who have carried holiness farthest who reproach themselves with deepest sinfulness" (p. 80). For, according to Freud, although misbehavior may activate a sense of guilt, much more does the potential for guilt suppress such behavior.

A second prediction implied by Freud's theories is that persons who have most successfully identified with the parent of the same sex will be those with the strongest consciences. It is, in other words, those who have most fully resolved the conflict of the oedipal situation (through identification with the parent of the same sex) who should have the most effective consciences.

A third expectation of Freud's theory of conscience that should be amenable to some kind of empirical test is that a strong conscience should provide for a high consistency in behavior. Since the superego is a major feature of personality developed at an early age, it should give continuity to a person's acts such that the degree of his morality in different situations should be highly consistent.

Some evidence regarding all three of these predictions is given in a study by Donald MacKinnon (1938). Ninety-three subjects were given a series of problem-solving tasks. Booklets containing solutions for all problems were available in the experimental room, but subjects were given instructions to consult these only for certain problems. Subjects worked alone, but through a one-way screen the experimenter watched to see how the subjects behaved. One of the things especially noted was that forty-three subjects violated the prohibitions against looking up solutions, whereas fifty did not violate prohibitions.

Four weeks later most of these subjects—sixty-nine, to be exact—were questioned about the experiment. In the course of this questioning, most, but not all, of the violators made at least partial admissions of their transgressions. But, more than admissions or nonadmissions of guilt, MacKinnon was interested in the feelings that seemed to accompany such memories. So subjects were asked, if they admitted peeking, "How do you feel about having looked at the prohibited solutions?" Subjects not admitting peeking, including both those who had and those who had not violated prohibitions, were asked a hypothetical question about how they would have felt if they had looked up prohibited solutions. The breakdown of results is indicated by Table 30. A similar pattern of results was obtained for the question, "Do you, in everyday life, often feel guilty about things which you have done or have not done?" These results together suggest much stronger feelings of guilt for nonviolators than for violators. This is very much in line with the prediction that people with strong senses of guilt will be those most apt to resist temptation.

TABLE 30   NUMBER OF VIOLATORS AND NONVIOLATORS WHO ASSO-
CIATED GUILT FEELINGS WITH VIOLATIONS OF PROHIBI-
TIONS

	Had or Would Have Guilt Feelings	*No Report of Guilt Feelings*
Admitted violators	6	16
Violators who denied violations	2	8
Nonviolators	31	6
	39	30

SOURCE: Adapted from MacKinnon (1938), pp. 494–495.

Most of the subjects (who were, by the way, mostly Harvard men) were also asked at one point, "Of which parent are you fonder?" The expectation, following Freud, would be that violators would be less apt to show identification with the father than nonviolators (who presumably had solved their oedipal conflicts more successfully). MacKinnon's data showed at least a trend in this direction. "Only 26% of the violators, as against 64% of the nonviolators, were at least as fond of their fathers as of their mothers" (p. 498). This line of investigation was followed with inquiries directed to twenty-eight of the male subjects as to how they recalled being disciplined by their parents in early childhood. There were no strong differences in the pictures of maternal behavior provided by violators or nonviolators, but there were differences in paternal discipline. Most of the violators reported fathers with much more physical punishment than the fathers described by nonviolators. Nonviolators were more apt to describe their fathers as using disciplinary "measures which seek to have a child feel that he has fallen short of some ideal or that he has hurt his parents and consequently is less loved by them because of what he has done" (p. 498). Most of these nonviolators suggested their father's psychological forms of punishment to be highly effective. This too is in line with what we would expect of boys who had successfully resolved their oedipal conflicts—whether because such conflicts were less intense or, as the last evidence suggests, because their fathers were more effective in asserting their influence.

MacKinnon did not observe the behavior of his subjects in a variety of situations. He observed only their behavior for one small moral dilemma. Therefore, he had no direct evidence on consistency of moral behavior as applied to different situations. But he believed that he did have good evidence of a consistency of personality, that actions in the test situation were highly consistent with other measured characteristics of the subjects. And his results showed the kind of consistency that Freud's theories would appear to predict.

An earlier and rather more ambitious study of cheating was made by Hartshorne and May (1928). They studied about eleven thousand students in the early 1920s in test situations that could involve lying, stealing, and (especially) cheating. The cheating studies mostly involved opportunities to cheat in classroom work. The results of these studies pointed to some variables affecting the tendency to cheat (for example, persons of higher socioeconomic standing and/or intelligence showed less cheating than those lower in either variable), but they also pointed to the wide variation from situation to situation in an individual's tendency to cheat. For example, the specific nature of test material and a student's ability to master it were particularly strongly related to the tendency to cheat. Also important was the particular classroom group in which a person was; "class groups differ from one another and tend to maintain these differences from year to year, each class building up a habit system which, without much consciousness on the part of the individual members, operates to differentiate it from other groups" (p. 338).

Hartshorne and May interpret their results as showing that

> . . . neither deceit nor its opposite, honesty, are unified character traits, but rather specific functions of life situations. Most children will deceive in certain situations and not in others. Lying, cheating, and stealing as measured by the test situations used in these studies are only very loosely related. . . .
>
> The motives for cheating, lying, or stealing are complex and inhere for the most part in the general situations themselves. The most common motive for cheating on classroom exercises is the desire to do well (pp. 411–412).

How can we harmonize the results of these two studies? MacKinnon found fairly high consistency between cheating behavior and background personality variables. Hartshorne and May found little consistency in honesty as related to personal variables, but, on the contrary, a great deal of situational variation. It need not be assumed that there is a direct contradiction between these two studies if it is noted that MacKinnon did not study different situations and thus could hardly be blamed for failing to note the great situational variation of dishonest behavior; and Hartshorne and May did not really include much personality data in their study. It might well be true that there is much more consistency in honesty behavior in situations than in persons, as the Hartshorne and May data suggest, but that there is still a significant continuity of such behavior by the same person from situation to situation.

A reanalysis of Hartshorne and May's data by Burton (1963) has indeed shown evidence of at least some underlying generality of moral behavior from situation to situation. Thus honesty may not be a highly general trait, but some persons are more generally honest than others. And to the degree that honesty or dishonesty is a general trait, it may be embedded in the kind of personality patterns MacKinnon pointed to.

Let us now add a much more recent study to further clarify, or confuse, the issues. This is a study by Sears, Rau, and Alpert (1965)[2] of nursery school children at Stanford, California. These children, mostly four-year-olds, were subjected to a number of test situations to observe the extent of their moral controls. For example, in one situation, they were given responsibility for carefully watching a pet hamster to see that it did not escape, then observed (through a one-way glass) to see their reactions when, in a moment of distraction, the hamster was made to disappear. In addition to such test situations, detailed interviews were conducted with the children's parents.

The most obvious thing about the findings of Sears, Rau, and Alpert is the lack of correlation between various measures of morality for different situations. Children who showed guilt or other signs of conscience in one situation may not be the same who showed it in other situations. And generally, as shown by Table 31, those who appeared to have the strongest consciences in data provided in interviews with parents were not necessarily the same as those who showed features of conscience in the test situations. Furthermore, measures of guilt showed little relationship to those of resistance to temptation; and parental reports of remorse had little correspondence to guilt shown in experimental situations. The investigators conclude that "the development of conscience cannot be considered a unitary process in any simple sense" (p. 238).

The authors believe that some of the lack of consistency in the moral behavior of children may be due to their age. Four-year-old children were deliberately selected because it was believed that at this age they would be in a particularly critical stage in their moral development. This is the time when, according to psychoanalytic theory, the primary infantile identification with the mother should be transformed into a

---

[2] Robert R. Sears, Lucy Rau, and Richard Alpert, *Identification and Child Rearing.* Stanford, Calif.: Stanford University Press, 1965. Quotations from this source are reprinted with permission of the publisher.

TABLE 31   CORRELATIONS OF RATINGS OF NURSERY SCHOOL CHIL-
DREN'S BEHAVIOR IN TEST SITUATIONS TO SIGNS OF
CONSCIENCE INDICATED BY INTERVIEW MATERIAL

Test Situation Behavior Rating	Correlation with Signs of Conscience in Parent Interview Material	
	Boys	Girls
Resistance to temptation	.18	−.06
Emotional upset	−.06	.45
Confessing behavior (after shortcoming)	−.27	.12
Fixing behavior (to repair wrongs)	−.31	−.06

SOURCE: Sears, Rau, and Alpert (1965), p. 216.

more mature identification. This more mature identification should be with the parent of the opposite sex, and it should be associated with the control of sexual and aggressive impulses. This, then, should be a time when very interesting patterns of moral development might be seen. It was something of a disappointment to find so little clear consistency in patterns shown by individual children. Still, within the data are at least some indications that the dynamics suggested by Freudian theory might be at work. The authors point out:

> Resistance to temptation is closely related to non-aggressiveness in both sexes, and we have been led to conclude that it represents an index of general impulse control. The child-rearing correlates of this type of behavior are different for the boys and girls, however, and suggest the possibility that the boys were being much influenced by the fathers' close attention and moral training, whereas the girls were being influenced more by the mothers' high standards and positive discipline. The ambivalence of the boys' fathers fits the pattern to be expected from defensive identification, and the girls' relation with their mothers is more in accord with what might develop through primary identification.
>
> The "guilt" reactions (emotional upset and confession) also present a difference in the parent-child relationships of the two sexes. The boys who showed high upset had mothers who tended to be cold, restrictive, and non-permissive about sex, and fathers who tended to be non-punitive but perhaps authoritarian. The girls, on the other hand, were strongly influenced by their fathers, and there was clear suggestion of a sexually tinged relationship that could be interpreted quite easily as involving an Oedipus conflict. Thus, again, the pattern of the data suggests defensive identification [identification as a solution to oedipal conflict] as a possible mediating process for the development of an important aspect of conscience (p. 240).

SUPEREGO OR EGO?

The principal view of morality followed in the previous section is that morality is a matter of conscience. People behave because they would otherwise have guilty consciences. And guilty consciences in turn grow out of childhood punishment and repression. But how adequate is this view? We have examined some evidence in MacKinnon's study and pointed to some more in the recent work of Sears and associates to support such a view of superego development and control. But there has been other evidence in which situational variation appears to be far more important than superego strength. Guilty consciences are either rather limited in the role they play or else they are highly variable.

Furthermore, how does a sense of guilt develop? Is it just from punishment—physical or psychological? More important than punishment, according to some reviews of the research, are techniques that "involve the direct stimulation of the child's capacity for moral self-judgment and guilt, rather than the creation of guilt out of punishment" (Kohlberg, 1964, p. 412). "Presumably," Kohlberg concludes, "discipline is effective in inducing guilt only within a context in which a child is capable of, and is stimulated to make, moral self-judgments."

The ability to make moral self-judgments is in turn something that may be much more relevant to situational variation than some automatic mechanism of guilt. It may rest in turn upon such other abilities as general intelligence, the ability to take a somewhat extended time perspective, to maintain stable attention, and to maintain self-esteem. All of these variables have been found to correlate strongly with moral behavior. Such findings provide, according to Kohlberg,

> . . . support for the interpretation of moral character as ego, rather than super-ego, strength. This interpretation implies that the major consistencies in moral conduct represent decision-making capacities rather than fixed behavior traits. It is thus consistent with the findings on situational variation, which suggested that moral conduct was the product of a situational decision (pp. 391–392).

Another approach toward resolving some of the ambiguity about the basis of morality suggests that we see moral behavior as resting on two principal bases: (1) an authoritarian conscience and (2) a situationally rooted sense of appropriate behavior. That the development of these two bases of morality may be somewhat different is suggested by the work of the Swiss psychologist Jean Piaget, especially in his book *The Moral Judgment of the Child* (1965). Piaget distinguishes between two kinds of morality. The first is heteronomous, a morality based on obedience to fixed standards, and the second he calls autonomous, a morality based on self-judgment. Heteronomous morality is seen as chiefly a product of obedience toward parents, reflecting the inequality of power and knowledge of parent and child and the adjustment the child must make because of this inequality. In accepting rules from his parents, often in a highly unconditional manner, the child is also accepting standards of society.

In contrast, as the child relates to others, especially his peers, under conditions of greater equality, he comes to realize that moral standards may be made by people to fit particular situations. Out of the reciprocity of his relationships to others he develops a sense of the relativity of moral rules. Also involved is a maturation of intelligence such that the child can come to see his world in terms of an *operational intelligence* —that is, understanding things as relative to the operations by which we may work with them—rather than simply experiencing them concretely. As this operational intelligence develops, a person gains a capacity for a greater relativity in his sense of moral behavior from situation to situation.

At one time, Piaget (1965)[3] and his associates asked children to give examples of what they considered unfair. Some replies follow:

Age 6: "Children who make a noise with their feet during prayers" or "telling lies."
Age 9: "The mother gives a lovely dog to one sister and not to the other" or "a worse punishment for one than for the other."
Age 12: "A mother who won't allow her children to play with children who are less well dressed" (pp. 314–315).

Paiget placed the above responses into the categories of forbidden behavior, behavior of inequality, and social injustice, respectively. The total distribution of answers Piaget reports by age levels are indicated by Table 32.

TABLE 32   KINDS OF BEHAVIOR GIVEN AS EXAMPLES OF WHAT IS UNFAIR

Age Level	Forbidden Behavior	Behavior of Inequality	Social Injustice	Other
6–9	64%	27%	0%	9%
9–12	7%	73%	11%	9%

SOURCE: Adapted from Piaget (1965), p. 314.

As can be seen in the table, examples of forbidden acts chosen to illustrate what is unfair decline sharply with age, and examples of inequality and social injustice increase. Piaget concludes:

These obviously spontaneous remarks, taken together with the rest of our enquiry, allow us to conclude, in so far as one can talk of stages in the moral life, the existence of three great periods in the development of the sense of justice in the child. One period, lasting up to the age of 7–8, during which justice is subordinated to adult authority; a period contained approximately between 8–11, and which is that of progressive equalitarianism; and finally a period which sets in towards 11–12, and during which purely equalitarian justice is tempered by considerations of equity.

The first is characterized by the non-differentiation of the notions of just and unjust from those of duty and disobedience: whatever conforms to the dictates of the adult authority is just. . . .

[3] Jean Piaget, *The Moral Judgment of the Child.* New York: Free Press, 1965. Quotations from this source are reprinted with permission of the Macmillan Publishing Co., Inc. and Routledge & Kegan Paul Ltd.

The second period . . . may be defined by the progressive development of autonomy and the priority of equality over authority. . . .

Towards 11–12 we see a new attitude emerge, which may be said to be characterized by the feeling of equity, and which is nothing but a development of equalitarianism in the direction of relativity. Instead of looking for equality in identity, the child no longer thinks of the equal rights of individuals except in relation to the particular situation of each (pp. 315–317).

Such developments, Piaget emphasizes, are closely related to the child's experience of cooperation and mutual respect with others, especially his peers.

Further Stages of Moral Development

SIDELIGHT

Lawrence Kohlberg (1964), following procedures similar to those of Piaget but with older children, believes that mature moral judgment develops even further than Piaget's morality of reciprocal cooperation. He identifies three main levels of development as follows:

1. Premoral—with subtypes of *obedience orientation* and *naïve instrumental hedonism*
2. Morality of conventional role conformity—with subtypes of *good boy morality* and *authority maintaining morality*
3. Morality of self-accepted moral principles—with subtypes of *democratic contact* and *individual principles of conscience*

In his studies Kohlberg found evidence that the first of these three levels of morality was clearly dominant at age seven. By age ten, the second level (morality of conventional role conformity) was almost as strong, and by age thirteen this conventionality was clearly dominant. The third level of self-accepted moral principles was not a significant feature of responses till about age thirteen, when such conceptions as political rights and social obligations began to show this form. However, role conformity seems to remain the dominant theme for most persons into adulthood.

Kohlberg believes the validity of his stages or levels is enhanced by their close correlations with age levels. He also points to evidence of the wide application of such stages, that one may find "the same basic stages of moral judgment in middle- and working-class children, in Protestants and Catholics, in popular and socially isolated children, in boys and girls, and in Formosan, Chinese, and American children" (p. 406). His general conclusion is that such moral judgment is a normal development of growing up within the context of institutions of moral authority (family, government, work, etc.) that must somehow be assimilated into the individual's organization of behavior. As he grows up, this assimilation usually becomes increasingly self-conscious and sophisticated.

RECAPITULATION

Let us review what we have learned in this chapter.

Freud's theory of the origin and basis of morality has served as our point of departure. His theory of morality, especially as contained in *Totem and Taboo* (1938), had several main aspects. These may be identified as (1) Freud's totemic theory of religious origins, (2) his oedipal interpretation of primitive sexual taboos, and (3) his superego interpretation of the continuing basis of moral judgment in the individual. Let us summarize our conclusions on each of these topics.

First, Freud's anthropology of religion was not one of his areas of greatest expertise. His views of totemism as the original form of both religion and morality may now be considered as having very little foundation.

Second, Freud's oedipal interpretation of primitive (and modern) moral taboos seems to be a more fruitful hypothesis. It may be questioned whether the oedipal conflicts are as specifically sexual as Freud suggests—perhaps a general struggle for power is more significant than sexual rivalry—nevertheless, there is some evidence that prohibitions are strongly affected by the nature of this early parent-child conflict. Even so, the complete explanation of these prohibitions—incest taboos, for example—requires sociological and anthropological interpretations to supplement psychological interpretations.

Third, Freud's superego interpretation of the basis of moral judgment provides only part of the picture. Guilty consciences are certainly a factor in moral behavior; and the basic habits for moral judgment reflecting such superego formation appear to develop in early family relationships, as Freud suggested. But what Freud did not adequately account for were (1) the extent of situational variation in moral judgment, (2) the extent to which moral judgments become matters of self-conscious choice, and (3) the extent to which moral judgments change their basis with the maturation of the individual.

More than a simple notion of the superego is necessary to explain the gross variation in moral judgment of a person from situation to situation. What is needed if such variability of behavior is to be understood is an analysis of the various meanings carried by particular situations. In other words, an understanding of social roles is needed.

Freud's view of the superego as exerting moral influence in an automatic, even largely unconscious, manner is another limitation of a superego view of morality. Morality may be much more a matter of ego functioning, of realistic and self-conscious choices.

Finally, and closely related to the previous two points, the patterns of moral judgment tend to change as the personality develops. As one matures, the operation of the conscience typically becomes less arbitrary and absolute. In so doing it becomes less of the kind of superego that Freud described and more a center for the organization of social cooperation in the give and take of daily life. In Piaget's terms, an autonomous morality of cooperation comes to largely (but never completely) replace the earlier heteronomous morality of restraint.

As is so often the case with Freudian ideas, here we have found in those views the basis of rich insight for social psychology; but these views need also to be supplemented to provide a fully adequate picture.

24
Social Norms: Review and Discussion

NORMS AS INSTITUTIONS

Norms are patterns of expected behavior. Many of these patterns of expected behavior are passed on from generation to generation as a part of the culture. Examples might be seen in language forms, in social roles, and in moral standards.

Languages have norms about pronunciation, word meaning, and grammar. These are institutionalized in the sense that they are well established by social usage and change little from generation to generation. We learn most of these language forms without a great deal of reflection, and they become an integral part of our behavior. We as individuals may use language in many inventive ways, but the basic forms are not matters for much individuality. They are quite well standardized by the conventions of past generations.

Social situations, especially those involving established groups, also carry with them norms about behavior. Some of the more general situations indicate norms that are well established through precedents of past generations. This is true for such general roles as wife, mother, or woman. It is also true for more specific roles like congressman, bartender, plant superintendent, and Sunday-school teacher. As we act in a social role, we perform the patterns expected by others. We do this with individual variation, to be sure, but the main structure of behavior is given by the nature of the situation. And many social situations in turn are presented in a manner prescribed by past generations of social organization.

Moral standards too are normative. They are passed on from generation to generation as a fabric of *do*'s and *don't*s. Often these standards are more diffuse than those of language norms or social roles, but they still operate to guide behavior (and especially its justification). To be sure, individual variations of ethical values exist, but these tend to be ordered around moral principles and particular taboos that are the legacy of past generations.

NORMS AS INDIVIDUAL FRAMEWORKS

However, to point to the institutionalized nature of social norms is only to indicate part of the picture. They are also frameworks for individual

279

behavior. And in becoming individualized, social norms undergo changes to fit with the organization of behavior characteristics of the person as well as of the particular social situation in which he finds himself. There is, therefore, always a degree of readjustment and reorganization as norms become patterns of actual behavior. Individual behavior always involves some variation of the normative patterns of language, social roles, and moral standards. But even when the individual is being his most "individual self" he is probably organizing his thoughts in terms of social norms—the norms of language that have become the key tools for his conceptual thought.

PARALLELS

Language forms, social roles, and moral standards have all been lumped together under the category of social norms. In some ways, these three elements may seem quite different, but there are basic analogues among them. Roger Brown (1965) has pointed to some close parallels between language and social structure:

> Social roles, such as male and female, guest and host, doctor and patient, as well as morpheme classes, such as article, noun, and verb, are defined in terms of the privileges and obligations of interaction enjoyed by their members. There are parallels also between the higher levels of linguistic structure and higher levels of social structure. The immediate constituents of a well-formed social event are as psychologically real as the immediate constituents of a well-formed sentence. A marriage ceremony, for instance, has such first level constituents as the procession, the vows, the reception, and the departure of the honeymooners. On a lower level of analysis the ceremony involves such roles as bride, groom, minister, and father-of-the-bride. The ultimate constituents are, of course, persons occupying the roles on a given occasion. The parallels between linguistic structure and social structure are not superficial. It seems likely that the two sorts of structure will turn out to be learned in the same way (pp. 303–304).

To this we could also add the parallel of moral standards. These, too, reflect obligations of interaction in a manner similar to roles. The elements of morality may not be so firmly structured as linguistic or role systems, but there is also a sense in which a given culture may be suggested to have a "moral grammar" for which dominant cultural values represent the main forms of structure (analogous to parts of speech); and specific moral obligations and prohibitions are related to each other within the framework of cultural values in much the same way as words are put together into phrases and sentences.

Impressed by the close parallels between linguistic structure and social and cultural structures, we are tempted to see one as the cause of the others. Is language the basic prototype, the model we unconsciously use for assimilating social and cultural structures? Or are social structures, such as those embedded in the human family, the prototypes of organization that become generalized (over the course of many generations) to other structures, including language? Or, more likely, is the influence perhaps in both directions, with social structure and linguistic structure reinforcing each other?

At any rate, linguistic structure, social organization, and a structure of cultural values have been developed side by side in the history of the species. And in each new generation, persons must accommodate themselves at the same time to already determined structures of words, structures of roles, and structures of moral obligations. The process of this accommodation has, in all cases, some general characteristics that can be considered as properties of the process of learning social norms.

THE LEARNING OF NORMS

The learning of norms may be summarized as a process that tends to take place in four phases. These should not be considered as distinct stages in a process of socialization, for there are no distinct age levels associated with them. They tend to proceed at the same time rather than in distinct periods. Still, there is a temporal order involved, in that later phases require the prior existence of earlier phases.

We may identify these phases of norm learning as (1) preliminary conditioning, (2) identification and imitation, (3) deliberate assumption of another's perspective, and (4) assimilation of a combined structure of the expectations of others.

Behind all learning of social norms is a background of experience in which the child has been dependent on other human beings. Through a process of basic conditioning, he directs his attention to those around him and finds his rewards primarily through an adjustment to their behavior.

Much of the early behavior of the child has a marked exploratory character. Within this exploration are the attempts to re-create patterns of response observed in persons of special importance. In this process of imitation, the child can feel a special sense of participation with the activities of these persons and thus can share in their importance. With this imitation, then, comes a sense of identification with those persons of greatest significance.

As the child imitates and identifies with significant others, he comes also to develop an imagination of how these specific persons view their actions. And as he does this, he begins also to see his own behavior as he thinks others see him. This provides a reflective quality to his behavior, a tendency to use the particular reactions of others as a guide for his own behavior. Through such an assumption of another's perspective a child learns basic roles, concepts, and habits of reciprocal cooperation. He thus enters more fully into social interaction than was possible earlier.

Finally, the child is able to organize a composite of these reactions of others. He develops a sense of a *generalized other,* to use a term suggested by George H. Mead. He views his own behavior in terms of what he has put together in his imagination from the reactions of persons in general. Thus, he forms an idea of what is generally expected and appropriate to guide his own behavior.

These four phases in the learning of norms can be seen in language learning as (1) a phase of early vocalization, (2) a phase of imitative babbling, (3) a phase of concept formation, and (4) a phase of the development of grammar. In learning of social roles, we can point to parallel developments with (1) a phase of primary dependency, (2) a phase of imitative behavior, (3) a phase of role taking in relationships with others of primary significance, and (4) a phase of developing a sense of generalized patterns of expectations. Somewhat similar is the development of morality. Although the development of moral standards is more complex, we can see here too the development in terms of (1) a phase of primary hedonism, (2) a phase dominated by standards of obedience, (3) a phase of reciprocal cooperation, and (4) a phase in which either distinctive cultural values or more universal ethical principles become predominant.

LEGITIMACY

Norms represent standards of what is expected. At the same time they represent standards of what is approved. Approval is always, at least to some degree, a necessary part of normative behavior.

How do patterns of expected behavior receive their stamp of approval, their legitimacy? We may here suggest that there are three fundamental ways that a norm obtains legitimacy: (1) usage, (2) utility, and (3) association with other forms of legitimacy.

Usage is the most obvious basis of legitimacy for most norms in most societies. In traditional societies time or age provided a special key to legitimacy. The longer a custom had been practiced, the more sure could people be of its propriety.

In the modern world, time-honored usages have probably become less important (though still significant—after all, not even the most modern American set *completely* dispenses with the English language), but crowd-honored usages provide another, and increasingly applied, form of legitimacy. What is popular at the moment suggests a standard for behavior just as surely as do the practices of past generations. Democracy as a form of government (compared, for example, to monarchy) is based very largely on this form of legitimacy.

Still another form of legitimacy-through-usage (in addition to the legitimacies of endurance and popularity) is that of generality of usage. The more universal a practice, the more it invites the stamp of legitimacy. For example, we tend to feel that certain sexual practices, such as incest avoidance, are made more proper by the finding that nearly all cultures share them; and, on the other hand, the norm of premarital chastity may be considered by some to be less binding as more evidence appears demonstrating its relaxation.

Utility typically supports usage as a basis for legitimatizing norms. That is, there are distinct gains to be realized through the following of particular norms. For example, the norms of language make possible the communication of ideas, which is presumably useful for everyone concerned. Correct role behavior ordinarily makes for more effective group action; and a general observance of the more prominent moral standards may also, in a general sense at least, make for a more effective society.

Sometimes it may be anticipated utility, more than proven value, that primarily supports a norm. One may learn and practice a foreign language in the anticipation of making use of it later, or one may prepare through rigorous training for an occupation, the rewards of which may be long delayed. Or a properly moral life on earth may be sought by some for the hopes of rewards that it may ultimately yield in heaven.

In some cases the utility of a norm may be concentrated in a limited group of persons. For example, some notion of property rights is presumably of general usefulness to a society; but the particular norms about property have, in most societies, been of primary interest to those few with major property rights to defend. And, on the other hand, moral obligations to give to the poor have usually been most supported, with whatever small power they could muster, by the poor or, more forcefully, by those who have collected, nominally or truly, on behalf of the poor.

Association with other forms of legitimacy forms a third main basis for a norm's legitimacy. This, in turn, may take several forms. We may mention in particular (1) group authority, (2) symbolic association, and (3) personal charisma.

Any norm is strengthened when stated by someone in authority. The legitimacy of the norm is thus supported by the legitimacy of group authority. A priest, therefore, can give greater legitimacy to a religious rule than can a layman; a president of a corporation can give greater legitimacy to a company policy than can an office worker; and a general can give greater legitimacy to a military order than can a lowly corporal. Group authority is almost always a major source of support for social norms.

Verbal and physical symbols also may provide important supports for social norms. Flowery rhetoric has often been used to support traditional norms, especially when doubt has been expressed about their validity. Liberals as well as conservatives use rhetoric to give symbolic sanction to norms; the main difference here is that the norms liberals seek are often those still to be established rather than those sanctioned by tradition. A particular form of such rhetoric can be seen in myths. Myths of particular appeal to traditionalists are those about early forms of accepted practices (for example, the democratic vision of the framers of the Constitution). In contrast, liberals and radicals tend to foster myths about the future to justify the forms they seek to promote (for example, the French revolutionists' image of liberty, equality, and fraternity; or the Marxian vision of the classless society).

Physical as well as verbal symbols often are used for their power to legitimatize. The colors of the flag are a must for the campaign materials of every candidate at election time. A person's dress may be another means of promoting a proper legitimacy for his actions (as the uniforms of many occupations from physician and nurse to priest and nun well illustrate). Other physical objects may provide additional support (such as the numerous artifacts of a doctor's office or the rich imagery of a sanctuary, which add legitimacy to the role performances of physician and minister, respectively).

A third category of legitimacy-through-association is that of personal charisma. Some individuals have a more distinctive personal appeal than do others, and persons with outstanding appeal may be said to have charisma. Just as the propriety of using certain products for grooming may be enhanced by TV associations with a beautiful woman (for either women or men), so association of norms with an especially appealing leader (for example, Abraham Lincoln or John F. Kennedy) may greatly enhance their value. And also in the cases of persons with less renown, personal appeal may provide considerable justification for actions. All is fair in love, it is said; and, while not exactly true, this piece of folk wisdom illustrates the power that even fairly ordinary individuals may have for justifying actions of others who are temporarily in awe. Charisma, especially in this democratic age, is not the exclusive property of gods and kings, but may be found in people in quite ordinary settings.

One final basis for legitimacy may also be mentioned. This is the legitimacy that comes through ego involvement. One's own language seems more naturally appropriate than others, which always seem so "foreign." One's own occupational role, if one is truly committed to a job, seems somehow more compelling than others. And moral standards whose demands have been met only with difficulty and strong resolve frequently have a special mark of rightness.

In one sense this legitimacy-through-ego-involvement may be considered as a fourth category of legitimacy-through-association. If one considers his own self as of very special legitimacy, then whatever has come to be most closely associated with the self will share in this generous self-approval. At any rate, ego involvement does seem to provide fertile ground for legitimization.

NORMS, AFFILIATION, AND GROUPS

Norms grow out of our dependence on other people. Thus, they naturally reflect our past associations with others, including the groups and organizations in which we have become members.

Norms are organized by groups. The division of labor in group activity takes place through norms organized as social roles. The goals and purposes of group activity are given by other norms. And the ultimate constituents of the content of the communication of groups are represented by other norms, those of the language system.

This is not to suggest that these norms always provide for smooth working relationships in groups. Norms may engender conflict as well as harmony. In most groups most of the time there is conflict, open or subdued, between norms. This is most painfully seen in cases of role conflict, when contradictory expectations are brought to bear upon the same behavior. Some positions (for example, factory foreman or city school superintendent) typically have normative conflict built into the heart of the role, as the man in the middle must constantly work among cross-pressures. But effective groups also provide means of dealing with normative conflict—even if it may require creation of a position (like superintendent or general manager) to operate at the very center of the storm.

NORMS AND INDIVIDUALITY

Norms are often seen as constraints, as limitations on our freedom and individuality. This is indeed the way they are often experienced. In fact, we are most personally aware of the existence of norms on those very occasions when the constraint is most clearly evident. This is, however, only one side of the picture. Norms provide opportunities as well as constraints.

Take, for example, language. The norms of language do constrain us, affecting the very innermost processes of thought. But at the same time they make possible new forms of individuality by providing the conceptual tools out of which new ideas and fresh insights may be developed.

This brings us to comment briefly on the popular but ambiguous concept of *freedom*. If by freedom we mean the complete absence of social influence, freedom can be only a myth. This should be apparent from all that has been said in preceding chapters. On the other hand, freedom may be conceived (among other meanings) as the individual's creative use of his own powers under whatever conditions he may find himself. Here the forms of social influence are to be reckoned with, but with a response selectivity that leaves the individual the center of his own action. Furthermore, certain social settings or patterns of social relationships should be expected to foster this kind of freedom, and others to inhibit it. For example, in Chapter 20 we indicated some conditions that may affect the degree of structuring of group behavior (how detailed prescribed behavior may be, the extent of consensus concerning appropriate behavior, the effectiveness of group surveillance and sanctions). These also are conditions that determine the range of individuality. Also, the presence of diverse groups, especially groups with competing claims, does much to enhance the opportunities for individual freedom. Such freedom grows in the context of relationships to other people, not in a general antagonism toward society.

This should leave us with an image that is somewhat different from the popular one of individual vs. society. It is true that sometimes there is a real tension between individual needs and social goals. But much more fundamental is the complementarity that exists between individual and society. We realize our individuality, the distinctiveness of our self-development, only in the context of society. Within this context are language norms that help us to think and social roles that help us achieve a sense of identity. It is the individual product we make out of such social norms that establishes our selfhood. More realistic, therefore, than the image of individual vs. society is that of individual-in-society. This, at any rate, is the central image of much of social psychology, and the image with which we may best approach the final chapters of this book.

part seven: PERSONALITY IN SOCIETY

Men make their own history, but they do not make it just as they please; they do not make it under circumstances chosen by themselves, but under circumstances directly found, given and transmitted from the past.

Karl Marx

The way we perceive persons is the subject of Chapter 25 ("Perceiving Persons"). In this chapter we examine the way an image of personality is constructed from the raw materials of sensation.

Chapter 26 ("Culture and Personality") deals with the cultural context of personality. In this chapter we give special attention to the variability of personality from culture to culture.

One particular theme of the relationship of personality to society, that of the spirit and scope of individuality, is the focus for Chapter 27 ("Individuality in Contemporary Society"). The question of the possible decline of individuality opens the exploration of this chapter, and leads to an examination of related matters, such as conditions and consequences of alienation and changing patterns of child rearing.

Chapter 28 ("Personality in Society: Review and Discussion") brings together the threads of the previous three chapters.

25
Perceiving Persons

VERBAL CUES

Imagine yourself hearing just seven words describing another person:

> intelligent
> skillful
> industrious
> warm
> determined
> practical
> cautious

What kind of person would you imagine this to be?

If you are like most experimental subjects who were actually given this problem by Solomon Asch (1946), you would soon develop a mental picture of such a person. Furthermore, certain other characteristics would be a part of such a picture. For example, if asked to check other adjectives to indicate whether or not you saw them as being descriptive of the same person, you would be likely to check all of the following: generous, wise, happy, humane, popular, and sociable.

Now imagine yourself hearing another seven adjectives describing a person:

> intelligent
> skillful
> industrious
> cold
> determined
> practical
> cautious

You will notice that this list is, with a single exception, the same as the first list. But could it describe a similar person? Not likely, according to the results obtained by Asch. Persons given this second set of adjectives instead of the first list, generally agreed that such a person could *not* be described by such further adjectives as generous, wise, happy, humane, popular, and sociable.

The difference is of course the difference between a person who is *warm* and one who is *cold*. Asch's work indicates that the dimension of warmth frequently takes a position of central importance in the formation of impressions of other persons. Other pairs of words (for example, *polite* and *blunt)* substituted for *warm* and *cold* in the above lists failed to give results that were nearly so differentiated.

There appear to be no simple physical cues that indicate the warmth of a person. Certainly body temperature is not at issue. Facial expressions may be more to the point, but why should we be so eager to perceive warmth in an expression? Apparently this has something to do with the way we might approach such a person, or if he is approachable at all—a matter of considerable importance as one anticipates possible interaction with another person.

Asch made several investigations with variations of the same basic technique. In each case a few adjectives were presented, then subjects indicated in other words what kind of person such verbal cues suggested to them. For example, another investigation involved the following set of words:

> intelligent
> industrious
> impulsive
> critical
> stubborn
> envious

Impressions this list created were compared to those created by the same words presented in reverse order. The differences were considerable, as Asch (1952) reports:[1]

> The accounts of the subjects indicate that the first terms set up a *direction* that exerts a continuous effect on the later terms. When one hears the first term, a broad, uncrystallized, but directed impression is born. The next characteristic is related to the established direction. The view formed quickly acquires a certain stability; later characteristics are fitted to the prevailing direction when conditions permit (pp. 212–213).

Does this suggest anything about how we form impressions about real people? Admittedly, Asch presents only a few verbal cues, not a real person. Still, experimental subjects do develop impressions of personality from just a few verbal cues. Asch believes that such a simplified procedure captures some of the main features of the formation of personal impressions. Among these, he indicates, belong the following generalizations.

1. One strives to form an impression of the entire person. The impression tends to become complete even when the evidence is meager. It is hard not to see the person as a unit.
2. The moment we see that two or more characteristics belong to the same person they enter into dynamic interaction. We cannot

[1] Solomon E. Asch, *Social Psychology*. Englewood Cliffs, N.J.: Prentice-Hall, 1952. Quotations from this source are reprinted with permission of the publisher.

see one quality and another in the same person without their affecting each other. If one person is intelligent and cheerful, and another intelligent and morose, the quality of intelligence ceases to be the same in the two. Interaction may produce a new quality, to which initial observations are subordinated. If, for example, we see one person as both warm and cold, we may conclude that he is moody.

3. From its inception the impression has a structure, even if rudimentary. The various characteristics do not possess the same weight. Some become central, providing the main direction; others become peripheral and dependent. Until we have found the center—that part of the person which wants to live and act in a certain way, which wants not to break up or disappear— we feel we have not succeeded in reaching an understanding (p. 216).

Other investigators have questioned whether the few words presented in Asch's technique are really enough to fairly represent the data we ordinarily use in forming impressions of other persons. This has led to variations in experimental design and other findings in subsequent research. But such later research has not decisively contradicted any of Asch's main findings or interpretations.

Luchins (1957), for example, used presentations in paragraph form and found strong evidence of a *primacy effect*—that is, that information presented first did in fact have an unusually strong impact upon the total impression. Kelley (1950), using the warm-cold variable, presented a live stranger with different introductions and produced in subjects both significantly different ratings of this person and different behaviors toward him. And Veness and Brierley (1963) presented tape recordings and asked subjects to indicate their impressions of the speaker; their results produced further confirmation of the importance of the warm-cold variable.

Implicit Personality Theory

THEORETICAL
POINTER

We are all theorists of a sort, in that we must act upon theoretical assumptions. Sometimes these assumptions are explicitly stated, but more often they guide our behavior without being specifically recognized.

Nowhere is this more true than in our perception and judgment of people. Each of us has acquired a set of habits of perception that we apply to our impressions of others. These habits of social perception are somewhat different from perceiver to perceiver, but they have some broad outlines in common. They include predictions of what features of behavior go with observed characteristics of personal appearance, assumptions of what traits are positively or negatively associated with each other, mental sets toward particular dimensions for interpreting other persons, and biases in value judgments used in such interpretations.

The concept of *everyday personality theory* has been suggested by Bruner and Tagiuri (1954) to describe these tendencies of person perception. "What kinds of naïve, implicit 'theories' of personality do people work with when they form an impression of others?" they ask

(p. 649); and their suggestion is that there is a lack of systematic knowledge on this subject. Heider (1958) has since added to our understanding of such naïve and implicit theories commonly used to understand human behavior. But our scientific knowledge in this relatively subjective area remains quite sketchy.

So long as the behavior of other persons does not contradict the assumptions of an implicit personality theory, it will tend to be maintained; for such theories are supported by their usefulness for interaction, not by their scientific evidence. In fact, it sometimes seems that a successful implicit personality theory is one that is relatively immune to direct scientific test (for example, the warm-cold variable). Nevertheless, social interaction sometimes contradicts our predictions about persons. Then it is that the theory by which we judge them may change—if we are unable to avoid further interaction with them.

PROJECTIVE PERCEPTION

The studies mentioned so far in this chapter focus upon the perception of persons in terms of the organization of impressions. A person receives cues about other persons and organizes these impressions in characteristic ways. It has been assumed that the basic data for these impressions come from cues given by other persons.

But is the person perceived the source of all cues built into personal impressions? May not some of the cues come from the perceiver himself?

Take, for example, a person who is prone to hold prejudice. His view of other persons will be colored by his own needs. Allport (1958) describes prejudiced persons as having cognitive processes generally different from those of more tolerant persons. For example, the prejudiced person is more likely to dichotomize his value judgments in either-or terms. And "his habits of thought are rigid. He does not change his mental set easily, but persists in old ways of reasoning—whether or not this reasoning has anything to do with human groups. He has a marked need for definiteness; he cannot tolerate ambiguity in his plans" (p. 171).

Probably the best-known study of how one's own personality may bias the judgment of other persons may be found in *The Authoritarian Personality* by Adorno and associates (1950). While this book deals more with the general development of attitudes than with the specific subject of person perception, it is clear from this work that more authoritarian persons have a tendency to make up for some of their own insecurities by rigid patterns of perceiving and judging other people. Part of the pattern is also a pronounced tendency among authoritarian persons to project upon others—especially upon rejected persons and groups—their own undesirable impulses.

SIDELIGHT

The Authoritarian Personality

In their studies of the authoritarian personality Adorno and his co-workers (Adorno, Frenkel-Brunswik, Levinson, and Sanford, 1950) have attempted to show the relationship between social attitudes and basic character traits. They began with a study of prejudice, conceiving of prejudice as but part of a larger personality pattern, and went on to develop scales to measure such authoritarian or antidemocratic trends in the individual.

A total of 2,099 subjects was used, mostly of middle-class origins and between twenty and thirty-five years of age. The persons studied included college students, prison inmates, psychiatric patients, and members of P.T.A. groups. Questionnaires included background questions, opinion-attitude scales, and projective questions. Opinion-attitude scales included (1) an anti-Semitism (A-S) scale indicating attitudes toward Jews, (2) an ethnocentrism (E) scale revealing attitudes toward minority groups generally, (3) a political-economic conservatism (PEC) scale measuring support for conservative ideas, and (4) a fascist tendency (F) scale suggesting the degree of susceptibility of an individual to antidemocratic propaganda. Individuals ranking in the highest and lowest 25 percent on these scales were further studied in clinical interviews. Interview data included discussion of a wide range of topics (for example, vocational ambitions, early family life, attitudes toward minority groups, etc.) and results of a projective test, the Thematic Apperception Test.

The results indicated a close relationship between the four opinion-attitude scales. There was not a very close correlation between prejudice and either intelligence or education; however, the unprejudiced subjects tended to be slightly more

intelligent and better educated. Among specified groups, prison inmates had the highest average on ethnocentrism; while studies of the sample of psychiatric patients indicated that disturbed people probably have prejudice scores about the same as similar groups of normal people.

The combined results of the opinion-attitude scales and interview data yielded a profile of a type of person especially prone toward prejudice. A rigid conventionalism, a tendency to stereotype, and the inability to form close personal relationships with other individuals all characterized the prejudiced person. In his early home life there was apt to be more harsh discipline and a high degree of dependence upon parents rather than free-flowing affection between parents and children. As the authors conclude:

The most crucial result of the present study . . . is the demonstration of close correspondence in the type of approach and outlook a subject is likely to have in a great variety of areas, ranging from most intimate features of family and sex adjustment through relationships to other people in general, to religion and to social and political philosophy. Thus a basically hierarchical, authoritarian, exploitive parent-child relationship is apt to carry over into a power-oriented exploitively dependent attitude toward one's sex partner and one's God and may well culminate in a political philosophy and social outlook which has no room for anything but a desperate clinging to what appears to be strong and a disdainful rejection of whatever is relegated to the bottom (p. 971).

But does it require an unusually prejudiced or authoritarian personality to find evidence of such bias in the perception of other people? And is a distortion in the perception of others necessarily in the direction of projecting unfavorable features of oneself upon undesirable groups? Analysis of research by Dana Bramel may help us answer such questions.

Bramel (1962; 1963)[2] has conducted a pair of interesting experiments dealing with what he calls defensive projection. The basic design of these experiments involves, first, a manipulation of self-concept, then the presentation of negative evidence about the subject, and, finally, the opportunity to make a judgment of a peer. The purpose of these procedures was to discover the conditions under which a person will tend to transfer undesirable perceptions he has of himself to other persons.

Let us note in some detail what occurred in one of these experiments (Bramel, 1962). Each subject (all were males) appeared for a preliminary session in which he took a variety of personality tests. He was told that these would be carefully analyzed by clinical psychologists, and that he would be informed of the results. His self-insight would be measured at the same session that he was informed about the results of the personality testing.

Appointments for the second session were arranged for two subjects at a time. Each pair of subjects was matched to make sure that they had similar scores on measures of self-esteem and self-conception of masculinity. The experimenter also made sure that the two subjects of each pair were not previously acquainted. Subjects were introduced to each other in a standardized manner.

The subjects were next interviewed individually (each by a separate interviewer) to go over the results of the previous personality testing. Actually, however, the interpretations were not based on their test performances at all. Rather, there were just two standard test reports: one generally favorable and one quite consistently unfavorable. The interviewer went over the report, whichever of the two forms it happened to be, spending about twenty minutes in discussing its implications. Explicit attention was given to the way in which the subject's self-concept was at variance with the fundamental "facts" uncovered by the testing. For each pair of subjects, one was given the favorable treatment in reporting on personality test results and the other was given the unfavorable report.

After the interviews concerning personality test results, the two subjects were brought together again. They then filled out questionnaires in which they made personality judgments of each other.

There seems to be nothing particularly surprising about these procedures as a means of studying what may influence judgments of another person. Apparently, Bramel was interested in seeing what effect raising or lowering self-conceptions might have upon judgments of another person. But what has been described so far is only preliminary to the crucial part of the experiment that was to follow.

The two subjects were then seated at a table facing a projection screen. On the table were two boxes with galvanometer dials, one facing each subject. Each dial was placed in such a way that it could be seen

---

[2] Dana Bramel, "A Dissonance Theory Approach to Defensive Projection," *Journal of Abnormal and Social Psychology*, 64 (1962), 121–129. Copyright 1962 by the American Psychological Association. Quotations from this source are reprinted with permission of the publisher.

by no one in the room except the subject. As Bramel further describes his procedures:

> It was explained that this part of the experiment would be con-
> cerned with the perception of sexual arousal. An elaborate ex-
> planation of the physiology of sexual arousal and the sensitive
> techniques for its measurement followed. . . . Considerable em-
> phasis was placed on the unconscious nature of sexual arousal
> and the impossibility of exerting conscious control over its ex-
> pression in the "psychogalvanic skin response." It was further
> explained that the experimenter was investigating the perception
> of homosexual rather than heterosexual arousal (p. 123).

Each subject was thus set to observe a measure of his own homosexual arousal as he looked at a series of photographs projected on the screen in front of him. After noting his own measure of sexual arousal, he was also to make an estimate of that of the other subject. Furthermore:

> All subjects were explicitly told that movements of the dial
> would indicate homosexual arousal to the photographs. As a
> precaution against excessive threat, they were told that persons
> with very strong homosexual tendencies would consistently "go
> off the scale." Further, the anonymity and privacy of the situa-
> tion were carefully spelled out, with the intention of convincing
> the subject that no one but he would know what his own re-
> sponses had been.
>   Unknown to the subject, the supposed "psychogalvanic skin
> response apparatus" was not actually responding to changes in
> his own level of sexual arousal to the pictures. Rather, the
> galvanometers in each of the two boxes were controlled re-
> motely by the experimenter. . . . Thus, the experimenter exerted
> complete control over the movements of the needles, which were
> identical for the two subjects. Each photograph had been as-
> signed an "appropriate" needle reading in advance, so that those
> depicting handsome men in states of undress received more cur-
> rent than did those depicting unattractive and fully clothed men.
> Both subjects were, thus, led to believe that they were sexually
> aroused by certain pictures and not by others, according to a
> consistent pattern. Both subjects were confronted with exactly
> the same stimulus input at this point of the experiment (p. 123).

Why would such procedures be introduced? Apparently, to give the subjects evidence that they had homosexual tendencies, then to see whether or not they considered other subjects to have similar ten-dencies. But why?

Before going on, we need to understand the theoretical context for this experiment. Bramel was attempting to study ego defensive proc-esses and the conditions under which such processes take the shape of *defensive projection*—that is, a tendency to protect oneself from con-cern about an undesirable characteristic by perceiving the trait as characteristic of other persons.

Psychoanalytic theory suggests that such projection is rather com-mon. An individual's anxiety and guilt can be reduced, psychoanalytic theory suggests, if the source of the disturbing impressions can be unconsciously transferred to other people, especially people who are disliked anyway.

Bramel prefers a dissonance theory interpretation, which makes predictions that are a bit more specific than psychoanalytic theory. Whereas psychoanalytic theory points to the general tendency of an undesirable characteristic to be projected onto other persons, dissonance theory suggests that this would be true mainly under certain conditions. When, for example, would evidence that he had unconscious homosexual tendencies create dissonance for a person? According to Bramel's interpretation of dissonance theory, this would occur primarily when a person has (1) a very high opinion of himself, (2) a very low opinion of homosexuality, and (3) little opportunity to deny the evidence of his homosexual tendencies. These, then, are the conditions under which we should expect to find a defensive projection of homosexuality.

The purpose of Bramel's most careful experimental procedures was to negate the opportunity to deny evidence of homosexual tendencies. Could a person reasonably doubt the evidence of the recordings of the so-called psychogalvanic skin response made before his very eyes? Apparently most subjects did not.

The selection of homosexuality as a characteristic to introduce experimentally was suggested both by its generally negative evaluation and by the fact that homosexuality is an emotionally charged subject. This would tend to be a characteristic that persons would very much want to reject, which might increase its potential as a candidate for projection.

But there is still a third requirement for dissonance. Not only should the evidence of the characteristic be undeniable and the characteristic be generally considered negative, but the individual must also have a generally positive image of himself. In this case (when a person has a very favorable image of himself but also sees himself possessing a negative trait), the dissonance should be especially marked. Less dissonance, and therefore less need for defensive projection, would be created if the person had a less favorable self-image to begin with.

It may be recalled that all experimental subjects were given bogus results of personality tests—half were presented with favorable results and half with unfavorable results. Questionnaire evidence indicates that this did indeed affect the subjects' self-esteem. What then is to be predicted? That subjects with higher self-esteem will be more likely to show defensive projection, which in this situation consists of rating their fellow subjects as possessing homosexual tendencies. That is, persons should be more likely to project such homosexual tendencies onto others when dissonance (in turn caused by the combination of a highly favorable self-image along with evidence of undesirable homosexuality) is higher than when there is less dissonance. Or at least so Bramel reasoned.

Did the results support this reasoning? As Bramel summarizes his findings:

> On the average, subjects in the high dissonance condition attributed to their partner about the same degree of arousal as they themselves appeared to be having. Those in the low dissonance condition in general attributed to their partner a level of arousal less than their own (p. 129).

Basically, these results support the predictions. But something new is also suggested. According to Bramel's results, high dissonance subjects projected only when they were with a partner they had previously rated favorably. Apparently, projection was more readily directed toward some people than toward others. And toward which other people? Those most *favorably* rated. This would seem to be the reverse of the commonly conceived pattern of projecting unfavorable characteristics upon unfavorable others.

In a second experiment Bramel (1963)[3] tested specifically the hypothesis that such defensive projection was more likely to be expressed toward someone in the same social category as the perceiver than toward someone quite different. And again the results were in this direction. Homosexuality (after evidence of its presence in the subject) was projected more upon speakers who were labeled as students than those labeled as criminals. How might this be explained? Suggests Bramel:

> There are several conceivable ways in which projection might produce a reduction in dissonance. For example, attributing an undesirable trait to favorably evaluated people might result in a change in the meaning of the dimension itself. Becoming less undesirable, it would then less strongly negate the person's favorable attitudes toward himself.
>
> Consider another way in which dissonance reduction might result from the kind of projection which occurred in the experimental situation There are many occasions in a person's life when he receives information about himself, but where an adequate context for comparison is not readily available. In the experiment described here, for example, the subject could clearly see that, in absolute terms, he was homosexually aroused by the photographs. The needle on the calibrated dial of his galvanometer indicated this unmistakably. But, lacking information concerning averages and ranges, the subject still had the problem of deciding "how homosexual is 23 milliamperes?" In order to apply necessary adjectives such as *very* or *slightly* to the label *homosexual*, the subject must have some further information about how he compares with other people (Festinger, 1954). Thus his subjective evaluation of his own position on the homosexuality scale is dependent upon where he perceives certain relevant other persons to be located on that scale. It is plausible to assume that a person's comparison group consists of people with backgrounds similar to his own and with whom he generally associates. It follows that if the subject can believe that other students like himself have about the same amount of homosexual motivation as he has, then his position on his subjective scale is not extreme. The cognition that one is average in homosexuality probably does not strongly negate a moderately favorable level of self-esteem and is certainly less dissonant than the cognition that one is more homosexual than others in the comparison group (p. 324).

[3] Dana Bramel, "Selection of a Target for Defensive Projection," *Journal of Abnormal and Social Psychology*, 66 (1963), 318–324. Copyright 1963 by the American Psychological Association. Quotations from this source are reprinted with permission of the publisher.

This strongly suggests that we see other people not just as objects in their own right, but rather also in relationship to (1) their social categories or group memberships and (2) our own characteristics and conditions. Under certain conditions (for example, when there is clear negative evidence about ourselves), this may lead us to project upon others what we perceive in ourselves, especially upon others we see as being like ourselves. (After all, what good are friends if they cannot share our faults?) Under conditions when the evidence is less clear, when a person may avoid seeing the evidence as applying specifically to himself, he would be more likely to project negative characteristics further away from the self—and more upon rejected groups of people.

METHODOLOGICAL POINTER

Experimental Ethics

After coming this far in this book, the reader will recognize that those who conduct social psychology experiments do not always tell their subjects "the truth, the whole truth, and nothing but the truth." Very commonly some feature of the experiment is misrepresented, or at least there is a lack of information as to the investigator's full interest in the study. The investigator does not usually inform subjects of his hypotheses; to do so would ordinarily prevent a fair test of them. Furthermore, misinformation is often given to subjects to create desired treatment groups.

To what extent is an experimenter justified in deceiving his subjects at particular points in an experiment or about what the experiment as a whole is designed to study? Are there no limits to such deception? The answer is that there are of course limits, but there is no simple way of deciding exactly where they are. In general the experimenter is limited by the ethical requirements that (1) any important deceptions that are a part of the experimental design must be explained and adequately justified to subjects after the experiment, and (2) no actual physical or psychological damage may be done to subjects in such experimentation.

An example of the first point is given by Bramel (1962), who reports:

A considerable amount of time at the end of the experiment was allocated to explaining the true nature of the study and demonstrating in detail that the personality reports and the apparatus were incapable of giving a correct evaluation of a person. The expression of relief which often followed the unveiling of the deceptions indicated that the manipulations had been effective. The necessity for the deceptions used in the experimental analysis of such delicate processes was carefully explained, and all questions were answered. Not until the subjects seemed quite restored and satisfied was the session ended. All available evidence indicates that the subjects considered the experiment interesting and worthy of their participation (p. 124).

Presumably such a final explanation or debriefing also answers the second requirement, that no actual damage may be done to subjects. Certainly without such debriefing there would be reason to consider psychological damage present—inducing subjects to believe they were homosexuals! Even with the debriefing afterwards, there still may remain some questions about this procedure.

But certainly Bramel's experiments are not alone in raising ethical questions. Milgram's studies of obedience, discussed in Chapter 7, have especially been singled out for debate (for example, by Baumrind, 1964). And, more generally,

Ring (1967) has questioned whether the whole climate in social psychology might not be too receptive to experimentation on "exotic topics with a zany manipulation." He complains that:

One sometimes gets the impression that an ever-growing coterie of social psychologists is playing (largely for one another's benefit) a game of "can you top this?" Whoever can conduct the most contrived, flamboyant, and mirth-producing experiments receives the highest score on the kudometer. There is, in short, a distinctly exhibitionistic flavor to much current experimentation, while the experimenters themselves often seem to equate notoriety with achievement (p. 117).

Such criticism may be overly harsh. Nevertheless, social psychologists cannot afford to be insensitive to such criticism, nor to ignore the provisions of their stated ethical codes. In this regard the following passages from the recently revised statement of ethics of the American Psychological Association (1973) may be noted:

Ethical practice requires the investigator to inform the participant of all features of the research that reasonably might be expected to influence willingness to participate, and to explain all other aspects of the research about which the participant inquires. . . . When the methodological requirements of a study necessitate concealment or deception, the investigator is required to ensure the participant's understanding of the reasons for this action and to restore the quality of the relationship with the investigator. . . .
The ethical investigator protects participants from physical and mental discomfort, harm and danger. If the risk of such consequences exists, the investigator is required to inform the participant of the fact, secure consent before proceeding, and take all possible measures to minimize distress. A research procedure may not be used if it is likely to cause serious and lasting harm to participants (pp. 1–2).

Questions of the ethics of experimental techniques may lead to even broader ethical questions concerning the consequences of experimentation. As a scientific strategy, there can be little doubt about the value of trying to control variables through experimental techniques. This facilitates more precise knowledge of principles of social behavior. But laymen, including the laymen who provide support for experimental research, usually have a more practical cast of mind. They want to *use* the findings of experimental research. And here is a real danger: that in the desire to make use of experimental work there will be inadequate recognition of its theoretical nature, that the laboratory approach to prediction and control of variables will be applied rather indiscriminately and generally to the prediction and control of persons.

We may be moving into a society in which there is ever more self-conscious and systematic manipulation of human behavior. If so, social psychology is bound to be a more and more popular discipline. Will the social psychologist use this opportunity to work harder to produce the bag of tricks—waving the scientific banner of prediction and control —most in demand for the manipulation of behavior? Or will he keep to the more fundamental scientific tasks of exploring the problematic and relating theoretical propositions to the full range of data available?

The answer to these questions may depend not just on the social psychologist himself but also on the kind of incentives he is given for his work. And these incentives come from a broader public than the limited fraternity of social psychologists. It therefore is important that such people as students taking an introductory course in social psychology see this subject as one that seeks a fundamental understanding of social behavior, and not as a collection of techniques for winning friends and influencing people. If this understanding can be more general, there will be less temptation for experimentation that appears to promote manipulation for its own sake.

IMPRESSION FORMATION: RECAPITULATION

Let us pause now to reconsider the main points of this chapter. The central topic has been that of impression formation. Key ideas developed so far have included the following:

1. We form impressions of other persons on the basis of limited information. As the work of Asch suggests, even very sketchy cues may yield a rather clear general impression.

2. We organize information about another person in terms of implicit theories about personality. These operate as intuitions about what different characteristics mean.

3. Our own inner personality patterns constitute one basis of the implicit personality theory we use for forming impressions about others. Thus, as Adorno's work suggests, we may sometimes project upon others those features we wish to avoid seeing in ourselves.

4. Our own level of self-esteem may be another key feature coloring the way we see others. Bramel's work suggests that the higher one's self-esteem, the more must the perception of another be consistent with a positive self-image.

5. Our tendency to compare ourselves with others is a key factor influencing what characteristics are most prominently featured in impressions formed. The more another person is seen as similar to us, the easier it is to transfer impressions about our own behavior to the way we see him.

Forming impressions of another is, however, only one aspect of the perception of persons. Perceiving the causes of behavior in ongoing interaction is another aspect, to which we now turn.

EXTERNAL AND INTERNAL

When we perceive the behavior of another, our perceptions go beyond describing the person. They also seek to explain his behavior. We look for the reasons why a particular act occurs, and we intuitively grasp for cues that might supply the answer.

This is, of course, a highly subjective process, and as such it may appear to be an area that would stubbornly resist scientific analysis. But there is at least a beginning of scientific analysis of the way we impute causes for the actions of other people, and a key distinction made in this work has been between external and internal causes of behavior.

We see behavior as externally caused when we identify something or someone else in the situation that makes the person do what he does. In contrast, behavior considered to be internally caused is seen as coming from the person himself. Internally caused behavior occurs because the individual wants or decides to do what he does.

A key question explored by Harold Kelley (1967) is the basis upon which we seek external or internal explanations for a person's behavior. The theory formulated by Kelley may be summarized as follows:

1. A person's behavior is perceived as having been caused by a condition external to him whenever the following obtain: (a) it occurs when that condition is present but does not occur otherwise; (b) it occurs in much the same way whenever that condition is present; and (c) it occurs when anyone else experiences that condition too.

2. A person's behavior is perceived to be internally caused whenever the opposite of the above three conditions obtain: that is, (a) it occurs regardless of whether the particular condition is present or not; (b) it varies in the way it occurs under the same conditions; and (c) its occurrence varies considerably from person to person.

Let us imagine an example. You are visiting in the home of a friend. You are chatting from time to time as you both watch television. At the end of the program, your friend turns off the TV and goes to the kitchen to find some refreshments. You said you'd have a coke. He brings you one, and for himself he has made an ice cream soda. Just as he is about to sit down, the telephone rings. He goes to the hall to answer it. "Hello," he says; then after a pause, "I'm sorry, you must have the wrong number." While still up, he goes to find a magazine which he mentioned earlier. He brings it to show you the article on a camping expedition in the far north. Then he sits down to his ice cream soda.

In that imaginary segment of behavior, you perceive some things that your friend did as externally caused and other things as being the result of internal motivations. The way he goes to the hall to answer the phone does not lead to speculation about internal motives. Why? He does this whenever the phone rings. He does it in about the same way whenever the phone rings. Furthermore, almost anyone else does about the same thing when the phone rings. You therefore do not attribute his behavior in answering the phone to internal causes. You do not see this behavior as expressing his uniqueness.

But that ice cream soda is another matter. He was the one who suggested refreshments. Since you suggested a coke, you see his bringing you a coke as not so much internally caused. But the ice cream soda is unique. It isn't naturally expected. It isn't what anyone else would do. Therefore it must be more clearly a matter of your friend's inner motivation.

Note that there are no physical cues that enable you to distinguish between internal and external causes of your friend's behavior. His internal physiological mechanisms are operating just as much when he answers the phone as when he opens the refrigerator. And external stimuli impinge upon him in the kitchen as well as in the hallway. The difference is primarily a matter of attribution, which is located more accurately in your mind than in his behavior. Nevertheless, it is an important dimension in your perception of his behavior.

Can these ideas about attribution be scientifically demonstrated?

Kelley (1967) presents them as part of a theory about the way we attribute motives to others, but he gives little direct evidence for his main propositions. Much more systematic evidence has been presented by Leslie Ann McArthur (1972). She developed questionnaires that described the behavior of an imaginary person and asked subjects to indicate what they believed caused that behavior. Questionnaires were planned to vary along three primary dimensions in the way behavior was described:

1. Distinctiveness—the extent to which the behavior fails to occur under other conditions
2. Consistency—the extent to which the behavior occurs in the same way
3. Consensus—the extent to which almost anyone would do the same

In conformity with the predictions of Kelley, McArthur generally found personal or internal attribution more common in situations of low distinctiveness, high consistency, and/or low consensus. In contrast, when there was high distinctiveness (that is, where behavior was different in different conditions), subjects tended to attribute causes to the nature of the particular stimuli (especially when consistency was high) or to the general circumstances (when consistency was low).

McArthur's findings also led her to conclude that there is a general bias in favor of attributing causes for behavior to the person rather than his environment. For example, the behavior of Sue when "Sue is afraid of the dog" is overwhelmingly attributed to the character of Sue rather than to the ferocity of the dog. And when "George translates the sentence incorrectly," it is George rather than the sentence that is usually seen as the problem.

Another variation in McArthur's experiment consisted in the use of different verb categories to describe imaginary behavior. Behaviors described as accomplishments or actions were more likely to be attributed to the person than those described as emotions and opinions. Emotions and opinions are more apt to be attributed to the nature of particular stimuli influencing the person.

Again, let us emphasize that we are not dealing with objective causes of behavior, or even with what a person sees as the causes of his own behavior. Rather, we are dealing with something that is, from our point of view, even more subjective: the causes we attribute to the behavior of another person. Still, despite the subjectivity, it is interesting to note that it is possible to devise scientific studies of the attribution process. McArthur's experiment is a case in point; it confirms the main tenets of Kelley's attribution theory, and also leads us to additional insights into the general process of how we perceive the behavior of another.

SELF-PERCEPTION

Prepare now for a sudden twist. Consider what we have said in this chapter about perceiving other people; now try to apply these ideas to the question of how a person perceives himself. Do not the same general processes apply?

There are of course differences between self-perception and the perception of others. One difference is that we are usually more preoccupied with ourselves than with another person. Therefore, with oneself the accumulation of past experiences is greater, the present emotional involvement is higher, and a greater impact is anticipated for the future. But these would not make self-perception processes different in kind from the processes of perceiving others. Rather, they would suggest that a greater variety of elements and a stronger consolidation of these elements may be characteristic of self-perception.

However, there is another way in which self-perception fundamentally differs from the perception of others. In self-perception we make direct use of internal cues. Internal physiological responses are parts of the data for self-perception in a way that has no parallel in interpersonal perception. Still, it would be possible to make too much of this point. These internal physiological cues seldom speak for themselves. They require interpretation. And their interpretation depends on the way we have learned to label these cues—in part by the reactions we have observed in others.

In his analysis of self-perception, Bem (1972) emphasizes the extent that even a person's internal state must be interpreted according to external cues. He therefore claims as fundamental ideas that

> Individuals come to "know" their own attitudes, emotions, and other internal states partially by inferring them from observations of their own overt behavior and/or the circumstances in which this behavior occurs. Thus, to the extent that internal cues are weak, ambiguous, or uninterpretable, the individual is functionally in the same position as an outside observer, an observer who must necessarily rely upon those same external cues to infer the individual's inner states (p. 2).

At any rate, it is reasonable to conclude that to some extent we use the same tools for self-perception as we use for perceiving other persons. The implicit personality theory we use to fill out the meaning of the behavior of another person may also be used to build meaning for our own behavior. The way in which we may project characteristics of ourselves upon others has a counterpart in the way we may assume characteristics in ourselves that we observe in others. And the same conditions that help us decide whether another person's behavior is caused by internal or external factors may also be used to decide whether our own behavior is to be interpreted as personally caused or as caused by external forces.

26
Culture and Personality

STUDIES OF SEX AND TEMPERAMENT

In the early 1930s the anthropologist Margaret Mead undertook some field studies in northeastern New Guinea (1950). A general objective was to add several cultures to those covered by the anthropological literature, but Dr. Mead had another objective as well. This was to discover to what extent the temperamental differences between the sexes are innate and to what extent they are culturally determined. A study of the patterning of sex roles in different cultures would apparently provide evidence on this question.

The first culture Mead visited on this trip was that of the Arapesh, who were living in a poor and mountainous region near the northern coast of New Guinea. Although these Arapesh lived a marginal physical existence, they provided an example of an unusually cooperative society, with individuals spending much of their time helping their neighbors. As children, both boys and girls received similar gentle attention from parents and other relatives. As adults, both men and women seemed to be predominantly gentle and responsive personalities. In fact, though there were of course differences in their social and economic division of labor, Mead found little along temperamental lines to distinguish males from females. The Arapesh of both sexes had the qualities that Americans would consider predominantly feminine.

About a hundred miles from the Arapesh, Mead visited several villages of the Mundugumor. Living along the banks of a river, these headhunters preyed on neighboring tribes and until recently had been cannibals. Physical vigor and self-assertiveness were prized qualities among the Mundugumor. Children were nearly universally unwanted, and both mothers and fathers sought to avoid child-rearing duties. As a result, the children developed their own assertive forms of coping with the human jungle that constituted their social world. As with the Arapesh, so with the Mundugumor, both males and females seemed to share generally similar temperamental qualities. However, among the Mundugumor this pattern, represented by women as well as men, was that of rough and rugged individualism.

Somewhat farther into the interior of New Guinea, along the shores of a lovely lake, Mead studied a third group, the Tchambuli. Tchambuli women ran the households and took care of most of the economic

activities, including fishing and marketing. Without personal adorn-
ment, they impersonally and industriously went about these pursuits.
On the other hand, it was the Tchambuli men who spent their time
decorating themselves, dancing, and gossiping down at their ceremonial huts beside the lake. Temperamentally, Mead suggests, it was
the Tchambuli males who (by Western standards) were feminine and
the females who were masculine. And to prepare for such differences,
it was the male children among the Tchambuli who were made more
emotionally dependent on their parents, whereas the girls were given
earlier encouragement in self-reliance.

Based on her studies of these contrasting patterns of culture, Mead
came to the conclusion that "human nature is almost unbelievably
malleable" and that:

> The differences between individuals who are members of differ-
> ent cultures, like the differences between individuals within a
> culture, are almost entirely to be laid to differences in condition-
> ing, especially during early childhood, and the form of this con-
> ditioning is culturally determined. Standardized personality dif-
> ferences between the sexes are of this order, cultural creations
> to which each generation, male and female, is trained to con-
> form (p. 191).

CULTURE AND BASIC PERSONALITY

Mead's view of the cultural relativity of sex roles goes a great distance
toward seeing personality as simply a particular reflection of culture.
Or as one sociologist has suggested, personality may be characterized
simply as the subjective aspect of culture. But such a simplification
would be premature for us, for we have not yet considered exactly how
culture works its effects upon personality development. In one sense,
nearly all the preceding chapters of this book discuss cultural influences upon individual behavior, but we have not given attention to the
way in which a culture *as an organized whole* produces its impact upon
personality.

Early anthropologists were not primarily interested in psychological
questions; and psychologists, for many years, concerned themselves
little with studies of different cultures. This, however, has changed
very much in the last three or four decades. A lively interest has developed in what has come to be known as the culture-and-personality
area, involving considerable cooperation between anthropologists and
psychologists.

The best-known example of this collaboration is the work led by
Abram Kardiner and Ralph Linton at Columbia University (Kardiner,
1939; 1945). Kardiner, a psychoanalyst, took very seriously Freud's emphasis upon early childhood experience, but he believed that the cultural content of this experience was far more important than Freud's
biological emphasis allowed. Linton, an anthropologist, believed that
culture should be seen as rooted in the psychological experience of
human beings. Together Kardiner and Linton developed a general
theory of culture-personality relationships and inspired anthropologists
to collect field data that would test elements of this theory.

Key concepts of the Kardiner-Linton theory may be identified as those of (1) primary institutions, (2) basic personality, and (3) secondary institutions.

The primary institutions are those cultural practices that predominantly shape the experience of early childhood. These are expected to vary from culture to culture, providing the basis for different problems of early adjustment.

Because the child-rearing institutions tend to be shared by persons in the same culture, the way a child adjusts to his early experience is also apt to have much in common with the way others in his society adjust. This typical pattern of adjustment found in a given society is termed *basic personality*. Although it is presumed to represent a key part of the individual personality, this conception of basic personality points not so much to what is unique in the individual as to what is shared with others. It refers not to what is biologically determined, but rather to what is culturally conditioned.

The pattern of basic personality found in any culture in turn serves to provide a pattern for other institutions. Cultural practices that take their form largely to express basic personality themes are known as secondary institutions. Common examples of such secondary institutions may be found in folklore and religion.

The analysis of Kardiner and Linton drew upon, and inspired further, researches of various primitive cultures (Tanala, Marquesas, Comanche, Alor) as well as a contemporary American community (dubbed "Plainville"). Generally, the evidence appears to be consistent with the main ideas of basic personality theory. Linton concludes (in Kardiner, 1945) that "in relatively stable cultures, such as those of 'primitive' societies, there is a close interrelation between the basic personality type and the culture as a whole" (p. viii). In such societies "the basic personality type and the culture configuration tend to reinforce and perpetuate each other" (p. ix).

THE CHEYENNES

To illustrate the congruency between cultural patterns and personality, let us note the example of the Cheyenne tribe discussed by Hoebel (1960). The Cheyennes, as described in the mid-nineteenth century, were a nomadic tribe of hunters and food gatherers. Skilled horsemen, they roamed the Great Plains in search of bison. Moving together in large bands consisting of several kinship groups, they lived in easily movable tepees. They were fierce warriors in battles with neighboring tribes, but within the tribe itself, aggression was kept in tight check. Exerting an almost unbelievable degree of self-control, the good Cheyenne was one whose impulses would never cause him to lose the perspective of his primary responsibilities to family and tribe.

Cheyenne children were highly prized and given careful attention. Babies were fed on a self-demand schedule. But their wishes were not always indulged. Even infants had to learn that a willful display of temper was not condoned. Not even crying was allowed. Could not a crying baby give away a camp position to enemy scouts at night? Besides, it was very disagreeable to have a screaming child around. So when an infant cried, it was simply left alone on its cradleboard tied to a bush out away from the camp. Thus it remained, cut off from all social contact, until it stopped crying. Very early this procedure taught the Cheyenne infant the necessity of basic self-control.

Children were always to be quiet and respectful before their elders. Elders, in turn, showered children with attention and constant sermonizing about the values of bravery, honesty, industry, and cooperation. Little boys learned to ride horseback practically as soon as they could walk, and little girls toddled along with their mothers to help get wood and water. Among themselves, children enjoyed games that closely approximated adult activities. This included play camps where children re-created nearly the full range of everyday life, with themselves filling the adult roles. Later, as early teen-agers, young Cheyennes entered gradually into the full round of adult activities.

What was the basic personality type produced by such child rearing? The adult Cheyenne was reserved, dignified, careful, and generous. He was quiet, slow to anger, and extremely repressed sexually. Highly practical, he went about his daily activities with steady concentration and skill.

All Cheyennes? No, not all fitted equally well into this type. In fact, the Cheyennes recognized a place for persons who could not fit the general image. Most interesting in this regard was the *Contrary*, a man who rejected all normal social relations to live alone and specialize in military exploits. The Contrary was expected to do everything backwards; when asked to do one thing, he would ordinarily do the opposite. This way of life represented a culturally accepted deviation for individuals who found it difficult to achieve the Cheyenne pattern in an integrated fashion. But even the Contrary represented a parody of the cultural ideal—supremely brave in battle and completely repressed sexually (he would not even sit or lie on a bed).

What kinds of secondary institutions may be observed in this kind of culture? In their highly developed ritual life the Cheyennes showed the imprint of their dominant concerns. Throughout their rituals were certain key themes: the universe has a limited store of energy which must be carefully applied; the human social order is likewise a fragile thing which must be carefully preserved; and both the harmony of the universe and the solidarity of human society must be renewed, when disrupted, by carefully planned acts of dedication and self-sacrifice. These themes are apparent in their great ritual ceremonies of the Arrow Renewal or the Sun Dance, performed when the tribe was gathered together just before the communal buffalo hunt held each summer.

Likewise, Cheyenne political structure showed great concern for the preservation of a proper moral order. A tribal chief was expected to embody dignity, courage, and generosity to a very high degree. The tribal council met with great form and decorum. And a key concern was always the control of all violence within the tribe, as well as a readiness for bravery in doing battle with enemy tribes.

In their ceremonial life and political institutions, the Cheyennes appeared to embody themes similar to those characteristic of individual Cheyennes: courage, chastity, and supreme dignity. Thus we see a basic congruency between (in the terms of Kardiner) the basic personality and the secondary institutions of Cheyenne culture, with the basic personality type in turn closely related to the primary institutions of child rearing.

RECONSIDERATION

The studies mentioned in this chapter have pointed to a general correspondence between the overall cultural pattern and the prominent features of individual behavior. To some culture-and-personality enthusiasts this has been sufficient to consider the main tenets of the Kardiner theory as demonstrated, namely: (1) that personality systems are organized to reflect the culture pattern, thus showing common personality forms in any common culture, and (2) that culture, in turn, is molded, and stabilized or changed, to fit with prevalent patterns of personality organization.

But where are the systematic studies using actual measures of personality organization in cross-cultural research? Results of projective personality tests (such as interpretation of Rorschach ink blots or the pictures of the Thematic Apperception Test) have been collected from a number of different cultural groups, and some comparisons using other kinds of personality data have been made. Still, as Inkeles (1959) has pointed out:

> No one has ever tested a national population or even a major sub-population using either an adequate sample or adequate psychological instruments. All assertions or denials of national, subnational, regional, or class differences of major magnitudes, therefore, remain mere statements of faith (pp. 267–268).

Although a few more ambitious studies have been published since Inkeles made this statement, his criticism remains approximately correct today.

One of the leaders in the attempt to collect personality data in systematic cross-cultural research, Bert Kaplan (1961), has pointed to a decline in interest in this field since the 1940s when "large numbers of workers eagerly embarked on cross-cultural personality studies and the swiftly mobilized interest almost had the proportions of a fad" (p. 1). The optimism for quick results and easy conclusions, however, was not fulfilled. "The materials were easy enough to collect," Kaplan further comments, "but were difficult or impossible to interpret and to integrate, with any reasonable claim to validity, into ongoing anthropological studies." As a result of this disillusionment there has been a subsequent decline in culture-and-personality research.

Furthermore, the more systematic studies that have accumulated point to fairly modest claims for the interrelation of culture patterns and personality organization. By and large, the personality data have shown greater variation within cultures than between cultures. Kaplan himself (1957) concludes that the key to the diversity of individual behavior is not to be found simply in cultural diversity, but rather in "a small number of motivational tendencies which could be found in any society in the world" (p. 121).

The earlier emphasis upon the extreme plasticity of human nature also has become somewhat moderated. Mead herself in later writings, such as in *Male and Female* (1949), has not emphasized the flexibility of human nature quite so much as she did earlier in *Sex and Temperament* (1935). In this reaction against an extreme cultural relativity, Kaplan (1957) goes so far as to conclude that "personality characteristics resulting from human biology overshadow in importance the special characteristics attributable to the particular social patterns in which development occurs" (p. 121).

SUBCULTURES

The culture-and-personality writers have pointed to a degree of correspondence between an overall cultural system and the personality patterns of individuals. Just exactly what may be the degree of correspondence, or its typical form, is not yet clear. But as a rough approximation it makes sense to say that personalities reflect their culture. It also makes sense to see widely shared personality patterns as setting some limits for the institutions of that society.

But this is not saying very much. This does not account for the great variability in personality within an area of common culture. Perhaps it fails to do so because it describes social patterns on too gross a level. Perhaps we can understand individual variations in behavior better if we see them as reflecting the particular cultural expectations rather than the culture in general. This is largely the approach taken in the earlier chapters of this book.

The concept of subcultures may serve as a useful mediating concept between particular cultural settings and the culture in general. Especially in the case of complex modern societies is it useful to distinguish among subcultures. In American society there are both regional subcultures in the nation at large and ecological subcultures within a given metropolitan area (the suburbs and the ghetto being typical examples). Correlated with such territorially based subcultures, and sometimes crosscutting through them, are occupational, social class, racial, nationality, and religious subcultures. Thus it is that one finds slightly different patterns of behavior in a Polish neighborhood than among the Dutch, Negroes, or Italians. Social-class subcultures may be even more important than ethnic divisions, especially in a relatively fluid and mobile society. Here the style of success or the consciousness of disadvantages may be especially important features in distinguishing middle- and lower-class ways of life. Even with such particular places as a manufacturing plant or a school, one can point to differences between production and management subcultures, or faculty and student subcultures.

As an individual identifies with a given subculture, his personality comes to mirror many of its values and expectations. So it is that whether a person becomes a salesman, a lawyer, or a social worker may be important in shaping personality patterns, as well as in reflecting that individual's personality.

RELIGION AND ACHIEVEMENT

As an example of subcultural influences, let us briefly examine some evidence on the effects of different religious subcultures upon achievement motivation.

We have, first of all, the thesis of Max Weber (1930) that at a particular point in European history a set of ethical ideas associated with Protestantism provided a setting favorable to the development of capitalism. The acceptance of a worldly occupation as a calling of God in which religious devotion might be expressed as disciplined work, the notion that man's relationship to God was one emphasizing individual responsibility, and the care with which man must limit and control his pursuit of individual pleasure—all of these ideas may be seen as expressive of early Protestantism, especially in its Calvinist, Baptist, and Quaker varieties. These ideas then fostered among Protestants a general outlook on life that was one of the important roots in the development of modern capitalism. Acceptance of systematic discipline, careful planning, and thrift—these were virtues encouraged by Protestant subcultures; these also provided a characterological base for the early growth of capitalism.

Weber never intended for his analysis to be simplified into the notion that Protestantism caused capitalism. Rather, his idea was that in the early modern period certain Protestant subcultures nurtured a type of personality that was especially favorable to capitalist development. His evidence was limited to citing examples of the convergence of religious and economic ideas and studies showing greater economic development in Protestant than in Roman Catholic areas.

There has been considerable debate over the historical validity of Weber's thesis (see, for example, Kitch, 1967), mostly concerning the degree of historical association between Protestantism and capitalism. But what about the contemporary world? Although Weber specifically avoided drawing a connection between Protestantism and capitalism for the twentieth century, we may still pose the question: Are Protestants today significantly different from Catholics in attitudes toward the world in general or toward economic activity in particular? Or do Protestants and Catholics no longer offer very significantly differing subcultures?

The best-known recent evidence on the social impact of religious differences is contained in Gerhard Lenski's book, *The Religious Factor* (1961). Based primarily upon a 1958 survey of the Detroit area, this work points to important differences among religious groups in political, economic, educational, and kinship matters. Among other things, Protestantism seems associated with a stronger drive toward economic achievement, with more of an individualistic family orientation, and with rationalistic rather than traditionalistic values. All of these are contemporary parallels of Weber's thesis about early Protestantism, supporting the idea that religious subcultures still play an important role in American society.

Unfortunately for a neat set of conclusions, other evidence is much more ambiguous. In a follow-up study of the Detroit area in 1966, many of Lenski's particular findings were not replicated (Schuman, 1971). One notable exception was the stronger tendency for Protestants than Catholics to seek work that gives "a feeling of accomplishment," a finding that still held in the later study. Other studies (for example, Jackson, Fox, and Crockett, 1970) have given additional evidence of a significant relationship between religious affiliation and occupational achievement.

In at least one area, that of achievement motivation, there thus appears to be a significant link to religious subcultures. This suggests that although the Protestant ethic may be dying as a central theme in American life, it still lives on within some Protestant subcultures.

As a postscript to our discussion of the differences in achievement motivation in different subcultures, let us note also a study in a non-European cultural context. Prothro (1961) studied child-rearing practices and early achievement motivation in twelve different samples in Lebanon. The samples varied in terms of religious community (Armenian Christian, Greek Orthodox, or Sunni Moslem), urban or rural (Beirut or Beqaa Valley), and social class (middle or lower). In general, child-rearing practices appeared to support earlier achievement training for urban middle-class children than for lower-class or rural families, and for Christian (Arab or Armenian) more than for Moslem communities. These factors tend to support the general patterns of economic achievement in Lebanon—associated most strongly with urban, middle-class, and Christian subcultures.

In Lebanon, then, as well as in Europe and America, we find evidence for a relationship between religious subcultures and achievement motivation.

27
Individuality in Contemporary Society

INSIDE THE LONELY CROWD

> We believe that music is a necessary part of life and its influence is felt in every phase of living. Singing and playing together can bring understanding and good-will and it seems to me that this world needs more of this kind of harmony.
>
> At X, we try to provide some kind of music participation for every child and wish to encourage more musical activity, especially that of playing with a group in an orchestra.

In *The Lonely Crowd,* David Riesman (revised edition, 1961, pp. 153–154) quotes the above explanation of a progressive school's music program as one among many bits of evidence of a profound change in the nature of the American character. Social adjustment seems to take precedence over private satisfaction for justifying the development of musical skills. This is characteristic of a shift in American society of the twentieth century from what Riesman calls *inner-direction* to *other-direction,* a shift that is also reflected in the character patterns of the individuals involved.

Riesman is especially concerned with understanding the link between the nature of society and the personality of the individual. He uses the concept of *social character* to represent this linkage. The social character is that part of personality that is the product of group experience and that is shared with others in society. Riesman sees this social character as rooted less specifically in particular child-rearing practices than other culture-and-personality writers; rather, what Riesman emphasizes is the *mode of conformity* or way of relating to society that becomes embodied in the social character. This is broadly shaped by the total configuration of society, though particular "agents of character formation" are given special attention in Riesman's analysis, namely parents, teachers, peers, and "storytellers" (including the mass media).

Riesman's main thesis is that as the overall pattern of society has changed, corresponding changes have occurred in social character or mode of conformity. In a static society, a *tradition-directed* type of social character was dominant. In a rapidly growing and industrializing society, a more *inner-directed,* individualistically oriented type became more prevalent. And on the contemporary scene we are finding the inner-directed type displaced more and more by an ever adjusting *other-directed* type. This is because of the importance of mobility and day-to-day adjustment in the contemporary world, and is generally related to an overall shift from an age of production to an age of consumption. Riesman also sees the contemporary social character as more specifically rooted in population patterns, with inner-direction related to high population growth and other-direction related to a more mature (more concentrated and slower growing) population structure.

Riesman supports his interpretations with a wide variety of references to changing institutional practices and citations of representative themes in popular culture. While his examples make his basic interpretation a plausible one, they hardly can be said to prove his thesis. In fact, in a later reconsideration (in Lipset and Lowenthal, 1961, pp. 419–458), he admits that the linkage to population structure was overdrawn, that the other-directed character of Americans was rooted in a longer history than *The Lonely Crowd* indicates, and that more attention might have been given to the direct power exerted by institutions upon individual behavior (rather than to see it primarily mediated by social character).

Work such as *The Lonely Crowd* is extremely hard to validate. The usefulness of the concepts of inner-direction and other-direction results from the general insight they bring rather than from specific research data. Nevertheless, some systematic research has used this typology with productive results. For example, Elaine Sofer (in Lipset and Lowenthal, 1961, pp. 316–348) developed a scale to measure other-direction and found it significantly related to the subjects' greater susceptibility to opinion change, greater field dependence in perceptual tasks (that is, less ability to discount environmental influences), less anxiety about their bodies, less assertive aggression, and possibly also greater authoritarianism and less intelligence. She concludes that "the results support the general hypothesis that the same underlying tendency toward other-direction versus self- or inner-direction found to operate in these subjects' choice of values may be seen mirrored also in their perception, their social behavior, and their underlying personality trends" (p. 335).

If we grant that the typology Riesman uses to describe American character may be useful, we may still doubt some of the particular meanings that he adds. Why, for example, talk about the other-directed man as being lonely? Riesman's answer is that in spite of all sociability, the other-directed man typically cannot feel at home in the shifting flux of others. He needs a firmer, more autonomous and self-conscious base from which to face his constantly shifting world. Without that base he remains lonely and lost amidst the mass.

ON ALIENATION

The quality of loneliness in mass society is most often discussed by social scientists under the heading of *alienation*. Alienation refers to the quality of feeling separated, of being outside the main processes of social life.

Many years ago—in 1844, to be exact—Karl Marx wrote an essay on

"Estranged Labour" (reprinted in Mills, 1960). In this essay he identifies certain key features of modern society that serve to accentuate the quality of alienation.

First of all, according to Marx, is the separation of the worker from the product of his work. He becomes enmeshed in the impersonal processes of production, making objects that have little value to himself. The output of his labor therefore becomes something alien, something with little direct meaning for his own life.

A second form of alienation pointed out by Marx is the separation of the worker from the process of work. Under conditions of industrial production, work itself becomes an alien activity. The work does not seem to involve the worker's own physical and mental activity. Work is not his own spontaneous activity but rather is made to order for the wishes of someone else. Work therefore becomes something external to the worker's sense of self, leaving the worker alienated from his own work.

Another aspect of the alienation of modern man lies in the separation of the individual from his species nature. Industrial work forces the worker into an artificial existence, where the regular routines of work become divorced from the basic life processes of his species. He thus becomes little more than an appendage of the machine, tied to it not as a free part of living but as a mere *means* to keeping his life going.

As a consequence of the above three kinds of separation experienced by workers in industrial society, Marx saw a fourth kind of separation growing: the separation of man from man. Relationships between men become artificial when encased in the structures of industrial society. And so men must necessarily become alienated from one another.

Believing that economic relationships are necessarily primary in the life of society, Marx saw the various estrangements experienced in the work setting as constituting the basis of a general alienation of modern man. Also believing that private property was the key link in the system that produced such alienation, Marx expected that a socialist system would be able to eliminate or markedly reduce man's alienation. When workers share the ownership and control of their own work, they should be able to change the nature and meaning of work into something both more self-fulfilling and more socially useful.

Although written well over a century ago, the views of Karl Marx on this subject (perhaps more than his distinctly economic or political writings) still have a contemporary ring. They give us a rationale for seeing the alienation of modern man rooted in his economic institutions. Updated in the hands of a contemporary philosopher such as Herbert Marcuse (1964, 1968), the Marxist theory of alienation is still very much with us.

But is it true? If we try to put the ideas of Marx or Marcuse into testable propositions, are they supported by empirical evidence?

In Marx's day there were no widespread social surveys using alienation scales developed by social psychologists. Today there are. And from some of these studies we may be able to get some further perspective on the alienation of modern man. In particular, let us review some of the work of Melvin Seeman (1959, 1967, 1971), a social scientist who has been particularly active in this area of research.

First of all, is there extensive work alienation among employees in industrial society? The answer seems to be yes. For many individuals, work is neither interesting nor challenging.

Does such work alienation create a broader sense of alienation from self and society? At this point it may be useful to distinguish several kinds of alienation and ask if they appear to be correlated. Seeman has delineated the following forms: work alienation, a general sense of powerlessness, social isolation, and value estrangement. Does alienation in work create a generalized sense of powerlessness, of social isolation, and of general meaninglessness—as Marxian theory suggests? The answer appears to be no. As Seeman points out, there seems to be almost no correlation between work alienation and the other forms of alienation; thus "alienation in work simply does not seem to make the difference it is supposed to" (1971, p. 138).

Does this mean that alienation is not a problem for contemporary society? Not at all. Work alienation is still a problem in itself, even if it does not create a broader alienation. And the sense of general powerlessness in society can be even more dangerous, for this is found to be strongly associated with ethnic prejudice and probably with a tendency to accept the use of violence. But this appears to be little affected by the quality of working conditions.

Another form of alienation is social isolation. Is this a general result of industrial society? Seeman finds little evidence that it is. Some people feel lonely, yes, but this seems to be a feature of their particular life rather than a widely shared pattern. Social isolation shows little correlation with other forms of alienation.

What about value estrangement—a generalized loss of social meaning and common purpose? Seeman's evidence points to a rather wide agreement across class, race, neighborhood, and sex lines on such matters as family patterns, goals for children, sentiments about people in general, and attitudes regarding conformity, materialism, and self-interest. Value estrangement does not appear to be as widespread as Sunday sermons and the popular press suggest.

Where, then, is that widespread alienation that is supposed to characterize the modern condition? It may be with us, but not in the generalized pattern suggested by Marxian theory. And it may be especially acute in particular segments of society. Segments that feel cut off from power over their fates may be expected to suffer a particularly frustrating form of alienation.

One group in which alienation may be particularly acute is that of intellectuals. Although intellectuals do not seem to be among the powerless, it may still be true that they feel relatively powerless in the face of the variety of forces with which they must deal. For the harsh forces of industrial organizations and national governments do not yield to words in the manner that an intellectual is wont to think they should. Meanwhile, the explosion of new knowledge and new cultural forms continues, stretching continually the world that he must try to get a grip on.

As more and more people come to share in higher education, we might expect the general alienation of intellectuals to be more widely experienced within society and to yield a greater and more generalized mood of alienation. But this is a far cry from the roots of alienation Marx saw in industrial work. Rather it is perhaps in leisure, not in labor, that the industrial age may open the greatest opportunity for alienation. And, as Alvin Toffler suggests in his provocative book, *Future Shock* (1970), it may be much more the stimulation of the variety of contemporary experience, rather than the monotony of work, that sets the stage for self-estrangement today.

THE DYNAMICS OF SELF-ESTRANGEMENT

The self, as viewed by social psychology, consists of those attitudes an individual has toward his own behavior. These attitudes, as has been emphasized earlier in this book, serve as the central focus for the organization of other attitudes.

If the self is so central in the organization of attitudes, how can we understand self-alienation, the feeling of estrangement from his own behavior that an individual sometimes has? If we examine the fundamental ways that the self system shapes our attitudes, we may find also the basic factors behind self-alienation.

One basic way in which the self shapes attitudes is in fostering self-consistency. We tend to take on attitudes selectively, favoring those that are congruent with our self-image. Conversely, when there is a notable failure to achieve self-consistency, self-estrangement is apt to be produced. When the parts do not fit, the result may be that the person is literally "beside himself," that is, part of his behavior is alien to the rest.

A second basic way that the self shapes attitudes is in fostering self-esteem. "We believe, first and foremost," Bertrand Russell (1950) has said, "what makes us feel that we are fine fellows" (p. 82). And attitudes that add to our sense of self-worth or self-importance tend to be fostered. Therefore, any notable blow to self-esteem may be an occasion for feelings of self-estrangement.

Role identification is a third key to understanding how the self shapes attitudes. Our sense of self is not just free-floating, but it is grounded in particular social roles. Those roles with which we identify provide an anchorage for the self system, and we come to depend upon them as bases for the elaboration of other attitudes. When something happens to destroy any of these key underpinnings—such as separation from a spouse or loss of a job—a sense of self-estrangement is frequently the result.

Self-alienation, therefore, is apt to occur whenever we experience a failure to achieve (1) self-consistency, (2) self-esteem, or (3) meaningful role identification. And when these failures occur together, self-alienation is especially likely to occur.

In his autobiography, Malcolm X recalled a key turning point in his life which well illustrates a sense of self-alienation. He was in a Massachusetts prison where his former career as a hustler had brought him. He could no longer take pride in what he had been, and instead was turning to the Muslim faith of Elijah Muhammad. Removing himself as much as possible from the prison life around him, he bent his knees, forcing himself to pray to Allah. In later recalling this process of conversion, Malcolm X (1966) commented:

> I still marvel at how swiftly my previous life's thinking pattern slid away from me, like snow off a roof. It is as though someone else I knew of had lived by hustling and crime. I would catch myself thinking in a remote way of my earlier self as another person (p. 170).

Reintegration of the self around new values, illustrated by the conversion of Malcolm X to the Muslim faith, is one possible outcome of self-alienation. The new values provide a new direction for behavior, a new focus for living.

A new organization for living is not the only outcome that may follow severe self-alienation. A general diffusion of values and goals is another possible response. This may lead to an accentuation of the present moment, allowing the individual to remain open to whatever may happen rather than committing himself strongly to any values. This is exemplified by a teen-age girl who expressed her life style to a reporter: "It's like do what you want to do now. . . . If you stay anywhere very long you get into a planning thing. . . . So you just move on." Toffler, who cites this example, considers the rootlessness it represents as increasingly characteristic of our society, where many now find their adjustment in a general style of living loose. "Spontaneity, the personal equivalent of social planlessness, is elevated into a cardinal psychological virtue" (pp. 450–451).

Another possible outcome of extreme self-alienation is psychosis. Rather than attempt to adjust to the world by either a new framework of social values or a general openness to new experience, an individual may respond by creating a substitute world encapsulated in inner privacy. This is the predominant response associated with schizophrenia, though milder forms far short of psychosis may also be cultivated. In the background of the development of schizophrenia is typically, as one study concluded, "a rash of insoluble, mutually reinforcing problems" (Rogler and Hollingshead, 1965, p. 413). As these problems seem to snowball, the individual feels caught in an impossible situation, a situation for which the creation of a substitute inner reality seems the only way out.

Self-alienation, the feeling of estrangement from one's own behavior, thus may be seen as having a variety of possible outcomes—including reintegration around new values and goals, a general attitude of openness to whatever comes, or an escape into an exclusively private world.

THE FUTURE OF INDIVIDUALITY

After surveying a quarter of a century of studies of American child rearing, Bronfenbrenner (1961) identified five "secular trends" that appeared to characterize changes in parental behavior. These were the following:

1. A general increase in permissiveness
2. More emphasis upon the expression of affection
3. Greater use of indirect or so-called psychological techniques of discipline rather than direct methods of punishment

4. A narrowing of the gap between social classes in the way
   children are reared (with working-class parents becoming
   more like middle-class parents)
5. A role of clearly reduced authority for fathers and somewhat
   increased authority for mothers

Speculating on the consequences of these changes, Bronfenbrenner
saw in their likely results the general fostering of a more conforming
and anxious and less enterprising and self-sufficient character pattern.
Especially would this change be apparent in males, for whom the
greater use of indirect discipline and reduced authority of the father
should have a stronger impact than it would for females.

These patterns of change are roughly similar to the long-term
trend suggested by David Riesman in *The Lonely Crowd.* They show
a general increase toward an other-directed pattern. They also suggest
some reasons why anxiety and alienation might be increasingly prominent themes on the contemporary scene. With a narrowing of the
gaps between behaviors of mothers and fathers and a general reliance
upon more indirect methods of control, parents provide less clearly
structured models of what their children might become. Greater uncertainty in role identification could be expected as a general by-product.

But we have little basis for stating how much such changes in
child rearing may limit the basic quality of individuality in contemporary Americans. Concern for the idea of individuality seems as strong
as ever, and the core of individuality in each of us may be less affected
by particular styles of child rearing than behavioral scientists usually
suggest. After all, most research relating child-rearing variables to adult
personality characteristics shows only very modest patterns of correlation. To pretend that such low correlations represent key causal determinants may be simply to exhibit a common professional bias of social
and behavioral scientists, identified by Dennis Wrong (1961) as "the
oversocialized conception of man." As Wrong correctly points out, we
should be careful about what we claim by a concept such as socialization. There can be little doubt that a cultural heritage is passed on
through a process of socialization, or that we become human in the
unique way that we do largely through interaction with other humans.
But this does not mean that any individual is *completely molded* by the
norms and values of his culture. Human uniqueness can hardly be
eliminated by a society of advanced industrialization. Though molded
by that society, the individual retains a wide range of opportunities
for expressing himself within the patterns provided, for choosing one
pattern rather than another—or for rebellion.

28
Personality in Society: Review and Discussion

PERSONAL IMAGES

When you watch a motion picture, what are you seeing? A very rapid sequence of individual pictures flashed upon the screen? That is what is physically present, but you certainly do not perceive it in this way. Rather, you have a sense of action occurring before your eyes, and the action you see is continuous. Somehow your nervous system takes you beyond the physical elements and enables you to construct a perception of continuous motion.

And those persons who are pictured on the screen are not simply perceived in terms of their individual acts. Rather, we relate to them as persons. Even when sitting in a crowded theater, we get from the image on the screen a sense of personhood that is irresistible. Temporarily, those persons are as real as any we know.

Is this sense of personality, like the sense of motion, an illusion? In several ways, yes. The character is portrayed by an actor, who follows a preplanned script. The motion picture camera is selective in what it records, and the film editors are even more selective in what they decide to include. All of this heightens the false impression that you are seeing an individual responding naturally as a person.

But the illusion that leads you to see the image on the screen as a personality has much in common with the way you see persons in everyday life. There too you refuse to see particular actions as discrete, but instead you build them immediately into a larger impression. In this manner you routinely construct an image of personality.

Is personality then a fiction or a real thing? Is it something artificial, or a phenomenon of the natural world?

The fact that we construct images of personality is certainly a real thing. This does not make it easy to study this phenomenon scientifically, but it does make person perception an appropriate part of social psychology. In Chapter 25, "Perceiving Persons," we gave an introductory consideration of this subject. Beginning with simple studies by Solomon Asch, we went on to build a general picture of the process of forming impressions, including the way self-conceptions may influence perceptions of another person. We then moved into the subject of how we attribute causes of the behavior of a person, including causes of our own behavior. Such factors as an individual's consistency in behavior lead us to see an act that is part of the consistent pattern as internally caused—that is, caused by the particular nature of the individual involved. On the other hand, when almost everybody does the same thing in a particular situation, we see this behavior as externally caused. These are examples of the way we attribute meanings in constructing images of other persons.

PERSONALITY AND CULTURE

The fact that there are individual differences is also real. Differences among individuals can be observed in contrived situations of tests or questionnaires. They can also be observed in more naturally occurring behavior. Some of these individual differences involve general patterns of personality that appear to vary with the cultural setting. This leads to the consideration of the area known as culture and personality— discussed in Chapter 26. There we observed that common personality patterns tend to reflect the culture in which they are found. This is true also for subcultures, as we saw in the case of achievement orientation of different religious subcultures. At the same time, we recognized that most personality variation cannot be accounted for on a cultural basis, that the personality variation within cultures still tends to be greater than that between cultures.

The range of individuality, however, may itself be different in different cultural settings. It has been suggested that contemporary Western society is especially constricting of individuality, albeit in subtle and indirect ways. This possibility served as the basis of our discussion in Chapter 27. Using David Riesman's *The Lonely Crowd* as our point of departure, we examined the thesis that modern man may be becoming more socially oriented and more alienated at the same time. This led us to an examination of the concept of alienation and the conditions that may give rise to it. Self-estrangement was an extreme form of alienation that we particularly noted. Although alienation appears to be severe in contemporary society, we found no systematic evidence that it is increasing. And while child-rearing evidence seems to support an other-directed trend for the American character, this does not necessarily undermine the fundamental uniqueness of each individual.

SCIENCE AND PERSONALITY

Earlier in this chapter we asked if personality is a real thing, a phenomenon of the natural world. We have partly answered by pointing out that the construction of an image of personality is real, and that individual differences (in part related to differences in society and culture) are real. But this evades part of the basis of asking the question. Science studies the world of nature by objective means. Is not personality largely a shadowy reality that must be grasped subjectively?

To put the objection plainly: personality is subjective, and science studies only objective things. How then can we presume to study personality-in-society in a scientific manner? To this there is not one answer, but several.

First, to say that science studies only objective phenomena means that the data must be observable in repeatable fashion. This does not mean we must necessarily limit ourselves to studying only physical things. If persons regularly give evidence of constructing their images of other persons along certain lines, this too can be a subject of scientific investigation.

Second, to say that personality is subjective is only partly correct. The organization of personality seems to be primarily subjective, but there may be objective indicators of this process in the way a person acts and what he says about himself.

Third, while it is extremely tricky to interpret personality data, and although what a person says about himself often cannot be interpreted at face value, this does not mean that we can make no interpretations at all. Rather, what all this does mean is that our results may be much more speculative than in other areas of scientific study. This is a caution, not an invalidation of the data.

Fourth, it must be noted that when all is said and done in terms of scientific study, most of the richness of personality still remains untapped. Psychologists and social scientists may point out important truths about personality, but most of our sense of understanding still comes from direct personal acquaintance.

THE BUILDING OF PERSONALITY

In Chapter 5 we suggested that personality may be considered as the organization of behavior at three levels: those of (1) the organism, (2) the private identity, and (3) the public identity. Let us use this classification as a basis for evaluating the social roots of personality.

The human person is, on one level, an organism. He is skin and bones and brain and blood. His body and its internal physiology provide an organization for behavior. Coordinated by the brain, his legs move to walk, his hands move to touch, and his lips move to talk.

Although the simple dichotomy of heredity versus environment is more a convenience of thought than a sharp line in nature, we find it useful to think of the organism as largely hereditary in nature. True, the food and oxygen we so vitally need come from the environment, and dietary differences can have an important effect upon body functioning. Also, we now know that different degrees of variety in early experience may affect the structural properties of the brain, and that conditioned responses may occur in internal visceral organs as well as in external actions. All of this clouds the simple association of the organism with heredity.

Nevertheless, it is possible to conceive of genetic factors as constantly present and affecting the behavior of the organism, sometimes directly and sometimes indirectly. By making numerous comparisons between identical twins and fraternal twins, as well as between other persons with different degrees of genetic relationship, it is possible to make calculations of the extent to which a given feature of personality is hereditary. Or, more correctly, we can calculate approximately how much of the variation of a given trait in a particular population at a particular time can be explained by genetic differences. Such "heritability indices" have been calculated to indicate that the genetic contributions range from 94 and 88 percent for height and weight, respectively, to about 50 percent for general neuroticism and schizophrenia, to extremely low measures for traits such as assertiveness and aggressiveness or for specific interests and attitudes (Heise, 1973). Intelligence appears to have an especially strong genetic component. Variations in measured intelligence (I.Q.) have been estimated in one analysis as 38 percent due to genetic variation within families, 49 percent due to genetic variation between families, 8 percent due to environmental differences among the individuals within families, and 5 percent due to environmental differences between families (Jinks and Fulker, 1970). Intellectual achievement, of course, has a much more important environmental contribution than such measures of I.Q. Among other characteristics that appear to have a very strong genetic base are introversion and extroversion; it has been estimated that genes control about two-thirds of the variation in these characteristics (Jinks and Fulker, 1970).

Again, it must be emphasized that genetic determinants are never separate from environmental factors in affecting the functioning of the organism. Therefore, to speak of a trait such as extroversion as being largely genetic is to say only that it is highly correlated with degrees of genetic relationship among individuals in a particular society. It is still a characteristic which requires certain environmental factors for its expression—such as, at a minimum, the presence of other people.

On another level, the human person is a private identity. He is an organization of thoughts and feelings about his own behavior. Society is far more important at this level than at the level of the organism, for it is on the basis of relationships to others that an individual develops his self-conceptions. As he interacts with others, he sees himself as stupid or smart, shy or gregarious, hard-working or lazy. And as he assimilates this interaction, he forms an identity. If his pattern of interaction changes, his sense of self also changes—generally in the direction which would be consistent with the evaluations of his friends (Manis, 1955).

Especially important in the private identity is the level of self-esteem. An individual's self-esteem tends to reflect the attention given to him by others. However, as Morris Rosenberg (1965) has shown in his study of adolescent self-conceptions, it is not so much the attention of others in general which fosters high self-esteem, but rather the attention of those of particular significance. For example, social class is positively associated with high self-esteem, especially for boys; but most of this association can be shown to be the result of the closer relationship to fathers at higher levels of socioeconomic status. Particularly damaging to self-esteem is parental indifference. Rosenberg found that even punitive parents produced children with higher levels of self-esteem than parents who were indifferent.

A third level of personality organization is the public identity—how we are known to other persons. The public identity is organized by the various social roles we play, and thus may also be called the role personality. Sometimes a job or a family role provides a central focus for other social roles, but only rarely does one role predominate over others to organize them all. We therefore tend to have different role personalities for different social situations. As William James (1890) observed long ago:

> *A man has as many social selves as there are individuals who recognize him* . . . as there are distinct *groups* of persons about whose opinions he cares. He generally shows a different side of himself to each of these different groups. Many a youth who is demure enough before his parents and teachers, swears and swaggers like a pirate among his "tough" young friends. We do not show ourselves to our children as to our club-companions, to our customers as to the laborers we employ, to our own masters and employers as to our intimate friends. From this there results what practically is a division of the man into several selves; and this may be a discordant splitting, as where one is afraid to let one set of his acquaintances know him as he is elsewhere; or it may be a perfectly harmonious division of labor, as where one tender to his children is stern to the soldiers or prisoners under his command (p. 294).

CONSISTENCY OF PERSONALITY

The functioning of the organism provides one kind of consistency for the personality. Temperature, for example, remains normally within a range of variation of about one degree Fahrenheit under the operation of internal physiological controls. The brain, too, has particular patterns of association and coordination that are fairly dependably wired into its functioning.

The strain toward consistency in self-conceptions is another key basis of consistency in personality. As we strive for consistency of our attitudes in general, we strive even more for consistency of those attitudes which have direct reference to the self.

Is there also a strain toward consistency in the public identity? Not directly in the sense that society decrees that all its roles must be in harmony. But indirectly, at least, there are several foundations of consistency in the public identity. For one thing, the search for self-consistency sets limits upon the variety of social roles a person will accept. For another, the reactions of others tend to be based upon the recognition of certain dominant roles (such as those of job and family) which are selected to give meaning to other roles. Finally, groups and social organizations have a tendency to standardize role relationships, thereby promoting another kind of consistency for the occupants of roles.

Thus, in several ways a rough consistency is fashioned for the behavior characteristic of a given person. This we perceive, in ourselves and in others, as personality. The personality we perceive may be a partial fabrication for the convenience of our perception, but it is never a total fabrication.

part eight: POSTSCRIPTS

The principle of the scientific method, in fact, is only a refinement by analysis and controls of the universal process of learning by experience. This is usually called common sense. The scientific addition to common sense is merely a more penetrating analysis of the complex factors involved, even in seemingly simple events, and the necessity of numerous repetitions and controls before conclusions are established.

A. J. Carlson

The final two chapters offer supplementary materials of a general nature.

Chapter 29 ("A Brief History of Social Psychology") gives a very brief historical survey of the development of social psychology.

Chapter 30 ("Research, Theory, and Practice") is an essay on the interrelationships of social psychological research, theory, and practice.

29
A Brief History of Social Psychology

The full history of social psychology may be pushed back in time almost indefinitely. Philosophers and practical men of affairs throughout history have provided many insights into social behavior. However, it is only in the twentieth century that social psychology has come to be recognized as an academic field. Our attention to its history will therefore be limited mostly to the present century. We shall also give primary emphasis to the United States, which has been, up to now, the home of most persons considering themselves to be social psychologists.

THE FIRST TEXTBOOKS

The year 1908 marked the first appearance of social psychology textbooks. There were in fact two textbooks published in that year, one by a psychologist, William McDougall, and one by a sociologist, E. A. Ross. McDougall (1908) saw social psychology as the study of the expression of instincts in the social life of man. These instincts are biologically rooted strivings that were assumed to represent the foundat.ons of all social behavior. In contrast, Ross (1908) saw social psychology as a field largely devoted to the study of "psychic planes and currents" in society. These psychic planes and currents take their form in such phenomena as crowds, fashions, and patterns of conventional behavior, all considered to be the consequences of the interaction of human beings.

What McDougall and Ross had in common was a functional approach to the study of social behavior; neither was content simply to describe and catalog forms of behavior. But they differed sharply in what they saw social forms as functions of. McDougall saw them as functions of biologically rooted strivings, whereas Ross saw them as functions of social interaction.

McDougall and Ross also differed sharply in their conceptions of the field of social psychology. McDougall saw it as concerned primarily with questions of motivation, whereas Ross considered social psychology to be a special phase of the study of society. However, neither of these continued long as the prevalent view. Among psychologists, a dominant concern to study social behavior as *behavior* soon displaced McDougall's concern for biological motivation. And among sociologists an interest in the social roots of personality soon displaced society's

327

planes and currents as the main focus of social psychology. By the early 1920s these newer trends were well established in social psychology textbooks and courses.

BEHAVIORISM AND INTERACTIONISM

Social psychology as presented by psychologists and social psychology as presented by sociologists have been somewhat different ever since the original works by McDougall and Ross. During the 1920s, however, these two disciplines came to contrast more clearly in their treatment of social psychology. Psychologists became more oriented to a behaviorist approach, while sociologists became more oriented to questions of the nature of the social self.

Behaviorism was primarily a revolt against speculation and introspection in psychology. Early behaviorists, such as John B. Watson, urged that psychology must be made thoroughly scientific and objective. This required the exclusion of subjective concepts and speculations, for only those aspects of behavior that may be externally observed and measured were considered suitable for a *science* of psychology. Psychology thus became the science of behavior rather than the study of mind. According to this view, mind was not a suitable concept at all for such a study; only the more elementary units of the behavior of organisms were considered as providing suitable handles for investigation. *Stimulus* and *response* came to be key concepts for research and theory. And favorite problems of investigation came to center around the modification of individual behavior—or, as it was usually called, learning. This was examined primarily in terms of particular responses and the stimulus conditions that produced them.

These themes of behaviorism never became quite so strong in social psychology as they did in some other areas of psychology. Social psychology did, however, come to be conceived by many psychologists simply as the study of individual responses to social stimuli. A leading influence in this direction was Floyd Allport (1924), whose very influential textbook was based on an individualistic conception of man as "essentially an enormously complex system of reflex arcs" (p. 139).

Sociologists, meanwhile, were eager to reject an individualistic conception of man and his behavior. Writers such as Charles H. Cooley and John Dewey had emphasized the unity between the individual and society since the early days of the century. And the University of Chicago, chief center for the training of American sociologists during most of the first half of the twentieth century, provided a setting where questions about personality and questions about society were not sharply distinguished. Important influences there were W. I. Thomas, Ellsworth Faris, Robert Park, E. W. Burgess, and George H. Mead. Mead (1934), even though technically a member of the philosophy department, was particularly influential in his lectures on social psychology. The point of view among such sociologically oriented students of social behavior (especially associated with the names of Cooley, Dewey, and Mead) has come to be known as *symbolic interactionism.*

Symbolic interactionism has as its key themes the social nature of the self and the symbolic nature of distinctively human behavior. The self is seen as originating chiefly through internalizing those patterns that are characteristic of an individual's interaction with others. He becomes a self-conscious entity by, in Mead's phrase, "taking the role of the other" and perceiving his own behavior from the standpoint of other persons. Such role-taking provides not only habits of responding to others but also standards for evaluating and organizing one's own behavior. This self-reflection, which organizes nearly all behavior, takes place through symbolic forms, which are themselves learned through interaction with other persons. Language provides the most obvious example of these symbolic forms, learned through interaction with others and then used as the basis for self-reflection and behavioral organization.

Although Mead liked to call his approach *social behaviorism*, it is clear that he was interested in questions that were much broader than the stimulus-response models of main-line behaviorism. It is also clear that investigations of such subjects as the social self, role-taking, or the symbolic organization of behavior are less susceptible to rigorous research designs than were studies of stimulus-response patterns. It is thus not surprising that by the 1930s a pattern of suspicion was already set between psychologically and sociologically oriented social psychologists. Psychologists were suspicious of sociologists for talking too much in general terms and providing very little clear-cut research, and sociologists were suspicious of psychologists for focusing on minor details and ignoring larger questions about relationships between self and society.

PSYCHOANALYSIS

While psychoanalysis has had more direct impact upon clinical psychology and psychiatry than upon social psychology, its impact upon social psychology has also been considerable. Most social psychologists, however, have been reluctant to accept psychoanalytic theories in their original forms.

Sigmund Freud made most of his great clinical discoveries, including the importance of unconscious motivation and the mechanism of repression, before 1900. However, his most systematic theories (especially his final theory of life and death instincts and his theory of the personality as composed of the subsystems of id, ego, and superego) were not elaborated until about 1920. Although there were some references to Freud in social psychology textbooks of the 1920s, especially that of Allport (1924), it was not till the 1930s that psychoanalysis began to be a major force in social psychology. Even then, social psychology showed about as much resistance to Freudian ideas as acceptance of them.

Behavioristically oriented social psychologists were naturally skeptical about Freud's emphasis upon the deep-seated motivational roots of behavior. They were accustomed to giving the emphasis to factors of the immediate stimulus situation. Furthermore, Freud, though claiming the mantle of science, had a rather unscientific style in using concepts without precise definitions and in formulating sweeping generalizations.

Sociologically trained social psychologists also were bothered by

Freud's views of motivation. They tended to consider Freudianism as both too biological in its view of basic instincts and too individualistic in its conception of the expression of these instincts. The symbolic interactionists (who came to represent most sociologically trained social psychologists) particularly objected to Freud's emphasis upon deeply rooted unconscious and emotional factors at the expense of what they considered to be the more important conscious and situational factors.

With such differences in perspective, it is not surprising that neither psychological nor sociological camps of social psychology showed a general conversion to psychoanalysis. However, many of the particular insights of Freud have been incorporated into working hypotheses for social psychological research. Even stronger have been the influences of some of the neo-Freudians, such as Karen Horney, Erich Fromm, Harry Stack Sullivan, and Erik Erikson. These psychoanalysts have tended to reject Freud's instinct theories, replacing them with an emphasis upon the social origins of basic motives. This has proved more acceptable to most social psychologists than orthodox Freudianism.

Psychoanalysis has not produced a sudden or total revolution in social psychology. But neither have psychonalytic ideas proved to be just a passing fad. The influence of psychoanalysis has been gradual and has focused primarily on particular questions (especially those concerning early socialization). Nevertheless, the general influence of psychoanalysis upon social psychology has remained strong to this day.

GESTALT PSYCHOLOGY AND COGNITIVE THEORY

Although it originated some years earlier in Europe, especially Germany, it was not till the 1930s that the gestalt tradition began to have a strong impact in America. Its influence upon psychology was felt especially as a counterweight against the earlier behaviorism, and its impact upon social psychology was particularly strong.

The German word *Gestalt* can probably best be translated as *configuration*. This points to the central idea of gestalt psychology: that is, that one must recognize properties of organization in phenomena. The whole is more than the sum of its parts, emphasized the early gestalt psychologists (including Max Wertheimer, Wolfgang Köhler, and Kurt Koffka), and one must avoid the behaviorist tendency to reduce phenomena to the simplest possible elements. Human behavior must also be seen as a structured whole, in larger *molar units* rather than simply in *molecular units*. The gestaltists were hostile to all forms of reductionism—not only the behaviorist reduction of complex phenomena to elementary units but also the sociological determinism that reduced the behavior of the individual to societal forms and to the *genetic fallacy* of psychoanalysis, which explained adult behavior in terms of long-past childhood experiences. A more holistic approach to human behavior was held to be required, and the study of the processes of perception and cognition was usually suggested as the proper place to begin.

The gestalt psychologist who undoubtedly made the greatest contribution to social psychology was Kurt Lewin. Departing somewhat from the more biological orientation of some of the gestaltists, Lewin emphasized that behavior was always a function of the entire field of forces operating at a given time. Some of these forces are features of the personality, and some are features of the social situation in which the individual is placed. Behavior, however, always reflects the total field, not just some of the factors. What is needed, then, is a *field theory*, for which Lewin tried to supply the main outlines. A key concept of Lewin's field theory was that of *life space*, the total situation as it exists for a person at a given time. Only by adequately perceiving a person's life space, Lewin insisted, could we understand his behavior.

Social psychology provided a fertile ground for the influence of Lewin and his field theory. Not only did he develop concepts to bridge the gap between person and group, but he also inspired careful experimental analysis of social behavior. Psychologically oriented social psychologists found in such an approach a way to deal more fully with complex social influences, and sociologically oriented social psychologists were impressed by the experimental rigor that Lewin and his followers introduced to the study of social behavior—even to the ambiguities of group dynamics, a field in which Lewin had come to take a special interest before his death in 1947.

Generally associated with the influence of gestalt psychology and field theory, but in some respects broader than either of these schools of thought, has been the growth of cognitive theory in psychology. The revulsion of the behaviorist against the use of mentalistic concepts has been to a large extent overcome as human cognitive processes have proven more and more susceptible to experimental study. This cognitive emphasis is very much in harmony with some of the primary themes of symbolic interactionism (seeing behavior as a product of internalized organizations of experience). Also, some of the more recent variations of psychoanalysis (especially the emphasis upon ego psychology by latter-day Freudians) have been at least compatible with most forms of recent cognitive theory.

In the last decade, cognitive theory has become an especially central concern of social psychologists. Theories of cognitive consistency, such as Heider's balance theory or Festinger's theory of cognitive dissonance, have been particularly prominent in their stimulus of current research.

CONTEMPORARY TRENDS

In this brief historical sketch we have emphasized the contributions of four dominant movements in twentieth-century social psychology: (1) behaviorism, (2) symbolic interactionism, (3) psychoanalysis, and (4) relatives of the gestalt school. There have of course been many other movements of schools of thought. While their impact upon the total field of social psychology may have been less than the four approaches specifically discussed above, the following have also had important influences:

1. The sociometric movement of J. L. Moreno
2. The human relations approach in industry, associated with such persons as Elton Mayo and Fritz Roethlisberger

3. The students of child development, most notably Jean Piaget
4. The culture-and-personality studies undertaken by numerous anthropologists
5. Studies of learning, especially recent work on operant conditioning inspired by B. F. Skinner
6. The interaction process analysis by modern sociologists such as Robert F. Bales

Each of these has been discussed at least briefly elsewhere in this book, and we shall not go into any further discussion of them now. Rather, let us attempt to indicate what appear to be some of the more significant trends of social psychology at the present time.

One of the important trends seems to be toward a convergence of the psychological and sociological approaches. There still tend to be some differences in emphasis between social psychology courses taught in psychology departments and those taught in sociology departments, but the differences are considerably less pronounced than they were thirty years ago. Increasingly, psychologists and sociologists are finding that they have much to learn from each other, at least so far as social psychology is concerned.

A second trend in contemporary social psychology is toward more demanding methodological standards. More emphasis is placed upon laboratory experimentation, and standards of experimental design have become more critical. Nonlaboratory methods of research, when used, have also become more sophisticated.

A third trend, related to the second, is that theory is becoming more precise and explicit. *Theory,* as used in much of this book, has implied a set of general ideas about some phenomenon. In contemporary social psychology, theory sometimes takes on the more formal meaning of a set of logically related propositions that, if supported, would take on the status of scientific laws. Theory, in this process, has become both more logically systematic and more empirically precise.

Finally, we may mention the ever increasing pattern of specialization. Anyone who attempts to keep up with the research literature (published in such journals as the *Journal of Personality and Social Psychology,* the *Journal of Experimental Social Psychology,* and *Sociometry*) must notice how specialized some of the research questions have become. Such specialization makes it more and more difficult to represent the entire field of social psychology in an introductory textbook. Thus this book is intended to serve as only the barest introduction to the field. Many varied and exciting opportunities, which have only been hinted at in the preceding pages, remain for further study.

30
Research, Theory, and Practice

Many examples of research have been cited in this book. They have varied in design from formal to informal, in locale from laboratory to field, and in results from dramatic to piddling. Is there anything that they generally have in common? Let us identify one common denominator: they have all aimed at improved conceptualization about social behavior. They may have done this in different ways—by calling attention to a variable not previously considered important, by demonstrating how variables combine in producing results, or by distinguishing what really causes an effect from what is only incidentally associated. In all of these cases the main purpose of research is to improve our image of reality. This image of reality, when carefully formulated into word pictures, is what we call theory. *The primary purpose of research is to improve theory.*

Theory consists of concepts and relational terms organized into propositions that assert something about the nature of reality. In social theory the propositions give a model of some recurrent aspect of social life. Scientific theory is aimed always at generalization; by this we mean that the purpose of theory is not to describe in detail the unique event, but to point to what is common among events. It thus gives us a handle for dealing with diverse events rather than a complete representation of any particular event.

Research aids in theory development by helping us know how well the predictions implied by our theories correspond to reality. A theory is almost never simply true or false; rather it is either better or less well supported by evidence than some other formulation. The gathering of evidence to test and revise theoretical formulations is the primary work of research.

But why theory? Why should we want to formulate general conceptualizations of events? Why should we want to develop models of reality?

These questions may be partly beside the point, for whether or not we want to formulate general conceptualizations, we do. And.why we do has something to do with the kind of cerebral creatures we are, animals whose peculiar adjustment has come to include taking thought. Reflection is an inevitable part of living. But how much does our reflection give us understanding? Here is the key point at which theory comes in. *The primary purpose of theory is to improve understanding.*

Understanding is the sense, supported by some kind of validating activity, that one's ideas have a fitness both with each other and with the world outside our heads. This sense can be cultivated by wishful thinking, and we all fool ourselves to some extent into thinking the world is the way we might wish. We must therefore allow for a distinction between understanding and the *feeling* of understanding. The clue to the distinction is in that qualifying phrase in the opening sentence of this paragraph indicating that understanding is *supported by some kind of validating activity*. The validating activity to support our sense of understanding is primarily of two kinds: logical and empirical.

We may logically analyze our ideas to see whether or not they fit together or whether they pose inconsistencies for each other. This need not be carried out through the formal discipline of logic, but may be done quite informally (for example, it just doesn't make sense that I'm not going to die if all people must die).

We may also validate our sense of understanding by empirical activity. This consists of making predictions on the basis of our ideas and then observing to see if the predictions are correct. Again, this need not be formalized into scientific hypothesis testing. Much more common is the informal checking to see if expectations are supported (for example, if I study harder, I'll do better on the next test).

With such activities we support our understanding by making the theoretical content of our understanding more valid. The personal validation of our own understanding through logical and empirical activities thus runs quite parallel to what research accomplishes on a more collective level. Much as research uses logical operations and empirical measurement to refine theory in a publicly stated manner, so in a similar manner on the personal level we use logical and empirical tools to refine our understanding. When we get support for our ideas through these tools, both our sense of understanding and our real understanding may be increased.

But what good is understanding? Why might we seek to know the truth even when the truth may be painful? The answer is that understanding must generally provide some kind of benefit for us, even if not always experienced directly. Let us suggest that most of the time increased understanding has its value in improved adjustment. With more intelligence we can act more effectively. That isn't always true, of course; but it is true more often than the converse. And so understanding is usually an asset for living. *The primary purpose of understanding is to improve practical adjustment in everyday life.*

We have made three main points in this discussion:

1. The primary purpose of research is to improve theory.
2. The primary purpose of theory is to improve understanding.
3. The primary purpose of understanding is to improve practical adjustment in everyday life.

Having made these points, we must hasten to add what they do not say. They do not say that the only purpose of research is to improve theory. Some research is done simply for methodological development;

on the other hand, some research may have a direct practical aim, such as market research.

Also, we have not said that the only purpose of theory is understanding. Theory building also may be pursued as an abstract exercise for its own sake, and some theorists may get a thrill from their work akin to the satisfaction of a musician with his composition.

Furthermore, not all understanding is necessarily practical. Some understanding may be relatively useless except for its satisfaction of pleasures of the mind.

With these points and qualifications, it should be evident that social psychology seldom comes to us in a form that will point out directly the way we should go about solving our personal and social problems. The data of the research findings of social psychology is highly relevant for the solution of such problems, as Alan C. Elms's recent book (1972) well illustrates. But the application and implications are generally indirect—through theory development and the understanding inspired by theory—rather than from the research directly.

References

Aderman, David. "Elation, Depression and Helping Behavior," *Journal of Personality and Social Psychology*, 24 (1972), 91–101.

Adorno, Theodor W., Else Frenkel-Brunswik, Daniel J. Levinson, and R. Nevitt Sanford. *The Authoritarian Personality*. New York: Harper & Row, 1950.

Allport, Floyd H. "The Influence of the Group Upon Association and Thought," *Journal of Experimental Psychology*, 3 (1920), 159–182.

———. *Social Psychology*. Boston: Houghton Mifflin, 1924.

Allport, Gordon W. *The Nature of Prejudice*. Garden City, N.Y.: Anchor Books, 1958; original edition published by Addison-Wesley, 1954.

———, and Leo Postman. *The Basic Psychology of Rumor*. New York: Holt, Rinehart and Winston, 1947.

American Psychological Association. *Ethical Principles in the Conduct of Research with Human Participants*. Washington, D.C.: A.P.A., 1973.

Aronson, Elliot. "Some Antecedents of Interpersonal Attraction." In W. Arnold and D. Levine (eds.), *Nebraska Symposium on Motivation, 1969*, pp. 143–173. Lincoln: University of Nebraska Press, 1969.

———, and Judson Mills. "The Effect of Severity of Initiation on Liking for a Group," *Journal of Abnormal and Social Psychology*, 59 (1959), 177–181.

Asch, Solomon E. "Forming Impressions of Personality," *Journal of Abnormal and Social Psychology*, 41 (1946), 258–290.

———. "Effects of Group Pressure upon the Modification and Distortion of Judgments." In H. Guetzkow (ed.), *Groups, Leadership, and Men*, pp. 177–190. Pittsburgh: Carnegie Press, 1951.

———. *Social Psychology*. Englewood Cliffs, N.J.: Prentice-Hall, 1952.

———. "Opinions and Social Pressure," *Scientific American*, November 1955, pp. 31–35.

Backman, Carl W., and Paul F. Secord. "Liking, Selective Interaction, and Misperception in Congruent Interpersonal Relations," *Sociometry*, 25 (1962), 321–335.

———. "The Compromise Process and the Affect Structure of Groups," *Human Relations*, 17 (1964), 19–22.

Bales, Robert F. *Interaction Process Analysis, A Method for the Study of Small Groups*. Reading, Mass.: Addison-Wesley, 1950.

———. "Task Roles and Social Roles in Problem-Solving Groups." In E. Maccoby, T. Newcomb, and E. Hartley (eds.), *Readings in Social Psychology*. 3rd ed., pp. 437–447. New York: Holt, Rinehart and Winston, 1958.

———, and Philip E. Slater. "Role Differentiation in Small Decision-making Groups." In T. Parsons, R. Bales, et al., *Family, Socialization, and Interaction Process*, pp. 259–306. New York: Free Press, 1955.

Bandura, Albert. "Vicarious Processes: A Case of No-trial Learning." In L. Berkowitz (ed.), *Advances in Experimental Social Psychology*, II, 1–55. New York: Academic Press, 1965.

———, and Aletha C. Huston. "Identification as a Process of Incidental Learning," *Journal of Abnormal and Social Psychology*, 63 (1961), 311–318.

———, Dorothea Ross, and Sheila A. Ross. "A Comparative Test of the Status Envy, Social Power, and Secondary Reinforcement Theories of Identificatory Learning," *Journal of Abnormal and Social Psychology*, 67 (1963), 527–534.

———, and Richard H. Walters. *Social Learning and Personality Development*. New York: Holt, Rinehart and Winston, 1963.

Bass, Bernard M. *Leadership, Psychology, and Organizational Behavior*. New York: Harper & Row, 1960.

Baumrind, Diana. "Some Thoughts on Ethics of Research: After Reading Milgram's 'Behavioral Study of Obedience,'" *American Psychologist*, 19 (1964), 421–423.

Bavelas, Alex. "A Mathematical Model for Group Structures," *Applied Anthropology*, 7 (1948), 16–30.

———. "Communication Patterns in Task-Oriented Groups," *Journal of the Acoustical Society of America*, 22 (1950), 725–730.

Bem, Daryl J. "Self-Perception Theory." In L. Berkowitz (ed.), *Advances in Experimental Social Psychology*, VI, 1–62. New York: Academic Press, 1972.

Berkowitz, Leonard. *Aggression: A Social Psychological Analysis*. New York: McGraw-Hill, 1962.

———, and Russell G. Geen. "Film Violence and the Cue Properties of Available Targets," *Journal of Personality and Social Psychology*, 3 (1966), 525–530.

Berscheid, Ellen, Karen Dion, Elaine Walster, and G. William Walster. "Physical Attractiveness and Dating Choice: A Test of the Matching Hypothesis," *Journal of Experimental Social Psychology*, 7 (1971), 173–189.

Bettelheim, Bruno. "Individual and Mass Behavior in Extreme Situations," *Journal of Abnormal and Social Psychology*, 38 (1943), 417–452.

Blau, Peter M. *The Dynamics of Bureaucracy*. 2nd ed. Chicago: University of Chicago Press, 1963.

———. *Exchange and Power in Social Life*. New York: Wiley, 1964.

Blumer, Herbert. "Collective Behavior." In A. Lee (ed.), *Principles of Sociology*. 2nd ed., pp. 165–198. New York: Barnes & Noble, 1951.

Bramel, Dana. "A Dissonance Theory Approach to Defensive Projection," *Journal of Abnormal and Social Psychology*, 64 (1962), 121–129.

———. "Selection of a Target for Defensive Projection," *Journal of Abnormal and Social Psychology*, 66 (1963), 318–324.

Brehm, Jack W., and Arthur R. Cohen. *Explorations in Cognitive Dissonance*. New York: Wiley, 1962.

Bridgman, Percy W. *The Logic of Modern Physics*. New York: Macmillan, 1928.

Brim, Orville G., Jr. "Family Structure and Sex Role Learning by Children: A Further Analysis of Helen Koch's Data," *Sociometry*, 21 (1958), 1–16.

Britt, Steuart H. (ed.). *Selected Readings in Social Psychology*. New York: Holt, Rinehart and Winston, 1950.

Bronfenbrenner, Urie. "The Changing American Child—A Speculative Analysis," *The Journal of Social Issues*, 17 (1961), 6–18.

Brown, Junius F. *Psychology and the Social Order*. New York: McGraw-Hill, 1936.

Brown, Roger W. "Language and Categories." In J. Bruner, J. Goodnow, and G. Austin, *A Study of Thinking*, pp. 247–312. New York: Wiley, 1956.

———. *Social Psychology*. New York: Free Press, 1965.

———, and Eric H. Lenneberg. "A Study in Language and Cognition," *Journal of Abnormal and Social Psychology*, 49 (1954), 454–462.

Bruch, Hilde. "Transformation of Oral Impulses in Eating Disorders: A Conceptual Approach," *Psychiatric Quarterly*, 35 (1961), 458–481.

Bruner, Jerome S., and Renato Tagiuri. "The Perception of People." In G. Lindzey (ed.), *Handbook of Social Psychology*, II, 634–654. Reading, Mass.: Addison-Wesley, 1954.

Buchanan, William, and Hadley Cantril. *How Nations See Each Other*. Urbana: University of Illinois Press, 1953.

Burke, Peter J. "The Development of Task and Social-Emotional Role Differentiation," *Sociometry*, 30 (1967), 379–392.

Burton, R. V. "The Generality of Honesty Reconsidered," *Psychological Review*, 70 (1963), 481–499.

Buss, Arnold H. *The Psychology of Aggression*. New York: Wiley, 1961.

Byrne, Donn. "Attitudes and Attraction." In L. Berkowitz (ed.), *Advances in Experimental Social Psychology*, IV, 35–89. New York: Academic Press, 1969.

———. *The Attraction Paradigm*. New York: Academic Press, 1971.

Cantril, Hadley, Hazel Gaudet, and Herta Herzog. *The Invasion from Mars.* Princeton, N.J.: Princeton University Press, 1940.

Carey, Alex. "The Hawthorne Studies: A Radical Criticism," *American Sociological Review*, 32 (1967), 403–416.

Carlsmith, J. Merrill, Barry E. Collins, and Robert K. Helmreich. "Studies in Forced Compliance: I. The Effect of Pressure for Compliance on Attitude Change Produced by Face-to-face Role Playing and Anonymous Essay Writing," *Journal of Personality and Social Psychology*, 4 (1966), 1–13.

Carroll, John B. (ed.). *Language, Thought and Reality: Selected Writings of Benjamin Lee Whorf.* Cambridge, Mass.: Technology Press, and New York: Wiley, 1956.

Carter, Lewis F., Richard J. Hill, and S. Dale McLemore. "Social Conformity and Attitude Change Within Non Laboratory Groups," *Sociometry*, 30 (1967), 1–14.

Chapanis, Natalia P., and Alphonse Chapanis. "Cognitive Dissonance: Five Years Later," *Psychological Bulletin*, 61 (1964), 1–22.

Chapple, Eliot, and Conrad Arensberg. *Measuring Human Relations: An Introduction to the Study of the Interaction of Individuals.* Genetic Psychology Monographs. Provincetown, Mass.: Journal Press, 1940.

Chemers, Martin, and George J. Skrzypek. "Experimental Test of the Contingency Model of Leadership Effectiveness," *Journal of Personality and Social Psychology*, 24 (1972), 172–177.

Coch, Lester, and John R. P. French, Jr., "Overcoming Resistance to Change," *Human Relations*, 1 (1948), 512–532.

Cooley, Charles H. *Social Organization.* New York: Scribner, 1909.

————. *Human Nature and the Social Order.* New York: Scribner, 1922; first printing, 1902.

Crutchfield, Richard S. "Conformity and Character," *American Psychologist*, 10 (1955), 191–198.

Darley, John, and Bibb Latané. "Bystander Intervention in Emergencies: Diffusion of Responsibility," *Journal of Personality and Social Psychology*, 8 (1968), 377–383.

Davis, Allison, and John Dollard. *Children of Bondage: The Personality Development of Negro Youth in the Urban South.* Washington, D.C.: American Council on Education, 1940; also New York: Torchbooks, 1964.

Davis, Kingsley. "Extreme Social Isolation of a Child," *American Journal of Sociology*, 45 (1940), 554–565.

————. "Final Note on a Case of Extreme Isolation," *American Journal of Sociology*, 52 (1947), 432–437.

Deutsch, Morton, and Harold B. Gerard. "A Study of Normative and Informational Social Influences upon Individual Judgment," *Journal of Abnormal and Social Psychology*, 51 (1955), 629–636.

Dollard, John, Leonard W. Doob, Neal E. Miller, O. Hobart Mowrer, and Robert R. Sears. *Frustration and Aggression.* New Haven: Yale University Press, 1939.

Elms, Alan C. *Social Psychology and Social Relevance.* Boston: Little, Brown, 1972.

Erikson, Erik H. *Childhood and Society.* 2nd ed. New York: Norton, 1963.

Festinger, Leon. "Informal Social Communication," *Psychological Review*, 57 (1950), 271–282.

————. "A Theory of Social Comparison Processes," *Human Relations*, 7 (1954), 117–140.

————. *A Theory of Cognitive Dissonance.* New York: Harper & Row, 1957.

————, and J. Merrill Carlsmith. "Cognitive Consequences of Forced Compliance," *Journal of Abnormal and Social Psychology*, 58 (1959), 203–210.

————, Henry W. Riecken, and Stanley Schachter. *When Prophecy Fails.* Minneapolis: University of Minnesota Press, 1956.

Fiedler, Fred E. "A Contingency Model of Leadership Effectiveness." In L. Berkowitz (ed.), *Advances in Experimental Social Psychology*, I, 149–190. New York: Academic Press, 1964.

Finck, H. T. *Romantic Love and Personal Beauty: Their Development, Causal Relations, Historic and National Peculiarities.* London: Macmillan, 1891.

French, John R. P., Jr., Joachim Israel, and Dagfinn Ås. "An Experiment on Participation in a Norwegian Factory," *Human Relations,* 13 (1960), 3–19.

Freud, Sigmund. "The Passing of the Oedipus-Complex," in *Collected Papers,* II, 269–282. London: Hogarth Press, 1924.

———. *Civilization and Its Discontents.* New York: Anchor Books, no date; first published by Hogarth Press, 1930.

———. "Totem and Taboo." In A. A. Brill (ed.), *The Basic Writings of Sigmund Freud,* pp. 805–930. New York: Random House, 1938; first printing, 1913.

Furth, Hans G. *Thinking Without Language: Psychological Implications of Deafness.* New York: Free Press, 1966.

Goffman, Erving. "On Face-Work: An Analysis of Ritual Elements in Social Interaction," *Psychiatry,* 18 (1955), 213–231.

———. "The Nature of Deference and Demeanor," *American Anthropologist,* 58 (1956), 473–502.

———. *The Presentation of Self in Everyday Life.* Garden City, N.Y.: Doubleday, 1959.

Goldenweiser, Alexander. "Totemism: An Essay on Religion and Society." In V. Calverton (ed.), *The Making of Man: An Outline of Anthropology,* pp. 363–392. New York: Random House, 1931.

Graen, George, Kenneth Alvares, James B. Orris, and Joseph A. Martella. "The Contingency Model of Leadership Effectiveness: Antecedent and Evidential Results," *Psychological Bulletin,* 74 (1970), 285–295.

Grimshaw, Allen D. "Urban Racial Violence in the United States: Changing Ecological Considerations," *American Journal of Sociology,* 66 (1960), 109–119.

Gudschinsky, Sarah C. "The ABC's of Lexicostatistics (Glottochronology)," *Word,* 12 (1956), 175–210.

Guttman, Louis. "The Problem of Attitude and Opinion Measurement" and "The Basis for Scalogram Analysis." In S. A. Stouffer, L. Guttman, E. A. Suchman, P. F. Lazarsfeld, Shirley A. Star, and J. A. Gardner (eds.), *Measurement and Prediction,* pp. 46–90. Princeton, N.J.: Princeton University Press, 1950.

Hahn, Emily. "Washoese," *The New Yorker,* December 11, 1971, pp. 54–98.

Harlow, Harry F. "The Heterosexual Affectional System in Monkeys," *American Psychologist,* 17 (1962), 1–9.

———, and Margaret K. Harlow. "The Affectional Systems." In A. Schrier, H. Harlow, and F. Stollnitz (eds.), *Behavior of Nonhuman Primates,* II, 287–334. New York: Academic Press, 1965.

———. "Learning to Love," *American Scientist,* 54 (1966), 244–272.

Hartshorne, Hugh, and Mark A. May. *Studies in Deceit.* Studies in the Nature of Character, vol. 1. New York: Macmillan, 1928.

Hayes, Cathy. *The Ape in Our House.* New York: Harper & Row, 1951.

Heider, Fritz. "Social Perception and Phenomenal Causality," *Psychological Review,* 51 (1944), 358–374.

———. *The Psychology of Interpersonal Relations.* New York: Wiley, 1958.

Heise, David R. *Personality: Biosocial Bases.* Chicago: Rand McNally, 1973.

Hendrick, Clyde, and Steven R. Brown. "Introversion, Extroversion, and Interpersonal Attraction," *Journal of Personality and Social Psychology,* 20 (1971), 31–36.

Hertzler, Joyce O. *A Sociology of Language.* New York: Random House, 1965.

Hoebel, E. Adamson. *The Cheyennes: Indians of the Great Plains.* New York: Holt, Rinehart and Winston, 1960.

Hoffer, Eric. *The True Believer.* New York: New American Library, 1958; originally published by Harper & Row, 1951.

Hollingshead, August B. *Elmtown's Youth: The Impact of Social Classes on Adolescents.* New York: Wiley, 1949.

———. "Cultural Factors in the Selection of Marriage Mates," *American Sociological Review,* 15 (1950), 619–627.

Homans, George C. *The Human Group.* New York: Harcourt, Brace & World, 1950.

———. "Group Factors in Worker Productivity." In E. Maccoby, T. Newcomb, and E. Hartley (eds.), *Readings in Social Psychology.* 3rd ed., pp. 583–595. New York: Holt, Rinehart and Winston, 1958a.

———. "Social Behavior as Exchange," *American Journal of Sociology*, 62 (1958b), 597–606.

———. *Social Behavior: Its Elementary Forms.* New York: Harcourt, Brace & World, 1961.

Huxley, Aldous. *Brave New World.* New York: Bantam Books, 1953; first published, 1932.

Inkeles, Alex, "Personality and Social Structure." In R. Merton, L. Broom, and L. Cottrell (eds.), *Sociology Today*, pp. 249–276. New York: Basic Books, 1959.

Isen, Alice M. "Success, Failure, and Reaction to Others: The Warm Glow of Success," *Journal of Personality and Social Psychology*, 8 (1970), 294–301.

Jackson, Elton F., William S. Fox, and Harry J. Crockett, Jr. "Religion and Occupational Achievement," *American Sociological Review*, 35 (1970), 48–63.

Jacob, Philip E. *Changing Values in College: An Exploratory Study of the Impact of College Teaching.* New York: Harper & Row, 1957.

James, William. *Principles of Psychology.* New York: Holt, 1890.

Jennings, Helen Hall. "Sociometric Differentiation of the Psychegroup and the Sociogroup," *Sociometry*, 10 (1947), 71–79.

———. *Leadership and Isolation: A Study of Personality in Inter-Personal Relations.* 2nd ed. London: Longmans, Green, 1950.

Jinks, J. L., and D. W. Fulker. "Comparison of the Biometrical Genetical, MAVA, and Classical Approaches to the Analysis of Human Behavior," *Psychological Bulletin*, 73 (1970), 311–349.

Kaplan, Bert. "Personality and Social Structure." In J. Gittler (ed.), *Review of Sociology: Analysis of a Decade*, pp. 87–126. New York: Wiley, 1957.

——— (ed.). *Studying Personality Cross-Culturally.* New York: Harper & Row, 1961.

Kardiner, Abram. *The Individual and His Society.* New York: Columbia University Press, 1939.

———. *The Psychological Frontiers of Society.* New York: Columbia University Press, 1945.

Katz, Elihu, and Paul F. Lazarsfeld. *Personal Influence: The Part Played by People in the Flow of Mass Communications.* New York: Free Press, 1955.

Keller, Helen. *The Story of My Life.* Garden City, N.Y.: Doubleday, 1954; first published, 1903.

Kelley, Harold H. "The Warm-Cold Variable in First Impressions of Persons," *Journal of Personality*, 18 (1950), 431–439.

———. "Attribution Theory in Social Psychology." In D. Levine (ed.), *Nebraska Symposium on Motivation, 1967*, pp. 192–238. Lincoln: University of Nebraska Press, 1967.

Kerner, Otto (chm.). *Report of the National Advisory Commission on Civil Disorders.* Advance ed. New York: Bantam Books, 1968.

Kitch, M. J. *Capitalism and the Reformation.* London: Longmans, Green, 1967.

Kohlberg, Lawrence. "Development of Moral Character and Moral Ideology." In M. and L. Hoffman (eds.), *Review of Child Development Research*, I, 383–431. New York: Russell Sage Foundation, 1964.

LaBarre, Weston. *The Human Animal.* Chicago: University of Chicago Press, 1954.

Langer, Ellen J., and Robert P. Abelson, "The Semantics of Asking a Favor: How to Succeed in Getting Help without Really Dying," *Journal of Personality and Social Psychology*, 24 (1972), 26–32.

Latané, Bibb, and John M. Darley. "Bystander 'Apathy,'" *American Scientist*, 57 (1969), 244–268.

————, and Judith Rodin. "A Lady in Distress: Inhibiting Effects of Friends and Strangers on Bystander Intervention," *Journal of Experimental Social Psychology*, 5 (1969), 189–202.

Leavitt, Harold J. "Some Effects of Certain Communication Patterns on Group Performance," *Journal of Abnormal and Social Psychology*, 46 (1951), 38–50.

LeBon, Gustave. *The Crowd: A Study of the Popular Mind*. New York: Viking, 1960; first published, 1895.

Leik, Robert K. "Instrumentality and Emotionality in Family Interaction," *Sociometry*, 26 (1963), 131–145.

Lenski, Gerhard. *The Religious Factor*. Garden City, N.Y.: Doubleday, 1961.

Levinger, George, and J. Diedrick Snoek. *Attraction in Relationship: A New Look at Interpersonal Attraction*. Morristown, N.J.: General Learning Press, 1972.

Lewin, Kurt. "Experiments in Social Space," *Harvard Educational Review*, 9 (1930), 21–32.

————, Ronald Lippitt, and Ralph K. White. "Patterns of Aggressive Behavior in Experimentally Created 'Social Climates,'" *Journal of Social Psychology*, 10 (1939), 271–299.

Lewis, Morris M. *Language, Thought, and Personality in Infancy and Childhood*. New York: Basic Books, 1963.

Lieberson, Stanley, and Arnold R. Silverman. "The Precipitants and Underlying Conditions of Race Riots," *American Sociological Review*, 30 (1965), 887–898.

Liebhart, Ernst H. "Empathy and Emergency Helping: The Effects of Personality, Self-Concern, and Acquaintance," *Journal of Experimental Social Psychology*, 8 (1972), 404–411.

Lilly, John C. *The Mind of the Dolphin: A Nonhuman Intelligence*. Garden City, N.Y.: Doubleday, 1967.

Lindesmith, Alfred R., and Anselm L. Strauss. *Social Psychology*. 3rd ed. New York: Holt, Rinehart and Winston, 1968.

Lippitt, Ronald. "Field Theory and Experiment in Social Psychology: Authoritarian and Democratic Group Atmospheres," *American Journal of Sociology*, 45 (1939), 26–49.

Lippmann, Walter. *Public Opinion*. New York: Harcourt, Brace & World, 1922.

Lipset, Seymour M., and Leo Lowenthal (eds.). *Culture and Social Character: The Work of David Riesman Reviewed*. New York: Free Press, 1961.

Lofland, John. *Doomsday Cult: A Study of Conversion, Proselytization, and Maintenance of Faith*. Englewood Cliffs, N.J.: Prentice-Hall, 1966.

————, and Rodney Stark. "Becoming a World-Saver: A Theory of Conversion to a Deviant Perspective," *American Sociological Review*, 30 (1965), 862–875.

Lorenz, Konrad Z. *King Solomon's Ring*. New York: Crowell, 1952.

Luchins, Abraham S. "Primacy-Recency in Impression Formation." In C. Hovland (ed.), *The Order of Presentation in Persuasion*, pp. 33–61. New Haven: Yale University Press, 1957.

Macaulay, Jacqueline R., and Leonard Berkowitz. *Altruism and Helping Behavior*. New York: Academic Press, 1970.

MacKinnon, Donald W. "Violation of Prohibitions." In H. A. Murray et al., *Explorations in Personality*, pp. 491–501. New York: Oxford University Press, 1938.

Malcolm X. *The Autobiography of Malcolm X*. New York: Grove Press, 1966.

Manis, Melvin. "Social Interaction and the Self-Concept," *Journal of Abnormal and Social Psychology*, 51 (1955), 362–376.

Marcuse, Herbert. *One-dimensional Man*. Boston: Beacon Press, 1964.

————. *Negations*. Boston: Beacon Press, 1968.

Maudlin, Bill. *Up Front*. Cleveland: World Publishing Co., 1945.

Mayo, Elton, *The Human Problems of an Industrial Civilization*. New York: Viking, 1960; original edition, 1933.

McArthur, Leslie Ann. "The How and What of Why: Some Determinants and

Consequences of Causal Attribution," *Journal of Personality and Social Psychology*, 22 (1972), 171–193.

McDougall, William. *Introduction to Social Psychology*. London: Methuen, 1908.

McPhail, Clark. "Civil Disorder Participation: A Critical Examination of Recent Research," *American Sociological Review*, 36 (1971), 1058–1073.

Mead, George H. *Mind, Self and Society: From the Standpoint of a Social Behaviorist*, ed. by C. W. Morris. Chicago: University of Chicago Press, 1934.

Mead, Margaret. *Male and Female*. New York: William Morrow, 1949.

——. *Sex and Temperament in Three Primitive Societies*. New York: New American Library, 1950; first published by William Morrow, 1935.

Michel, Dom Virgil. *The Liturgy of the Church*. New York: Macmillan, 1937.

Milgram, Stanley. "Behavioral Study of Obedience," *Journal of Abnormal and Social Psychology*, 67 (1963), 371–378.

——. "Liberating Effects of Group Pressure," *Journal of Personality and Social Psychology*, 1 (1965), 127–134.

Miller, Delbert R., and Guy E. Swanson. *The Changing American Parent*. New York: Wiley, 1968.

Miller, Neal E. "The Frustration-Aggression Hypothesis," *Psychological Review*, 48 (1941), 337–342.

——, and John Dollard. *Social Learning and Imitation*. New Haven: Yale University Press, 1941.

Mills, C. Wright (ed.). *Images of Man: The Classic Tradition in Sociological Thinking*. New York: George Braziller, 1960.

Moreno, Jacob L. *Who Shall Survive?* New York: Beacon House, 1934.

Mowrer, O. Hobart. "The Autism Theory of Speech Development and Some Clinical Applications," *Journal of Speech and Hearing Disorders*, 17 (1952), 263–368.

——. *Learning Theory and the Symbolic Processes*. New York: Wiley, 1960.

Murdock, George Peter. *Social Structure*. New York: Macmillan, 1949.

Murstein, Bernard I. "Physical Attractiveness and Marital Choice," *Journal of Personality and Social Psychology*, 22 (1972), 8–12.

Newcomb, Theodore M. *Personality and Social Change: Attitude Formation in a Student Community*. New York: Dryden Press, 1943.

——. "The Prediction of Interpersonal Attraction," *American Psychologist*, 9 (1956), 575–586.

——. *The Acquaintance Process*. New York: Holt, Rinehart and Winston, 1961.

——, Kathryn E. Koenig, Richard Flacks, and Donald P. Warwick. *Persistence and Change: Bennington College and Its Students After Twenty-Five Years*. New York: Wiley, 1967.

Nielsen, Waldemar A. "Moochie the Magnificent," *The New Yorker*, February 1, 1947, pp. 55–59.

Orne, Martin T. "The Nature of Hypnosis: Artifact or Essence," *Journal of Abnormal and Social Psychology*, 58 (1959), 277–299.

Osgood, Charles E., and Percy T. Tannenbaum. "The Principle of Congruity in the Prediction of Attitude Change," *Psychological Review*, 62 (1955), 42–55.

Piaget, Jean. *The Moral Judgment of the Child*. New York: Free Press, 1965; first published, 1932.

Piliavin, Irving M., Judith Rodin, and Jane A. Piliavin. "Good Samaritanism: An Underground Phenomenon?" *Journal of Personality and Social Psychology*, 13 (1969), 289–299.

Piliavin, Jane Allyn, and Irving M. Piliavin. "Effect of Blood on Relations to a Victim," *Journal of Personality and Social Psychology*, 23 (1972), 353–361.

Premack, David. "Language in Chimpanzee?" *Science*, May 21, 1971, pp. 808–822.

Pribram, Karl H. "Neuropsychology in America." In B. Berelson (ed.), *The Behavioral Sciences Today*, pp. 101–111. New York: Torchbooks, 1964; first published by Basic Books, 1963.

Prothro, Edwin Terry. *Child Rearing in the Lebanon*. Cambridge, Mass.: Harvard University Press, 1961.

Ragan, Dennis T., Margo Williams, and Sondra Sparling. "Voluntary Expiation of Guilt: A Field Experiment," *Journal of Personality and Social Psychology*, 24 (1972), 42–45.

Riesman, David. *The Lonely Crowd: A Study of the Changing American Character*. Rev. ed. New Haven: Yale University Press, 1961; original edition, 1950.

Ring, Kenneth. "Experimental Social Psychology: Some Sober Questions About Some Frivolous Values," *Journal of Experimental Social Psychology*, 3 (1967), 113–123.

Roethlisberger, Fritz J., and William J. Dickson. *Management and the Worker*. Cambridge, Mass.: Harvard University Press, 1943.

Rogler, Lloyd H., and August B. Hollingshead. *Trapped: Families and Schizophrenia*. New York: Wiley, 1965.

Rohrer, John H., and Munro S. Edmonson. *The Eighth Generation: Cultures and Personalities of New Orleans Negroes*. New York: Harper & Row, 1960.

Rosenberg, Milton J. "Cognitive Reorganization in Response to the Hypnotic Reversal of Attitudinal Affect," *Journal of Personality*, 28 (1960), 39–63.

———. "When Dissonance Fails: On Eliminating Evaluation Apprehension from Attitude Measurement," *Journal of Personality and Social Psychology*, 1 (1965)), 28–42.

Rosenberg, Morris. *Society and the Adolescent Self-Image*. Princeton, N.J.: Princeton University Press, 1965.

Rosenthal, A. M. *Thirty-eight Witnesses*. New York: McGraw-Hill, 1964.

Ross, E. A. *Social Psychology: An Outline and Source Book*. New York: Macmillan, 1908.

Rubin, Zick. "Measurement of Romantic Love," *Journal of Personality and Social Psychology*, 16 (1970), 265–273.

Rudé, George. *The Crowd in History: A Study of Popular Disturbances in France and England, 1730–1848*. New York: Wiley, 1964.

Russell, Bertrand. *Unpopular Essays*. New York: Simon & Schuster, 1950.

Samuelson, Robert J. "Riots: The More There Are, the Less We Understand," *Science*, August 11, 1967, pp. 663–665.

Sarbin, Theodore R. "Attempts to Understand Hypnotic Phenomena." In L. Postman (ed.), *Psychology in the Making: Histories of Selected Research Problems*, pp. 745–785. New York: Knopf, 1963.

Schacter, Stanley. "The Interaction of Cognitive and Physiological Determinants of Emotional State." In L. Berkowitz (ed.), *Advances in Experimental Social Psychology*, I, 49–80. New York: Academic Press, 1964.

———, and Jerome·E. Singer. "Cognitive, Social, and Physiological Determinants of Emotional State," *Psychological Review*, 69 (1962), 379–399.

Schellenberg, James A. "Homogamy in Personal Values and the 'Field of Eligibles,'" *Social Forces*, 39 (1960), 157–162.

———. "Dependence and Cooperation," *Sociometry*, 28 (1965), 158–172.

Schelling, Thomas C. "An Essay on Bargaining," *American Economic Review*, 46 (1956), 281–306.

Schulman, Gary I. "Asch Conformity Studies: Conformity to the Experimenter and/or to the Group?" *Sociometry*, 30 (1967), 26–40.

Schuman, Howard. "The Religious Factor in Detroit: Review, Replication, and Reanalysis," *American Sociological Review*, 36 (1971), 30–48.

Scott, John Paul. *Animal Behavior*. Chicago: University of Chicago Press, 1958.

———. "The Development of Social Motivation." In D. Levine (ed.), *Nebraska Symposium on Motivation, 1967*, pp. 111–132. Lincoln: University of Nebraska Press, 1967.

Sears, Robert R. "Relation of Early Socialization Experiences to Aggression in Middle Childhood," *Journal of Abnormal and Social Psychology*, 63 (1961), 466–492.

———, Eleanor E. Maccoby, and Harry Levin. *Patterns of Child Rearing*. New York: Harper & Row, 1957.

————, Lucy Rau, and Richard Alpert. *Identification and Child Rearing.* Stanford, Calif.: Stanford University Press, 1965.

Secord, Paul F., and Carl W. Backman. "Personality Theory and the Problem of Stability and Change in Individual Behavior: An Interpersonal Approach," *Psychological Review*, 68 (1961), 21–32.

————. "Interpersonal Congruency, Perceived Similarity, and Friendship," *Sociometry*, 27 (1964a), 115–127.

————. *Social Psychology.* New York: McGraw-Hill, 1964b.

Seeman, Melvin. "On the Meaning of Alienation," *American Sociological Review*, 24 (1959), 783–791.

————. "On the Personal Consequences of Alienation in Work," *American Sociological Review*, 32 (1967), 273–285.

————. "The Urban Alienations: Some Dubious Theses from Marx to Marcuse," *Journal of Personality and Social Psychology*, 19 (1971), 135–143.

Sewell, William H. "Infant Training and the Personality of the Child," *American Journal of Sociology*, 58 (1952), 150–159.

Shaw, Marvin E. "Communication Networks." In L. Berkowitz (ed)., *Advances in Experimental Social Psychology*, I, 111–147. New York: Academic Press, 1964.

Sherif, Muzafer. *The Psychology of Social Norms.* New York: Harper & Row, 1936.

Sherman, Steven J. "Effects of Choice and Incentive on Attitude Change in a Discrepant Behavior Situation," *Journal of Personality and Social Psychology*, 15 (1970), 245–252.

Shils, Edward A., and Morris Janowitz. "Cohesion and Disintegration in the Wehrmacht in World War II," *Public Opinion Quarterly*, 12 (1948), 280–315.

Simmel, Georg. *The Sociology of Georg Simmel*, ed. by K. Wolff. New York: Free Press, 1950.

Slater, Philip E. "Role Differentiation in Small Groups," *American Sociological Review*, 20 (1955), 300–310.

————. "On Social Regression," *American Sociological Review*, 28 (1963), 339–364.

Smith, M. Brewster, Jerome S. Bruner, and Robert W. White. *Opinions and Personality.* New York: Wiley, 1956.

Smith, Ronald E., Lisa Smythe, and Douglas Lien. "Inhibition of Helping Behavior by a Similar or Dissimilar Nonreactive Fellow Bystander," *Journal of Personality and Social Psychology*, 23 (1972), 414–419.

Spilerman, Seymour. "The Causes of Racial Disturbances: A Comparison of Alternative Explanations," *American Sociological Review*, 35 (1970), 627–649.

Spiro, Melford E. "Is the Family Universal?" *American Anthropologist*, 56 (1954), 839–846.

Spitz, René A. "Hospitalism." In A. Freud, H. Hartmann, and E. Kris (eds.), *The Psychoanalytic Study of the Child*, I, 53–74. New York: International Universities Press, 1945.

————. "Hospitalism: A Follow-up Report." In A. Freud, H. Hartmann, and E. Kris (eds.), *The Psychoanalytic Study of the Child*, II, 113–117. New York: International Universities Press, 1946.

———— *The First Year of Life: A Psychoanalytic Study of Normal and Deviant Development of Object Relations.* New York: International Universities Press, 1965.

Staats, Carolyn K., Arthur W. Staats, and William G. Heard. "Attitude Development and Ratio of Reinforcement," *Sociometry*, 23 (1960), 338–350.

Stephan, Walter, Ellen Berscheid, and Elaine Walster. "Sexual Arousal and Heterosexual Perception," *Journal of Personality and Social Psychology*, 20 (1971), 93–101.

Stephens, William N. *The Oedipus Complex: Cross-Cultural Evidence.* New York: Free Press, 1962.

————. *The Family in Cross-Cultural Perspective.* New York: Holt, Rinehart and Winston, 1963.

Swadish, Morris. "Diffusional Cumulation and Archaic Residue as Historical Explanations," *Southwestern Journal of Anthropology*, 7 (1950), 1–21.

———. "Toward Greater Accuracy in Lexicostatistic Dating," *International Journal of American Linguistics*, 21 (1955), 121–137.

Tannenbaum, Percy H. "Mediated Generalization of Attitude Change via the Principle of Congruity," *Journal of Personality and Social Psychology*, 3 (1966), 493–499.

Thibaut, John W., and Harold H. Kelley. *The Social Psychology of Groups*. New York: Wiley, 1959.

Toffler, Alvin. *Future Shock*. New York: Random House, 1970.

Touhey, John C. "Comparison of Two Dimensions of Attitude Similarity on Heterosexual Attraction," *Journal of Personality and Social Psychology*, 23 (1972), 8–10.

Veness, Thelma, and Dorothy W. Brierley. "Forming Impressions of Personality: Two Experiments," *British Journal of Social and Clinical Psychology*, 2 (1963), 11–19.

Verba, Sidney. *Small Groups and Political Behavior*. Princeton, N.J.: Princeton University Press, 1961.

Vroom, Victor H. "Some Personality Determinants of the Effects of Participation," *Journal of Abnormal and Social Psychology*, 59 (1959), 322–327.

Waller, Willard, and Reuben Hill. *The Family: A Dynamic Interpretation*. Rev. ed. New York: Dryden, 1951.

Walster, Elaine, Vera Aronson, Darcy Abrahams, and Leon Rottmann. "Importance of Physical Attractiveness in Dating Behavior," *Journal of Personality and Social Psychology*, 4 (1966), 508–516.

———, and Ellen Berscheid. "Adrenaline Makes the Heart Grow Fonder," *Psychology Today*, June 1971, pp. 47–50, 62.

Warner, W. Lloyd. *The Family of God: A Symbolic Study of Christian Life in America*. New Haven: Yale University Press, 1961.

Weber, Max. *The Protestant Ethic and the Spirit of Capitalism*. London: Allen & Unwin, 1930.

———. " 'Objectivity' in Social Science and Social Policy." In E. Shils and H. Finch (eds.), *The Methodology of the Social Sciences*, pp. 89–99. New York: Free Press, 1949; this essay first published, 1904.

White, Leslie A. "The Symbol: The Origin and Basis of Human Behavior," *Philosophy of Science*, 7 (1940), 451–463.

———. *The Science of Culture*. 2nd ed. New York: Farrar, Straus & Giroux, 1969.

Whiting, John W. M. "Resource Mediation and Learning by Identification." In I. Iscoe and H. Stevenson (eds.), *Personality Development in Children*, pp. 112–126. Austin: University of Texas Press, 1960.

Whyte, William Foote. "Corner Boys: A Study of Clique Behavior," *American Journal of Sociology*, 46 (1941), 647–664.

———. *Street Corner Society: The Social Structure of an Italian Slum*. 2nd ed. Chicago: University of Chicago Press, 1955; original edition, 1943.

Winch, Robert F. *Mate Selection: A Study of Complementary Needs*. New York: Harper & Row, 1958.

Wrong, Dennis. "The Oversocialized Conception of Man in Modern Sociology," *American Sociological Review*, 26 (1961), 183–193.

Yankelovich, Daniel. *The Changing Values on Campus*. New York: Washington Square Press, 1972.

Glossary

affiliation—the process of forming a positive relationship between persons; also, the sense of this relationship on the part of one of the persons.

aggression—any behavior designed to hurt another person or group of persons. Aggression may be further identified as *habitual* (if characteristic of the behavior of an individual) or *occasional* (if characteristic of particular kinds of situations). Occasional aggression can further be divided into instances of *angry aggression* (in response to frustration) and *strategic aggression* (in which aggression is only a means to other ends).

alienation—the feeling of being separated from the main processes of social life. Different types of alienation include work alienation (lack of a sense of purpose in work), powerlessness (feeling of being unable to affect social conditions), social isolation (being unable to have frequent contact with others), value estrangement (feeling of a lack of meaningful values), and self-estrangement (lack of a clear sense of identity).

angry aggression—*see* aggression.

assertion (Osgood)—*see* congruity.

assimilation effect—the tendency to merge together cognitions that are similar, treating them as nearly a single thing. *See also* contrast effect.

attitude—a relatively enduring evaluative orientation toward some object of experience. Components of attitudes include cognitions, feelings, and action tendencies.

attitude scale—a set of questions designed to measure an attitude on a single dimension.

attribution—the everyday process of interpreting social events, including perceptions of characteristics of other persons and explanations of their behavior. Explanations of causes of behavior include *external* (conditions of the environment) and *internal* (nature of the person) factors.

authoritarian personality—according to Adorno, a pattern of organization of perception and behavior that includes conventionalism, an intolerance of ambiguity, and a desire for highly structured relationships with other persons.

autokinetic effect—the tendency to perceive motion that is not actually present.

autonomous morality—*see* heteronomous morality.

balance—according to Heider, a condition of consistency between associated cognitive elements, especially between *unit relations* and *sentiment relations*. Unit relations represent the groupings of cognitions with each other, while sentiment relations represent positive or negative feelings toward cognitive elements. Balance obtains when similar sentiments are felt toward all elements of a unit relation; *imbalance* occurs when this is not the case.

basic personality—according to Kardiner, the pattern of personal adjustment shared by persons of the same culture as a result of their similar early experiences. *See also* social character.

case study—an intensive study of a particular person or situation.

catharsis—the reduction of an emotion, such as aggressive feeling, through its expression.

charisma—the property of special

appeal associated with particular persons. Once used to refer to divine sources of personal appeal, the term is now used to apply to any form of personal magnetism having wide appeal.

class—*see* social class.

classical conditioning—*see* conditioning.

coefficient of correlation—a measure of correlation. *See also* correlation.

cognition—the internal processing of perceptions, memories, beliefs, and other forms of thought.

cognitive balance—*see* balance.

cognitive dissonance—psychological contradiction between associated cognitive elements. A state of consonance occurs when there is an absence of dissonance.

collective behavior—a term usually used to represent the general class of social behavior that is relatively unstructured by customs or institions. *See also* crowd, mass, and public.

collective excitement—*see* crowd.

commitment—the extent to which the self is involved in a given choice.

communication—*see* natural communication and symbolic communication.

communication network—an arrangement of positions in which ability to communicate is used as the criterion for relating positions.

compromise process—according to Backman and Secord, the process by which an individual adjusts his aspirations for friendship with other persons. In taking into account availability as well as desirability, a person normally comes to accept friends at approximately his own level of popularity.

concept (Osgood)—*see* congruity.

conditioned reflex—Pavlov's term for a conditioned response. *See also* conditioned response.

conditioned response (CR)—in classical conditioning, a response elicited by a *conditioned stimulus* after this stimulus has been associated with an *unconditioned stimulus;* the conditioned response is similar to the *unconditioned response* that was originally elicited by the *unconditioned stimulus*. *See also* conditioning.

conditioned stimulus (CS)—*see* conditioned response.

conditioning—the alteration of response patterns following changes in the presentation of stimuli. In *classical conditioning* responses are elicited to a new stimulus by associating it with a previous stimulus. In *operant* or *instrumental conditioning* a response is emitted with greater frequency following its association with reinforcement.

conformity—standardization of behavior in group settings. *Normative conformity* represents adjustment to group needs for interdependent action. *Modal conformity* represents more simply the trend toward a generalized uniformity.

congruity—according to Osgood, a condition of evaluative consistency between associated cognitive elements (especially between the cognitive representatives of the *source* of a message, the *concept* indicated by the message, and the *assertion* made by the source about the concept). *Incongruity* refers to the relative absence of such consistency. *See also* interpersonal congruity.

consensual validation—*see* social reality.

consideration—leadership behavior that emphasizes empathy with other group members. *See also* initiation.

consistency—*see* evaluative consistency. *See also* balance, congruity, and cognitive dissonance.

consonance — *see* cognitive dissonance.

contingency model of leadership effectiveness—Fiedler's theory that group productivity is variously affected by the particular combinations of four variables: (1) psychological distance of leader, (2) authority position of leader, (3) the amount of social acceptance of the leader by other members, and (4) the degree of structure of the task to be performed.

contrast effect—the tendency to divide cognitions that are dissimilar, treating them as something approaching polar opposites. *See also* assimilation effect.

conversion—relatively sudden and drastic attitude change.

correlation—a measure of the degree to which variables are similar in their pattern of variation. *Direct correlation* refers to a positive association between variables (high points in one variable match highs in the other, and low points match lows); while *inverse correlation* refers to a negative association between variables.

critical periods—*see* primary socialization.

crowd—a temporary group, focused on a common object of attention, in which mutual stimulation among members is a main basis of behavior. This mutual stimulation typically includes a *milling* of persons in close physical contact, *collective excitement* aroused by an unusual event, and the *social contagion* of mood and action from one member to another. *See also* collective behavior.

cultural stereotypes—*see* stereotypes.

culture—*see* society.

deference—acceding to the power of, and showing respect toward, another person.

dependence—the value of a social relationship for a person as compared to the perceived value of alternatives to the relationship. *Instrumental dependence* occurs when what is valued consists primarily of means to other goals. *Orientational dependence* occurs when what is valued consists primarily of information and its interpretation. *Ego dependence* occurs when what is valued is primarily a positive or consistent self-image.

dependent variable—*see* variable.

direct correlation—*see* correlation.

dissonance — *see* cognitive dissonance.

dyad—a group consisting of two persons. *See also* pair events.

ego—broadly, the organization of conceptions an individual has of himself and of his behavior. Also called the self or private identity. In Freudian theory, the subsystem of personality organization based upon the testing of reality. *See also* id and superego.

ego dependence—*see* dependence.

evaluative consistency, principle of —the idea that closely associated cognitions tend to be evaluated in a similar way. *See also* balance, congruity, and cognitive dissonance.

everyday personality theory—*see* implicit personality theory.

experimentation—the observation of phenomena under controlled conditions. In *laboratory experiments* the investigator himself creates the setting for his observations, whereas in *field experiments* he manipulates only some of the variables in an established social setting. A third category of *natural experiments* is sometimes used to refer to cases where the investigator actually controls nothing, but where events happen to occur in a way similar to that which an investigator might wish to create through controlled conditions.

face—Goffman's term to refer to the claims that a person makes for himself and which he finds accepted by others in social interaction.

field experiment—*see* experimentation.

formal organization—*see* human relations approach.

frustration—felt interference with goal achievement.

glottochronology—the use of measures of language differentiation for dating estimates.

grammar—*see* language.

group—any two or more persons whose interaction results in some degree of concerted action.

group conformity—*see* conformity.

group membership—*see* membership.

habitual aggression—*see* aggression.

heteronomous morality — according to Piaget, a morality of obedience and fixed standards based on external constraint. In contrast is *autonomous morality*, a morality of voluntary cooperation that emerges out of the reciprocity of social interaction.

human relations approach—in the study of organizations, an emphasis upon informal rather than formal organization. *Informal organization* includes the primary groups and their informal pressures; whereas *formal organization* refers to the pattern of positions, duties, and rules as formally defined by top officers.

hypnosis—a sleeplike condition in which a subject limits his attention to the suggestions of a hypnotist, which he follows fully.

id—in Freudian theory, the original and most basic form of personality organization, based upon pleasure-seeking impulses. *See also* ego and superego.

ideal types—purified concepts constructed by an investigator to give a frame of reference for his discussion.

identification—the process of an individual's concentrating his adjustment, including his sense of self-identity, upon a relationship with another person. This typically involves imitation of the behavior of the object of identification. *See also* imitation.

imbalance—*see* balance.

imitation—behavior by one individual designed to match that of another. The person whose behavior is matched or copied is known as a *model*.

implicit personality theory—the set of assumptions a person uses in perceiving and judging other persons.

imprinting—the early learning, observed in certain species, that normally creates an apparently permanent attachment to an adult of the species. *See also* primary socialization.

incest—forbidden sexual intercourse with a close relative.

incongruity—*see* congruity.

independent variable—*see* variable.

influence—*see* social influence.

informal organization—*see* human relations approach.

initiation—leadership behavior that emphasizes directing the actions of other group members. *See also* consideration.

institutions—sets of established patterns of thought and behavior that are passed from generation to generation as part of the cultural heritage.

instrumental conditioning—*see* conditioning.

instrumental dependence — *see* dependence.

interaction process analysis—a set of techniques developed by Bales to measure features of interaction in small groups.

interpersonal congruency—according to Secord and Backman, the consistency a person strives to create between his own self-concept, his behavior toward others, and the way others seem to relate to him.

interpersonal power—the ability to influence others in person-to-person interaction.

inverse correlation—*see* correlation.

isolates—*see* sociometry.

laboratory experiment—*see* experimentation.

language—a comprehensive system of symbols, plus rules for their usage. These rules of usage provide the structure or *grammar* for the language. Forms of such structure include *morphology* (the formation of *morphemes*, words or parts of words, which provide the elementary structural units of meaning) and *syntax* (the arrangement of morphemes into conventional patterns, especially sentences). *See also* symbolic communication.

leadership—influence exerted in a group setting, based on voluntary following rather than on the control of formal sanctions. *See also* social influence.

learning—any modification of response tendencies that follows experience in a new situation. *See also* conditioning.

legitimacy—the quality of acceptability, especially as applied to a social norm. Norms become legitimate primarily through usage, utility, and association with other forms of legitimacy.

libido—in Freudian theory, the energy of pleasure-seeking impulses, especially those of a broadly sexual nature.

linguistic relativity—the doctrine that language forms predominantly determine forms of thought.

looking-glass self—Cooley's term for pointing to the social origins of the self. *See also* role-taking and self.

mass—a form of collective behavior characterized by physical dispersion, indirect communication, anonymity of members, and inability to carry out concerted action. *See also* collective behavior.

membership—being a part of the group. *Official membership* is indicated by listings of persons in the group. *Psychological membership* is indicated by the presence of both attraction toward the group by an individual and acceptance of him by the group.

milling—*see* crowd.

model—*see* imitation.

morphemes—*see* language.

morphology—*see* language.

multiple correlation—a measure of correlation among several variables. *See also* correlation.

national stereotypes — *see* stereotypes.

natural communication — the communication through natural signs or signals. A *natural sign* is anything that stands for something else through natural association. *See also* symbolic communication.

natural experiment—*see* experimentation.

natural sign—*see* natural communication and signs.

negative reinforcement — *see* reinforcement.

norms—standards of expected and approved behavior.

nuclear family—a group of parents and their children sharing a common residence.

occasional aggression—*see* aggression.

Oedipus complex—Freud's term for the condition of a young son's rivalry with his father for the affections of his mother. Freud held this to be a universal human phenomenon, normally resolved through the son's identification with his father.

official membership—*see* membership.

operant conditioning—*see* conditioning.

operational definitions—concepts identified by a specification of the operations used in making observations.

organism—the organization of physiological activity of the individual.

orientational dependence—*see* dependence.

pair events—events involving only two persons at the same time. *See also* set events.

partial correlation—a measure of correlation between two variables, holding constant the effects of their intercorrelations with another variable or other variables. *See also* correlation.

personality—the organization of behavior characteristics of a particular person. *See also* organism, private identity, and public identity.

phonology—the system of sounds used in a spoken language.

physical reality—*see* social reality.

positive reinforcement — *see* reinforcement.

power—*see* interpersonal power and social influence.

prejudice—stereotyped attitudes toward a person or group, held without adequate evidence. Prejudices are usually thought of as negative attitudes, though they may also be positive. *See also* stereotypes.

primary group—a group characterized by relatively close person-to-person relationships. Such intimate relationships, in which persons involve their total personalities, may also be called *primary relationships*. In contrast to primary groups, groups in which relationships are impersonal and involve only segments of the lives of participants are frequently called *secondary groups*.

primary institutions—according to Kardiner, the culturally determined practices that predominantly shape early childhood experience.

primary relationship—*see* primary group.

primary socialization—the early development of a social relationship with (normally) adult members of the species. This apparently takes place within a *critical period* (different for different species) during which time a basic framework for the animal's self-identity is formed. *See also* identification.

private identity—the organization of conceptions that an individual has of himself and of his behavior. Also called the self or ego.

projection—the tendency to see one's own characteristics as belonging to others.

psychological membership—*see* membership.

public—a form of collective behavior characterized by discussion of a particular issue of common concern to members. Typically, a public is physically dispersed, but members have means of communication and influence that make common action possible. *See also* collective behavior.

public identity—the organization of social roles that a person plays in his various interpersonal relationships and social groups.

questionnaire—a planned set of questions presented to respondents.

reinforcement—according to Skinner, any stimulus that strengthens a response tendency. More popularly, *positive reinforcement* is sometimes given the general meaning of any reward, and *negative reinforcement* represents interference or punishment.

reliability—the degree to which repeated observations present the same results.

resources (for interpersonal influence)—anything that a person has, represents, or is able to give that may be useful to another person. *See also* dependence, interpersonal power, and social influence.

response reinforcement—the strengthening of a response tendency through reinforcement. *See* reinforcement.

role—the pattern of behavior expected of a person by others in a given social context.

role-taking—assumption of the perspective of another person or persons as a framework for considering one's own behavior.

rumor—a tentative belief based primarily on widespread hearsay evidence.

sample—*see* sampling.

sampling—the selection of part of a population for purposes of study, with the expectation that data gathered from this part, or *sample*, will also be representative of the entire population, or *universe*, of cases.

satisfaction—the degree of rewards realized relative to the level of rewards expected.

secondary group—*see* primary group.

secondary institutions—according to Kardiner, cultural practices primarily formed on the pattern of basic personality prevalent in a given culture. *See also* primary institutions and basic personality.

secondary reinforcement theory of identification—that an individual will tend to select as a model for imitation and identification a person who is associated with his own past enjoyment of rewards.

self—the organization of conceptions an individual has of himself and of his behavior. Also called the ego or private identity.

sentiment relations (Heider)—*see* balance.

set events—events involving more than two persons at the same time. *See also* pair events.

significance—*see* statistical significance.

signs—any word, action, or physical object that carries meaning. Signs include natural signs and symbols. *See also* natural communication and symbolic communication.

simplicity, principle of—the idea that cognitions tend to be organized into a framework of maximum simplicity.

social character—according to Riesman, that part of personality that is the product of group experience and is widely shared with others of the society. *See also* basic personality.

social class—a grouping of persons with similar levels of favorable evaluation in the hierarchy of a given society.

social contagion—*see* crowd.

social exchange—the idea that social relationships are structured by the positive or negative values of actions that persons present to each other. The assumption is that "goods" (such as social approval or recognition) will tend to be given in return for positive actions from other persons.

social facilitation—the stimulating effect of the presence of other persons upon an activity being pursued by an individual.

social influence—any effects, deliberate or unintended, upon the behavior of other persons.

social institution—*see* institutions.

social power theory of identification—that an individual will tend to select a person with control of rewards as a model for imitation and identification.

social reality—the view of reality that is known primarily through social cues. Its truths are matters of *consensual validation*, that is, checked through the conceptions of others. This is in contrast with *physical reality*, which is checked through observing actions of the physical world.

social regression—according to Slater, the tendency of an individual to withdraw emotional attachment from broad social forms in favor of its concentration in himself or in highly intimate groups.

socialization—the process of an individual's adjustment to living with other people, including adjustment to individuals, to groups, and to the culture as a whole.

society—the most inclusive pattern of social relationships of persons who share a common culture. *Culture*, in turn, represents the totality of socially acquired ways of thinking and behaving, which are shared by a social group. A *subculture* refers to the ways of thinking and behaving of some segment of a larger culture.

sociogram—*see* sociometry.

sociometric matrix—*see* sociometry.

sociometric test—*see* sociometry.

sociometry—the measurement of relationships within a group, especially if following procedures suggested by Moreno. Moreno developed the *sociometric test* (a questionnaire designed to determine social choices in a group), the *sociometric matrix* (a means of expressing these choices in the form of a table), and the *sociogram* (a graphic form of picturing such choices, showing also subgroup formation and calling attention to highly chosen persons, or *stars*, as well as persons not chosen, or *isolates*).

source (Osgood)—*see* congruity.

stars—*see* sociometry.

statistical significance—a measure of the extent to which a pattern of results would be unlikely to occur through random variation.

status envy theory of identification—that an individual will tend to select a successful rival as a model for imitation and identification.

stereotypes—simplified and standardized images (often highly evaluative) applied to the perception and judgment of social objects. *Cultural stereotypes* are those stereotypes that have become standardized in a given cultural tradition and thus are accepted as part of the culture. *National stereotypes* are stereotypes commonly held about the people of another nation.

stimulus generalization—the tendency of a response conditioned to a given stimulus also to occur with a similar, or otherwise closely associated, stimulus. *See also* conditioning.

strategic aggression—*see* aggression.

subculture—*see* society.

sublimation—the modification of an unacceptable impulse into a form of behavior that is more socially acceptable.

superego—in Freudian theory, the organization of social standards that are internalized by the individual to serve as the basis for evaluating the rightness or wrongness of his actions, thoughts, and feelings. *See also* id and ego.

symbol—*see* symbolic communication.

symbolic communication—the communication through symbols. A *symbol*, in turn, is anything (a word, an action, or a physical object) that stands for something else in an artificial (without natural association required) and conventional (through collective habits of association) manner. *See also* language and natural communication.

syntax—*see* language.

target (of aggression)—the person or group that is the object of aggressive behavior. *See also* aggression.

temperament—a dominant mood or style of personality, considered by many to be determined by biological heredity.

theory—a body of concepts organized to assert something general about the nature of reality.

totemism—a form of primitive religion and social organization in which a natural object (usually a particular species of animal) is revered as representative of the family, clan, or tribe.

unconditioned response (UR)—*see* conditioned response.

unconditioned stimulus (US)—*see* conditioned response.

unit relations (Heider)—*see* balance.

universe—*see* sampling.

validating activity—in general, any logical operation or empirical test used to ascertain the correctness of a sense of understanding. In particular, a scientific operation that shows the extent to which scientific conclusions follow from the evidence presented (*internal validity*) and/or may be generalized to other situations (*external validity*).

validity—the degree to which results of a given investigation apply to the subject matter for which generalizations are made.

variable—any feature that can be observed by an investigator to show variation. An investigator pays particular attention to two classes of variables: (1) *independent variables* which may be at least partially controlled to observe their effects on other variables, and (2) *dependent variables*, the variation of which is assumed to reflect the independent variables.

verification—the process of obtaining and evaluating new evidence to check the adequacy of previous scientific findings.

AUTHOR INDEX

SUBJECT INDEX

Affiliation, 1–50, 346; and aggression, 50, 100–101

Aggression, 51–101, 141–142, 346; angry, 85–90, 97–98; frustration, 82–83; habitual, 96–97; and influence, 101, 141–142; obedient, 90–94; occasional, 97–99; strategic, 98–99

Alienation, 313–317, 346

Alternatives, 48, 135–136

Animals, 27–32, 37–38, 248, 249

Assimilation effect, 184, 346

Attitude change, 144–158, 163–181

Attitude scale, 152–153, 346

Attitudes, 144–189, 346; and attraction, 18–24; components of, 151; and conditioning, 160–163; and groups, 189, 237; and influence, 142, 189

Attraction (interpersonal), 12–26

Attribution, 300–302, 346

Authoritarian personality, 292–293, 346

Autism theory (of speech), 247–248

Autokinetic effect, 117–118, 346

Balance (cognitive), 20–21, 24, 166–167, 346

Basic personality, 305–306, 346

Behaviorism, 328–329

Case study, 66, 95, 346

Catharsis, 83–84, 346

Charisma, 283–284, 346–347

Child rearing, 32–34, 45–47, 57–60, 68–80, 96–97, 243–247, 251, 258–260, 306–308

Class (social), 15–18, 62–65, 347, 352

Cognition, 37, 151, 166–167, 169–170, 171–181, 184–186, 252–255, 347

Collective behavior, 206–217, 347, 348

Commitment, 49–50, 177–181, 188–189, 347

Communication, 9, 166, 200–205, 243–255, 347, 350, 353; natural, 248, 350; symbolic, 248–249, 353

Communication network, 200–205, 347

Compromise process, 18, 347

Conditional response, 160–163, 347

Conditioning, 72–73, 96–97, 160–170, 347; classical, 160–161, 347; operant (or instrumental), 160–161, 347

Conformity, 117–122, 347

Congruity, 166–169, 172, 347

Consideration (in leadership), 200, 347

Consistency (attitudinal) 20–23, 163–181, 185–186, 189, 347

Consistency (of personality), 323

Contingency (leadership model), 198–200, 347–348

Contrast effect, 184, 348

Conversion, 144–158, 348

Correlation, 74–75, 100, 348, 350; direct, 348; inverse, 348; multiple, 75, 350; partial, 75, 351

Critical periods, 37–38, 348

Crowd, 206–215, 217, 348

Culture, 204–211, 218–219, 249–252, 253–254, 262–264, 267–269, 304–311, 320, 348, 353

Deference, 262–264, 348

Dependence, 48–49, 114, 134–138, 232–233, 348; ego, 48, 134–135, 348; and influence, 114; instrumental, 48, 134–135, 348, 349; orientational, 48, 134–135, 348, 351

Dissonance (cognitive), 171–181, 187–189, 347, 348

Divine Precepts, 145–150

Dyads, 111, 348

Ego, 57, 348

Ethics, 298–300

Exchange (social), 231–235, 352

Experimentation, 36, 42–43, 87, 298–300, 348, 350; and ethics, 298–300; field, 36, 348; laboratory, 36, 87, 348, 350; natural, 36, 348, 350

Face, 131, 348

Facilitation (social), 215–216, 352

Family, 218–221, 262–264, 350; nuclear, 218–219, 350

Feelings, 123–128, 151

Frustration, 82–83, 97–98, 349

Gestalt psychology, 184, 331–332

Glottochronology, 251–252, 349

Group, 105–114, 121–122, 130, 189, 191–237, 260–262, 284, 349

Hospitalism, 32–35

Hypnosis, 169–170, 256–258, 349

Id, 57, 349

Ideal types, 213–214, 349

Identification, 38–44, 284, 349

Identity, 56, 128–133, 321–323, 351; private, 56, 351; public, 56, 351

Imitation, 37–38, 40–42, 44, 243–244, 246–248, 281, 349

Implicit personality theory, 291–292, 349